FREE LABOR

FREE LABOR

The Civil War and the Making of an American Working Class

MARK A. LAUSE

UNIVERSITY OF ILLINOIS PRESS
Urbana, Chicago, and Springfield

Manufactured in the United States of America
1 2 3 4 5 C P 5 4 3 2 1
♾ This book is printed on acid-free paper.

Library of Congress Cataloging-in-Publication Data
Lause, Mark A.
Free labor : the Civil War and the making of an American working class / Mark A. Lause.
pages cm.—(The working class in American history)
Includes bibliographical references and index.
ISBN 978-0-252-03933-1 (hardcover : alk. paper) —
ISBN 978-0-252-08086-9 (pbk. : alk. paper) —
ISBN 978-0-252-09738-6 (e-book)
1. Working class—United States—History—19th century. 2. United States—History—Civil War, 1861–1865—Social aspects. 3. Working class—United States—Social conditions—19th century. 4. Labor movement—United States—History—19th century. 5. United States—Social conditions—19th century. I. Title.
HD8070.L39 2015
305.5'62097309034—dc23 2015008312

Contents

Acknowledgments

Work on this subject has gone on for decades, as I gathered up what has become the bits and pieces of this study from almost every library or archive I've ever visited. These included the Library of Congress, the National Archives, the American Antiquarian Society, and the state historical societies and archives of New York, Pennsylvania, Ohio, Wisconsin, Indiana, Illinois, Missouri, and Kansas. The staff of these instituions have never failed to impress me with their expertise. The staff of the Langsam Library at the University of Cincinnati, particularly Milkaila Corday, who has managed the interlibrary loan services there for almost as long as I have been here, has always provided essential support with similar expertise.

That said, this kind of sweeping research project could not have been possible without the massive technological changes in recent years. The Civil War Soldiers and Sailors System Web site of the U.S. National Park Service and the even more informative American Civil War Research Database have precluded what would have been innumerably repeated research trips to the military records in Washington, D.C. I ruthlessly exploited the availability of digital sources from Google Books and the Internet Archives to the burgeoning newspaper-digitalization projects, notably Chronicling America from the Library of Congress and state newspaper digitalization projects, as well as the ProQuest subscriptions available by subscription to libraries. It should be added that many of these for the period had already been culled, transcribed, and indexed by Vicki Betts's powerful little site on "Civil War Newspapers" at the University of Texas at Tyler.[1]

I frankly confess that I tend to be a much more solitary worker in researching these projects than I should be. Nevertheless, bringing such a long project to fruition has benefited tremendously from periodic short exchanges with too many people in the field to name without serious risk of missing someone. However, I would be remiss without noting my appreciation of the encouragement for this project by Bruce Laurie, Bruce Levine, and Nikki Taylor, as well as Laurie Matheson, the editorial staff, and the manuscript readers at the University of Illinois Press who forced the reshaping of part of this manuscript. As they have for years, my colleagues Janine Hartman at the University of Cincinnati and L. J. Andrew Villalon at the University of Texas have provided a sounding board, the former also adding a needed second pair of eyes to the more troublesome parts of the manuscript. All contributed to whatever the manuscript can achieve, while the mistakes and errors are my own.

Introduction

The Civil War proved central to the making of an American working class. Yet the intersection of labor history and the conflict itself with regard to the future nature of labor in the country has stirred remarkably little interest among historians in either field. Historians have certainly written about a struggle that subsumed large sections of the workforce and transformed the working-class experience forever. Yet the role of workers in shaping the course of that conflict and the role of the conflict itself in shaping the future nature of labor and the labor movement has stirred remarkably little interest in the field as a whole. Interest in the demise of slavery has turned largely on the evolution of government policies. Too, free laboring people, as such, usually find a place in the war's history only in the brief cameo in the New York City draft riots, and the admirable interest in slavery still often turns on the evolution of institutional policies rather than slaves as active agents in the making of their own history. Workers themselves understood this. Indeed, an Iowa harnessmaker once described the war as "a great labor movement." Conversely, historians of labor, with a few exceptions, usually do no more than mention the subject in passing, focusing instead on the later institutional development of unions or the social conditions that cultivated the postwar movement.[1]

The U.S. census provides a crude measure of the workforce. For these years associated with the war, it offered gendered counts by age groups without enumerating skilled and semiskilled adult workingmen or even distinguishing between master craftsmen and hired men, but the numbers do provide some grounds for reasonably estimating the non-agricultural wage-earning workforce, which grew from around two hundred thousand in the 1820s to nearly 1.5 million on the eve of the Civil War. The census also reflected the presence of several million workers and their children owned as slaves, a small proportion of African Americans working for wages, and a portion of the laboring women; but mixed-race persons, slaves who also worked for wages, or a domestically constrained population of female labor remained largely invisible.[2]

* * *

Our concern is the role of the Civil War experience in the "making of an American working class" in the sense that E. P. Thompson envisioned that process in England. Thompson resurrected the insights of Karl Marx, understanding class as a process of self-definition through which workers come to see themselves as playing a distinct role in society. Workers express this shared sense of themselves through their organization of demonstrations, picket lines, unions, parties, and other material activities. Conversely, "class" has little material meaning for participants in a workforce who do not see themselves as having a distinct set of concerns. Finally, seeing this as a process understands the "making" as an issue of degrees.

The war wrought major changes on this working population. Most obviously, it ended slavery and radically expanded the numbers of hired laborers. War-related industrialization expanded the manufacturing base, and the massive exodus of enslaved workers into the wage-earning population roughly doubled this greater size. More subtly, the military experience imposed a qualitatively new discipline and regulation that made for a more easily managed labor.[3]

Getting at how these workers actually saw themselves takes real effort. They expressed this partly through associations where workers chose to unite with each other *as* workers to formulate and foster common concerns, but these organizations marked the documentary record only when they reached a certain size or engaged in mass meetings, demonstrations, or strikes. Certainly, a cross-section of workers in America had begun to behave and to explain themselves in much the same way as Thompson's English workers had, suggesting that they saw themselves and their relationship to society in distinct ways, but the manifestation of this was not always the same. That is, the organizations and rhetoric that served their peers in Britain and Europe appeared in a system with an endemic labor shortage, growing amid massive resources with an insufficient workforce to exploit those riches. The masters and rulers of American society resolved this problem, in part, by expanding the enslaved population of African Americans. For their part, these "owned workers" came to understand themselves and their social realities in class terms that proved quite distinct from that of the organized white-labor movement.

Nevertheless, politicians, statesmen, and generals penned the dominant sources in the library of published and unpublished materials, shaping a top-down view of history. Antebellum Democratic politicians had claimed to speak on behalf of the white workingmen of the North as they warned of the threat of abolition and possible competition with blacks in the labor market. The riots in New York City or the Pennsylvania coalfields leave little room for doubt that partisan appeals against war, against conscription, and against blacks could still find an audience among some white workers during the war. For various reasons—including the partisan affinities of organized labor in the mid-twentieth century—scholars have tended to accept those elite voices claiming to speak for workers as an authentic expression of the views of laboring people. This essentially leaves the working-class presence in Civil War history exactly where contemporary businessmen, politicians, and military commanders chose to position it.[4]

Yet a closer look discloses much greater complexity. While some working-class New Yorkers, ready to take their cue from Democratic politicians, rioted against the draft, no known trade-union members were actually even associated with the rioting and the violence. Among the troops rushed to the city were members of the Seventh Ohio of Colonel William R. Creighton, formerly of the Cleveland Typographical Union. So, too, the hundreds of Pennsylvania coal miners fighting Republican bosses and the war effort—egged on by Democratic officeholders—seemed to speak for workers in the industry, as thousands of their peers had gone to war. This includes the Forty-Eighth Pennsylvania Volunteers, whose men proposed sinking the mine shaft beneath the Confederate lines at Petersburg.

We also know that other differences divided hired workers. A number of historians have focused on European ethnicities. Quite a number have focused on the Irish, while others have explored the German American labor experience. Less immediately obvious, workers in the United States of every ethnicity tended to approach the wider world with preindustrial and traditionalist, revivalist, or radical assumptions.[5]

Most dramatically, perhaps, racial slavery marked the most important contradiction in the American labor system, because it created the crisis that threatened the nation's life in 1860–61. Over recent years, Marxist historians have introduced sociological insights drawn from the Caribbean invention of "whiteness" as a cultural construct to studies of the mainland. Certainly, race constrained the vision of most hired white workers, but what interests us here is how this shaped the sense of shared experience among African Americans.[6]

Different sociological issues have drawn other scholars into other areas, such as the nature of the sectional conflict and whether or not slavery provided a brake on capitalism. Certainly, however one chooses to define it, the economic and social order after the war changed fundamentally from what was there before.[7] The extent to which this distinguishes slavery from capitalism is primarily a matter of how we define these terms.

Notwithstanding the mid-nineteenth-century clash between their rhetoric and ideology over slavery, the gentlemen in the North and the South had gotten on famously for generations and shared throughout some fundamental assumptions about the subjugation of labor. Slavery had many forms over thousands of years, and that which existed in the antebellum South functioned alongside a reliance on wage labor in a money-making enterprise integral to a global economy. Nevertheless, though many of the institutions and ideologies used to reconstruct the country came from the older hierarchies and structures,[8] workers of any condition found an understanding of themselves as workers virtually unavoidable.

Indeed, getting at that distinct sense of self among laboring people requires stalking it within a seemingly familiar language. Historians of the Civil War have consistently found that men on both sides, from the top to the ranks, used the same language of self-government, liberty, and republicanism to explain why they slaughtered each other. They obviously did not mean the same things by it. However, even from the perspective of one side or the other, any conflict requiring that scale of mobilization at the front and at home assuredly involves people who used similar words to describe a broad spectrum of views among themselves.[9]

Free workers certainly saw themselves and their organizations as an organic part of a wider republican tradition. After all, the evidence among the well-documented printers reveals the presence of men who remembered Washington and the founders of the nation. Some had fought in the War of 1812 and gone on to form some of the country's oldest unions, including the Columbia Typographical Union, founded in the ruins of Washington after the British had burned the city in 1814.[10] Similar though less documented associations affected other crafts.

Yet historians of labor have honed a useful concept of an "artisan republicanism," suggesting a distinctive producers' ideology in which laboring people saw themselves. For decades workers had invariably couched their grievance in the republican ideology of the age. Enlightenment thinkers described a natural law that included essentials for human survival and implied natural rights to meet those needs.

Civilization required a social contract that translated some of these rights into civil rights, while others remained "inalienable." The English, American, and French revolutions established the idea that the social contract required the consent of the governed. As early as 1809, New York City carpenters explicitly described the workplace as a "social compact" that mandated employer respect for workers' inalienable natural rights. Among those rights, they enumerated the length of the workday, a wage sufficient to raise a family and sustain themselves in their old age, and other familiar trade unionist themes. A society that failed to meet its obligations essentially nullified the claims of the social contract on the people. That left former participants in the social contract free to alter, abolish or remake it.[11] Such language certainly could cloak a direct challenge the assumptions of capitalism, but it did not necessarily require it.

Certainly, the very act of organization implied something of a common understanding of what the social contract of the workplace required, and it moved toward an agreement around a plan of action. Printers, shoemakers, and others in the traditional crafts found organizing a useful way of discussing how economic development devalued their skills. The progressive division of labor in the workplace allowed for using cheaper labor with less training to perform much of the work. Apprenticeships evolved into a form of child labor, flooding the craft with "half-way" and "two-thirds" craftsmen. In the new occupations associated with the mechanization and industrialization, not even feeble traditions restrained the growing specializations. Living machinists recalled when their employers had worked alongside them in a job that represented "a compound of handiwork, a kind of cross between a millwright and a whitesmith, a fitter, finisher, locksmith and so forth."[12]

Rapid economic growth actually made the lives of most workers and their families more miserable, particularly in the cities. Hired men in boarding houses doubled and tripled up on the room rentals. Married men enjoyed a somewhat better life, as the labors of their wives and children often contributed to the household budget. Most of the time, enough workers were coming and going to cushion an immediate awareness of the long-term, general trends in wages relative to the cost of housing and food.

That to which hired workers aspired was "free labor." The appeal of "free labor" or "free soil" was their very elasticity. Scholars have explored the many ways the term has proved to be a complex and troublesome concept. Employers of labor may have understood this in terms of the superiority of wage labor over slave labor, but surely the black workers coming out of slavery rarely understood it as the mere absence of formal enslavement.[13] It seems quite clear that most working people in Civil War America had an understanding of such things that included elements unshared with their social betters.

Conversely, workers from early in the century juxtaposed an idea of free labor to what they called "wages slavery" to describe grievances running from the workplace into government. For generations, Northern workingmen had argued that freedom without the material wherewithal to act freely—or the realistic hope of acquiring it—constituted a "wages slavery" comparable to the condition of "chattel slavery." Although Southern politicians took up the term to rebuke Northern critics of the South's "peculiar institution," historians embraced their top-down assumptions to describe a situation wherein free workers "echoed" the slaveholders as conscious apologists for slavery. This grotesque misunderstanding actually ignores the source of the term and the timing of its use.

Workers using an expression like "wages slavery" obviously did not necessarily mean the same thing. However, a growing number did so with a clear eye to the role of racially owned labor and an appreciation of the struggle against it, particularly the struggle by the owned workers themselves. Among the land reformers and many other radicals, they explicitly made this connection.

Then, too, for all the differences in their experience, African American laboring people spoke the same language of free labor and liberty to express their own aspirations for personal independence, particularly through land ownership or its equivalent. What differed for most, of course, would be not only slavery but also their persistent attempts to surmount it. African American writers had long described black resistance, more generally appreciated with the twentieth-century war against fascism, as a civil rights movement and "black pride."[14]

No less an authority than Samuel Gompers—future head of the American Federation of Labor—proposed his own alternative to the model of Thompson or Marx. The thirteen-year-old London-born Jewish immigrant had begun pondering these questions from his first look at the American working class in the summer of 1863. He worked as a cigarmaker, learning his organizing principles among the socialists and radicals of the city, generally followers of Karl Marx. In the end, Gompers concluded that the *Klassen Bewustzein* (class consciousness) posited by social scientists, statisticians, and vulgar Marxists meant little in America. While the workers of other advanced industrial nations waged mass strikes, organized industrial unions, launched and carried to victory their own labor and socialist parties, Gompers discerned a *Klassengefühl*, a feeling of class American workers naturally followed into the business unionism of the American Federation of Labor, which Gompers came to lead into the next century.[15] This explanation for a distinctly conservative workers' movement grew from a sense of exceptional American conditions that derived directly from the Civil War.

Gompers's view raises serious issues. On the surface, two German terms provides a strange way to distinguish an American answer to the views of a German social thinker. More substantively, though, class formation in other industrial nations had actually proved to be no less uneven and confused—and no less liable to institutional manipulation from the top down—than in the United States. All Western industrial societies have an ethnically stratified workforce, varying widely from region to region. Workers might well resent their bosses and voice that resentment, but a feeling of solidarity certainly tends to fade as one goes beyond the workplace to an entire industry, and the feeling becomes even more tenuous with regard to the workforce as a whole, so it provides a weak reed on which to rest unionism and national unions. As we shall see, however, it does explain an important dimension of the American class formation.

Whether we ascribe these efforts to express their common interests to their *Gefühl* or their *Bewustzein*, it took a conscious choice for workers to formulate and give priority to solidarity, however compromised, in the workplace over matters as important as religion and politics. This had immense implications as working people faced the sectional conflict. As one social commentator, Jennie Collins, wrote, "The late Civil War brought nearly as many great changes in the North as it did in the South."[16] The war took America and its entire laboring people through a series of rather distinct processes.

The events of 1860–1863 forced workers to draw heavily upon antebellum ideas of their identity in facing the realities of war. Working people responded to the imminence of civil war in with very clear and legitimate concerns that they would, as in any war, bear the burden of its waging. Certainly, the advent of war did absolutely nothing immediately to moderate the low standing of workers at home, and arguably the threat of war even intensified the subjugation of work and the power of the employers.

As the war became "irrepressible," large numbers of workers associated with labor organizations responded in traditional ways, though they did so in unprecedented numbers. The younger, unmarried white men expected to face violence, but few relished participation in a conflict on the scale of an impending civil war waged against their own countrymen. Significantly, Southern white workers turned out to fight dutifully, and these in far fewer numbers and with considerably less enthusiasm and determination than their peers in the North. The escalating human cost of the war drew ever-larger circles of men into the conflict. The new armies battling for "free labor" swallowed much of the union memberships and entire locals, virtually destroying the movement that had gone into the war.

Additionally, the war restructured the workforce. This diminishing of the Confederate labor supply and the imperatives of the Federal war effort resulted in an official emancipationist policy that sanctioned the largest mass strike in U.S. history to that point, rolling over the South as the proximity of the Union forces and the exodus of hundreds of thousands from slavery into the wage-earning workforce came to pass. The economic and industrial course of the war expanded the importance of unskilled labor in the expanding industries associated with war and wartime necessities and coincided with the wartime emphasis on ethnic identities, initiating a wave of desperate actions among the unskilled and generally immigrant workers. At the same time, the disappearance of available male labor left behind mothers, wives, sisters, and daughters who had to make their own arrangements amid this booming wartime demand for workers. In short, the war that shattered the old movement and then created a much broader hired workforce from which another could emerge.

As well, new organizations emerged in 1863–1864 in what amounted to a rebirth of the American labor movement. Across the North workers rebuilt old unions and forged new ones, drawing them together in new trades assemblies. Southern communities experienced this in uneven ways, depending directly on the collapse of the slave system and the Confederate power structure, as well as, ultimately, the fortunes of war, but the documentation offers us real insight into the spectrum of experience in their major cities. North and South, as the war entered the most intense phases, workers faced a new authoritarianism on the part of employers, backed by civil authorities using the hard hand of war among civilian workers on the home front.

Finally, by 1864–65—and contrary to all of the shallow rhetoric and the deep assumptions of laissez-faire—these new labor movements struggled under the heavy hand of government, north and south. The owners and managers of the new or newly expanding industries operated behind the authority of war and with an almost military imperative in offering conditions and wages simply on their own terms. Neither a unifying community identity among workers nor the institutionally feeble remnants of the older labor movement offered any deterrent to the employers. In the end, the Union victory for "free labor" poses a series of questions about the nature of the labor movements that could emerge, ambiguities that remain central to the making of an American working class.

Labor in the Civil War years not only had to address these issues but also did so while under fire, not only from a sectional slaveholding elite attempting secession but also from unprecedented repression by a centralized state power, itself new to the American experience. This is not to counterpose wage labor to the emancipationist goals government pursued for its own reasons but instead to acknowledge the complexities of the processes at work.[17] In the end, coming to grips with its innate lack of power and its own status as a subject class came naturally not from emancipation but from the wartime experience of dealing with government. Moreover, the black experience of war, reconstruction, and its results left African Americans with similar insights, alabeit from a particular perspective.

PROLOGUE

The Antebellum Labor Crisis

Organized Workers as a Force in Mid-Nineteenth-Century American History

March 1860 saw the largest strike to date in American history. At 8:00 A.M. on March 8, some fifteen hundred "ladies" led a march of thousands of shoemakers bearing "several hundred banners" through Lynn, Massachusetts. The townspeople, "with flags and streamers," and several local militia and fire companies paraded as bands of music escorted them, as did "delegations of ladies" from nearby communities. Overall, some seventeen thousand New England shoemakers—including two thousand women—noisily walked off their jobs and contested the local elites for control of the streets. While visiting the region, Abraham Lincoln claimed no special understanding of the issues, but he added, "I am glad to know that there is a system of labor where the laborer can strike if he wants to! I would to God that such a system prevailed all over the world."[1] On the eve of civil war, organized labor already moved in impressive numbers to its own martial beat.

Americans built their labor movement in a society, parts of which permitted employers to buy and sell workers. Trade unionism before the Civil War reached its impressive proportions only within a very restricted fraction of the workforce. Despite this, an uncompromising advocacy of "free labor" emerged from that workforce as surely as it did in other Western industrial societies. However, it too remained confined to skilled hired workingmen, though unskilled white immigrants, enslaved African Americans, and female workers performed vital labors. These deeply rooted institutional distinctions within the workforce became inseparable from the crisis that carried the entire nation to the brink of its destruction.

Organizations of Hired Workers

Like so many other features of American life, its labor movements, an organized expression of workers' self-awareness, reflected the British foundations of the civilization, though sometimes heavily accented. Trade unionists organized workplaces through the local organizations strong enough to make short-lived efforts to maintain citywide bodies at Philadelphia briefly in 1796 and again in 1827, followed by a succession of such "trades' unions" in other cities. Given the often-transient nature of that workforce, individual participation in the labor movement proved episodic, with a membership regularly responding to the seasonal ebb and flow of demand for labor, and their unions tended to collapse when the financial panics of 1819, 1837, and 1857 blighted job markets and scattered the membership. By 1834 the city associations tried to launch a National Trades' Union, said to represent an estimated thirty thousand to thirty-five thousand workers in half a dozen communities before its implosion later in the decade. As the economy and workers' organizations recovered, city-centrals reemerged after 1849, and, by the early 1850s, likely involved more than 120,000 participants.[2] A good portion of those hired workers with enough freedom to organize did so.

By then, better transportation grew markets that gave rise to new kinds of national unions, despite the growing sectionalism that strained the wider society. Working printers had organized episodically in New York, Philadelphia, and other cities for decades. In December 1849 twenty-seven New York compositors formulated a new wage scale for the newspapers, which revived their local union and sparked a series of national conventions. After reassembling in September 1851 and May 1852, they formed the National Typographical Union (NTU) in 1853.[3] Unlike its predecessor, the NTU weathered the national economic crisis in 1857.

So, too, the national unions of the hat finishers and stonecutters prevailed. In 1854, the National Silk and Fur Hat Finishers' Association superseded the older and more guild-like "Hatters Society" and promised to arbitrate workplace issues and insure "amiable" relations with employers about apprenticeships. The Journeymen Stone Cutters Association of the United States and Canada boasted locals at Albany, Baltimore, Buffalo, Cincinnati, Cleveland, Detroit, Hamilton, Hastings-on-Hudson, New York, Philadelphia, St. Louis, Toronto, and Washington, D.C., which claimed to be the same local that had marched at the 1792 laying of the cornerstone of the U.S. Capitol.[4]

Other national unions had formed but did not survive the Panic of 1857. In 1849 an ambitious National Union of Building Trades combined housepainters, stonecutters, plasterers, house carpenters, bricklayers, plumbers, and masons, and participated in New York's citywide federation. An Upholsterers National Union and some sort of general Mechanics' Trade Union Association of the United States formed in 1853, the Plumbers' National Union in 1854, and National Silver Platers in 1857. New York cigarmakers hosted an 1856 national convention of their craft, presaging a national organization. Locomotive engineers attempted a "National Protective Association of the United States" in 1855, and moved over workplace issues in 1856, when it began authorizing strikes.[5] At least some locals survived the collapse of national bodies, sometimes in secret, as did the train engineers.

After the panic, workers built new national unions. The National Cotton Mule Spinners' Association formed in 1858, based on strong locals, such as that at Fall River. Shoemakers had unionized locally since the eighteenth century and had a short-lived national organization in the 1830s, but the Cordwainers National union that formed in 1859 had to grapple with new issues of mass production and mechanization. Local unions of painters, representing between one-third and one-half of the men in the craft, had failed to organize nationally several times before the New York body, "the oldest and best-governed union of the trade," successfully established the Painters Grand Lodge. English, Welsh, and Irish miners brought their taste for organization into the American coalfields, braving severe repression in Pennsylvania but establishing strong locals in Illinois, which started the 1861 organization of the American Miners Association.[6]

Two particularly important new national unions grew from new industries centered at Philadelphia. In March 1859, the year-old local union launched the Jonathan C. Fincher's National Union of Machinists and Blacksmiths, which, by November 1860, had 2,828 members in fifty-seven locals, which cooperated with American members of Britain's Amalgamated Society of Engineers, Machinists, Smiths, Millwrights, and Patternmakers in America. The National Union of Iron Molders formed in July 1859, winning a much-touted "complete victory" against pay cuts at Sputen Duyvull and surviving a year-long strike against the Excelsior Stove Works, which tried to break the union at St. Louis. By 1860, its dozen founding locals grew to forty-four, with 2,744 members.[7]

These new national unions required tough-minded and pragmatic leaders, such as William H. Sylvis. The son of a Pennsylvania wagonmaker and boat builder, he obtained much of what education he could in return for doing farm chores in the home B. F. Pawling. When only nine years old, Sylvis experienced the Panic of 1837 and, when his father's shop went under, lived with Pawling for the next six years. Although he helped in his father's trade for a while, Sylvis gained an apprenticeship as a helper in an ironworks and continued near Curwensville in a foundry. A temperance advocate and Methodist Sunday school teacher, he married in 1852 and settled in Philadelphia. Before the war, he won national office in the union and arguably became the most important labor leader of his generation.[8]

Hundreds of local unions functioned on the eve of the Civil War without ever participating in these new kind of national unions. A decade before the war, the New York City Industrial Congress listed groups from more than sixty organized occupations, and those in the bodies at Philadelphia, Baltimore, and Pittsburgh brought the total to well over a hundred various crafts. In New York and similar Northeast urban settings, free blacks account for some of these local unions. Some of these had made it through the Panic of 1857 in one form or another.

The Ideology of Self-Organization

At the most basic level, participants in these unions shared a belief that their own concerted actions could improve their lot. The role of religion in formulating that sense varied widely. Bruce Laurie's work clarified categories of preindustrial traditional sensibilities, evangelical faith, or rationalism that shaped workers' approaches to life.[9] Individuals, however, likely migrated across these barriers as suited them at any point and rarely challenged an underlying drive for secular success and material well-being.

Many tried to do as expected, only to find that the path of Benjamin Franklin (or Horace Greeley) had become increasingly steep and narrow. Some minimal successes at upward mobility usually involved other moves, particularly to the West. In 1859, Missouri printer John Merrick gathered what type he could and loaded the little Mormon press salvaged from the river at Independence almost a generation earlier and joined the Pike's Peak Gold Rush. When he reached Denver, he began setting the first number of the *Cherry Creek Pioneer*. Shortly after, an entrepreneur—neither a printer nor an editor—brought a well-funded, well-equipped operation that put hired printers to work on the *Rocky Mountain News*. There followed an uneven race, ending on April 23, when the *News* beat Merrick's paper into the streets by twenty minutes. "Jolly Jack" accepted his fate and went to work for the *News*, but he presided over the Denver Typographical Union, "the city's second oldest surviving institution." When the *News* celebrated its first anniversary with a pay cut, the union declared "Denver's first strike."[10] In fact, Merrick's success, like that of so many of his peers, had turned out to be a failure in the end.

The same considerations that moved competing businesses in the same craft or industry toward uniform standards and conditions affected workers. While the moral suasion of the owners remained central, the ultimate source of union power rested on the threatened withdrawal of labor in the "turn-out" or "strike." As this closed the shops of the employers who refused to accede to those demands, unionists established picket lines to publicize the employer's noncompliance. These also patrolled for strikebreakers or "scabs," inflicting the greatest scorn on those union members who crossed the line—"rats," in the lexicon of the printers. Without an intervention by the courts, unions usually succeeded when their goals generally reflected the distinctive interests of organized workers, a labor movement.

The history of antebellum unionism remained inexorably intertwined with the larger milieu of labor reform, even in the most successful and conservative craft organizations. Workers on the New York City newspapers established the Typographical Union, and, in April 1853, two hundred book and job printers formed "a protective trade union, co-operative with the Printers' Union." Their New York Cooperative Printers Union elected Keyes Arthur Bailey president and strove to improve wages and working conditions without paying the NTU's higher dues to sustain generous benefit features. After enrolling several hundred members, the "cooperatives" asked the NTU to recognize two locals in the city, one for newspapers and another for everyone else. From 1854 into 1857, the two bodies clashed not over cooperationism and unionism but over how inclusive unionism should be. In the end, they combined.[11]

James Gordon Bennett's antilabor Democratic *New York Herald* strove tirelessly to distinguish between labor reform and unionism. In 1850Bennett had urged participants in the local Industrial Congress, including his own employees, to "limit the membership to the trades, and . . . make a clean sweep of the politicians and socialists." Although scholars anachronistically read into this a distinction between "pure and simple" trade unionists and the reformers, those Bennett named among the latter included Bailey and Henry Crate, representing both printers' unions, and Ben Price the carpenter and J. J. Franks the hatter. So, too, they have misunderstood "benevolent" or "benefit" societies as mere fraternal associations, distinct from "protective unions" engaged in trade regulation. In reality, contemporaries called some cooperatives "protective unions," and "benevolent" or "benefit" societies could function as unions, even as a self-described "literary society" among nailmakers called a strike.[12] Then, too, Bennett never proved more sympathetic to any single federation of the trades, though composed of "solid unions" among hatters, stonecutters, machinists, molders, printers, bricklayers "and others."

In reality, even the conservative printers' union had a long tradition of free thought. As Horace Seaver wrote, "We owe every improvement of the age, every advance in science, government, and art, to agitation." Ideas of serious change nested most comfortably among "those who were apparently the least calculated to advance them; among those who were weak in power and influence." Liberty could not progress left to the "powerful princes and barons." His friend and union member, Joseph N. Moreau, sought to root his radicalism in the ideas of Tom Paine, whose biography he aspired to write.[13]

A broad tradition of worker skepticism about capitalism grew in the first half of the century, broadly analogous to developments in other industrializing societies, where laboring people experienced the reality of how little justice the marketplace would produce for them. At the onset of the century, the loose circles of freethinkers had applied their reasoned skepticism to society with an 1802 account of life in a fictional Lithconia. There, "the acquisition of property was every thing, and the cunningest knave was the best man." There, the upper classes maintained "an order of men to teach the people that all the evils which afflict the generations of men were appointed by God the Supreme Ruler." Lithconian reformers dated the rebirth of their civilization from their decision to think past the lies of these "hired deceivers" to share the land and the bounties of Nature.[14]

Over these years, workers periodically expressed this skepticism politically in response to overt government action against them, and, in 1860, any fifty-year-old craftsmen who had been in those cities remembered outbursts of mass insurgency. Thirty years before, the gradual elimination of the property requirements for voting resulted in the rise of local workingmen's parties at Philadelphia, New York, Boston, and elsewhere. In its wake came citywide federations of labor, coupled in places with various reform currents, such as the Locofocos in New York City. Scholars have traditionally believed that the Jacksonian rhetoric against banks and "monopoly" may have drawn many workers to the Democratic Party, and the identification of the Whigs with exclusionary elites particularly tended to drive immigrant or Catholic workers toward the Democrats. Such a scenario certainly jibed with the later partisan associations of labor organizations and the predisposition of scholars. However, government encouragement of economic development also interested workers and led some just as easily to the Whigs and other major oppositional currents, including the American or Nativist currents in some cities. After the Panic of 1837 the more radical workers looked for labor emancipation through an egalitarian restructuring of land ownership.[15]

For decades, labor reform included advocates of land reform, cooperation, and socialism, as advocated by Robert Owen in the 1820s and by Charles Fourier in the 1840s. They argued, as did Seaver, that "man requires the full supply of his physical necessities." Meeting those needs, they believed, required the formation of scientifically humanitarian communities grounded in equality and justice. Some old Owenites survived to the Civil War, but larger numbers of often-influential Fourierists did, most notably Horace Greeley and the old *Tribune* people, such as Assistant Secretary of War Charles A. Dana. Warren B. Chase expressed their general response to Paine's pamphlet series *The American Crisis* not primarily as a power struggle or a clash over specific issues but as a struggle over the future of democracy and progress.[16]

Land reform represented the most political manifestation of working-class aspirations. At the time of the Civil War, labor reform included figures such as John Commerford, who had begun his career as a leader of the cabinetmakers' union in 1830. He subsequently became involved in one of those pioneering local Workingmen's parties and the insurgent Equal Rights Democrats, known as "Locofocos." In the mid-1840s, Commerford joined other veteran Workies to launch the land reform movement, which had contributed to the emergence of mass "free soil" politics. Joshua K. Ingalls, Henry Beeny, Lewis Masquerier, and Ben Price led these efforts until the war.

The "agrarianism" of the National Reform Association (NRA) involved: the complete exemption of all family-operated farms from foreclosure for debt; the establishment of a Federal Homestead Act to assure access to land by those presently without it; and land limitation, clearly the most radical feature of its program but one essential to equitable land distribution. Over time they expanded their program to call for a ten-hour workday, cooperative workshops, and a wide range of other measures, ultimately including abolitionism and woman suffrage. Using time-honored language, they described wage labor as "wages slavery" and hoped to secure "free labor" through what they called "free soil."[17] In the massive petition drives of the NRA, tens of thousands of Americans regularly called for legal limits to land ownership as a means for encouraging its broader distribution, reflecting just how widespread the appeal of such radicalism could be.

When a handful of union printers established the *United States Mechanics' Own* on the eve of the sectional hostilities, the publication reflected all of these currents. The articles and letters from across the country underscored the necessity of self-organization, of assisting each other across craft lines. These reflected activities beyond the big cities at places such as Bergen Hill, Wilmington, or Zanesville. In May 1860, one of the editors, Charles B. Church of the Typographical Union toured the west with the express purpose of organizing unions wherever he could, in any craft. Fred Oberkline, the Cincinnati molder, toured industrial communities from Pittsburgh to St. Louis. Another of their collaborators, Sylvis would also follow this course, and do so for some years beyond the war.[18] Certainly, the *Mechanics' Own* articulated a fighting spirit usually associated with later labor movements.

The concerns of the most important labor paper in the country hardly echoed those of the Democratic would-be voices of the worker, though they hardly shunned political commentary. "Will you leave this country to those who come after us a model republic or a despotism?" a coach painter asked his union. The *Mechanics' Own* embraced land reform, discussed the distribution of wealth, and challenged the assumptions of the class structure. It also endorsed cooperative ventures, particularly early experiments by Philadelphia workers with the Rochdale Society of Equitable Pioneers consumer cooperative plan brought over from England, as well as a shorter workday: "Eight hours work, eight hours sleep, eight hours study and recreation will preserve one's life eighty years." The paper and the unions that supported it frankly acknowledged "the hostility of the relations which now exist between Capital and Labor," which "involuntarily" pit workers wanting as much as they could get for their labor against bosses hoping to get that labor for as cheaply as they could. This amounted to a struggle of "the greater the number of dollars" against "the greater the number of laborers."[19] In America, as elsewhere, large numbers of skilled workers rejected the assumptions, values, and positions of their social betters, and they articulated the rudiments of a distinctive social consciousness with a great potential for influencing change.

Several peculiarities, however, afflicted the emergence of a genuine class sensibility.

The Unfree and the Nominally Free

Vast sections of the American workforce labored in very different conditions that made participation in such a clear and structured labor movement largely impossible. The mechanisms of trade unionism simply offered such workers no real agency for addressing their concerns. Instead, slaves found an extraordinarily broad and creative range of asserting their interests, everything from slowdowns and feigning sickness to active attempts to harm their masters or flee their enslavement. Conversely, of course, such practices would be of no real use to their contemporary trade unionists.

Since the mid-twentieth century, race has moved to the fore of scholarly interest. Students of race in America have shrewdly drawn upon sociological studies of slavery's origins in the Caribbean, emphasizing the cultural and ultimately subjective distinction of "whiteness." However useful the insight, it often smudges vital differences with slavery on the North American mainland, in the scale of the institution, the overwhelming proportion of black slaves to free whites, and the overwhelmingly plantation nature of slavery in the islands. More fundamentally, the legal and social restrictions imposed on race mixing would have been superfluous had it not been a continual worry for the rulers.[20] Understanding the legacy of race involves nuances and complexities.

A similarly sharp legal or constitutional line between slavery and "freedom" hardly encompassed the complex social realities of slavery. In the southern United States, slavery had to remain far more flexible in order to permit a vast spectrum of labor under diverse circumstances in terms of family and community identities, and under supervision with varying severity. While all slaves shared a common legal status, much turned on the kind of work they did, their relationship to a household, and the size of the community in which they performed their labor. A significant portion of slaves lived in cities, some having trades or working in industrial jobs. Masters also rented slaves to perform different work for wages, and, particularly in the lower South, some slaves negotiated additional time on their own to seek employment and earn wages.[21] In reality, different categories of labor involved variations in the degree of control and implied a complex spectrum of experiences.

Some free African Americans attained enough wealth to own property, with a well-publicized handful even owning slaves themselves. On the other hand, free blacks faced enough pervasive impositions to merit their description as "slaves without masters." Some lived and worked in situations where participation in unions made sense. In the early 1850s the United Association of Colored Waiters used those barriers to protect jobs and, with the later New York Waiters Protective Union, raised pay to sixteen dollars and then eighteen dollars per month. These included what was later called the Coachman's Union League Society. However, even in a slaveholding city such as Baltimore, black ship caulkers, laboring alongside whites, had some sort of association that established sufficient unity of action to have been protested by the whites, who appealed to race ties and to their loyalty to the employers in an effort to break the hold of the union. Increasing sectional tensions translated into overtly racial clashes in that craft during the summers of 1858 and 1859. The prestigious NTU included at least two black members, one acknowledged to be an African American in Providence and the other "passing" as white in New Orleans.[22] Yet antebellum black trade unionism represents the defining margins of the African American workforce.

Although "white," European immigrants faced an even more diverse experience. Roughly one-eighth of all white Americans had actually been born elsewhere. The several million Irish or German newcomers and other foreign-born people disproportionately concentrated in the North and, particularly, in the cities. They shaped urban life, the Irish having a special influence in New York and Boston and the Germans in the great cities of the interior: Cincinnati, Milwaukee, St. Louis, and Chicago. The numbers of the latter usually included German-speaking Swiss, Austrian, Poles, Hungarians, and Czechs. In addition, French and French Canadians concentrated in places, and ten thousand Italians lived in New York; Scandinavians clustered in places as well.[23]

These newcomers performed an even greater range of work than did African Americans, but they disproportionately ended up doing less skilled labor with less pay, less job stability, and under worse conditions than those whites who had been here longer. Those with skills that landed them alongside the native-born craftsmen had participated in the trade unions from their origins in the United States. As later arrivals, they naturally tended to fill the entry-level, lowest-paying, hardest-working, least-stable new industries. Their presence certainly cushioned workers with deeper roots and longer experience from those sectors of the workforce most likely to inspire the kind of political radicalism or cultural hooliganism the press associated with immigrants. Even the most radical of them, though—such as the German molders at St. Louis—spoke of "the rights that belong to white men."[24]

The coherence of these immigrants depended on where they settled and what they faced. The largest numbers of the Irish in these years landed at New York City. Yet most did not settle into the colorful and distinctive neighborhoods of the Sixth Ward but passed on into the rest of the country, seeking their personal destinies, and many of the few who did not might well have done so, had they been able to afford it. No less than native whites, though, immigrants strove for survival and success as individuals on their own behalf or for their household and family.[25] The experience of being Irish in rural Illinois was never the same as in the Sixth Ward, however.

Still, while Cornish miners in Illinois or German furniture makers in New York found a place in the trade unions, the kind of work most immigrants did proved much rougher. In a large road construction crew, workers knew that their employers had little investment in their presence and well-being, and the workers, in turn, felt little investment in the job. The jobs themselves tended to be for an indefinite tenure, and a treasury large enough for mutual assistance often made no sense. In good times, they had less to lose by moving on in search of something better.

If, in hard times or otherwise, bosses tried to get by with paying less than agreed, workers would respond knowing that they would taste no victory without a speedy win. Workers in this position knew that they had only their own numbers to achieve what they needed, and they never hesitated to do what was necessary to persuade their peers to join them. In the decades before the war, the growing number of reports of their strikes used terms like "riotous" and "violent," alongside descriptions of "foreigners" and, even more often, "Irish." On one level, these extended the old distinctions between the worthy poor and the vicious classes, dependent and dangerous.

These workers had never been as spontaneous or unorganized as they seemed from the outside, but their level of organization did not exceed what was needed. To a great extent, it suited workers and protected their leaders to appear as a largely disorganized "mob" instinctively barring the way to strikebreakers or clashing with the authorities. As with the enslaved condition of most African Americans, the unskilled immigrant in such jobs simply developed means for most effectively and safely asserting their interests in the position into which they were kept.

Professions of solidarity did not come easily between the native-born and immigrants and were more infrequent between "whites" and African Americans. The radical proponents of free labor spoke of enduring a "wage slavery" implicitly placed on all laboring people in the same class as enslaved blacks. An 1850 report to their National Industrial Congress described all labor in America as ultimately coerced and representing different layers of slavery. They sometimes addressed each other as "fellow slaves." While such language often meant different things to different people in different contexts, it certainly did not constitute an ipso facto apology for slavery and held the germ of an idea of solidarity. In any event, the 1851 National Industrial Congress voted overwhelmingly to admit a black delegate, throwing the Democratic press in hysterics.

Gender proved a still harder sell for antebellum labor. Notwithstanding the dramatic example of the Lynn shoemakers, only a very small portion of female labor worked where unions had any practical meaning and use. Almost all women worked in their own personal setting, and most of those who also worked outside the home tended to be extending their domestic sphere of work, taking in laundry, for example. A growing number had begun to bring contracted piecework back into their domiciles as well, but this remained the most atomized kind of labor one could do. For decades, a very small number participated in the industrial concentration of such work in the new factory system, and women had participated in strikes. As with unskilled immigrant work crews, they surely had a greater level of organization than they generally presented to the world.

However, the atomized and overworked position of most female labor in America also inspired its own methods of resistance. The paternalistic values of the society imposed ideas about the sanctity of womanhood, motherhood, marriage, and children. Gentlemen unmoved by efforts at "moral suasion" over racial slavery found themselves vulnerable to such appeals to their own chivalry. This course did not permit women to determine what might be done to meet their needs, but it provided an almost certain avenue of appeal.

Male workers sometimes did support their female peers, particularly when imposed upon by vicious male bosses. However, few understood as well as the anti-institutional radicals around Cleveland's *New Republic* that "woman must be made entirely independent of men," particularly in an economic sense. This, it was argued, represented "a first step towards social reorganization."[26] Solidarity would always be a hard-won lesson.

* * *

Before the Civil War, laboring people experienced work less as a class than as individuals in specific occupations, but this did not preclude an underlying sense of where they stood in the social order. They had precious little to say about their views on the social contract, because they knew that talk would have no real influence with the owners of their workplaces and the rulers of their country. Notwithstanding of national independence, American courts even used common law to prosecute unions as criminal conspiracies. Their governments followed the British example of encouraging businesses with legislated privileges, protective tariffs, and charters, but they extended no such privileges or protections to human labor.[27]

Radicals such as Commerford appealed to the logic of laissez-faire, claiming for labor organizations the same freedom to manage the only capital they had. They wanted the same protection for their labor as government willingly extended to other forms of capital held by privately owned, profit-making organizations.[28] Whether urging that their organizations retain the same freedom from state interference or the same legislative sanction as a business, they wanted their organizations on equal footing before the law with capital. A common argument for equality underlay the diverse antebellum solutions to "the labor problem," but the nature of work in America institutionalized the most glaring of inequalities.

PART I

Labor, Liberty, and Union

Bone and sinew of the land,
Know your rights, and by them stand!
On this glorious day retrace
Deeds of your own working race!

—"The Working Men's Fourth
of July Anthem"

CHAPTER 1

Workers and the Crisis of Nationhood

The Social Republic, Peace, and the Union

In April 1861 twenty-one-year-old Wesley Washington Pasko skulked through the streets of Charleston, South Carolina. After joining the New York City Typographical Union, he had also helped to organize the Troy local before returning in January 1861 and leaving for Charleston in March. Unwilling to rely on more easily recognized and detained editors and reporters, the *New York Tribune* sent one of its young printers to cover the confrontation over Fort Sumter. Older and more well-traveled union members would have been ducking the Charleston printers and newspapermen who might have recognized them.[1] Pasko had his own difficulties trying to remain incognito as he witnessed the onset of a conflict that would transform labor, liberty, and the union.

The secessionist guns in Charleston harbor aimed at the survival of both the American republic and the aspirations workers had within that republic. The year 1860 had been a banner one for organized labor, with the largest strike in American history to that time and the prospects of rebuilding the national unions lost in the recent financial panic. A new Republican insurgency swept the nonslaveholding states, based in large part on a sufficiently amorphous idea of "free labor" to inspire even the most radical workers and supporters. As secession confronted Republican victory, organized workers briefly stepped from the shadows to repudiate both sectionalism and the prospect of sectional warfare. As it became clear that nothing short of armed conflict would sustain the republic, workers had to become conscious of another dimension of their place in society.

Sectionalism and the Old Trades: Shoemakers and Printers

Sectional disparities and tensions certainly shaped the course of the most well-documented labor organizations. For all of the many and diverse locations in which workers organized, it is rare to see an account of any successful efforts venturing far into slaveholding territory deeper than the border cities of Wilmington, Baltimore, Washington, Louisville, and St. Louis. Letters reached the *Mechanics' Own* from Vicksburg, Mississippi, and Macon, Georgia, but no further reports indicated any unions formed there.[2]

Sectionalism shaped the emergence of unionism among printers and shoemakers, two trades that had been organizing since the eighteenth century. Shoemakers minimized the practical importance of their national organization to focus on local and regional cooperation. Long a center for shoemaking, Lynn, Massachusetts, also pioneered large-scale shoe production. For a quarter-century shoemakers there had sought to establish permanent labor organizations. By the 1840s admirers of French socialist Charles Fourier and American land reformers had won a broad local following for their cooperationist and political goals. Even as the Panic of 1857 loomed, local workingmen launched the Lynn Mechanics' Association.[3]

Although not yet twenty-five years old, Alonzo Granville Draper, who chaired that association by 1859, became one of the most important organizers of antebellum labor. Born in Brattleboro, Vermont, he had attended the English high school in Boston and had found at least seasonal work teaching. However, his marriage to Sarah E. Andrews united him to a family of local shoemakers, and the early arrival of at least two children likely kept him working at whatever he could. He became the editor of the *New England Mechanic* and commanded a militia unit, the Lynn Mechanics' Phalanx, largely composed of men of that trade.

By early February 1860 prices had begun to rebound from the depression figures, but New England shoe bosses stubbornly resisted any pay increase. A Natick circular quickly began galvanizing those workers intent upon raising wages. The strike spread quickly until it reached Lynn, after which it caught fire; Draper and other well-drilled, militia-trained strike leaders organized a highly disciplined movement at Lynn that conducted itself with military precision. On Washington's birthday Draper and other strike leaders presided over a mass meeting of some three thousand that dispatched "missionaries . . . all over the State converting the shoemakers to the true faith." They effectively prevented strikebreaking and brought shoe production to a grinding halt through much of the region. Pressured by the shoe bosses, town officials began hiring Boston policemen in an unsuccessful effort to maintain order by protecting scabs. Under Draper, the strikers carefully focused on winning the hearts and minds of their communities. The strike enjoyed the support of Lynn clergymen, such as Rev. Charles C. Shackford, the black preacher Thomas Driver, and Father Patrick Strain.

The issue quickly assumed national prominence. Lynn and Essex County remained the epicenter, but Middlesex and Worcester County shoemakers walked off as well. Boston-area shoemakers declined to strike but did organize support, and the movement failed to reach many south of Boston. However, shoemakers in at least seven New Hampshire towns struck, as did some as far as Maine. In fact, by mid-March, inspired shoemakers at Lafayette, Indiana, went out as well. Supporters raised money not only at New York City, Brooklyn, and Newark, but also at Philadelphia, Baltimore, and as far west as St. Louis. The strike committee discussed sending missionaries from New England "as far as Lynn shoes go, even to New Orleans."[4]

The strike lasted into April and beyond. Determined shoemakers in Lynn prevented the work finished by strikebreakers from reaching the railroad depot in what the press called "more or less rioting." The authorities asked neighboring towns for police support but were refused. However, Boston sent a detachment, even as the state's attorney general sent "a hundred special policemen," and the Lynn Light Infantry mobilized. The final outcome of the strike varied, with localized successes and defeats.

The Yankee shoe strike quickly became part of the sectional debate over the nature of free labor. Seeing it as an effective counter to the abolitionist agitation, one Southern capitalist offered to pledge one hundred dollars to the strike, and the West Baton Rouge *Sugar Planter* imagined a discussion among the strikers in which one of them asked, "Shall we assert our superiority over Southern niggers?" In reality, though, the twenty-five-year-old strike leader Napoleon Wood had returned to New England from the Free State efforts in Kansas, and the strike regularly made effective use of antislavery analogies. Abolitionists and prominent Republicans as far south as Newark contributed both public support and strike funds. When Draper spoke at New York City, he shared the platform with Horace Greeley. Further, when one Congressional Democrat blamed the strike on declining shoe orders from the South, "the result of the unfortunate warfare brought about by this sectional controversy," a newspaper got a response from a nationally prominent Midwestern Republican visiting Hartford for a comment. Abraham Lincoln frankly acknowledged that he knew little of the shoe markets. "I know one thing," he added, "*there is a strike!* And I am glad to know that there is a system of labor where the laborer can strike if he wants to! I would to God that such a system prevailed all over the world."[5]

While in the northeast, Lincoln also spent time with Amos Jay Cummings, an eighteen-year-old union printer. After his masterful address at New York's

Cooper Union, he stepped into the crowded frenzy of a gas-lit composing room at the *Tribune* to check the galleys before going to print. An adventurous and ambitious native of Broome County, Cummings retained his Jacksonian politics and had actually gone to Nicaragua in a filibustering expedition as a boy. Despite his Democratic predispositions, though, Cummings had a "pleasant" conversation with Lincoln in a quiet corner of the large composing table. The future president impressed the printer by concentrating on the task at hand amid all the noise and chaos of his surroundings.[6]

Newspapers and government contracts gave printing a particularly political dimension. As early as the 1830s, a member of the New York union, Ely Moore, won election to the House of Representatives. Even as Lincoln and the Republicans sought to admit Kansas to the Union, that territory selected Martin F. Conway, a Southern-born founder of the NTU, to represent it in Congress.

Cummings's particularly well-documented national union remained essentially an organization of the large Northern cities, the locals at New York and Philadelphia alone accounting for a thousand members. That said, the craft existed across the country, and the national character of the union required Southern locals. With the Panic of 1857, national membership dropped to only 1,286 but bounced back in 1858 to 2,181 and in 1859 to 2,362; the union reached 3,592 members in 1860. This process of rebuilding the national union made it all the more important to alleviate sectionalism when the NTU's representatives assembled at Nashville, Tennessee, May 7–12, 1860, to deliberate over a hopeful future.[7]

Membership in the small Southern unions generally reflected the demographics of the skilled white workforce in the region, which consisted disproportionately of Northern or foreign-born journeymen. A veteran of the Mexican War with his health broken, DeWitt Clinton Roberts of Illinois went south to recover, though he returned north in 1858 as a New Orleans delegate to the NTU convention. Still, those Southern whites who were members used language identical to that of their Northern peers. S. P. Bassett spoke the language familiar to unionists at Boston when he addressed members of his union at Montgomery, Alabama. "Labor was before property, as God was before the creation," he declared, "for it is the former which produces the latter, and gives the possessor a title."[8] This reflected the nature of Southern trade unionism as buffered entirely from the broader workforce and slavery.

Nevertheless, contemporary trade unionists certainly acknowledged the sectional peculiarities of their organizations in the antebellum South. White printers who ventured there might have had better prospects of gaining and retaining proprietorship of a newspaper than in the North, should they be personally willing to negotiate the conditions shaped by the region's institution. On the other hand, the 1859 election of officers in the New Orleans local ended in a knife fight, the news of which horrified Northern members.[9]

The most important issues the NTU faced at its 1860 national convention in Nashville broke down along sectional lines. Locals regularly circulated the names of "rats" who had betrayed the union, but a border state case resulted in a national dispute. Objecting to their circulation, E. A. Patterson of Charleston urged a federation of autonomous local unions with their own standards, for which ratting in one community might have no effect on one's possible standing in another. William Madigan of Boston led a successful floor fight to block Patterson's innovation, and this largely sectional standoff over a national policy on "rats" framed the election of the NTU's president. On the first ballot, the thirty-nine delegates split between Patterson, Bassett—then at Memphis—and the Yankee Madigan. In the end, the delegates settled on John M. Farquhar. Intelligent and self-reliant, the dark-complexioned five-foot-ten-inch Scotsman in the Chicago local had not yet reached age thirty but had earlier lived and worked in the South.[10] As in the Federal Union, so it was that an adopted Illinoisan with Southern connections came to the presidency of the NTU.

Free Labor in National Political Debate

By 1860, a six-year-old third-party movement carried the presidency. The Democratic employer, James G. Bennett, who regularly clashed with his union printers, found the convergence of labor reform with antislavery politics intolerably vexing. Democrats in Congress not only passed the 1854 Kansas-Nebraska Act, but they bent every effort to foist a proslavery government on the territory. In Wisconsin, veteran radicals Alvan Earl Bovay and Warren Chase detonated a new third-party effort, while pioneering Republicans in Michigan included Bovay's old colleague from New York, Donald C. Henderson, as well as William Harsha, "a strong abolitionist" in the Detroit Typographical Union. Across the country insurgents proclaimed their faith in free labor.[11] Certainly, their ideas about the subject remained contradictory enough to appeal to a broad constituency.

The Democratic Party presided over the economic Panic of 1857, undercutting rhetorical professions of sympathy with the common people and handing the Republicans a vital issue. Then, Southern Democratic intransigence against even the most moderate land-reform legislation culminated in Buchanan's veto of the Homestead Bill.[12] Finally, Democrats denounced Lincoln's supporters as "mudsills" and "greasy mechanics," which helped assure the new Republican Party of getting a realistic hearing among working-class voters.

A generation of efforts by Southern leaders to cultivate sectional fears of abolitionism and slave rebellion had already shaped Northern fears about a "Slave

Power Conspiracy." While some Republican office seekers may have employed the rhetoric to appeal to a "paranoid style," many articulate working citizens in the North had come to understand slavery along with land monopoly and other trends as a concrete threat to the "the republic." In short, the Republican insurgency tapped a deeply rooted working-class discontent with the older rivalry of Democrats and Whigs.

The issue of "free labor"—and its studied vagueness as to what it meant—contributed much to the Republican victory. Delegates to the national convention of May 1860 included those with the most radical ideas possible on the subject. Their candidate, Lincoln, had Edward Kellogg's book rethinking *Labor and Capital*. Land reformers in Illinois, including Benjamin J. F. Hanna, participated in the new party, as did John L. Scripps, Lincoln's campaign biographer; but other radicals, such as the Chartist and socialist Richard J. Hinton, wrote another life of Lincoln. *The Printer* pointed with pride to the fact that Lincoln's vice president, his postmaster general, as well as his secretaries of the War Department and the Navy had all been printers.[13]

Wise Republicans cultivated this identification with the laboring white people. "The Democrats who affect to be above all aristocratic notions, sneer at Lincoln, because he was a rail splitter," declared one of these orators, James A. Briggs. He described his as "preeminently the party of the workingmen," which was "opposed to slavery then because it degraded men of his own race and color," for "free labor and slavery could not dwell together in one territory." As to the old working classes' concerns about access to the land, Briggs added, "Uncle Sam was rich enough to give us all a farm, but if he filled up his territories with servile hosts he crowds out freemen."[14]

Radical labor reform became an important vehicle for bringing the Republican message to working-class and ethnic voters, even in slaveholding border states. Joseph Weydemeyer, August Willich, and other émigré radicals took up the Republican cause here with as much enthusiasm as they had in their homelands during 1848–49, partly reversing the earlier immigrant predisposition to the Democrats. This process even extended into slaveholding states, where Maryland coal miners displayed placards for Lincoln and union printers such as John L. Bittenger of the St. Louis local labored diligently for the Republican ticket.[15]

In New York City's Lower East Side, radical labor reformers provided the core of the Republican effort. In the overwhelmingly Democratic Fourth Congressional District, Benjamin F. Price and other land reformers secured the Republican nomination for "Honest John" Commerford, the veteran leader of the cabinet and chair makers, whose activities began with the Workies of the 1820s and continued through his presidency of the citywide General Trades' Union and the pioneering National Trades' Union in the 1830s. In 1844 Commerford had become a founding member of the National Reform Association, agitating the land question. In the 1850s, Commerford, Price, and their comrades formed a circle of the Brotherhood of the Union. It participated in antislavery politics through the local Free Democratic Party but helped draw that party locally into a broad coalition that the English Garibaldian Hugh Forbes had formed from French, Italian, German, and other radical associations. Calling themselves "Universal Democratic Republicans" in 1853–55, they affiliated with the new "International Association" overseas.[16]

During these years, Commerford had acquired his own little shop but remained a spokesman for the movement. In early October 1860 eighteen of the twenty-eight elected Republican delegates voted at their district convention to nominate Commerford for Congress. The politicians running the state party had little enthusiasm for a candidate who looked very much to them like a working-class revolutionary, and they actually made several efforts to overturn the nomination. However, members of the local *Kommunist Klub* and the Garibaldi Wide-Awakes embraced the campaign. At one point, hundreds of torch-bearing supporters marched to a rally where orators recalled the Sons of Liberty, who had once moved through the same neighborhoods to defend artisans' rights and republican aspirations.[17]

In the wake of the election, Commerford and his radical Republicans joined this new Commonwealth Association, which had emerged from spiritualist circles to involve many of the most iconoclastic of the American labor reformers.[18] It called the new National Industrial Congress "of working men and women" to meet on Tuesday, November 20, "to discuss questions connected with the laboring interests." These annual gatherings had met from 1846 to 1856, when escalating tensions indirectly related to the emergence of the Republicans made them less relevant. In the wake of the 1860 Republican triumph, labor reformers hoped to revive interest in "the various questions connected with Labor and Land Reform." The *Herald of Progress* summarized its resolution.

> That the present system of commerce is false—that the laborer should receive the full net product of his labor—that all intermediates between producers and consumers are non-essential; they should exchange with each other the produces [sic] of their own labor—that the legal recognition of paper currency should cease—that land monopoly is an evil—that the public lands should be given to actual settlers—that a homestead exemption law should be passed—that women are entitled to an equal voice with men in the administration of government, and to the same freedom of industrial pursuits, and the same compensation enjoyed by men.

Before closing, the resolution revisited the idea of "a new and distinct political party" but informally seemed to agree that the Republican Party loomed as a vehicle to implement workers' interests.[19]

On December 10, just after that final antebellum National Industrial Congress, veteran shoe strikers went to the polls at Lynn. These voters helped send Lincoln to the White House but seethed with anger at the municipal officials who had called in the Boston police against them. They elected Hiram N. Breed, "the Citizens' and Workingmen's candidate for Mayor," by a majority of about three hundred. A longtime reformer, Breed remained "a working shoemaker, and quietly occupied his bench for the greater part of the day of election." After the count, several hundred workers, led by former strike leader James Dillon, turned up to present Breed with "a mammoth broom, saying that it was the wish of the parties for whom he presented that he would 'sweep clean.'" Breed appointed strike leader Alonzo G. Draper as town marshal, and Draper replaced the police with prominent strikers.[20]

However, on December 20, South Carolina seceded, challenging not only the survival of the American republic but the agenda of all serious labor reformers and trade unionists. Workers' hopes for peaceful change by the ballot could not survive a system where part of the ruling elite could simply veto the result of a national election. Most immediately, it provided a political justification for the Southern states to cancel any debts its people owed residents of the United States. Secession destroyed all hopes of men such as Commerford for collecting any of their debts from the Southern trade. In his case, he was forced at age sixty to abandon his hard-won furniture business and return to the journeyman's bench. This shook the confidence of investors and caused an immediate financial crisis, over which a gloating *Charleston Mercury* reported a Northern economy on the brink of collapse that would leave "the laboring classes . . . employed half time, or at reduced wages."[21] While wishful thinking, the fears were real enough and fueled the genuine complexities of worker reactions to the sectional crisis.

Peace and Union

By all indications, most free workers had no desire for civil war. George Lippard, a radical writer in sympathy with the workers' movement, had warned them, "Disunion only means this—the Poor Men of one State shall cut the throats of the Poor Men of some other State." A decade later, the *United States Mechanics' Own* resurrected Lippard's concerns about the dangers of internecine warfare. A week after secession, Louisville labor figures helped bring citizens together at city hall. Although billed as "a mass meeting of the mechanics and workingmen," the assembly on December 27 included employers and capitalists alongside officers of the local unions, particularly the iron molders. They declared themselves ardently for the Union and warned secessionist agitators to leave the city. On January 4, 1861, "a large meeting of workingmen" assembled at Cincinnati, resolving that "the only safety for the Union is in maintaining and enforcing the Constitution."[22]

Politicians scrambled to establish leadership of these meetings, the first of which took place in U.S. Senator John J. Crittenden's state of Kentucky. The Louisville meetings confirmed interest in the Crittenden Compromise, which aimed at resolving the crisis with a compromise that would, among other things, make slavery explicitly sacrosanct where it existed. They issued "a whole-souled Union Address to the mechanics, laborers, manufacturers, farmers and merchants of the country" and heard ardent Unionist speeches that clearly understood "peaceful secession" as "an utter impossibility." The last urged "Northern workingmen and naturalized citizens" to unite with "the industrial masses everywhere" in a February 22 convention at Philadelphia. Nevertheless, they voted to "rescind their former resolution, warning secessionist missionaries to leave Louisville within a given time as conflicting with free speech and open discussion," and the press reported that the Crittenden plan was "evidently approved by the large gathering to-night." In the interests of peace, some seemed willing to barter the successful Republican electoral mandate and the fundamental elements of a representative Union.

On the other hand, that meeting of Cincinnati workingmen clearly believed that Union would best ensure peace. A few weeks later, Fred Oberkline, one of the union molders participating in the meeting assured President-elect Lincoln that the Cincinnatians had no interest in compromising a fairly won victory at the polls. "We spurn such compromise," he continued. "We firmly adhere to the principles which directed our votes in your favor."[23] In other words, some participants were more willing to risk peace to insure the triumph of representative government and an elected government.

Other meetings took place from Pittsburgh to Boston. On January 11, the former gathered under President Henry B. McCarty of the Pittsburgh Trades' Assembly, endorsing the Philadelphia convention, as did the "meeting of the Mechanics and Working-men of Evansville" on January 12. Plans for a January 17 meeting at Reading failed, allegedly because the workers could not find a place to meet. The rally of "the mechanics and workingmen of Boston and vicinity" met on February 20, featuring politicians and philanthropists, but including Dillon of Lynn who "was for the union out and out and he wanted all workingmen to go with him."[24]

The involvement of businessmen, industrialists, officeholders, and office seekers increasingly overwhelmed the views of "workingmen." The *New York Times* objected to a meeting of Newark's unemployed that endorsed the Crittenden Compromise. The paper correctly ascribed the New York City meeting to "the Working Men's Anti-Republican in-aid-of-South Carolina-Party," which included no prominent figure from the workers' movement but declared against "coercion" of the South and its rights to enslave labor. One suspects the decision of a similar meeting in Brooklyn "to exclude all demagogues" actually aimed at excluding any workingmen unwilling to go along with the Democratic agenda.[25]

At Philadelphia, "delegates representing the various industrial interests of our city" deliberated on January 16 at the Spring Garden Hall "upon the great political issues which now agitate and threaten to destroy the Union." The prominence of local employers and industrialists eager to speak on behalf of the workingmen should caution against an optimistic interpretation of the gathering. On January 26 the local movement did get some six thousand workingmen in ankle-deep snow of Independence Square, and the "employees in all the large manufacturing establishments in the country marched to the place of meeting bearing torches and lanterns, accompanied by bands of music." At this large demonstration, though, the self-appointed "representatives" of the workers equated peace with the Crittenden Compromise.[26]

At such meetings in the South, secessionists pushed their way to the fore to speak for the free white worker. Undisturbed by any talk of compromise, the "Mechanics and Working Men's Southern Rights Association" at Memphis voted on January 25 to "indorse the action of the southern seceding States" and endorsed the secession of Tennessee "if we do not get our rights." Some dissenting voices at the ward meetings inspired plans to coordinate with the former Union Party.[27] Most such gatherings did little more than provide some fig leaf of popular justification for secessionism.

Significantly, workingmen at Richmond contested the secessionist hold on the mid-January gatherings there. Since the secessionist employers, particularly the newspaper proprietors, officered the meeting, it crushed a motion from the floor "that none but mechanics and working men be allowed to address the meeting." When it looked as though the workers would call their own Unionist meeting, the officers turned off the gas, but Robert V. Priddy—likely a relative of Thomas Priddy of the local Typographical Society—managed to assemble some two hundred workingmen, who appointed a Unionist committee of vigilance. The secessionists reconvened the meeting on January 29 and proposed blaming the crisis on "anti-slavery fanaticism," declaring that "we, the non-slaveholding working men of Richmond, will stand by our slaveholding brethren and make their cause our cause, believing our interests to be the same." However, participants defeated resolutions under leaders such as Samuel Huffman and Captain Martin Meredith Lipscomb, a "workingman" who one Richmond secessionist likened to Lincoln, both of whom spoke for the Union and wanted to "give every poor man a cow."[28]

At the height of this movement, the molders held their national convention in Cincinnati and designated as its official publishers not only the *Mechanics' Own* but also Willich's *Cincinnati Republikaner*, the local German-language paper of the Republicans. Oberkline, the officer of the Cincinnati local, headed the delegation of German workingmen who made the key point to Lincoln: "Our vanquished opponents have, in recent times, made frequent use of the terms 'workingmen' and 'Workingmen' Meetings,' in order to create an impression that the mass of workingmen we in favor of compromise between the interests of free labor and slave labor, by which the victory just won would be turned into a defeat."[29]

The thrust of these meetings often remained obscure. A "large meeting of workingmen" on February 19 at Indianapolis "unanimously recommended" a more general national convention, which may have aimed at the February 22 for the Crittenden Compromise or one slated for February 28 "of all those Republicans who are in favor of a settlement of our troubles upon the Border State, or any other equally fair plan of adjustment."[30]

Ultimately, compromise faltered and fizzled because it had nowhere new to go. On February 21 some of the local Committee of Thirty-Three tried to meet with Lincoln. Two days later, representatives from Delaware, Maryland, Virginia, Kentucky, Tennessee, Indiana, and Ohio joined the local delegates and slated another national gathering for March 4 in Louisville.[31] All such efforts placed the fate of the nation and its workers directly in the hands of the very people and institutions that had created the crisis, and the process of secession continued. With no more regard for what their own "mudsills" wanted than for Northern workers, when their representatives convened at Montgomery to establish their own Confederate States, they effectively ended any realistic hopes for compromise.

Washington's birthday opened in Philadelphia with a mass demonstration of the visiting representatives from the various workingmen's meetings. The city found ten times as many "multitudinous early risers" on the streets, which were "densely thronged with people" by noon. "The Workingmen's procession is now passing through Third and Chestnut streets. A large number are in line. All the various trades are represented. The Machinists drag along in carts their implements of labor rendered useless by the political troubles of the country. Salutes are being fired as they march along to their destination," the "National Convention of Workingmen" gathered at the National Hall. Militia units also marched that morning.[32] The procession represented funeral cortege for faith in the democratic will, in the patriotism of the ruling classes, and for the countless thousands of laboring people, who would survive the next four years.

President-elect Lincoln, who had arrived the previous night, expressed all of these concerns in a flag-raising at Independence Hall. When a member of the Select Council told him that the Union had to "be preserved by every concession short of eternal principle itself," Lincoln responded, "[A]ll the political sentiments I entertain have been drawn . . . from this hall in which we stand." The Declaration "gave promise that in due time the weights should be lifted from the shoulders of all men, and that all should have an equal chance." When Lincoln reached the White House, Confederate flags fluttered within view in Virginia and Maryland. Plausibly, the authorities were said to have employed the union stonecutters at the capital, made idle by the inauguration, as makeshift bodyguards for Lincoln.[33]

Over the coming weeks, the new administration refused to surrender Federal installations to local authorities in the South, who acted, often without secession, to seize those assets through threats and posturing. Everything came to a head when the U.S. government sought to reinforce the garrison in Charleston harbor. Eager for a confrontation that would revive the flagging interest of the Lower South in secession, Confederate authorities delivered an ultimatum and then had to follow through by opening fire on the flag and its defenders at Fort Sumter. The incident dissolved the wistful ruminations on peace, as stonecutters, carpenters, printers, mill hands and workers of all sort formed ranks once more.

Throughout these weeks, workers in New Orleans, the strongest trade-union center in the South, seem to have remained silent as a group. This proved all the more remarkable given the importance of labor in local politics. In the years leading to the war, political rivalries in cosmopolitan and urbane New Orleans, tensions pitting Creoles, Anglos, and more recent immigrants had long provided some of the strangest politics in the South. Mayor John T. Monroe had come to the city penniless and became president of the predominantly Irish Screwmen's Union, the specialized craftsmen using mechanisms to fit cotton bales into place for transport. His predecessor as mayor, Gerard Stith, had been the president of the Typographical Union.[34] Remarkably, labor politics in that case blunted none of the class deference characteristic of most American workers.

That said, at the level of the union, many seemed less than enthusiastic about secession. New Orleans printers apparently planned to send delegates to the national convention, even after the January secession of Louisiana. Not until April 21, after Fort Sumter, did delegate-elect Daniel C. Byerly resign and the body resolve that, as "civil war having been inaugurated by the acts of President Lincoln," it became "impolitic and inexpedient for the New Orleans Typographical Union to be represented at the coming annual Convention."[35] By then, though, more than one Southern union had already begun to disintegrate.

* * *

"The Times are out of Joint," complained the *Printer*.[36] In the end, though, it was not the times but decisions by those who owned human labor to brush aside the modest aspirations of those who wished merely to continue working for a living. Secession forced the Federal authorities either to defend its installations in the South or to concede a de facto surrender of its own sovereignty and legitimacy. Indeed, secession backed the secessionists themselves into a corner where they had either to surrender their claims to sovereignty over those installations or to exercise their authority over them. The political leaders began talking more earnestly about accepting the judgments of God, even as the masters of the nation had followed their short-term business interests into surrendering rule to the logic of events. In this setting, American workers found themselves virtually helpless.

Still, even free white workers hardly entered the war united. As one of them later wrote in a letter to Lincoln from Britain, many of his peers "affect to believe that Slavery had nothing to do with the cause of the revolt." Nevertheless, Southern leaders such as James Henry Hammond had repeatedly and consistently made their views clear, and groups such as William Oland Bourne's "Iron Platform Democrats"—which soon became the Workingmen's Democratic Republican Association—regularly quoted them in such tracts as *White Slaves*. Hammond claimed "a Solution of the great problem of reconciling the interests of labour and capital. By making the labourer himself capital, the conflict ceases, and the interests become identical."[37] Ultimately, the secessionist dissolution of the United States offered all workers one very clear, horrifically antilabor vision of their future in North America.

CHAPTER 2

Continuities of Class

The Persistence of Labor Struggles

After Bull Run shattered hopes for a short war, some of the more radical socialists proposed concrete relief measures to ameliorate the burden of a longer conflict. On Friday, July 24, 1861, the *Arbeiterbund* at New York assembled some two thousand people at the Harmonic Gardens to suggest that a society that chose to go to war bore the responsibility for its economic impact and needed to provide jobs or income for workers whose livelihoods had been disrupted. The organizers had not proposed Utopia, but planned to form "sections" in the wards and trades to promote these goals, with an ultimate aim "to effect a general organization of workingmen of every description on a socialistic basis." After another mass meeting on August 9, at Metropolitan Hall on Hester Street, the *Courier des Etats Unis* tried to dismiss it as the work "principally of Germans, not in New York alone, but also in Philadelphia and Newark, and at other places." It asked if the Union would now be plagued by "bands of unemployed workingmen infesting the streets, with demands for bread, to be responded to, perhaps, by the bullet?"[1] The effort addressed the economic dislocations of the war's first weeks from the perspective of a persistent antebellum urban understanding of class.

The advent of civil war imposed a series of crises on American labor. While their unions struggled to keep their balance on rapidly shifting grounds, workers still faced the traditional old grievances with the tried and true responses of organization, protests, and strikes. With war, however, the civil authorities had made themselves a growing factor in resolving workplace issues. At the same time, workers in uniform brought their own experiences and skills to the war, contributing a reshaping of the ways in which the conflict reshaped the workforce and its perceptions.

Wartime Economies and the Crisis of the National Unions

The escalating sectional tensions almost immediately began to unravel the national unions. As early as February 2, Charleston printers announced meetings of their "Typographical Society" in the afternoon, followed in the evening by one of "the Southern Typographical Union No. 1." On February 13 they formally announced, "The Typographical Union here has dissolved its connection with the national body." A prime mover in this, John F. Britton had become an ardent secessionist, and both the local political authorities and newspaper owners naturally gave a disproportionate weight to such persons.[2] All that proved decisive in the smaller Southern locals.

The preparation for the National Typographical Union convention slated for New York on May 6 continued, with locals as far as California electing delegates. Union vice president William Madigan likely told the *Boston Herald* that the convention would open as scheduled, and "representative printers will be present from every State except South Carolina." Nevertheless, on April 22, Thomas J. Walsh, the national secretary of the NTU, issued a statement in New York at Madigan's urging, recognizing "the present distracted state of political affairs through the country." For this reason, the NTU board "deemed it best for the interest of the Craft to postpone until further notice the Convention of Delegates which was to have met in this city in May." President John M. Farquhar disagreed, believing the cancellation would concede too much legitimacy to the secessionists. Indeed, only on May 1—five days before the convention was to begin—Farquhar "consented to its postponement."[3]

Other national unions faced similar problems to that of the printers. On one level, regionalism drained the Cordwainers' National Union. Although the Machinists and Blacksmiths had convened in November 1860, the next year's convention assembled representatives from only four states a year later, with a single national officer, Secretary Jonathan Fincher. As noted, after holding their convention in January 1861, the Iron Molders but could hold another until January 1863.[4]

As Washington girded itself for war, its population grew and cost of living rose. The local printers demanded a pay hike, and "succeeded without friction owing to the necessities of the time, the Government Printing Office readily conceding the demand." In November their Columbia Typographical Union also voted to amend their requirements to require an eight-hour day but reconsidered it, owing to the difficulty of enforcement. When the leadership of the depleted Philadelphia local recommended accepting the proposal for "a temporary wage abatement" by the *North American and U.S. Gazette*, their membership voted it down 135 to 16. In December, Journeymen Pattern Makers at Boston became beleaguered enough to attempt their own Protective Union.[5]

Over time, government policies would loom ever larger in such considerations: to pay for the war by printing paper currency made it easier to win. In February and July 1862, Congress authorized the Treasury Department to inject $300,000 in paper currency into the economy and added another $750,000 in January and March 1863. This allowed prices to rise far beyond the ability of wages to keep pace. By one reasonable measure, the cost of living rose overall 76 percent during the war, while wages increased only 50 percent.

The specific character and effect of those economic changes remain in dispute. Scholars have debated over the extent to which the statistical evidence reflects a pace of investment and capitalization well under way. On the one hand, war initially torpedoed the flagship of the new factory system, which had been textiles, particularly mills processing cotton. Notwithstanding the fact that American industrialists, like their British counterparts, had stockpiled a reserve from the bumper crop of 1860, access to cotton fell off very dramatically with the isolation of the South. By June 1862 two-thirds of the 4.5 million cotton spindles in the northeastern states had gone idle, and the remaining did not work to their prewar capacitics.[6]

On the other hand, wartime demand spurred other kinds of industries. Due in part to military uses, wool production soared to an annual peak of 208 million pounds. Then, too, the demand for shoes sped the application of sewing machinery pioneered in textiles to leatherwork. The dislocations of war created a vast demand not only for industrially produced ships, wagons, weapons, rations, uniforms, and supplies, but also for photographers, jewelers, tobacconists, and other services generally run on a modest scale, even as spiritualists and self-appointed healers found growing demand.[7]

Iron foundries and machine shops appeared or expanded rapidly to meet the wartime need for firearms, cannons, ironclads, and other materiel. Federal arsenals such as the one at Springfield, Massachusetts, swelled to include several thousand workers who daily fed the war a thousand new rifles. The government operations transformed installations such as the West Point Foundry at Cold Springs, New York, into a military research site of unprecedented scale and international importance. The Confederacy made a noteworthy and centralizing effort to do the same, physically evident in its industrial complex at Augusta, Georgia.

These industrial developments radically remade the critical margins of the urban landscape. The production of a blockade fleet expanded the navy yards on the Atlantic coast to unprecedented scale, but the need for an inland navy on the rivers created vast new industrial districts along the waterfront of Pittsburgh, Cincinnati, Louisville, and St. Louis. The construction and frequent reconstruction of railroads and the infrastructure they required shaped innovations from which the country would not retreat after the war's end.[8] The impact came most drastically perhaps in the smaller cities of the heartland.

The cost of all this grew quickly to unprecedented proportions. To arm and equip a military force in the first months of the war, the government spent $50 million, of which contractors pocketed an estimated $17 million, according to congressional investigators. Over and above the cost in lives, by 1863 the Federal government spent $2.5 million per day on the war. The burden of blood and treasure fell most heavily on the social base.

Workers who did not go to war found themselves embattled to preserve their quality of life at home. The spiritualist *Banner of Light* noted that the war exposed "one of the most atrocious arrangements of the whole social system." "For a novelty, *prices* go up now-a-days and *labor* goes up with them." Usually, prices became "exorbitant," with the cost of labor "the very last thing to advance, and simply because it never yet has been able to command its own wages and prices." Simply put, "the armies must be fed, and those who stay at home must be fed; and it will take labor, and any quantity of it, to supply the demand." Yet wages persistently lagged behind prices as the war continued. In places, the *Banner of Light* reported, workers earned enough to pay the rent without "touching the bottom of their purses before they begin on ordinary living expenses." This problem would deepen "as wealth accumulates in this country and the population of our cities and towns becomes denser every year. Even with this civil war's bloody exactions, it is found by the last popular vote that the several loyal States show an increased population over that of four years ago." The growing population of New York, Philadelphia, and other American cities—like the populations of Paris and London—sheltered in "overcrowded and foul tenements."[9]

From early days, workers responded to the wartime conditions by sending representatives to their city governments looking for assistance. In the summer of 1861, a delegation of twenty-five Boston tailors called on the mayor to ask for work from the city. The local press called it "the first case of a delegation of workmen applying to the city authorities for relief, though individual instances have been somewhat numerous." New York established a joint special committee to discuss how "to relieve the condition of our working classes, and aiding the families of volunteers." They considered employing the unemployed in Central Park and the area's fortifications, and the Croton Board could provide many more jobs. Initially, though, even a relatively small city like Cincinnati faced a rising unemployment rate that, by early 1862, left some thirty thousand people out of work.[10]

German radical groups raised issues about sharing the burdens of the war effort from its inception. Chicago had several mass meetings on the subject in May 1861. The July 24 proposals of the Arbeiterbund of New York that the warring government assume the responsibility for guaranteeing the incomes of working-class families horrified the ruling powers on both sides of the Mason-Dixon Line. Branches of the organization at Philadelphia, Newark, and elsewhere shared their insistence that the society in general should participate in the burden of war rather than to drop it squarely on the workers.[11] As near as can be discerned, the political authorities ducked the question entirely.

Predictably, the press universally howled about it. James Gordon Bennett's Democratic *Herald* fumed at the effrontery of the workers, foreigners to boot. The trouble, it reported, originated "less with the workingmen, as a class, than with a small knot of restless and unprincipled agitators, who for the last twenty years have been endeavoring to make use of them as a stepping stone to political notoriety and influence." The local correspondent of the *Philadelphia Inquirer* ascribed the resolutions to "a little clique of German Socialists in this city" with "very *Frenchy*" politics and "pestilent theories." These, he wrote, "are not the times, and New York is not the place, for 'trying on' any of these imported and mischievous 'isms.'"[12]

Secessionists thought it symptomatic of a mad radicalism that had seized the North. A Texas paper claimed that the Confederacy had joined Europe in accepting no more than a "few gleams of enlightenment" to avoid "spiritualism, socialism, and a thousand and one other isms." Now, "Yankee fanaticism" sought "to enlighten and civilize us at the sword's point." The *Memphis Daily Appeal* and the *Richmond Daily Dispatch* lifted from the Northern papers and provided their own fictional background story. In the conditions of war, workers found themselves "reduced to a condition bordering upon distress . . . with destitution staring them and their families in the face." In the end, though, the secessionist press shared the response of the established Unionist papers in denouncing the idea that "the State is bound to protect them in the fruits of their honest tell, and all the rights and immunities guarantee to them by the Declaration of Independence and the Constitution or Charter of American Liberty." A British observer added that the social disruptions convinced him that "Agrarian and Socialist Riots may be expected pretty soon."[13]

Over time, though, conditions in the South became so miserable that it began eliciting some modest expressions of sympathy by the press. After a year of war, the *Houston Tri-Weekly Telegraph* described the dire circumstances of many people owing to "the high prices now charged for the necessaries of life." A letter from "Junius" acknowledged "incalculable suffering among a large class of our population.... There might be some sense in this if mechanics' wages had advanced in a proportionate degree with the prices, but that such is not the case requires no great effort to demonstrate." He continued, "If the wages of the working class were double what they now are, they would not then be in proportion to the enormous advance in the price." All this fell particularly heavily on "the wives of soldiers who are compelled to earn their living by sewing for contractors at starvation rates."[14] Free workers responded to these larger issues in the same way they had addressed such matters on the small scale of a particular workshop.

The Persistence of Trade Unionism

Hard times elicited a renewal of trade-unionist activities, but the economic and industrial dislocations of the war caused greater problems. The production of uniforms created scandalous conditions in Philadelphia. By late September more than five thousand seamstresses rushed to get work in the Schuylkill Arsenal to avoid the rank exploitation of taking outwork through contractors. Women from the arsenal held a protest meeting at Temperance Hall. They declared themselves willing to take a wartime pay cut from the government but objected to doing so for private contractors. The knapsack strappers had been getting fifty-six dollars per hundred before the war, but contractors tried in October 1861 to reduce this to only forty or fifty dollars per hundred. In November, when the German tailors failed to secure a uniform scale for government clothing work, a thousand of them went on strike.[15]

Government policies regularly provoked walkouts, starting with the midwinter attempt to slash wages in the Navy Yards. One victim of the policies complained, "If the Hon. economist who would screw down the working man to starvation point, would look nearer home and commence retrenchment there, it would tell better for his disinterested honesty." In January, workers at the New York Navy Yard sent Joseph Archibald to Washington. There, however, "the workmen in the Washington Navy Yard . . . resolved that is as highly imprudent to follow in the footsteps of those employed in the northern years by carrying their opposition to a strike."[16]

The news also caused "much excitement in the Boston Navy-yard.... A strike is talked of, and efforts are making to secure the cooperation of the workmen in other yards." Shipwrights there had organized a union before the war. Workers in Maine's Kittery Navy Yard did walk off the job over the question.[17]

After the January 16, 1862, announcement of pay cuts in the Philadelphia Navy Yard, "a general strike ensued, and an indignation meeting was held in the spar shed, where a very exciting scene took place." Depending on the trade, the reduction would cost the men twenty-five to fifty cents per day, but the press blamed the strike on their "imbibing pretty freely." Over the next few days, the absence of between eight hundred and fifteen hundred strikers left work unfinished on roughly half a dozen ships, including the *Hartford*. One of their leaders declared it "hardly fair that workingmen should be sufferers, when so much pillaging of the Government had taken place by those in higher positions." The strike sometimes assumed "a riotous character." "Several very severe fights occurred, during which the participants were pretty roughly handled. After a few days, the men returned with the understanding that the problem would be addressed in Washington. According to some accounts, detectives used a trance medium to identify and fire troublemakers.[18]

Meanwhile, the close-knit immigrant communities of the coalfields caused more problems that increasingly involved the military. In Lincoln's own Illinois, the first year of the war saw major strikes by the American Miners' Association in the Belleville coalfields. In August, as the army built a base of operations at the tip of the state near Cairo, twenty-three overworked and underpaid teamsters—possibly blacks—had walked off the job there and went to St. Louis to collect their pay. Provost Marshal Justin McKinstry—later dismissed for administrative irregularities in the Federal Army—did not give them the wages they had earned. Instead, he "furnished them . . . with a file of soldiers, and sent them to prison to live on bread and water."[19]

Starting in the spring of 1862, matters became even more serious in the Pennsylvania coalfields. In May some fifteen hundred of a largely Irish contingent of workers had the temerity to strike to get miners ten cents per wagon and laborers twenty-five cents per day. When strikes closed the mines at Hewett's, Forestville, and Thomaston, authorities feared "that the supply of Government coal will be partially stopped." Moreover, "many of the strikers were three months' volunteers, and well drilled in the use of arms," so the government sent two companies of troops "with four howitzers and detachments of others." They soon returned to Philadelphia and Pottsville, declaring the strike "amicably settled," but the grievances festered. Confederate papers repeated the exaggerated account of the *New York Herald*, implying a virtual armed insurrection, and the *Charleston Mercury* anticipated "the many 'rebellions' that must soon take place among the poor and laboring classes of the North from the effects of the war."[20]

At the other end of the country, optimistic printers attempted to launch unions like those back east. In May, diggers leveling the streets of San Francisco demanded a raise from $1.75 to two dollars per a day and "promenaded the principal streets . . ., bearing the stars and stripes at the head of their column, which grew rapidly as it marched." They launched a Protective Union, with a dollar admission fee and weekly dues of a quarter, agreeing not only to a minimum pay scale but also to abstain from alcohol, violence, and threats of violence. The Stockton papers apparently acquiesced when the journeymen organized a local there. The Eureka Typographical Union at San Francisco held its second ball in August 1861. In November, day laborers employed by local contractors walked off to get thirty dollars per month rather than twenty-five. Only a "few contractors" held out, and the strikers held fast. The *Evening Bulletin* indirectly lectured them that they had "a right to set their own price on their own labor. They know well, however, that nothing but moral means can be safely used to induce other laborers to join them in their movement."[21] Despite the problems of their national unions, organized workers hoped to maintain their wages and sustain their locals.

Labor troubles resumed in the textile industry almost as soon as the industry began its slow rebound. Fifty handloom weavers won an 1862 strike for higher pay in the Pontoosuc mills at Pittsfield. Workers in the Berkshire Woolen mills at nearby Great Barrington won a strike to reduce the hours of labor from thirteen to eleven hours per day. An 1863 summer fire in the mills at Cohoes likely contributed to the April 1864 strike there.[22]

The industry also produced a new word essential to any discussion of the wartime economy. The demand for such goods on an industry unbound by much of anything in terms of regulations inspired an increasing modification of standards. In the end, the new industries began turning out products made from the sweepings and scraps, delivering what became known as "shoddy." The word seemed to fit so much about the work of government contractors, that it soon came to be applied almost universally.

Commenting on social conditions at the time, Jennie Collins noted that the war "brought nearly as many great changes in the North as it did in the South." Union printer George Washington Beidelman concurred adding that it "has been, and is, a terrible thing to an unmilitary people." After working at his native Bloomsburg and at Norristown, he had moved to Philadelphia and joined the union. A pious Lutheran who had taught Sunday school and promoted temperance back home, he resisted the impetuous initial excitement after Sumter. Nevertheless, he enlisted as a private on May 21 in what became the Seventy-First Pennsylvania.[23] Beidelman's letters continued to document how the war had transformed him, his comrades, his class, and his country.

Laboring for Victory

With the outbreak of a new American Revolution, armed workers began seizing the means of production from the employers. An unused press at Hagerstown,

Maryland, inspired an "'irrepressible impulse'" among the four editors and forty compositors in a Wisconsin regiment who seized it to publish their own *Camp Record*, promising its subsequent number would be published in Richmond. An Indiana regiment at Winchester published the *Army Bulletin* daily, and printers in blue at Leesburg issued the *Advance Guard*. Soldiers elsewhere in the Shenandoah Valley sustained their own "Typographic Fraternity," which seized a press at Berryville to print the *First Minnesota*. Three years later, soldiers at Philadelphia issued *Our Daily Fare*. At Hilton Head, one such paper, the *Camp Kettle*, published such humorous items as a slave advertising for his runaway master.[24]

Officers often turned a blind eye to the practice, but they sometimes also participated. William R. Creighton, of the Cleveland union, commanded the men who descended on a "defunct rebel paper office in western Virginia, on the 4th of July," from which they issued the *Ohio Seventh*. Joseph M. Kinkead—likely the Pittsburgh land reformer of that name—became the adjutant of the regiment that used a local secessionist press to print their own *Pennsylvania Thirteenth*, but got marching orders after printing only three hundred copies. So, too, the *Virginia Republican* became the *American Union*. Frederick S. Davis, formerly of the spiritualist *Banner of Light* office became detailed to help print the *Newbern Progress*.[25]

Other units with union printers participated in General U.S. Grant's movement across the Ohio to occupy Paducah, Kentucky. Once there, Federal soldiers seized the abandoned office of the secessionist *Herald*. Grant used it to issue his proclamation. The unionists, however, used the equipment to publish their own paper, the *Union Picket Guard*. "The printing and publishing are done by the soldiers of the Ninth Illinois regiment, and of Company A of the Chicago Light Artillery." On Ship Island, Mississippi, on the Gulf of Mexico, a group likely headed by Alfred W. Eastman of the Eighth Vermont printed the *Soldier's News-Letter*.[26]

Missouri saw a series of these soldiers' papers. In addition to the *First Kansas*, G. N. L. Scott wrote his fellow printers that the printers of the Thirteenth Illinois at Camp Polk had begun issuing *Our Regiment*. Rolla had the *Camp Sweeny Spy*, and nearby Otterville the *War Eagle and Camp Journal of the Army of the West*, succeeded by the *First Division Proclamation*.[27]

Even farther west, Private John Howard Kitts of the Lawrence Typographical Union and others found an old printing office in Arkansas with type, probably taken earlier from the *Cherokee Messenger*. Kitts and his fellow printers in Company E of the Eleventh Kansas were aided by officers familiar with the craft—perhaps by Colonel William A. Phillips, the land reformer, abolitionist and newspaperman then commanding the Third Indian Home Guard as well. They transformed the little cabin into a printing office, issuing their own *Buck and Ball*. They returned from a raid with newer, more ornate type, and refitted their paper as the *Arkansas Traveler*, though the high command ordered the enterprise abandoned. Fort Gibson later had its own *Cherokee Tomahawk*.[28]

In the midsummer of 1861, Bates and the other printers in the Eighth Missouri occupied the secessionist press at Mexico and issued the *Star-Spangled Banner*, claiming it to have been the first Union newspaper printed in the Confederacy. The First Iowa had "no less than forty printers" when it passed through Macon, where they took possession of the *Register*, "a hot Secession sheet," and "promptly issued a spicy loyal journal, called *Our Whole Union*." Albert D. Richardson of the *New York Tribune* described it as one of "a number of freaks which startled the natives."[29] Before moving on, the Iowans addressed the absent secessionist owner:

> We leave you to-night. We're going where bullets are thick and mosquitos thicker. We may never return. If we do not, old boy, remember us. We sat at your table; we stole from your "Dictionary of Latin Quotations"; we wrote Union articles with your pen, your ink, on your paper. We printed them on your press. Our boys set 'em up with your types, and your galleys, your "shooting-sticks," your "chases," your "quads," your "spaces," your "rules," your every thing. We even drank some poor whisky out of your bottle.

Such things represented more than a "freak" or a boyish prank. Working printers clearly nursed a sense of grievance against the trade's proprietors for contributing to a war that could be resolved only through the shedding of their employees' blood. The exigencies of that war permitted working printers to express their resentment through the expropriation—however brief—of the workplace. As Union forces advanced into the South, secessionist journalists fled, abandoning their equipment and offices. The units who occupied such communities often included men well trained in such matters.

With such printers in uniforms involved in such activities, it should be no surprise that some soldiers organized in hopes of getting a union charter. In September 1861, the eighteen printers in the Fourth Iowa at Rolla, Missouri, announced that they had "formed a Typographical Union" and wrote the national body to apply for a charter."[30] By January 1862, however, the regiment had moved on to other business.

Workers brought their experience and skills with them when they went to the war as citizens. Train engineers performed essential service not only in supplying the troops and making the military operations possible, but in the spring of 1862 two of them earned Medals of Honor by volunteering to slip into Confederate lines and steal a train. Before Vicksburg and, later, Petersburg, coal miners planned and dug shafts under the enemy lines in which to plant explosives.

More than in the Union, conditions in the Confederacy tended to subsume every issue into the war. Printers from Richmond to New Orleans adopted the same measures as their Northern counterparts to care for members going to war, but without much enthusiasm. The Charleston printers voted to leave the NTU in mid-February 1861, and pressure of employers and the weight of the militarizing society around them pushed members elsewhere to do the same. In mid-March the Jackson local appointed a committee "to draft an Ordinance of Secession from the 'National Typographical Union,' with a view to the formation of another grand body in the Confederate States." Those in New Orleans, Atlanta, and other cities followed. In June, the Petersburg Typographical Society "severed its connection with the National Typographical Union." The following month, the *Macon Daily Telegraph* boasted that "the numerous Typographical Unions in the Confederate States have declared their independence of the National Typographical Union."[31] Some seceded locals had already begun to refer to themselves as the "Southern Typographical Union," although any such body existed only on paper.

As with secession generally, the implicit threat of violence accompanied the decision, explicitly in some cases. Despite his standing opposition to circulating lists of "rats," S. P. Bassett presided when a Memphis local voted to issue a list of members who had "fled from us to aid the ruthless invading army of Lincoln" and circulate it nationally, and threatened to "tar and feather" any such member who ever returned to the city. It also called on other unions "to act in a similar manner, if any coercion sympathizers have quitted them for the land of Abe." Not until September, though, could the *Nashville Union* report that local's passage of "an ordinance dissolving all connection with the National Union was adopted by a unanimous vote."[32]

Nevertheless, Southern trade unionists and labor reformers proved much more likely to resist the dominant trend in their section. Many printers pointed that, regardless of grievances against the Federal Union, their locals had no such complaints against the NTU. Some, such as Mobile, simply refused to leave their national union. Several officers of Southern locals wrote the NTU acknowledging that their locals had nothing to excuse, much less justify, its dissolution. One added that secession and war—with their paper shortages, skyrocketing cost of living, and job losses—had imploded his local of 163 members. "God help us," he wrote, "if you northerners don't." Defiant in the context of the time and place, the correspondent signed his letter, "Yours for the Union."[33]

Antisecessionist clubs organized at St. Louis by January, in Louisville in May, and in Maryland and along the Ohio River in the early months of the war. Tennessee Unionists had more secretive "Union Leagues" that "sought refuge in inaccessible places and caves in the mountains of their State." In June 1862 a dozen persons, including a Tennessee refugee at Pekin, Illinois, launched the first lodge of the Union League of America, which quickly spread to Peoria, Bloomington, Kingston, Decatur, and Chicago, resulting in a state convention that September. Union Leagues spread across Indiana, Ohio, Wisconsin, Michigan, Minnesota, and Iowa by spring 1863, and chapters soon formed as far away as San Francisco. As late as early 1864 the Lincoln administration continued to make it easy for Southern workers to change sides.[34]

In terms of labor organizations, the Union Leagues initially sought the same kind of ambiguity as the Republican coalition itself. Joshua K. Ingalls recalled how the New York City remnants of the working-class land-reform movement "was absorbed during the war by the Union League." Overall, though, local elites prevailed in the groups at the nation's capital, followed by the leagues at Philadelphia in late 1862, New York City in January 1863, and Boston the following month. The Union Leagues in such places, however, often remained aloof from the national organization and sometimes survived as select gentlemen's clubs, as did the Chicago Union League.[35]

The Confederate press responded with insistent bluster on the loyalty of the Southern printers. A Nashville paper boasted that "from no body of men has the present war drawn so largely, in proportion to its members, as from the Typographical Societies of the South." The legislature exempted printers from service, yet the *Nashville Banner* claimed the war left "barely enough . . . to supply the actual need on our local papers." Yet when the Confederates abandoned the state capital, an "Association of Journeymen Printers" formed among those left behind, publishing their *Nashville Evening Bulletin* daily through March.[36] This represented an independent bid to be taken seriously, regardless of which side held the reins of power.

In the end, though, the development of a wartime Confederate economy actually fostered trade-union activities. In November 1861, the Richmond press reported Lynchburg shoemakers "on a strike for higher wages." Toward the close of the year, those same papers reported that after making an equitable pay settlement with the union, the comptroller simply stopped payment for the government printers. He declared, "While the men in the Army and in the Navy were worked night and day, and the clerks in the Departments many nights until 10 o'clock, and while printers throughout the Union work at least ten hours, he did not see why those printers in the Government employ could ask full pay for a day of less than ten hours." The printers, who had voted not to strike in November, closed ranks in midwinter to wage "a general strike."[37]

The entrepreneurial Kentucky secessionist Blanton Duncan opened his own printing operation at the national capital. Almost immediately, his bullying helped inspire workers to form the Richmond Typographical Society and build it into a force formidable to the Confederate Treasury Department itself. In his efforts to break to the Union, Duncan solicited the assistance of the former Baltimore police detective, John H. Winder, whose image Duncan subsequently put on a thousand-dollar Confederate bill.[38]

* * *

The exigencies of a wartime economy raised new issues for working people. North or South, East or West, some workers turned to concerted action in response to immediate problems in their workplaces. Yet the general conditions in which laboring people formulated and asserted their self-interests had changed radically. Beyond the economy loomed the stark realities of the American Civil War.

One of the most dramatic features of the war was its rapid escalation. In the first battles of 1861, thousands clashed for hours, while April 1862 saw nearly one hundred thousand slaughtering or maiming each other over two days around Shiloh. Shortly after, nearly twice that number clashed almost daily over weeks in Virginia. Most immediately, the Federals pushed relentlessly into Confederate territory, securing key cities such as St. Louis, Louisville, Nashville, and Huntsville, taking large sections along the Mississippi River, seizing New Orleans in the south and threatening Memphis. Confederate hopes rested heavily on the generalship of Robert E. Lee and his lieutenants in Virginia, who had failed only when they invaded Maryland in September 1862. After defeating yet another larger Federal army near Chancellorsville in May 1863, Lee's army opted to relieve Virginia of the weight of those contending armies, and gambled a second invasion reaching Gettysburg.

CHAPTER 3

Organized Labor Goes to War

The Fate of the Old Workers' Movement

William R. Creighton of the Typographical Union married and put his affairs in order before he went to war on April 22, 1861, when his company of the Cleveland Light Guards mobilized as part of the Seventh Ohio. The Pittsburgh native had gone to work at age ten, and he had little formal education before entering the printing trade. There, though, he joined the local fire company and became active in the Light Guards. Contemporaries spoke of "his love of adventure" that was hardly appeased in the experience of the workshop. More than this, though, as Creighton's pastor explained later, the working-class patriot cherished the idea that "the most indigent son of toil stands before the law the equal peer of merchant princes" and scorned the notion "that 'Capital shall own labor,' the non-capitalled [sic] to be the chattel of the rich." He particularly resented that "the forum, pulpit, and press should be enslaved, and intelligence among the masses be rendered contraband."[1] The very same concerns that had moved workers to oppose a war they thought might be avoided drew men like Creighton to a war for free labor they deemed to be inevitable.

War quickly drained the antebellum workforce. The workers themselves took up arms because they understood the importance of the conflict in shaping the future value of "free labor" to themselves and their peers. A brief survey of the presence of men associated with the labor movement at Gettysburg demonstrates the simply ubiquitous nature of their contribution to the war. However, the extent of this involvement came at the price of depleting labor organizations, taking a particularly heavy toll on their leaderships and the most ardently radical of the old labor reformers.

Taking Up Arms

"The mechanics from every large centre enlisted in the army, and among those who were foremost would be found the officers of the local union," recalled Terence V. Powderly, later the head of the Knights of Labor. In Philadelphia, he said, "One union enlisted to a man; the entry made upon the records of the union reads: 'It having been resolved to enlist with Uncle Sam for the war, this union stands adjourned until either the union is safe or we are whipped.'"[2]

Only days after Fort Sumter, the well-documented printers began joining in large numbers. The newspapers of Boston, Newburg, and Albany reported the loss of many workers. Cincinnati reported "fully seventy-five printers of this city have enlisted in the service of Uncle Samuel," clustering in the "Franklin Guards," a company of the Fifth Ohio. Union members rose to officers' ranks in the Twenty-Fifth New York, the Seventeenth, Eighteenth, and One Hundred Fourteenth Pennsylvania, and the Second Pennsylvania Cavalry, and were prominent in the Third, Fourth, Fifth, and Sixth Ohio, as well as Creighton's Seventh. Others had similar prominence in the Eleventh Indiana, the Seventh and Ninth Illinois, and the Tenth Illinois Cavalry, in addition to the First and Eighth Missouri. Leavenworth reported "many enlisting in the U.S. service to fight for the glorious old 'Stars and Stripes.'" Even on the west coast, San Francisco's Eureka Typographical Union procured "a drill room" to train its members as a company "ready for any service that the authorities may demand of them." One newspaper suggested that every volunteer regiment raised in April 1861 had enough printers to run an office of their own.[3]

Captain Alonzo Granville Draper's Lynn Mechanics' Phalanx led the remnants of the 1860 shoe strike into a unit that retained its identity throughout the war. Fifty-nine of the ninety-six original enlisted men of his company identified themselves as shoemakers, and many of the rest who gave no occupation or described themselves as farmers or laborers had also worked at the trade. The old strike network also shaped similar companies like the Salem Mechanic Grays, which also joined the Fourteenth Massachusetts, initially under the command of Colonel William Batchelder Greene, a West Pointer and Fourierist won to the mutualism of Pierre Joseph Proudhon. When he returned from France, he advised his nephew, Robert Gould Shaw, who later took command of the black soldiers of the famous Fifty-Fourth Massachusetts.[4]

The same dynamic moved workers in other, less documented industries. Martin Boyle, the national lecturer for the American Miners Association, left to raise troops in Illinois. He recruited one company that elected him captain, but he chose to leave and raise another, after which he died of natural causes. Union miners filled the ranks of other companies as well. In the aftermath of Bull Run, the governor of New York announced plans for a new engineer's regiment "composed of machinists, carpenters, boiler makers, bridge-builders, steam-engineers, civil-engineers, railroad men, miners, teamsters, masons, blacksmiths, and similar artisans. The officers are to be educated civil and military engineers."[5]

Trade unionists who did not go to war quickly voted to sustain the membership and even maintain the families of those who volunteered. In the Navy Yard in Brooklyn, "a meeting of the mechanics and laborers" voted a day's pay "to assist the families of those who have left their situations in the yard and volunteered to defend and maintain our beloved Constitution and its glorious and unconquerable flag." The Philadelphia printers immediately "resolved to keep all the members volunteering for the war, in good standing during their absence at the seat of actual conflict," and the entire NTU followed suit in its 1862 convention, even restoring several printer-soldiers whose membership had lapsed for nonpayment of dues under the previous rules.[6]

Southern papers claimed a similar response. "Our typographical force having been reduced," wrote the *Augusta Constitutionalist*, "we must ask our readers to excuse any short comings in the paper for a few days." It continued, "In these war times when so many of that patriotic class of men—printers—are enlisted in the service of the country, it is no easy matter to keep a sufficient force of compositors in a newspaper office." In Louisiana, the *Sugar Planter* bemoaned the fact that "our journeymen having left for the wars, places us under the necessity of editing and publishing the paper alone."[7]

The responses of white workers in the Confederacy ran the gamut. A few did take up arms as eagerly as their brethren in the North. From March 1861, J. Holbrook Estill of the Savannah Typographical Union assured his Northern union brothers that three officers and ten members of that local were garrisoned at nearby Fort Pulaski. However, most had usually come from the North or overseas, and many of these reacted to secession with flight, as did Richard F. Trevellick, a native of Cornwall and a veteran Chartist, who had traveled as far as India and Australia before settling in New Orleans. He had married a local woman and lived peacefully until the new secessionist authorities insisted that he officer a gunboat or, at least, join the army, at which point he used a British consulate pass to get to Detroit. There Ship Carpenters' and Caulkers' Union No. 4 elected him president, from which he became the leader of the national union by the war's end.[8] While this almost exaggerated the proportion that had volunteered, enough had taken up arms to make maintaining a labor organization doubtful.

Trevellick's neighbor, newspaper printer Dewitt C. Roberts found getting out of the South far more complicated. The Illinois native responded sharply when co-workers on the *Commercial Bulletin* demanded that Roberts stand by his native state, and the journeyman faced arrest as "an enemy of the South and a dangerous man." When released, he consulted the Pennsylvania-born secessionist foreman Daniel C. Byerly, a fellow veteran of the Mexican War, who helped his union brother get work at the new Confederate capital, Montgomery. When the government moved to Richmond, he escaped military service to Georgia and ended his flight at Charleston. Roberts did not exaggerate the danger, as Confederates executed Unionists without strong connections to protect them, as when they hanged James McGaff, "a compositor in the *Congressional Globe* office, and a member of the Columbia Typographical Society."[9]

The *Richmond Daily Dispatch* noted the presence of George McK. Luken, a Chicagoan who had formerly presided over the Richmond local present with the Federals "at Cairo, to spot such Southerners as he may chance to know."[10]

In their initial flush of martial glory, these armies of unprecedented size in North America shocked each other into facing the cruel realities. On July 21, 1861, Estill in the Eighth Georgia and James P. Floyd of the Atlanta local in the Twelfth advanced across the green fields along Bull Run to meet a Federal advance that included Timothy P: Kavaneaugh of the Cincinnati Typographical Union and Samuel Lincoln of the Columbus local in the Second Ohio, with Detroit's John Witherspoon serving in the First Michigan. The day left Witherspoon with a mangled hand, and Estill and Floyd so severely wounded as to receive discharges for disabilities. Even in the smaller and more isolated clashes, such as Wilson's Creek in Missouri, the First Iowa included First Lieutenant William H. Clark and First Sergeant Joseph Utter of the Burlington local and Edwin M. Newcomb and Joseph O. Shannon of Dubuque. Captain George Harry Stone of the St. Louis local served in the First Missouri, while Captain L. Brown and Corporal George C. Smith of the Leavenworth Typographical Union joined a number of printer unionists in the First Kansas.[11]

Consider one small corner of the May 1863 Chancellorsville campaign, that diversionary probe through Fredericksburg. Sergeant John A. Lant, a protégé of the land reformers, volunteered for the advance, which captured the heights above town, and the Federals met no serious and effective resistance until Salem Church. There, the freethinker and union printer Joseph Moreau "rushed from the line to the head of the company, evidently desiring, by word and example, to lead them into the deadly woods," becoming "the mark for a hundred rifles, and he fell pierced with many balls." When the Confederate counterattack near the church threatened a Federal battery, Amos Jay Cummings of the New York City Typographical Union rallied some of the men to challenge the rebels hand to hand and roll the cannons off to safety, earning a Congressional Medal of Honor.[12]

The Example of Gettysburg

A brief survey of the first day of the battle of Gettysburg on July 1, 1863, demonstrates the ubiquitous presence of veterans of the labor movement on the battlefields of the war. As the Confederate army entered Pennsylvania, Isaac J. Neall, the former president of the National Molders' Union, though earlier wounded, raised volunteers for the emergency, as had his successor, William Sylvis. However, the relatively complete rolls of the Typographical Union provide our best sense of what organized workers in uniform experienced in this campaign.[13] Further restricting our focus to labor figures who were officers or became casualties will hopefully moderate any Homeric overtones.

July 1 began as a Confederate corps moved on the town from the west. A member of the Atlanta Typographical Union in the Thirteenth Alabama and another of the Savannah local in the Second Georgia Battalion marched in the ranks. The Twelfth Virginia included Captain J. Richard Lewellen, who had represented Richmond at the national printers' convention of 1851, as well as two other Richmond unionists, and a member of the Petersburg local.[14]

Several units of Federal cavalry met the rebels on the high ground just northwest of Gettysburg. In this desperate action, the twenty-six-year-old Major William H. Medill of the Chicago local commanded the left of his Eighth Illinois Cavalry, a regiment with at least one other member of that local. The brother of Joseph Medill of the *Chicago Tribune*, the major had lost his own paper in the Panic of 1857 and eventually found himself working for wages. An avid reader of history, he became a "radical Republican" and "an ardent, thorough devotee of Liberty; his whole soul was in the holy cause of Union." With the news from Fort Sumter, he had ridden with the Chicago Dragoons into western Virginia and survived to rise through the ranks until he shared responsibility for the efforts of the Union cavalry in holding the terrain west of Gettysburg until the Federal First Corps came rushing from the road through the fields west of town into position.[15]

With them came the "Iron Brigade" of Midwesterners. An entire company of the Second Wisconsin consisted "of foundry-men and iron-workers," but the presence of so many printers in the Twenty-Fourth Michigan made this the bloodiest day in the history of Detroit labor. Union member Corporal Charles H. McConnell wrote the story for the *Detroit Advertiser and Tribune*. Raised the previous summer, the regiment had already lost four union members by Gettysburg. The union also accounted for several officers and Sergeant John Witherspoon, who had been wounded at Bull Run, and would be again at Gettysburg. The local also provided First Sergeants Samuel W. Church and Joseph R. Boyle, Corporal James S. Booth, Privates John McCutcheon, and probably James F. Clegg, discharged for disability after the battle. Reports cited for gallantry Second Lieutenant Michael Dempsey, vice president of the union. In addition, Thomas S. Orton lost his life, as did Captain Malachi J. O'Donnell, last seen waving the sword his fellow workers at the *Detroit Free Press* had given him. "In the hands of an O'Donnell," he promised them, "it will never cause a blush to mount the cheeks of these kind friends." He fell at the last barricade they defended, near the seminary.[16]

The next brigade included other members of the Typographical Union. The Eighty-Fourth New York had about a half-dozen men from the New York local, and its participants in the day's action included William G. Magonigle and John T. Ryan, wounded. Other members may have been in the nearby Ninety-Fifth New York and the Fifty-Sixth Pennsylvania. That division included still more. In the Thirteenth Massachusetts, Captain Augustine Harlow of the Boston local fell wounded. The Twelfth had other members of that local, William L. Kimball and George Kimball, the latter having been wounded at Antietam and the former in the fields above Gettysburg. Nearby, Second Lieutenant James S. Bonsall of the Philadelphia local tried to stabilize the ranks of the Ninetieth Pennsylvania. John Paulding Conn and Myron H. Matthews of the Rochester local frantically worked the guns of the First New York Light Artillery, Conn falling mortally wounded.[17]

Despite the lack of any comparable membership lists of other trade unions, other participants in the labor movement turned up alongside these printers. One man recalled glimpsing First Lieutenant George A. Deering of the Sixteenth Maine, the former leader of the firefighters' strike at Saco. To steady his beleaguered company, he picked up a musket himself, stood beside them and fired it, but the rammer had been left in the barrel and it shot away "with a crazy whizz that set the boys of his company to laughing. It was strange to hear laughter there, with dead men by." When the Confederates overwhelmed that part of the line, they captured Deering, who spent a year and a half as a prisoner.[18]

At a critical moment, a second Confederate corps appeared north of Gettysburg, and its advance threatened to cut off the First Union corps from the rest of the army. The Thirty-Eighth Georgia had two members of the Atlanta local. A single division had the Twelfth Georgia with two members from Atlanta. The Third Alabama had four members of the Mobile local and two from Montgomery. At least three of the five members of the Raleigh Typographical Society serving in the Fourteenth North Carolina participated in the battle, including First Lieutenant Jefferson McKinny Henson and First Sergeant Leonidas N. Keith, wounded severely enough to be reassigned to the invalids corps.[19]

Meeting them were parts of the small Federal Eleventh Corps. Quartermaster Sergeant Charles F. Sheldon of the Indianapolis local, serving in the First Indiana Cavalry at the headquarters of the Eleventh Corps, charged to meet that advance. Several members of the Boston local served in the Thirty-Third Massachusetts, including Captain Albion W. Tibbetts, destined eventually to make lieutenant colonel. A cluster of other union printers identified were associated with these regiments. It is worth noting that, in the Twenty-Sixth Wisconsin, Lieutenant Colonel Hans Boebel of Milwaukee's antebellum land-reform movement lost his leg and likely had it removed by his co-thinker and comrade, Dr. Francis Huebschman.[20] Overwhelming Confederate numbers swept the Federals back through Gettysburg from north and northwest of town, but the resistance allowed reinforcements to secure the high ground to the south.

This narrative could be extended, as the next two days brought more unionists with the greater numbers of both armies into the field. July 2 found Creighton commanding his Ohioans on Culp's Hill. He had just returned from time at home to recover from wounds received at Cedar Mountain. While there, he too received a sword from his old co-workers at the *Herald*, who called him "the immediate representative of this, their own particular circle." Within months, a Cleveland shop produced sheet music for a "Seventh Regiment March," dedicated to Creighton and bearing the picture of the local hero on the cover. He used these accolades, not surprisingly, to recruit replacements for the losses his regiment had experienced.[21] The day also found Ben Price of the land reformers in the Peach Orchard, and John Tobin of Madigan's old regiment in the Wheatfield.

After yet a third day of carnage, the battered and bloodied soldiers who endured to greet the dawn on July 4 remained uncertain as to whether the fighting would begin anew. Bracing for an attack that did not come, the high command sent Creighton and his men to scout along what had been the sweep of the Confederate line. They returned with a few prisoners and the welcome news that the battle had ended and the Confederates had turned south. Later, news arrived from beyond the field that the Confederate army, besieged at Vicksburg, Mississippi, had surrendered. Gettysburg had severely bloodied both sides but left the Federals more capable of replacing their losses.

Two days later, Union cavalry pushed the rebels near Williamsport, and Medill personally borrowed a carbine to take half of his regiment forward as skirmishers, falling mortally wounded. The carpenter and national officer of the land-reform association, Captain Benjamin F. Price had rejoined his regiment the previous fall after having been taken prisoner of war on the peninsula. At Gettysburg, he and his men had faced such withering fire that initial accounts erroneously reported him killed in action, but, on July 23, as acting major, Price took half of his regiment forward against a well-positioned rear guard at Manassas Gap, only to lose his life there.[22]

A crude tally indicates a significant presence of members of the prewar labor movement through the three days of the battle. To focus strictly on the well-documented rolls of the printers union, some eighty-three members from New Haven to Chicago served in the Army of the Potomac, including seventeen as commissioned officers. Some twenty-eight of them—about one-third—fell as casualties. In addition, the Army of Northern Virginia included twenty-one members of locals from Richmond to New Orleans, two of them officers. In total, the NTU contributed well over one hundred soldiers to the fighting at Gettysburg.[23] Something like this sketch could be written of virtually any engagement.

What is essential to remember is that there were a dozen or more unions as large or larger than the NTU, and that printers often had a special exemption from military service. By any measure, the actual fighting of the Civil War had a major impact on working-class history.

Long-Term Consequences

The escalating scale of the war quickly reached beyond the ranks of the younger, single men to mobilize older workers, who were sometimes married and with considerable obligations. The generation of men who led the unions had passed their childhood and adolescence in an ideological climate shaped by optimistic possibilities of a more egalitarian and just society through rational and ethical social persuasion. William H. Sylvis of the Molders' Union raised a company of volunteers that elected him an officer, but his wife insisted that he not go with them, but a number of others did. The war took a serious toll among land reformers, of whom Joshua S. Valentine, Solomon Shepherd, William Haddock, Ben Price, James Penn Bennett, and David D. Irons entered the army, the first two returning in broken health and the last three never coming back. At age fifty-six, Joel Brown, the Yankee carpenter and friend of Frances Wright, was the oldest man in his Ohio regiment.[24] Those who most ardently believed in the idea of "free labor" disproportionately went to war.

Younger men poised to take up the leadership of the old cause also died in the war. One of the old antebellum radicals, Horace Seaver, viewed Joseph N. Moreau as a protégé of sorts. Certainly, Moreau stood at the edge of an old labor radicalism that saw the conflict of 1861 as "a war for liberty" in a world where everything seemed "unequal and unnatural and unjust." Seaver thought he had little military ambition and sought "no glory, except in the glory of the cause he defended." A related strain of émigré radicalism experienced similar losses, such as First Lieutenant Fritz Jacobi of New York's *Kommunists Klub*.[25]

The reports of the Typographical Unions indicated that the national organization had entered the crisis with fifty-five locals, of which secession removed fifteen. Of the remaining forty, only six continued to file reports through 1861. While that number tripled in 1862, some twenty-two locals posted nothing beyond the list of officers. Over the entire course of the war, eleven of those forty locals never reported anything and had surely ceased to function at all.

Events hardly encouraged members of those locals that did survive. By the fall of 1862, the Philadelphia membership had dropped from around six hundred to a mere 254, with nearly seventy more noted as being in the service. During this same period, New York membership fell from around four hundred to 242 with more than forty having gone to the war. Cincinnati's officers hoped the local would "swell up to its original goodly proportions" because their numbers had been falling. In the summer of 1862, the Boston union formed part of a broader contingent of the local craft marching beneath a banner proclaiming: "The Printers of Boston—One Hundred Men in the Union Army." Toward war's end, the local itself claimed eighty-two members but knew of another fifty-six in the army and navy. New Haven and Harrisburg reported proportionately similar losses, and locals like Peoria, which had eleven of its twenty-eight members in uniform, winked out of existence. Chicago claimed that fifty-six had joined by the fall of 1862, adding that "most of these now hold commissions; besides three or four majors, there are several captains, and a large number of lieutenants."[26] These losses in the antebellum leadership and therefore the postwar leadership potential would be sorely missed.

The losses had been even more extensive in other crafts. The eighty-seven locals of Machinists and Blacksmiths collapsed to thirty, and Secretary Jonathan Fincher showed up for its November convention at the war's start to find only a handful of delegates present. The National Cotton Mule Spinners' Association "was almost dead during the war, as most of its members had gone to shoulder the musket and to fight for the maintenance of the Union of States, and to strike the shackles from the negro." In that union, as in others, "a large number of the old members" died in the war.[27]

Workers were going to take their own shot at shaping the revolution into which the war was growing. Newspaper proprietors, eager to take every patriotic advantage of their workers, tried to use the mobilizations to clear the unionists out of their shops. Indiana authorized the owner of the Valparaiso *Republic* to raise a company for the Sixty-Third Indiana, which he proposed to fill with printers, and the Chicago bosses quickly concocted plans for a "Chicago Typographical Battalion" to be "composed exclusively of members of the craft," even dangling a commission before NTU president John M. Farquhar.[28] Similar commissions had been offered other presidents of the national unions.

President Farquhar consciously repudiated the project, which would have been suicidal for the union. With the NTU's vice president William Madigan and many local officers already gone, Farquhar had remained at his post and even accepted reelection to the presidency in May. Nevertheless, on August 13 he joined Chicago's "railroad regiment," the Eighty-Ninth Illinois, in hopes it would remain close enough to permit performance of his limited duties as a union president. By early September, though, Sergeant Major Farquhar and his regiment rushed into Kentucky to meet the Confederate invasion at Perryville. (In the east, another union president, William H. Sylvis, served as an orderly sergeant for moving another company up in support of the Federal Army at Antietam.) The end of the year found him west of Murfreesboro along Stone's River to the rear of the extreme right of the Union army. As the Confederates swept down on them, Farquhar took charge of what was left of his own regiment, rallied fugitives of different commands, and established a temporary line. A superior reported Farquhar's "gallantry in rallying to my colors fugitives from other commands," and the overall Federal report cited Farquhar with others to whom "a nation's gratitude is due them for their conduct."[29]

Some certainly pursued a traditional printer's route to respectability, particularly with the mid-nineteenth-century boom in the market for the written word. Franklin J. Ottarson, involved in efforts to unionize the craft since 1844 had represented the city's crafts in the founding national conventions but made a remarkable transition to newspaper writing and magazine work. War made other union members such as Mortimer C. Misener and George Bowerem into reporters. Members of that union left a considerable literature on the war. One of them wrote a self-deprecating *How Private George W. Peck Put Down the Rebellion; or, The Funny Experiences of a Raw Recruit* but branched into a series on "Peck's bad boy" and wound up governor of Wisconsin. Others, such as Theodore C. Tracie, wrote a history of his unit, the *Annals of the Nineteenth Ohio Battery Volunteers Artillery*. George F. Williams proved remarkably prolific: he compiled *The Memorial War Book* and a novel, *Bullet and Shell: War as the Soldier Saw It*.[30]

The Pennsylvania-born printer John Lawrence Bittinger followed the path of Benjamin Franklin into government. He had participated in the founding of the Republican Party in Illinois before coming to St. Louis in 1855, where he worked on what became the *Missouri Democrat*. After briefly operating the *St. Louis Evening Bulletin*, he left in 1860 for St. Joseph, where the Lincoln administration appointed him postmaster. Although enlisting as a private, he soon rose to a staff position, which he held while serving the organization of the state's Unionist government as speaker pro tem of the General Assembly.[31]

Craft identities even survived Andersonville. John Ransom's famous diary from the Andersonville prison camp recalled his being given small cowpeas for rations. He wrote, "Being a printer by trade, I spread the peas out on a blanket and quickly pick them up one at a time, after the manner of picking up type," though often unconsciously consuming them all. "I have trials of skill with a fellow named Land, who is also a printer. There are no other typos here that I know of." At least one other passed through briefly. As Confederates brought John C. Reid, the quartermaster sergeant of an Ohio regiment, to the prison camp, he overheard a Southern printer, who had known him earlier, say, "He won't last long in such a place as this!" Reid risked everything to escape and, "assisted by friendly negroes, he reached the Union lines greatly emaciated after the privations he had endured both at Andersonville and following his escape."[32]

Many of these members would not return. From the early summer of 1862—and for most of the next three years—the surviving larger unions in the east hardly saw a month without bad news from the front. Rochester early got the news that William R. Wells had been killed at Williamsburg. A few weeks later, William Madigan, vice president of the NTU, fell at Gaines' Mill, brandishing the sword given him by his co-workers before he went off in charge of a company and commanded one side of the line of the "the Fighting Ninth" of Massachusetts. The Columbus Typographical Union survived throughout the war, periodically passing resolutions, such as those "expressive of the sense of the Union relative to the death of our late fellow craftsman, Dr. Henry Y. Smith," Assistant Surgeon of the 24th O.V.I. in the flower of manhood."[33]

The poor records of the western war eclipsed other cases. Denver's pioneer unionist, John L. Merrick, disappeared into the poor records of the western war. He headed back east when the war broke out and joined the Sixteenth Illinois, later transferring to become an officer in Seventh Kansas Cavalry, known for its marauding "jayhawking" along the Missouri border. Merrick resigned and reenlisted in the Fourteenth Kansas Cavalry as a private but became part of General James G. Blunt's bodyguard. In that capacity, he was severely wounded, likely at the Baxter Springs ambush in October 1863. Returning to service as a scout, he returned from one expedition sick and then succumbed to disease.

Both sides built mass armies from very little. For this reason, if no other, in no subsequent conflict did so many members of labor organizations participate more fully as leaders of the military effort. From the onset of the war, trade unionists and labor reformers won commissions as officers and helped lead the war effort at that level. Indeed, proportionately larger numbers of commissioned officers had associations with the labor movement than had been or would be the case in any American war.

* * *

Lucius Alonzo Hine of the *Cincinnati Gazette* stood among the reporters straining to hear the words of Abraham Lincoln's address dedicating the cemetery at Gettysburg. A Fourierist socialist, spiritualist, abolitionist, and land reformer, he had participated in virtually every phase of the workers' movements at Cincinnati. He had also edited a series of reform newspapers and spent most of the decade before the war on the road, lecturing and agitating. For the *Missouri Democrat*, he had covered the overthrow of the state's secessionist government but later returned to the *Gazette*, which sent him to cover the president's speech on November 19, 1863. This longtime advocate of radical social reconstruction heard the president's hope "that these dead shall not have died in vain—that this nation, under God, shall have a new birth of freedom—and that government of the people, by the people, for the people, shall not perish from the earth."[34] At no point in Hine's long career had the prospect of serious radical change seemed more likely, though it now faced not only all of the old obstacles but a series of new ones unimagined a generation earlier.

Then, too, as organized workers sought to influence the course of the war, they found the kind of success that eluded them in the workplaces at home, particularly as attrition and experience brought them to higher rank and greater authority. Toward the close of 1863, as Union armies stirred to action at Chattanooga, the Cleveland union printer William Creighton led the Seventh Ohio as it approached Lookout Mountain, where they fought within the view of his Chicago union brother Owen M. Stuart, then commanding the Ninetieth Illinois. In the course of the attack, the loss of his superior forced Creighton to take charge of the entire brigade as it seized the Confederate defenses. A few days later, Creighton fell at the head of that brigade's assault on the Confederate rear guard positions on Taylor's Ridge.[35] Though elements of it clung on tenaciously, the old labor movement, like so many of its members and leaders, perished in the Civil War.

The cause that had given rise to them clearly did not.

PART II

Remaking the Workforce

No ban, or race, or creed, but free
As air is to mankind,
Let all the rights of manhood be
As a just God designed.

—"Equal Rights for All" from the
Daily Evening Voice

CHAPTER 4

The Great Slave Strike

Emancipation and Race

Workers in the Washington Navy Yard moved into action, along with the general wartime labor unrest that swept the capital. There, "most of the colored hands employed in the anchor shop struck for higher wages, demanding one dollar and seventy-five cents instead of one dollar and fifty cents, which they have been receiving heretofore." The bosses refused the raise and decided to replace twenty-nine black strikers with twenty-five white strikebreakers.[1] The frequent portrayal of black workers as strikebreakers not only oversimplified the complexity of wartime race relations but also sometimes inverted what actually happened.

In terms of numbers and militancy, the black strike of 1861–1865 moved hundreds of thousands, eclipsing the shoe strike of 1860. While the demands of war subsumed most of the older labor organizations, a mass strike by the most downtrodden and oppressed of the American working class redefined the national identity and transformed the nature of the Civil War. The scholarship on slavery and race has increasingly emphasized the importance of black self-emancipation as a vital corrective to the dominant, politically motivated portrayal of African Americans as passive recipients of Unionist policies.[2] While most slaves took whatever measures they deemed necessary to free themselves, many shared a broad realization that, under the circumstances, the quality of that freedom they gained would rest heavily on the army and the government. This forced a clearer negotiation about the nature of "free labor," and it also made the newly centralizing American State the vital mechanism for defining and institutionalizing what the term would mean in the real world.

The Mass Strike

The story of slavery and emancipation has long been told and is retold in virtually every list of newly published books. Several million slaves, with various degrees of militancy, walked off their jobs over the course of the Civil War. As in most such disputes between workers and the employers of their labor, the latter provides most of the documentation and predisposes our perspective to theirs. Slaveholders rarely resisted the temptation to exaggerate the threat of violence and rationalized the most brutal repression with a blessed lack of self-awareness. Yet they had little reason to exaggerate, particularly in the course of the war.

The workers engaged in these activities left little in terms of sources, while the slaveholders never left any doubt as to their predictable reactions. Secession dissolved the South's reliance on the large-scale commercial farming of crops for export such as cotton, which meant that slaves began experiencing their condition differently. Matters became increasingly confused and confusing, as slaves began performing new kinds of work or doing what they had done differently or under new conditions. Whether they fled slavery or not—and before those who did so acted to free themselves—African Americans naturally tended to play a greater role in redefining themselves as individuals, families, and communities.

From the onset of the war, slaves became increasingly forthcoming about their views. On Christmas Eve 1861, Kentucky whites watched as sixty slaves paraded "singing political songs and shouting for Lincoln." That winter, as white Unionists sabotaged railroad bridges in the upper South, Confederate authorities also began blaming disgruntled slaves for arson. At year's end they blamed unsupervised slaves encamped in Charleston for a fire that swept through the city, destroying hundreds of buildings. Elsewhere in South Carolina, authorities followed rumors into a swamp where they found an encampment of runaways growing their own crops. Soon after, Confederates in Adams County, Mississippi, found that field slaves had stashed arms and supplies in a similarly isolated maroon. Even as slaveholders repeated rumors of armed slave insurrections, they reported remarkably more pragmatic plans, such as that for "a stampede" of a hundred slaves into the wilderness or toward Union lines.[3]

The authorities responded ruthlessly to maintain their power. Arkansas slaveholders executed blacks for an alleged plot at Monroe, while similar executions took place in May and June across the river in Mississippi. At New Orleans a dozen ships burned at anchor and, "on more than one plantation, the assistance of the authorities has been called in to overcome the open resistance of the slaves." Similar rumors stirred central Kentucky and Tennessee.[4]

The crisis exacerbated the almost pathological concern about the dangers that black resistance involved white nonslaveholders. For generations before the war, slaveholders had used race to keep most whites docile, if not cooperative, in the interests of slaveholding. Secessionists felt little need for more than the most cursory mandate from their deferential inferiors to embark on their project to destroy the United States. The grotesquely undemocratic nature of secession and the unexpected costs of an unwanted war increasingly strained those old allegiances. At the beginning of the conflict, Southern gentlemen shared terrifying stories of whites ready to assist plots by slaves to rush from their plantations en masse. Frequently, their accounts of slave conspiracies involved white allies.

At first, though, the Federal authorities—even those who later became prominent emancipationists—balked at allying themselves with slave insurrection. In the war's first weeks General Benjamin F. Butler assured Maryland officials that his troops would prevent a servile insurrection there. As late as August 1862, Butler, then in Louisiana, worried that "an insurrection [that] broke out among the negroes" threatened whites. He squelched "the incipient revolt . . . by informing the negroes that we should repel an attack by them upon the women and children." That fall, a threatened rebellion north of Thibodeaux concerned officials of the Federal occupation.[5]

Confederate paranoia aside, African Americans sustained organizations of their own that pressed their own agenda. Without speculating on its extent or strength, older antebellum networks of communications and action existed among slaves and helped foster concerted responses to the war. Black resistance to slavery had forced white supporters to help shape a new "underground railroad." Moreover, even in the most contested and supervised circumstances in Virginia, enslaved black workers established and maintained their own associations. A Union prisoner at Staunton and a spy at Richmond stumbled onto these societies "composed almost exclusively of colored men."[6]

The Confederate paradox was that the very slavery that secession has sought to protect ultimately crippled the war effort as reversals in the field whittled away both the territory and the labor supply of the Confederacy, making those who remained all the more important to the war effort. The remaining slaves increasingly found themselves doing new kinds of work and, often, for wages. The proximity of Federal alternatives required competitive responses among the Confederates, whether private employers, civilian authorities, or the military. Quick studies in terms of wartime inflation, slaves and free blacks commanded unprecedented high wages at just the point the Southern economy could least afford it. In March 1865 as the Confederate Senate authorized the War Department to arrange with governors to hire slave labor, it expressed that standard American disregard of laissez faire ideology as it applied to workers by prohibiting "higher wages for the hire of such slaves than is allowed by law to privates in the army."[7] Such regulations were often honored more in the breach.

The problem became acute where slaves worked alongside wage labor at places such as Tredegar Iron Works. Years before, the employers at Tredegar had opted to replace white wage earners with slaves, but what resulted became a terribly stratified workforce in which the division of labor in industry came to define lines of race and gender as well. The industrial demands of war expanded Tredegar, particularly its reliance on slave labor. The labor disputes there left the Confederate authorities in May 1864 to face what it viewed as mutinies. As elsewhere, repression only made matters worse, and June brought the arrest of a black waiter named Bob Richardson, charged for conspiring with the Union Army that had begun encircling the Confederate capital.[8]

The growing numbers of aggrieved nonslaveholders, including armed Confederate deserters and escaped Union prisoners, provided slave rebels a growing number of whites ready to transgress the color bar. Civilian authorities far from Federal lines clamored for martial law and the assignment of troops to suppress small bands of armed blacks. Increasingly, Confederates feared a convergence of "deserters from our armies, Tories and runaways." By early 1864 Confederate officials in South Carolina reported "five to six hundred negroes" not in "the regular military organization of the Yankees" who "lead the lives of banditti, roving the country with fire and committing all sorts of horrible crimes upon the inhabitants." Florida officials reported "500 Union men, deserters, and negroes . . . raiding towards Gainesville," while similar groups formed to commit "depredations upon the plantations and crops of loyal citizens and running off their slaves." At Yazoo City, Mississippi, they not only attacked such private estates but successfully burned the courthouse.[9]

At times, black resistance fueled the worst Confederate fears, nowhere more famously than in Jones County, Mississippi. A Confederate conscript and deserter named Newton Knight organized and captained a small but effective band of guerilla fighters. Recent work has emphasized the biracial nature of these activities and how they influenced the local course of Reconstruction and the emergence of Populism at the close of the century.[10] In hindsight, no white resistance in such parts of the South would have been possible without places of refuge in the swamps or mountains or other unfarmable enclaves, of which blacks had cultivated a special understanding and knowledge.

The rolling strike of the slaves had actually defied the official policies of both governments. However, it made itself the great incontrovertible and irreversible fact of the war. It established the foundations for a substantive interracial cooperation and forced the capitulation of one of the those contending governments to rethink and expand its war goals. Through the summer of 1862, even as President Abraham Lincoln remained aloof from abolitionist proposals, he decided to expand the Union's goals as commander-in-chief. In September, though, the president issued his "preliminary proclamation" of emancipation.[11]

Government and the Transition to Wage Labor

The Federal government accepted emancipation because it had no alternative. The farther the Union armies penetrated into the South, the more dense population of slaves responded with a general, though not universal, abandonment of the plantations. On the Carolina coast, in the lower Mississippi Valley, and in the later march through Georgia, the numbers of enslaved workers who abandoned their labors and escaped to freedom came to outnumber the Union troops that seized and garrisoned these areas. Those who had been the most powerless and downtrodden people on the continent had placed emancipation beyond the control of presidents and generals.

Yet the same Union officials who had balked so long at emancipation scrambled quickly to manage the process. Slaves opting for freedom found that they not only had to plan the logistics of their escape from bondage, and also had to negotiate the space for building a new life, primarily through the Federal officials. For their part, those authorities understood the potential of black labor unrest and the slaves' strike without necessarily agreeing on what they hoped to achieve beyond the military defeat of secession. Certainly, the demands of war and production ultimately challenged the older assumptions of whiteness (or paternalism) without requiring their abandonment.

On one level, the same institutions and values that had sustained slavery continued to define and regulate race relations. They fretted over how to officially structure the black transition to "free labor." Paradoxically, the first experience of freedom for most African Americans coming out of slavery became markedly unfree. Legal emancipation became inexorably associated with military service, labor associated with refugee camps and fortifications and other fiercely circumscribed circumstance. Former slaves who tried to bypass war work tended to find themselves competing for jobs previously performed by whites.[12] The service of African Americans attained food and shelter that matched the low pay, slow pay, or no pay.

Essential to this persistence was the fact that the initial experience with free labor of most former slaves usually took place under conditions of martial law. Union authorities had few other options but to place blacks to work on military projects and to create the largest series of public works projects in American history to employ these unemployed.

Most conservatively, though, were those schemes by which planters in 1864 welcomed the military "settled plan" in sponsorship of a free labor plan for "employing such negroes as the Government does not require." Some called for "dragooning" blacks into the army or other such forced labor projects because the labor shortage had become so acute that they could often been seen "loafering about town or at work for themselves."[13]

In fact, African Americans had never entirely been strangers to wage labor. Former slaveholders often lacked the means or intentions to employ their former chattel, and some adopted the tactic of leaving them as "vagrants" for the military to handle. The more sympathetic Federal authorities mandated an arbitration of negotiations over wages.[14] Elsewhere, former slaves could be arrested for vagrancy and sentenced to terms of labor.

Some slaves as well as free blacks had participated in labor activities and organizations. The Waiter's Protective Union at New York, a decade before the war, had surely not been unique. Almost as soon as the war ended, ongoing black labor discontent gave rise to local "ringleaders" and "troublemakers." A South Carolina freedman named Sandy was described as one who "works when he chooses, and only such work as he chooses to do . . . all the time exciting the people with falsehoods and rebellions principles." He and his followers appealed persistently to the Freedmen's Bureau, but Federal concerns proved to be nothing if not ambiguous.[15]

Associations for mutual aid sprang up across the South, some achieving considerable size and influence. The Church Pension Society of Freedmen at Columbia, South Carolina, appeared quickly enough to hint at older networks among blacks. African Americans in Tennessee established two prominent mutual-aid societies at Memphis and Chattanooga, the former strong enough to support on its own two hundred indigent freed people.[16]

Other associations, such as the Union Progressive Association, organized blacks or sometimes racially mixed memberships. This "literary society of the colored men of Boston" sponsored a celebration of emancipation that drew "a very large attendance, a considerable portion of those present being white." Among the speakers, old Chartist and labor radical John C. Cluer "alluded to the mistaken idea the people in this country have of the feeling of the working classes of England in regard to the North and their hatred of slavery."[17]

The antebellum Typographical Union—hardly the broadest and most welcoming of the skilled crafts—had actually included a few black members despite the sweeping and mistaken generalizations about their antebellum exclusion. Alexander Niger worked at Providence for years and openly identified himself as a Negro member of the tiny local there. On the other hand, John Clovis Laizer held a long and active membership in the antebellum New Orleans local, though he did so by passing as white.

Black workers in Washington, D.C., clustered in such large numbers not only because of the city's proximity to their general origins in the South but because the demands of war created real opportunities for work and the building of life beyond slavery. Many worked for twenty-five dollars per month, more than twice the wage set by the Militia Act. Societies grew from this, such as the Colored

Union Benevolent Association of Washington, which provided "charity and mutual assistance in time of need" and secured "a small property in real estate." It evolved into the postwar network of "Colored Citizens and Tax-payers."[18]

Certainly, what looked like evidence for such an organization could be something else. One suspects that the "African Protective Union" advertised by "Colonel" C. W. Worster of Tean and Worster represented something other than the kind of "protective union" that existed among whites, though it is interesting that the owners chose to present themselves as such. It claimed to be "organized by colored men who have at heart the colored man's interest, in preserving him from the fraudulent representation." However, there was no "Colonel" Worster and the company actually seems to have itself been an employment agency for which "60,000 Colored men [were] wanted."[19] Opportunistic entrepreneurs certainly took advantage of this influx of new workers, and many whites in authority envisioned little beyond continued exploitation.

As part of this the authorities launched and optimistically named *The New South*. By midsummer 1863, "the employees in the Quartermaster's department, who are chiefly negroes, have, it appears, threatened to strike for higher wages, and been in other ways mutinous." Faced with an interracial, if not exclusively black movement, the army issued a stern warning "to the Employees of the Quartermaster's Department," threatening serious reprisals against "the least holding back or want of interest, or willingness to work all day, and all night too, when called on, or hesitation in obeying the order of the officer or chief man under whom you are placed." Those guilty of failing to follow orders, the warning stated, "shall be sent to work in the trenches and in the works in the very front at Morris Island." Further, "any man that will 'strike' for higher wages in this emergency should be shot."[20] Of course, having nipped such interracial cooperation at the workplace in the bud, the successors of those authorities would decry its absence and blame the backwardness of the workers.

Most dramatically, the unexpectedly disastrous level of casualties opened one avenue of work, traditionally reserved for whites, to African Americans. As events drove the white South to an ever-heavier reliance on conscription and coercion, the Union turned to black troops. Strikers accounted for most of the roughly quarter-million soldiers who served in the "colored volunteer" regiments, where they performed the same work being performed by whites, though not at the same pay or under the same terms.

Nevertheless, military service imposed similar experiences upon black and white men, and many responded with an acknowledgement of the familiar. "You would be astonished," Sergeant George Washington Beidelman of the Philadelphia Typographical Union assured his father, "to see in what short time these rough and uncouth, and hitherto despised and ignorant men, attain proficiency as good soldiers—both in drill and discipline. We have many visitors daily—both citizens and soldiers, and all are surprised and delighted. . . . I think the Government has 'hit the nail on the head' in this instance; for it is evidently fast becoming its strongest arm for the suppression of the rebellion."[21]

Workers generally, not just the former slaves, had an interest in making emancipation more than a new way to exploit labor. To be meaningful, new national standards of labor rights required a common, national market. Coal-fired railroads and the telegraph wove the infrastructure for such things, though in and of themselves, they would do nothing. The future would itself turn on what workers would insist upon, precisely the process against which the prominent newspapers North and South warned.

Beidelman's former union brother, Colonel John H. Taggart, had played a crucial role in the fielding of those regiments. He resigned his commission as the Army of the Potomac withdrew from the Peninsula. Returning to Philadelphia, he set up a training school for white soldiers volunteering to take commissions in these new units, an important forerunner of what would later be the Officer Candidate School.[22]

The decision to officer black soldiers could not be taken lightly. Despite the Lincoln administration directive to commission black officers, the military high command placed whites in charge of such regiments. Many in power retained the racist expectations that the entire project was but a disaster in the making. Other white officers generally ascribed lesser status to a "nigger colonel" and, with many of the white soldiers, initially accorded black men in arms little respect. Finally, Confederate policy was to regard all black soldiers as slave rebels and their officers as instigators of slave rebellion, liable to summary execution.

Quite understandably, some advocates of labor reform became involved in this transition. Early on, radical abolitionists such as Elizur Wright urged black recruitment as an essential mechanism of a sweeping social reconstruction. A periodic ally of the land reformers back in New York, General Daniel Ullman got the White House to send him to Louisiana, where he became their tireless recruiter and advocate of black troops. Taking command there of the Ninth Corps d'Afrique, grown from the efforts of free blacks in New Orleans, was Samuel F. H. Learned, a union printer from Boston who had risen from the ranks to take a commission in the Eighty-First USCT.[23]

Certainly, various African Americans became involved in such military activities through the work of a number of important recruiters. Martin R. Delany, James Macune Smith, William H. Day, and Peter Humphries Clark—who had longstanding, if selective, association with white radicals and labor reformers—seemed to see equal participation in the military as a means of fostering a more equal participation in the wider society.[24]

Few illustrated this association better than Captain Alonzo G. Draper, the former leader of shoe strikers. When Colonel William Batchelder Green resigned from the Fourteenth Massachusetts in September 1862 and headed home from garrison duties around Washington, Draper, athough promoted to major, decided to leave for one of the new black regiments. July 1863 found him raising troops on for the "African's Brigade" on coastal South Carolina, where Green's nephew, Colonel Robert Gould Shaw, had just been killed at the head of the black Fifty-Fourth Massachusetts. Draper spent the rest of the year near Norfolk and Portsmouth, organizing some of the more than thirty-seven thousand black recruits into the Second North Carolina (African Descent) alongside the "only Benevolent Soc. in Portsmouth" for burial of the dead.[25]

Assigned to garrison the prison camp at Point Lookout, Draper took his men, their dependents, and other civilian refugees to the camp with him, though he made several expeditions into Virginia to sustain the "Government Farms," where he settled blacks on confiscated rebel estates. The prison population climbed from under eight thousand to almost twenty thousand by late summer, given the unwillingness of the Confederates to treat blacks as prisoners of war and the Federal disinterest in trading for whites only.[26]

With Colonel Greene now back in the field with Butler, the latter directly wrote Secretary of War Edwin M. Stanton, "Might I not have the 36th U.S. Colored Regiment from Point Lookout?" Butler also pleaded with General U.S. Grant to cooperate in getting Draper "a valuable officer" to the front. When Draper found himself detained to take command at Fort Monroe while en route to Butler's army, the general again complained to Grant that Draper "is very much needed here." The end of July brought Draper to command of a full brigade in the Richmond-Petersburg defenses. By the spring of 1864 Butler took charge of the Department of Virginia and North Carolina and organized most of the USCT into a new Army of the James.[27]

Along the western border of the war, former Chartist and socialist Richard J. Hinton served in the First Kansas Colored, and then the Second Kansas Colored, the Seventy-Ninth and Eighty-Third USCT. William H. T. Wakefield, future vice presidential candidate of the United Labor Party, served as a lieutenant among Arkansas black soldiers.[28]

Consideration of the role of Native Americans in the war is in order. In the military setting, where workers expected to be deferential and follow orders, at least half a dozen union printers from the Denver local, most from the *Rocky Mountain News*, enrolled in what became "the Bloodless Third," which perpetrated the horrific 1864 Sand Creek massacre. Yet they also demonstrated genuinely newer approaches, as did Illinois land reformer Col. William A. Phillips, who raised, commanded, and advocated the rights of the Indian brigade of the Union army at Fort Gibson.[29] While racial attitudes could be mixed among working people, their social betters would certainly settle on one policy, and it always tended to be more reminiscent of Sand Creek than Fort Gibson.

The presence of such officers should not obscure the generally miserable experience of African Americans in uniform. Whites generally chafed under the brutal discipline and hardship of nineteenth-century military life, but most black soldiers faced far worse. More than whites, they got pay, food, and shelter that often looked more symbolic than real. When they responded, as did members of the Corps d'Afrique at Fort Jackson December 1863, the full force of military law fell upon them.[30] While the shadow of such insubordination and its repression might be short among whites, it remained a long, dark, and brooding presence over the African American experience.

The Politics of Class and Slave Liberation

Military service on this scale represented something peculiar to the war and, when the war ended, blacks would find themselves in the same workforce as whites. But they found that emancipation had not been abolition. It did not eliminate race but most immediately melded hitherto distinct parts of the black population, subjecting all African Americans to conditions that no longer had anything clearly to do with enslavement. Emancipation delivered, as was said, "nothing but freedom."[31]

Class interest had moved white workers to defend the survival of the Federal Union and had informed their hostility toward slavery, but this was a far cry from extending the same solidarity to black workers as whites. Democrats and Republicans alike, bosses as well as white workers tended to think of blacks in terms of objects of white philanthropy rather than their peers. Even radical white workers, like the molders in St. Louis, described themselves as defenders of "the rights that belong to white men," a formulation open to many interpretations.[32] At issue, however, was whether blacks and whites could and should perform the same kinds of jobs.

Over generations, though, the Democratic use of white fears about black equality, competition, and miscegenation became increasingly important to the party's success and survival. Democratic papers regularly published exaggerated or entirely fictional stories about Federal troops firing on a Democratic parade, shooting babies, and even desecrating the U.S. flag. The *Jonesboro Gazette* in Illinois reported that Ohio Republicans had been "crowding into every available locality" free negroes and runaways, who would "naturally interfere with the interests of the white laborer by greatly reducing wages of labor, without being of any advantage to the State as a class." The paper continued: "To prevent this, memorials are being extensively circulated throughout the State, to be presented to the Legislature, asking that body to pass laws prohibiting the immigration of negroes into their midst." The *Gazette* urged Illinois to act before it, too, "shall soon be overrun with fugitive blacks," urging a constitutional ban "prohibiting the immigration or settlement in this State of free negroes or mulattoes." Only in this way could it "promote the interests and welfare of the white man."[33] Well practice at these arts for decades, the Democratic Party found it the best means to blunt the appeal of Republican "free labor" rhetoric among white workers, particularly the most vulnerable, the Irish and foreign born.

To a lesser extent, the Democratic *New York Herald* experimented with its own brand of nativism, selectively warning about foreign radicals. Bennett denounced Proudhonism and similar efforts "to assail the rights of capitalists and property owners in the North, as the anti-slavery fanatics have assailed the rights of the slaveowners in the South." Once implemented, the "policy against the right of property in the Southern States" would inspire "the doctrine that property is robbery promulgated here in the North, and the laboring masses by and by instigated to sack our cities." So, too, it denounced its rival, the Republican *Tribune*, as "the metropolitan organ of free love, spiritual affinities, the amalgamation of the white and black races, and other kindred subjects." By late 1863 it charged that the *Tribune* ran advertisements by "two full-blooded likely niggers, away down South, who desirous of testing the beauties of the new doctrines, advertise for young ladies to aid them in doing so."[34] The Democratic crusade against abolitionism, free love, and radicalism never became as effective as the simplistic focus on the threat black emancipation posed to white jobs in the North.

In the midst of the strikes on the New York City and Brooklyn docks, rumors swept the strike "that two more slavers are fitting out, not very far from the Roosevelt street dock. One of them is said to be a clipper barque, and Captain Rynders has accordingly been notified, but the Captain, of course, knows nothing about it."[35] Almost surely, the source of the story had been Isaiah Rynders himself, a Democratic gang boss and rabid white supremacist with a long record of filibustering and thuggish attacks on antislavery meetings.

Dewitt C. Roberts, the Illinois printer, had hardly been immune to this as he watched the July 18 assault by the black Fifty-Fourth Massachusetts on Battery Wagner from the flat roof of the three-story building of Evans and Cogswell, his workplace in Charleston. Among the defenders, Captain John H. Lopez and five other members of the Savannah union of Roberts' union were in one company of Sixty-Third Georgia. Another had Sergeant David M. Middleton, four other Savannah members, and one from the Augusta local. The assault killed Middleton, and Roberts watched the flag briefly appear on the works, but the defenders prevailed, sending "a large number of Federal prisoners, white and black, bloodstained and powder-begrimed" back into the city. Roberts "closely observed the countenances of the negro wounded but could learn very little from their stolid and downcast features. They certainly uttered no complaints, and showed but slight emotion."[36] What brought armed blacks to the doorstep of Charleston was the manpower shortage that afflicted Charleston as well.

Shortly after, conditions had deteriorated to where Roberts mustered what resources he could and made a dash to reach Federal lines back in Mississippi. As he passed through Holly Springs, Confederate cavalry had just passed through with sixty-three prisoners, with Federal horsemen in pursuit. Cold weather held Roberts for several freezing days in January. When he set off on foot, he soon became exhausted and sought shelter in a cabin "occupied solely by negroes." His new friends provided him a warm bed with shelter and arranged for him to get a ride into Union lines with a neighbor taking his wagon to Memphis.[37]

The conduct of African Americans, together with the logic of war, mellowed the intensity of racial feeling in some quarters. "A spectacle for the ethnologist, a problem for the statesman, a theorem for the Christian: six thousand curly-headed, dusky-skinned, immortal-souled humanities!" wrote Colonel August J. H. Duganne, a writer with ties to the antebellum Brotherhood of the Union. He mused that "the horse I bestride is likewise black, and I see, not far from me, a score of lusty oxen sable-skinned. I do not remark the instincts of white ox or white horse pitting him against his fellow of a darker hide. It is left for Man to learn those loftier prejudices which regard the hue of his poor clay, ere it returns to dust." At that moment, he looked beyond race to "see only six thousand men, women and children, lying in mire and dust, after their weary marches . . . resting here by the waters of the Atchafalaya as another enfranchised slave-race rested, forty centuries ago, on Jordan's banks, after Exodus from Darkness and Bondage." Duganne rejected "the etiquette of cuticular priority" accorded "Anglo-Saxon pigment."[38]

As NTU brother Beidelman struggled to recover from wounds in both legs gotten at Gettysburg, he reflected on the war's impact on his own racial views. He entered the war a small-town Jacksonian Democratic with no love for abolitionists or blacks. However, he decided that emancipation came from "the house of the Lord—the refiner's fire that will purify our nation." He publicly challenged a bishop back home who had sermonized that slavery had not in itself been a sin. Recovering at a camp where they trained new black regiments, Beidelman had a transformative experience of interracial camaraderie. "Thank God, the inhuman and hell-begotten prejudices, which would deprive these people of the dearest privileges of men and citizens, are fast disappearing; and a new order of things will no doubt attend the results of this great rebellion and the cleaning out of the Augean stables of our political system."[39] By his death on March 14,

1864, Beidelman messed and socialized with his new black comrades and wrote of them with open admiration.

African Americans found some strong allies for equality, often with close ties to the abolitionist and antebellum labor currents. However, they were too few, too far between, and too preoccupied with the war to matter greatly until later, and then it proved far too little to counterbalance the great social weight of the plantation elite, particularly as it forgave the nation for its defeat and came back to the exercise of power.[40] Moreover, even as the mass slave strike secured emancipation, Federal responses struggled to translate the achievement into an act of government philanthropy that had nothing to do with what the slaves or abolitionists had done.

* * *

The example of Senator Jim Lane, one of the most persistent western advocates of emancipation, reveals less an abolitionist spirit than an entrepreneurial opportunism when confronted with the shortage of labor, and not just military labor. The pro-emancipation newspaper *The Conservative*, which spoke for Lane, supplemented the usual reform rhetoric with the suggestion that emancipation might provide that state's property owners with cheap labor "if the contrabands hereabout could be distributed throughout Southern Kansas." Too, the *Baltimore Sun* warned that labor shortages would give workers power they might retain at the war's end, and that paper suggested supplementing emancipation with measures to encourage immigration.[41] Such white Unionist politicians and entrepreneurs—not all, by any means—saw the war as simply a sectional conflict over whether the planters or elites in the North would be able to exploit labor rendered vulnerable for racial or ethnic reasons.

From a labor perspective, the slave strike repressed an uncompromising and overwhelming appeal to numbers. It introduced a qualitatively new kind of mass action, systemically shunned by those who would later describe themselves as "free, white, and twenty-one." White workers hardly welcomed the idea that employers would drive them to such desperate actions to secure their rights. This desire to think well of their place in society provided skilled white workers a means of distancing themselves from what Allan Pinkerton described as the source of mass militancy among blacks: "the mercurial nature of that childish and ignorant race."[42] Civil war opened the tendency to racialize modes of worker resistance.

CHAPTER 5

The Alienation of Militancy

Immigrants and the New White Workingmen

The contemporary American press tended to use ethnic terms to describe labor struggles in the stratified workforce. When unskilled Brooklyn laborers clashed with strikebreakers, the *New York Times* reported that a "general *melee* ensued; brickbats, stones and shillelaghs flew about briskly," for which the papers blamed "the bad whisky." The police turned up and arrested the strike leaders "while the rank and file took to their heels, to the tune of St. Patrick's day in the morning." Two years later, as representatives of the various local labor organizations—almost all of them very new—gathered at the Cooper Union, Charles McCarty, (also called McCarthy) a shoemaker and episodic office seeker, took the chair. Under his gavel, they planned a convention of the local trades that would establish a central body, which they discussed less as a combination of workers in various crafts and industries than as "a union of nationalities."[1]

These escalating struggles reflected the ethnic realities of class formation in the United States. A brief look at labor activism across the Union in the first part of the war demonstrates the particular ascendancy of the unskilled and immigrant workforce. A closer examination of strikes and labor troubles in the spring and early summer of 1863 at New York City demonstrates how central this stratification became in the making of an American working class. This exploded most dramatically in what became known as the "Draft Riots," in which the Democratic politicians of the city goaded impoverished Irish to stop the implementation of conscription by the Republican administration and tried, with some success, to direct their ire against African Americans in the city. Usually the only brief cameo of the white working class into Civil War history, the disorders draw a great line. This not only represented a racial divide, but one separating the older ideas of the worthy poor from the rabble and respectable trade unionism from rowdy aliens.

Renewed Labor Struggles along Ethnic Lines

Immigrant and ethnic identity proved central to understanding the Civil War, as its military record indicates. The heroes of the failed 1848–49 German revolutions like Frederick Hecker and Franz Sigel became symbols for the crusade to save their new country from the disunity that plagued the old fatherland. German radicals like Hans Boebel, August Willich, Joseph Weydemeyer, and others quickly rushed to the task of raising and leading troops. Units like the Third Missouri carried the red flag of the workers' movement into the struggle to overthrow that state's secessionist government.[2]

The Irish disproportionately filled the ranks of many regiments, including the Ninth Massachusetts. Vice President William Madigan of the National Typographical Union not only enlisted but raised volunteers for one of its companies. In response, his former co-workers gathered at Boston's Hancock House to present him with "an elegant regulation sword, belt and sash," acknowledging evidence of "your lasting fealty to our *trade* Union, when we see you go forth as the commander of a body of men who have volunteered their services to defend that large and glorious UNION under which we have enjoyed the blessings of a free and independent government." In response, Madigan pledged to use the sword in defense of "the Union—THE Union of ALL Unions." After his death in battle, Madigan's spirit returned to console his comrades and co-workers: "Say to my friends that I died without fear, and am content." By May, the Boston local also provided another Irishman and former compositor, First Lieutenant John Michael Tobin, with "a serviceable and handsome regulation sword and belt." The regiment also included Captain Bernard S. Treanor, a prominent Irish Fourierist, and John W. Mahan, a Boston lawyer with political ambitions.[3]

The ethnic-based labor reform communities also contributed. Outside endangered St. Louis, the Icarian community of Cheltenham, French communists, organized and marched to the defense of the city, the state, and their new country. So, too, the Swedes at Bishop Hill fielded a company for an Illinois regiment. The aged German pacifists of the Harmony Society at Beaver County, Pennsylvania, "determined to do all that loyal citizens can do for a Government which they love" and sent $5,500 to help raise and equip local troops.[4]

Nevertheless, the social and economic burden of the war fell most heavily on those at the base of the workforce. Ambulance drivers—likely black or Irish—revolted after Bull Run, when the War Department tried to cut their pay and rations. After voting to strike, they began "storming the Government mess-room," where violence erupted, ending with the killing of one striker. Early in the war Irish deck hands at the Cincinnati landing drove off the Germans from their jobs, and, by July 1862, rioted for several days to ensure that "no d——d nigger shall work on the levee." Over the next weeks, racial clashes also took place between Irish stevedores at Buffalo, where a black man supposedly shot a white worker who attacked him.[5] Immigrant communities outraged by such stories struck back, to the detriment of all who worked there.

Perception of the ethnic dimension of the working-class experience in America remained inexorably tied to the level of skill involved and, therefore, generally to the scale of the work process. The nature of wartime labor disputes through 1862 and early 1863 created increasingly sharp distinctions between the relatively more well-focused, traditional, and orderly strikes of the craftsmen and a new scale and type of labor struggle. Westfield cigarmakers and Rochester printers won their strikes, as did those at Philadelphia, where housepainters, carpenters, tailors, bookmakers, and the sailmakers also went on strike. In addition to Rochester and Philadelphia, the printers' unions at Milwaukee, Columbus, Indianapolis, and Washington sought to meet the requirements of worsening wartime conditions.

New struggles, however, began regularly breaking precedents in terms of numbers, violence, and bitterness. Workers on Philadelphia's Arch Street Railway went out over the long hours—sixteen hours a day—and tried to block trains, leading to clashes with the police. Down the street began what William H. Sylvis called "the most protracted and the most stubbornly contested 'strike' that has ever taken place within the history of 'Trades Unions' on this continent." On February 11, 1863, a reported 218 members of the molders union walked out on four of the industry's largest local employers, who simply decided to set aside their agreement with the union over apprenticeship and work rules. When Sylvis went to the Stewart and Peterson's foundry to discuss the issue with strikebreakers, employers had him arrested for trespassing. By the end of May, other unions had raised $4,500 for the strike fund, and, as late as February 1864, only twenty-three men had returned to work.[6]

This growing wartime distinction among labor activities extended well into traditional New England. Certainly, the printers at Cambridge, the tailors in Boston, and the plasterers in East Boston waged militant strikes within the context of a craft. Even the strike of the Morocco leather finishers at Lynn and Charleston won support from as far away as New York without going beyond a familiar kind of trade unionism. Still, none of that could have prepared the community for the roughly two thousand longshoremen, coopers, blacksmiths, carpenters, shipwrights, and caulkers who walked off the job. Even in Maine, the strike of fifteen hundred shoemakers at Auburn and Lewiston overshadowed the relatively modest yet important strikes of firefighters and carpenters.[7]

The significance of this became most apparent during these months at New York City, which experienced an escalating wave of strikes and organizing.

New York Labor in the Wake of Emancipation

Nowhere did these new kinds of turbulent mass strikes become as obvious as among Gotham's unskilled and largely immigrant workforce. In mid-1862, "about two thousand men" shoveling grain at the harbor formed a Protective Union and walked off the job to protest the use of new machines. These devices not only mechanized jobs, but their rapid removal of the cargo shifted the weight on the boats too quickly, and the process raised "great dust which . . . is injurious to life." The *New York Evangelist* advised that "that no combinations of laborers or mechanics can successfully resist the introduction of labor-saving machinery, and that it is most unwise to attempt it." However, a July 8 meeting at Tammany Hall called a strike, joined by the stevedores. On July 13 strikers crossed to Brooklyn to stop work on an elevator there, after which they returned to march on the Produce Exchange. Their efforts left newly arrived vessels loaded with grain untouched at the dock.[8]

October 1862 saw two "riotous" strikes by local unskilled and immigrant workers. Mayor Wood's Democratic administration decided to contract the work of the city's street sweepers to a private contractor who would only pay $1.25 a day. Determined to get "the old Corporation rate" of $1.50, the strikers not only stopped work, they also "kept the ash-carts from doing duty." The police intervened, but a committee of strikers met the mayor "who received them kindly in this private office" and made sympathetic noises and promised to revisit the issue.[9] It was, after all, an election year.

At about the same time, the largely Irish workers at the Manhattan Gas Company struck for a raise from $1.50 to $1.75 or more. The strikers organized and marched throughout the city until some four hundred men had joined them. The employers hired Germans to replace them, leading to a "serious disturbance . . . for some days past." The police arrested two strikers for "assault and battery and rioting."[10]

As the November voting approached, the Democratic press *Philadelphia Inquirer* gave heavy coverage to the "a delegation of workingmen and mechanics, representing the various trades of the city" heading to Washington. They would carry "a petition against such a course of public policy as will be likely to add to the free negro population of the Northern cities." Democrats hoped their presence would remind the president "of the hardships which the white laboring population are suffering from the exorbitant price of the necessaries of life, while any measure which may have a tendency to unduly increase the number of laborers among us, and, by consequence, a further increase in the cost of living, will be remonstrated against."[11] As far as the newspaper readers might be concerned, this perceived labor movement with all the racial concerns of the Democrats confirmed the fiction that the anti-Lincoln party spoke for the white workingmen.

By the election, the developments across the East River in the Navy Yard overshadowed almost everything. The works employed five thousand men in Brooklyn, "many of them by night and day." The press reported that "a complete revolution has taken place in the mode of doing things in the various shops." On November 22, a mass meeting of carpenters, foundrymen, sailmakers and others voted to raise wages from $2.50 to "the New York standard, which is understood to be $3 a day." Their strike "almost paralyzed work on the new ships," while employers agreed "not to employ one of the malcontents." Ship caulkers, coopers, and other mechanics also went out. The problem was that workers addressed immediate grievances that management easily passed to the Navy Department. By late December the strike committee recommended that they return to work until they got some feedback from the authorities in Washington. By then, house painters clashed with employers over wages, as did hackmen and horse shoers. However, the overarching troubles at the shipyards festered into the new year.[12]

Through early 1863 so many trades and industries had gone into action that it created a dynamic of its own. A unified spirit inspired a February 6 meeting, which resembled something like an attempt to reconstruct the old citywide central bodies of a decade before, with Greeley in the chair and the discussion revolving on how to convince employers to cooperate without strikes. On March 24 McCarthy of the shoemakers' union chaired, while familiar faces sat in the crowd, including Daniel Walford the plasterer, William Hardinge the coach maker, and other labor leaders.[13] Nevertheless, the involvement of large numbers of immigrant workers made these efforts a bone of partisan contention.

Over the previous year, militant struggles had erupted sporadically across the metropolitan area. Between forty and fifty laborers working on the Court House at Brooklyn walked off the job in April 1862 hoping to raise their dollar-per-day wage to $1.25. Workers on the Brooklyn Central City Passenger Railroad walked off when the bosses told them that they would be required to be on duty seventeen hours. One of the local bosses became obsessed with breaking the wool hat finishers' union and bankrupted his business in the process. Tailors there also took steps toward organizing their own union, culminating in plans to promulgate a new wage rate on May 1. On the Jersey Shore, harness makers at Newark not only struck but also marched through the streets "in large numbers and calling upon all workmen to join them." About two hundred laborers at Secor and Company's monitor yard paraded as well, demanding a raise from ten to twelve shillings a day.[14]

At New York City, within weeks of the promulgation of the Emancipation Proclamation, Tammany hosted what it billed as a labor meeting "for the purpose of preventing a further strike, and to devise the best means to prevent the further importation of foreign labor, thereby causing a reduction of their wages, and thus throwing their services on the market." The organizers invited Greeley, but neither he nor any particularly prominent trade union officers attended. Speakers denounced Greeley as "a hoary headed traitor" and charged "that 'they' had commenced to introduce contrabands in their midst; that as long as they were able to work, their employers would pay." One speaker, possibly Moses Platt, the Brooklyn trade unionist, complained of politicians speaking for the workers, adding that workers were currently in no position to speak for themselves.[15] Yet Tammany and the Democrats were hitting on an issue that they had long employed.

Over these same weeks, workers on other rail lines walked off as well. Discontent had simmered for nearly a year among workers on the South Amboy and Camden railroad. The previous spring about sixty of them went on strike, but the bosses replaced them with strikebreakers the mayor protected "with a strong police force." By March 1863, about two hundred went on strike to raise a week's pay from seven dollars to nine dollars. The bosses hired unskilled and "principally aged men" to break the strike, most who had just landed at Castle Garden from Ireland. At the same time, hundreds on the Hudson River railroad walked off the job, some gathering at the depot, where one of the bosses told them he would bring black workers from the South to replace them very cheaply.[16]

That same month, longshoremen on the Erie Railroad docks, who had earlier won a pay increase to $1.25 a day, went on strike for $1.50 with Sundays off. On March 23, about a thousand of them gathered to find strikebreakers, including "some negroes" working at Pier No. 36. By 9:00 A.M. the strikers drove them off with "a shower of clubs, stones and other missiles." The Democratic *Herald* blamed the violence simply on the tactlessness of the bosses hiring "negro laborers." The police did make some arrests, but the employers realized around noon that it would be best to cave in on wages, but they "determinedly refused to take about sixty of the men back." Many returned to work, though some who did not glared as "several colored men lounged around the dock."[17]

On March 24—a day after the clashes on the docks—the city's labor organizations held a citywide meeting at the Cooper Union. Five hundred street sweepers marched in with music. Spokesmen took the platform for the hatters, tailors, shipwrights, bakers, painters, bookbinders, coopers, carpenters, and cartmen, and the list included antebellum leaders, such as McCarthy, Hardinge, and Walford. They agreed to "a general Convention to be held in Military Hall, No. 193 Bowery" on March 31. One of them asked, "Should it be said that they who could build palaces and adorn them—who build ships, and man them, and navigate them, and guide them to all parts of the world—should it be said that such men had not intellect to organize a great trades organization?" Stating their goal as the uniting of New York's "nations," some of the leaders used language that jibed with the understanding of Mayor Wood's administration, rumored to have helped in financing the meeting.[18]

The crafts certainly continued to move. Tailors, largely German and socialist, proved remarkably good at unionism. On March 18, 1863, the "'Central Journeymen Tailors' Association'—a very respectable organization, with a somewhat elongated name" voted to charge $1.25 on business coats, fifty cents on fine coats, and twenty-five cents on pantaloons and vests. On March 23, four hundred workers employed at Brooks Brothers marched to their workplace, with other groups doing the same, resolved to "stand or die till the desired end is attained." On March 28 the Journeymen Tailors Protective Union reported the capitulation of Brooks Brothers and other firms, with Hurston and Hastings holding out. The city's eighty fresco painters, "almost exclusively Germans," had once earned five dollars a day and were down to two dollars a day, and they wanted a raise to $2.50. So, also, the Piano Makers Association, organized by German cooperationists more than a decade before, functioned as a union. By the start of April the Waiters' Protective and Benevolent Association of the city and county of New York waged a strike that wrung concessions from some of the city's leading hotels.[19]

Nevertheless, the very real conflicts persisted along the waterfronts on both sides of the East River. April saw strikes "at the Greenpoint, Continental, and other ship yards," leaving work on several rams and ironclads "nearly suspended." However, the *Daily Eagle* reported the first attempts to start a citywide body in Brooklyn had been "conducted entirely by New York men, connected with the New York Trades' Union, and the speakers, with one exception, were all New York men." The *Eagle* reported that half of the roughly two hundred men present "left the Hall before the proceedings closed." Moses Platt, a ship carpenter from the Navy Yard "made an extravagant speech about capital and labor" and another named Newbern talked about "France during the last revolution, when the combination of labor became so strong that capitalists in all countries became alarmed and combined to put it down, and they did so through Napoleon." His ignorance about parts of his own country were evident when he added that workers "called themselves free men, but in some respects they were not so well off as the negroes [in the] South, who are worked only five days a week, and have one-day to work for themselves and buy their freedom if they saw fit." Many called for a citywide body in Brooklyn but none took place until after the events that summer.[20]

By June 1863 longshoremen at New York made another stab at getting more than $1.50 per day, particularly since they were only getting three or four days of work each week. A Yankee wag quipped that such trades "average two strikes per month, with a few small strikes daily, just by way of diversion." On June 8, though, an estimated three thousand walked off to get a raise to twenty-five cents an hour up to 6:00 P.M. and fifty cents an hour for later. The bosses planned to hire two thousand strikebreakers, but the workers continually frustrated their efforts. On the morning of the strike, some five hundred strikers drove off "some laborers who were loading a ship at the old rates, at pier No. 11, East River," and the police turned up to haul "the ringleaders off to the station-house." Later, a force crossed to Brooklyn, where several more arrests were made. Rather than suffer "the extortionate demands of the laborers," the government brought deserters from the prison on Governor's Island and convalescents from Bedloe's Island to load army transports with ammunition and supplies under the protection of army bayonets with hundreds of police in reserve. In short, across "almost the entire length of the wharves of the city the greatest inactivity prevails."[21] Rumors that the government would bring in legions of former slaves never materialized and surely originated with the Democrat Party.

In another corner of the waterfront, labor troubles steamed up the rails. Workers on the New York and Erie Railroad struck, and authorities expected "a serious riot" when they moved freight from one point to another on the East River. The bosses decided to try raising wages to two dollars a day and "employ none of the old hands." After the predictable violence, the police arrested two strikers as "ringleaders of the attacking party."[22]

At the same time, workers of all sorts seemed chronically discontented, partly because government and employers cooperated to ignore them. Street sweepers "besieged the rooms of the Board of Councilmen . . . clamoring for their back pay" and forcing an appropriation of $3,200 to pay them. Meat inspectors, grain shovelers, and possibly the grain measurers walked off for more wages. Ira B. Davis's antebellum Protective Union resurfaced with some five hundred members, along with a new Journeymen Bakers' Association of 250 members, the two agreeing to reduce "the working hours to twelve hours per day or night, to which many bosses have agreed."[23]

Conservative observers saw in these efforts the reemergence of working-class radicalism. Early in the war, the *Arbeiter-Verein* at Chicago dropped its entrance fee, and its rapid membership growth would have added to the concerns of the elites. Its militant resolutions for emancipation certainly disturbed conservatives, and its finding leadership among figures like the radical and future socialist Caspar Butz consoled them little. The threat, they believed, particularly centered on "a dangerous element among the Germans, in various parts of the country—we mean the portion who have brought here the Socialism, or Red republicanism, of the old world and are trying to realize it." "The Reds who congregate with the Radicals are aiding to destroy our country."[24]

Ethnicity, Politics, and the Draft Riots

Nothing better represents this description of ethnically "dangerous classes" as a substitute for a working class than what came to be called the New York City Draft Riots. After Shiloh and the Seven Days, the authorities on both sides took measures that would eventually place more than five million men under arms. The initial mobilization tended to be young, unmarried, and adventurous, along with those most ideologically committed to the war's goals, but they now needed to bring in larger portions of older men, often married and with children.[25]

The Confederacy needed a bold new solution to meet the related problem of manpower and morale after Shiloh. Dewitt C. Roberts, the Illinois printer trapped by the outbreak of hostilities, struggled to keep his exemption as a printer to avoid conscription, implemented earlier and in a more thorough fashion than the Unionists would ever match. He had evaded permanent incarceration in New Orleans as well as an attempt to dragoon him into the army at Montgomery, and he found work at the *Charleston Courier*, in "a pleasant place for the rich man to live in, but the very worst for the working man that I have ever seen." Their coverage of Shiloh recalled that of Bull Run, the press simply not reporting on the second day's defeat for more than a week. "The Government has seemed afraid to let the people know of reverses, to regard them as children, unable to look danger in the face, and has accordingly always been prompt to tell good news, slow to acknowledge bad."[26] The Confederacy would not be the last American government to do so, but where misrepresentations fail to inspire, other imperatives pushed workers to the military.

In the Union, Democratic partisanship stoked these tensions until they erupted in the wake of Gettysburg.[27] The Federal military draft remained much smaller and more limited than in the Confederacy, but it affected a much-less-deferential population. The Union equivalent of the Confederate "twenty negro" provision permitting anyone selected to hire a substitute for three hundred dollars. As the date for drawings approached, the Democrats particularly urged their Irish supporters toward resistance and promised assistance in financing substitutes. Minor disorders took place at Buffalo and other cities before the scheduled drawings on July 11, but the initial draft provoked no reaction in New York City, even with the state militia absent to assist the army in the Gettysburg campaign.

However, news of the tremendous losses from Gettysburg, particularly among the Irish, swept new concerns through streets of Gotham, escalating into fear and rage. On July 13 officials at a provost marshal's office on Forty-Seventh and Third Avenues prepared for the second drawings. Before they began, the Black Joke Engine Company No. 33 led a crowd of hundreds against the office. Hurling paving stones, they broke the windows, knocked down the doors, and torched the office. The mob recognized Police Superintendent John Kennedy, whose presence tapped a deeply rooted resentment over the Republican's earlier displacement of the local Democratic police force. The crowd attacked, beat, and stabbed the superintendent. On July 15 rioters went through the city, going from factory to factory, and bringing commerce and production to a halt.[28]

On that day discontent inspired "an impromptu meeting of artisans, laborers and others" in Brooklyn's Fourteenth Ward. By 8:30, "about 600" assembled on lot to be addressed by "Col. Edmund Powers, who lived nearby." The small but spirited gathering expressed its hostility to the draft and to the Republicans. However, when one man cheered Jeff Davis, "so great was the disfavor manifested that the rebel sympathizer was glad to quickly leave the crowd, followed by hisses and threats." They cheered Governor Horatio Seymour, General George B. McClellan, and the Union. Seymour himself arrived in the city but, rather than to quell the rioters, declared that he, too, opposed conscription.[29] Fanning race hatred and fears had been a staple of the Democratic formula for maintaining its hold on the city, and it should surprise no one that it would be applied in this situation.

The crowd also cheered for Jeff Davis as it turned its attention toward the *Tribune*. Several writers who showed up there, found only one man in the editorial rooms, while Amos Jay Cummings—just back from fighting rebels in Virginia—prepared to defend the composing room with his brother and two other printers, who scurried about to procure muskets. By the second day, they had hand grenades, bombshells, and a howitzer, as well firearms and more NTU members, such as Sylvester Bailey and Peter Hackett, to help man the barricades. Workers also manned two Gatling guns, covering the neighborhood in its defense. At midday Greeley himself showed up and, while unhappy with having arms in the building, remained there alongside his men.[30] The riots provided one of the last occasions for Greeley and his men to revisit the old days of craft solidarity.

Meanwhile, the crowds attacked and sometimes burned various hotels, police stations, the mayor's residence, newspaper offices, and the homes and workplaces of prominent Republicans. "Yarber Bros., and J. A. Gray, printers, and others been warned that their establishments [would] be destroyed, if the workmen are kept on duty." Blacks "are fleeing in all directions."[31]

Rioters specifically vented their fear and rage on black New Yorkers. Blacks faced beating, torture, and death at the hands of large crowds of whites, who set fire to the lynched body of one of their victims. The police managed to hold back the tide for hundreds of children to escape the Colored Orphan Asylum on Fifth Avenue before the rioters destroyed that. Scholars tend to ascribe the viciousness of these racial attacks to the Irish fear of black competition at the bottom of the job market. However, such fears were not new, and the wartime economy hardly created scarcity in such employment. Then, too, the neighborhoods historically most prone to such activities on Lower Manhattan remained relatively quiet.

By then, though, the army made available hundreds of troops at various points in the harbor and West Point. The local militia also started back to the city from Pennsylvania. On the third day of the outbreaks, the provost marshal's office also announced a suspension of the draft, and thousands of troops began occupying the city. A final clash near Gramercy Park ended the riots, which left at least 120 civilians dead and two thousand more injured.

The realities of the draft riots are not only far more complex, but the complexity itself demonstrates that the time for such approaches had, for the present, passed them by. Indeed, one finds workers and labor reformers quite articulate on the subject. Among the Federal troops briefly in the city to prevent a recurrence of the rioting was the Seventh Ohio, under Colonel Creighton, the trade unionist. Much of the city's own workforce was also in uniform, of course, and most who were not uniformed simply did not participate in the "draft riots." Within days, William Oland Bourne's Workingmen's Democratic Republican issued its warning *To the Laboring Men of New York* about their political manipulation by Democratic demagoguery on race, with other statements leading to its tome titled *A Challenge* aimed at the mayor and other politicians. The position of this largely Republican association would be echoed shortly after by *Fincher's Trades' Review* and, more clearly, by labor voice.[32]

This Workingmen's Association, Bourne admitted, "does not at present hold *public meetings*. The expense of such meetings, if they are to be of real value, is too great, and the Executive Committee believe that their work now can be accomplished in a far more effective and economical manner by correspondence with other Associations and the circulation of documents. The Association will enter the field *when its turn comes*."[33]

German radicals most decidedly held meetings. They became notoriously noisy in differentiating their general working-class distaste for conscription from the "riots" instigated by the Democrats. The Chicago *Arbeiter-Verein* even declared that the riots demonstrated the dangers to the republic and the necessity of conscription. "Germans, Americans, and Irish must stand together" in opposition to "everyone who awakens internal strife by creating prejudice."[34]

More tellingly, perhaps, organized labor remained unaffected by the draft riot and unencumbered by its repression. Before the riots, in May, the Typographical

Union had written a new pay scale, and when a minority of shops refused to raise wages, the union struck. It had no qualms about coming back in September to get a new scale for the book compositors. The union sponsored "a numerous attended public meeting" at Tammany Hall that called on nonmembers to join the union.[35]

The record also provides glimpses of old labor reformers assisting the efforts to protect African American residents of the city. Near where George S. McWatters, a "bohemian" and radical newspaperman then on the police force, battled rioters in City Hall Park, John H. Keyser, the old land reformer who had done well enough to become a philanthropist, volunteered to help the "large numbers of poor, persecuted colored men, women, and children," many injured. The municipal authorities appointed Keyser "to superintend these wretched victims of violence and prejudice," and he "devoted unwearied days to the duty."[36]

Union Army general Gustave Cluseret, revolutionary émigré and bohemian, reported to the *Siècle* that he had followed the crowd "with two officers," one most likely McWatters, another bohemian radical who had been a private detective before joining the Republican reconstruction of the city's police force. The three followed the crowd at a distance "in order to study it well. Based on their observations, they determined that the acting and paid crowd did not consist of more than three hundred persons." While thousands of "ragged wretches from the Five Points district" had followed along as observers, "the real working men, the laboring classes, did not take part in the movement, which was directed, as everything proves, by the slavery party."[37]

Most important, workers as a group took measures to free themselves from politicians eager to speak on their behalf. Instead, workers and their organizations grappled toward finding a new voice of their own to address new issues. New York maintained some sort of trade assembly from before the war but organized a new statewide Workingmen's Union. In fact, the dust had hardly settled from the riots when the representatives of various unions in the city met to elect the officers of their new citywide organization.[38] This would be a prerequisite for the hired men and their organizations in gaining the stature they needed to speak for themselves.

Civil War histories often use the draft riots to provide a singular brief cameo by the American working class, as such. James Gordon Bennett, Seymour, and other Democratic figures presumed to speak for the worker and had every reason to identify with the sentiment of the rioters, if not the rioting itself. Then, too, the Republican *New York Times* denounced strikes as "symptoms dangerous alike to the peace and quiet of our community" and ascribed them to "the spirit which some of our Copperheaded citizens have endeavored to infuse into the channels of labor."[39] In short, the dominant currents in both parties had reasons to ascribe the rioting and the sentiments of the rioters to the views of the white working class in general.

When a similar wave of rioting erupted in Boston and the city fathers blamed it on "workmen in the Gas Works," the workers insisted on a retraction. The *Boston Herald* noted that they "feel much aggrieved" but would go no more than to say that "the disturbance began near the Gas House, but the men there employed deny that they commenced them."[40] The New York papers never bothered.

* * *

Certainly, the much larger and more overwhelming draft in the Confederacy created a much greater persistent resistance. As paper, ink, and supplies dwindled, printers in the Confederacy faced unemployment and the loss of their exemptions. Roberts went from Charleston to Atlanta for work, but, as the weeks wore on, the prospect of Confederate conscription once more threatened him. He had gotten a thirty-day leave from his employer, the *Southern Confederacy*, to visit Charleston, and then told the provost marshal that he wanted to visit his relatives near Oxford, Mississippi. On December 20, 1863, he abandoned his "trunk, books, and clothing," saving what he "could carry in a handtrunk." He found that war had crippled the Southern railroads, but he reached Oxford nevertheless, eight days later. There, he persuaded the Confederate cavalry to permit him through the lines to Holly Springs. Circumstances soon forced Roberts, who had thought so disparagingly of the blacks attacking Fort Wagner, to rely entirely upon African Americans for assistance in reaching Union lines.[41] Regardless of personal preferences—or the ultimate limits upon it—a Second American was underway.

Labor struggles during the Civil War bore a legitimate resemblance to antebellum organizing drives and strikes, but they differed in their composition, as well as their scale, and the wartime context. More than ever, the employers and the press identified these as "riotous" disruptions of normal social relations. More important, they increasingly identified the riots in ethnic terms, as disorders among the Irish, the German, or generic "foreigners" and aliens. Having long distinguished between the worthy and unworthy poor, this process used ethnicity to conjure a difference between the respectable conduct and the riotous, violent and subversive means unworthy of how Americans did things.

"The Republican Party going to the right House" [1860, by Currier and Ives, has Greeley carrying Abraham Lincoln into the Lunatic Asylum, as the candidate promises "The millennium is going to begin." One ragged follower wants "everybody to have a share of everybody else's property," even as free lovers and women suffragists make their case. A woman uses the Fourierist term "passional attraction" to express her feelings for Lincoln, and a black man inverts the Dred Scott decision to claim: "De white man hab no rights dat cullud pussons am bound to spect' I want dat understood." Courtesy of the Library of Congress, Prints and Photographs Division (reproduction no. LC-USZ62-1990).

In March 1860 Lynn City Guards lead thousands of striking shoemakers, including near a thousand women who braved a snowstorm to march through Lynn bearing their banners. Courtesy of the Library of Congress, Prints and Photographs Division (reproduction no. LC-USZ62-62100). Original from *Frank Leslie's Illustrated Newspaper*, March 17, 1860, 242 and 251.

Strikers at Lynn attack an express wagon attempting to bring goods from a shoe shop to the railroad station. Courtesy of the Library of Congress, Prints and Photographs Division (reproduction no. LC-USZ62-132550). Original from *Frank Leslie's Illustrated Newspaper*, March 17, 1860, 239.

Carpenter shops near the railroad yards at Alexandria, Virginia [1862 or 1863]. Courtesy of the Library of Congress, Prints and Photographs Division (reproduction no. LC-DIG-ppmsca-10381).

Black workers on the James River in Virginia. Courtesy of the National Archives (item 111-B-400).

Blacksmith shop in the field. From *Harper's Weekly*, September 21, 1861, 593.

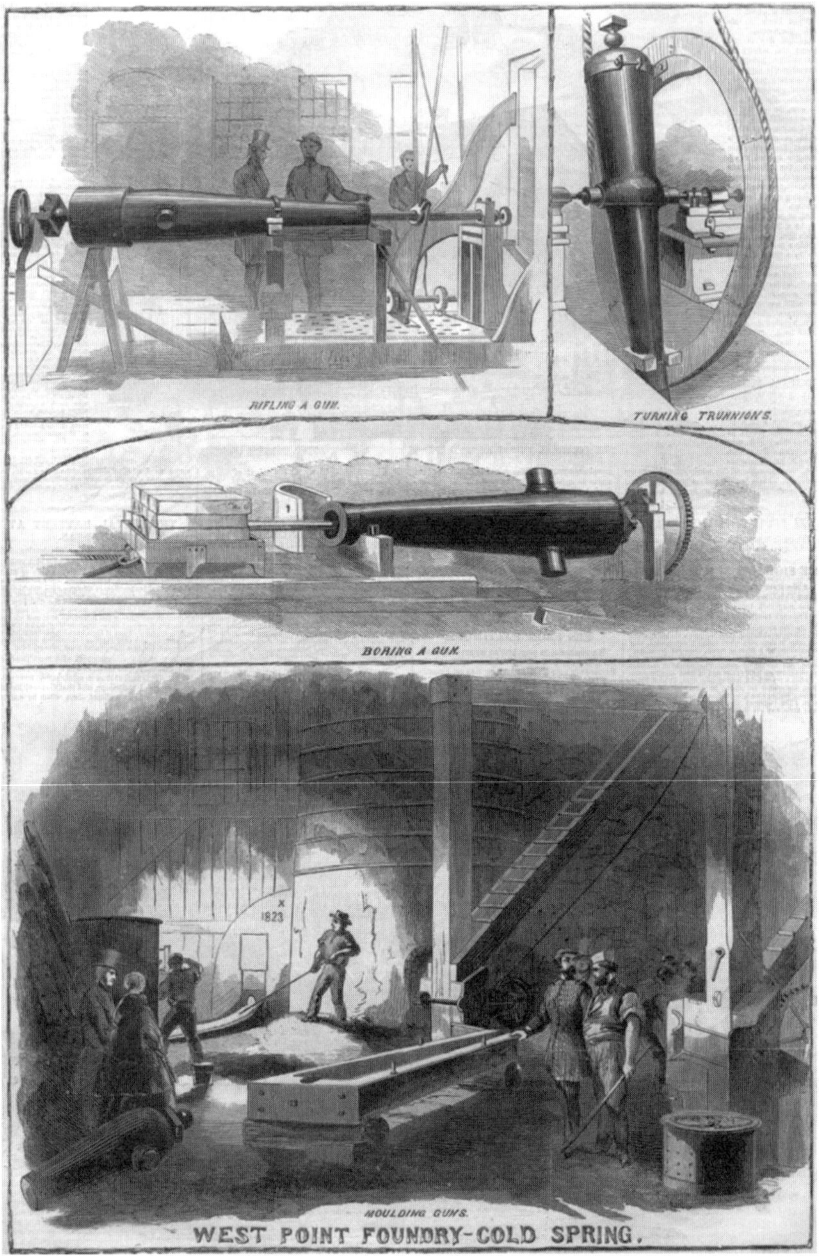

The Cold Springs Foundry, site of a major strike. From *Harper's Weekly*, September 14, 1861, 588.

Post–Civil War reunion of the wartime founders of the Knights of Labor. Courtesy of the Terence V. Powderly Papers, Catholic University, Washington, D.C.

William H. Sylvis. Courtesy of the Terence V. Powderly Papers, Catholic University, Washington, D.C.

William H. Sylvis with Jonathan Fincher, leader of the Machinists and Blacksmiths Union and editor of *Fincher's Trades' Review*. Courtesy of the Terence V. Powderly Papers, Catholic University, Washington, D.C.

Telegraph battery wagon with the Army of the Potomac near Petersburg. Courtesy of the Library of Congress (reproduction no. LC-DIG-cwpb-04330).

Tredegar Iron Works on the James River at Richmond, Virginia. Courtesy of the Library of Congress (reproduction no. LC-B817-7542).

Women of the 1863 Richmond "Bread Riot." Courtesy of the Library of Congress (reproduction no. LC-USZ62-42028).

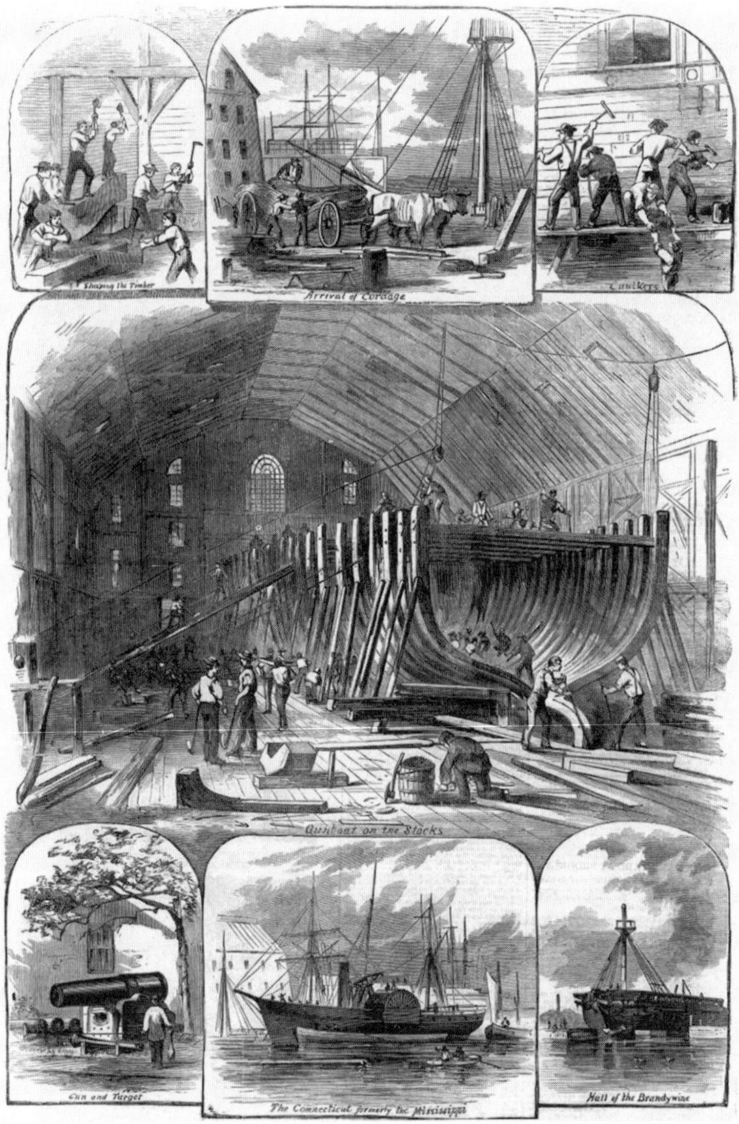

Wartime Navy Yards employed thousands of workers and created modern industrial standards on an unprecedented scale. From *Harper's Weekly*, August 24, 1861, 534.

Horace Seaver, former minister and freethinker who became the editor of the *Boston Investigator*, and an active proponent of labor reform since the 1830s, from his *Occasional Thoughts of Horace Seaver: From Fifty Years of Free Thinking*.

Plantation Police or Home Guard checking passes for African American workers near New Orleans. Courtesy of the Library of Congress (reproduction no. LC-USZ62-138395). Original from *Frank Leslie's Illustrated Newspaper*, July 11, 1863, 252.

Workers on the Military Railroad. Courtesy of the Library of Congress (reproduction no. LC-DIG-ppmsca-10395).

President of the NTU, John M. Farquhar, one of the three members of the union to win a Congressional Medal of Honor in the Civil War. Farquhar was recognized for meritorious conduct at Stones River; John M. Tobin and Amos J. Commings won medals, respectively, for service at Malvern Hill and Salem Church. From Tracy, *History of the Typographical Union*, opp. p. 200.

Nashville. The expanded rail yards below the capital hill. Courtesy of the Library of Congress (reproduction no. LC-B811-2652).

The Army's explosive industrial expansion of the Tennessee Capital created these Quartermaster's Repair Shops on the Nashville Pike. Courtesy of the Library of Congress (reproduction no. LC DIG-ppmsca-33612).

The machine shops in the eastern yard of the Orange & Alexandria Railroad. Courtesy of the Library of Congress (reproduction no. LC-B8184-10217).

CHAPTER 6

The Survival of Moral Suasion

Solidarity, Sisterhood, and Paternalism

The wives, mothers, and daughters of men off to the war joined other women who had already been making their own way in New York City to establish the Working Women's Protective Union. On October 26, 1863, they sought to highlight the plight of female labor in the city by presenting their grievances before the mayor and other such luminaries. The spiritualists, who tended to move toward an early version of social work during the war, had already begun organizing relief for impoverished women. Philanthropy doubtlessly created a new kind of sisterhood with working-class women, but a very limited kind of sisterhood. Working-class women were finally accorded a distinctive voice, but it would not be their own.[1] To be sure, those women who might build or join unions faced complex problems in doing so. For many in that paternalistic culture, it seemed that sharing their problems with their social betters might provide a more rapid and certain means of resolving them.

The war that drew hundreds of thousands of men out of the workforce left their mothers, wives, sisters, and daughters to their own resources without any new social consensus about improving their earnings, skills, or opportunities. The result not only challenged expectations of a masculine workforce but also folded into it new sectors characterized innately by a deep, inescapable, and gendered poverty. Too, the presence of vast numbers of laboring female poor forced society to face issues about the role of women in terms of the family, community, and nation. The wartime efforts to address some of these questions would continue for generations to come.

Working-Class Women and the Exigencies of War

Women had long worked beyond the farm, the home, and the neighborhood, but war extended and sped this process by removing millions of husbands, fathers, brothers, and sons from their families. Yet Horace Seaver of the *Boston Investigator* complained that it remained "common to speak of woman as a perfect nonentity." Moreover, "every step taken by society towards her political emancipation is spoken of as a *favor* to the sex." "Either a woman is no whit above a horse, in the political and civil scale," he wrote, "or she is part and parcel of society, entitled to her voice and vote and property."[2]

Traditional female labor in the needle trades provided the easiest opening to the workforce. They found ready work as makers of dresses, cloaks, tassels, tents, corsets, hoop skirts, caps, vests, and umbrellas, as hatbinders, shirt-sewers, wool sorters, and sewing-machine operators. The demands for uniforms, coats, and caps for soldiers grew quickly, making more work. However, increased mechanization tended to shrink earnings.

A New York letter in the *Philadelphia Inquirer* acknowledged that "a stranger coming among us might be led to believe we are rapidly going to the bad." The press reported people building "marble stables for their horses, and of others who are constructing edifices for private theatricals, who are giving dinner parties that cost $1,000, and parties to children where every child was clad in dresses entirely imported from Paris." Others reported on "the equipages which whirl through the aristocratic avenues almost every hour of the day, and the ostentatious prodigality which prevails elsewhere." The *Daily News* admitted that "while the rich are thus getting richer, the poor are getting poorer." The writer mentioned "the working men's strikes for higher wages" and how "the woes of the poor needle women are as usual made the burden of elaborate lamentation."[3]

Cultural sensibilities saw women as an essential part of the worthy poor, fit objects for charity, and the views persisted but with an increasing emphasis on the essential contribution their labor meant. War added some urgency to the question. Spiritualist poet Lizzie Doten recalled the war's start when "the battle cry went up and down in the length and breadth of your land. Women who never worked before, had a chord touched in their natures, which gave the ready response." "Modern civilization has established one doctrine beyond reach of cavil," declared the *Banner of Light*, "that in proportion to the care which is bestowed upon woman, and the opportunities which are thrown open to secure her independence, and the freedom she enjoys to make herself a position and an influence in society, does the community progress in refinement and advance in general culture."[4]

Some women worked in factory conditions or in overcrowded, dark, filthy rooms, but most worked in their homes. Paid by the piece, many had to supply material for lighting their workspace, their own thread, needles, and tools. The women themselves said that a pair of drawers earned them sixteen cents, but took eighteen hundred stitches by machine, and they could only finish four between 7 A.M. to 9 P.M., earning sixty-four cents a day. Shirts paid sixty cents a dozen, but it took two long days to finish that many. A fast worker might turn out nine to a dozen flannel shirts for a daily wage of thirty-six cents to seventy two cents. However, employers and contractors made more by shaving the pay, so the fine shirts that sold for three dollars to $3.60 each that paid a dollar a dozen at the war's start wound up earning eighty cents. A milliner said her earnings had been cut from seventeen-and-a-half cents a shirt to only eight cents by 1864. "I may as well starve without work," quipped one of the women, "as to work and starve at the same time."[5] Of course, the rising cost of living sharpened these immiserations.

The sample household budget written by the Typographical Union indicated a 257 percent increase in the cost of living over the course of the war in New York, to which the union had fought hard to get advances amounting to a 72 percent increase in wages. Workingwomen faced the same cost of living, albeit without a union, and actually lost ground in terms of wartime pay. They probably ate cheap meat or fish periodically, but most of their diet likely consisted of bread, supplemented by tea or coffee, these drinks being easily watered.[6] The danger was sickness.

Women workers also found ways to stretch their rent money. Working-class people had generally aspired to save enough to move "a little way out of town" for "more healthy and comfortable and much cheaper residences in the suburbs." Children might be an asset if they did something to bring in some money and did some of the marketing additionally. However, the easiest solution for women on piecework involved doubling up or tripling up to save on rents.[7] If home was also where they worked, they faced a fairly brutal existence.

In contrast, what they faced were wartime dynamics that favored the most villainous. Lizzie Doten described army contractors growing rich by plundering "the brains and nerves of the girls they employ." Of these "vast accumulations of wealth" periodically dropped "occasional *mites*—proportionately considered—to the Sanitary Commission, and to public charities." However, the capitalists created the need for these charities by underpaying the women. A movement needed to see itself as a counterforce facing a natural "opposition from the '*Shoddyites*.'"[8]

When such information became readily available, reformers of all sorts expressed horror. John T. Amos, a Rochester spiritualist, wondered whether "such a paltry, miserable remuneration for labor be given in this latter part of the nineteenth century? After all the preaching of 'do as thou would be done by,' and 'love thy neighbor as thyself,' which we have had, and with the present high rate of every article of necessity and comfort?" With a rare bluntness, he described the bosses "in palatial homes, surround by all that art and science can bring to bear upon them," with their workers "living in the homes of misery, surrounded by every deteriorating influence and temptation." He urged Americans to "look the miserable system square in the face."[9]

Acknowledging women as workers entitled to respectable wages might bend traditional gender roles, but not doing so fostered poverty, which, in turn, created a prostitution that threatened the sanctity of the family. Society, said the *Chicago Journal*, "relies more upon the purity, refinement and intelligence of woman, for its elevated tone, than upon any other element." Underpaying women is not only an injustice to labor but a subversion of women's "purity." It has "the effect of disheartening those poor women in our land who are dependent upon their earnings for a livelihood, and of discouraging woman's ambition for industrious usefulness? Does it not have the effect of driving many a poor girl to desperate and fearful alternatives—of reducing those who, by their efforts in the industrial or professional avocations of life, might raise themselves to high positions in society, to be ornaments in social life, to the lowest scale of dependency and of moral and social degradation?"[10]

The most common of those "desperate and fearful alternatives" to which working-class women resorted had already reached proportions that remain almost entirely unacknowledged by later generations. Later peoples, including scholars, have found the contemporary estimates of prostitution in the industrializing cities to be excessive. When one reads that London had a population of 2.4 million in midcentury and estimates of eight thousand women engaged in prostitution of one sort or another. Estimates for New York ran from ten thousand to fifty thousand, the total adult female population being eighty thousand. Later writers, including scholars, have found the contemporary estimates of prostitution in the industrializing cities to be excessive.[11] Much of the disparity turned on the extent to which women may have used the practice irregularly to supplement particularly dire circumstances.

On the eve of the Civil War, the London-born spiritualist Emma Hardinge tried to introduce ideas common in the East End of her home city. She proposed organizing alternatives for workingwomen driven into prostitution through cooperative shelters, job training, and even colonization to the West. Even as secession ripped at the country's future, she raised subscriptions along the East Coast, reported to "a very large audience in Tremont Temple that she had raised several thousand but needed $50,000 to finance a start in the cities." She hoped to start "a practical horticultural school" with other branches of industry that would employ "a hundred inmates." In addition to a broad range of other spiritualists and clergymen, she had won the endorsement of such Boston luminaries as James Russell Lowell, Mrs. Julia Ward Howe, and Henry Wadsworth Longfellow.[12]

In the end, though, Hardinge abandoned the effort and returned to England to proselytize for spiritualism there. She purchased some land for the enterprise in New Jersey, left it to her trustees, and departed. "The disastrous war, which is still unhappily aging, broke out just as my Committee were forming their preliminary arrangements, and at once scattered their ranks, and engrossed all their energies in the national crisis; and though I believe many of them are still as benevolently interested in my work as ever, yet, I have never since found it possible to assemble them together, or induce them singly or collectively to withdraw their attention from the nation's calamities to this movement of mine."[13]

For some, perhaps, all these problems grew from the muzzling of women as a civic force. After the war, observers such as Jennie Collins saw suffrage as essential. She saw the enfranchisement of working-class women as contributing a vital new voice to the civil society: "Factory-girls are always politicians; they must discuss something; and in the absence of fashionable balls, dinner-parties, new styles, and the amusements of high life, they turn their attention to the solid affairs which concern the welfare of the State and nation." Doten claimed disinterest in suffrage but urged women to press for legislation to protect their rights.[14]

"Ours is a democratic country," declared Doten, "and women have more rights and a higher degree of respect shown them than in any other country. . . . Yet it is not enough. They need something more." Others described the inequality of pay as "a degree of wrong and injustice done to laboring women in this country that is reproach to us, and a good reason for which we have even been at a loss to find." The sewing girl did "more difficult work, and more of it, than a man sewing in a tailor's shop" for "hardly one-quarter as much." A female teacher "performing precisely the same duties and quite as efficiently as a male teacher, receives scarcely half as large a salary."[15]

Working Women's Protective Union: The New York Model

Labor organizations had directly addressed this issue for some years. Female schoolteachers had become virtually iconic and often took the lead in fighting for women's rights in the workplace and generally. When California made provisions to reward them equal pay with the men, the *United States Mechanics' Own* called it the "Right Kind of Woman's Rights." Later, *Fincher's Trades' Review* advocated more pay and unionization as the solution to their issues.[16]

The crisis of the sewing women moved some to attempt harnessing these Victorian sensibilities to their advantage. The *Banner of Light* reported that initially "none but working women [were] present and participating in the proceedings." In June 1863, the sewing women launched the Working Women's Protective

Union [WWPU]. "Not that the men workers alone have been engaged in—but the women are combining to assert their rights and their power, and demanding that wrongs . . . this day be righted, which have been left to work their evil effects through a long course of generations." "For the protection and employment of women, other than house servants, providing them with legal protection from the frauds and impositions of unscrupulous employers." While New York certainly had the lead on this question, a Cleveland paper not especially friendly to unionism acknowledged, "The cruelty of this unjust distinction between the man and woman worker is beginning to be realized by the public."[17] Events that summer both on the battlefield and in the city delayed its public activities until the fall.

Certainly, workingwomen themselves seized the initiative of documenting their impoverishment before the wider community, particularly those capable of doing something about it. None of the "some three hundred girls" making haircloth on Sixth Avenue attending their meetings made more than $1.50 per week. "Many of the girls have parents to support, and this sum is wholly inadequate." By early November, they went "on strike for 5 cents more per yard." The spiritualists' *Banner of Light* pointed out that the women's wages were from a fraction of what had been paid at the war's onset, "while every article purchased has nearly *doubled* in its price." Even the *New York Times* supported them. Hundreds of "plainly dressed, but tidy-looking, intelligent and handsome girls" turned up for the subsequent meeting of the WWPU to initiate a "movement among the working girls in the city for an increase of prices." Before several gentlemen, including "a representative of the Workingmen's Union," they presented concrete examples on the pay they received laboring as photographers, working as book stitchers, tasselmakers, sewing machine operators, silver burnishers; makers of shirts, shelter tents, vests, hoop skirts, parasols, and umbrellas. The body also adopted resolutions.[18]

Women repeated this technique before an even more prestigious gathering in March 1864. Various officials, including former mayor James T. Brady, presided over the meeting, which included Judge Daly and other luminaries. They began with Mrs. Anne S. Stephens's poem "Song of the Working Women" and declared their goal "to protect and find employment for all workingwomen, without regard to creed or nationality, saint or sinner, virtuous or vicious." Press and politicians warned against trusting "the tender mercies of the Shylocks."[19]

By June 1864, *Banner of Light* published the discussion of "The Laboring Women" by Amos. He recited the statistics on wages and budgets, but less to foster self-organization among the women than to shame the city fathers into action. "Let the principle of cooperation once obtain a foothold upon a truly spiritual basis," he suggested, "and it will then be discovered that therein lies the embryo of health, happiness, progression, peace, and the millennium of harmony." The

Banner labeled the plight of workingwomen "a crime appalling to contemplate; and must be expiated by the nation either by hastening to do justice or by sufferings not now thought of." It wondered whether "the rich men, and the ambitious men of a nation are willing to build themselves up at the expense of woman" who seemed "an appropriate subject for philanthropy, along with contraband freed people or sick soldiers.[20]

In the end, prominent patrons, excellent press, and big plans could offer the workingwomen a clear course of action. Patrons and the press supported the women, not in terms of equal pay, of course, or the encouragement of trade unionism, but as objects of paternal largess. "That such reforms as these are urgently required in New-York, no one can deny who is at all acquainted with the quarters of the City inhabited by our laboring classes," declared the *New York Times*. "Practical philanthropy can have no better or higher object; and it is our belief that private and associated capital could find no safer or, in the end, more lucrative form of investment."[21]

Prominent male philanthropists took the major offices and made fundraising essential to the WWPU's future. Contributions allowed it to open a placement bureau that found connected reputable employers and contracts with several thousand women seeking work, and the organization also provided some legal help against employers who simply failed to pay their wages. By December 1864, the WWPU had become a going concern and held a first anniversary celebration at the Cooper Institute, attended by prominent preachers, philanthropists, and politicians.[22]

The circumstances naturally gave rise to rhetoric about wages slavery, and Cora Wilburn explicitly declared the condition of white workingwomen a form of enslavement. The rhetoric is subject to conflicting interpretations, telling us little, in itself, about the view of the speakers or their audiences on abolition.[23] However, the association of the contractors with the war and government contracts permitted those critical of the Lincoln administration to place the blame on the Republican war for slave liberation.

More substantively, the use of the reform movement to establish a placement bureau for finding jobs for women raised other possibilities, as entrepreneurs elsewhere in the country saw advantages to themselves. "Why don't some of our rich men establish associations for the express purpose of aiding such poor sewing-girls to obtain homes at the West?" These could bring "thousands of poor girls and women in our Eastern cities, too, who cannot earn money enough to keep soul and body decently together, but who are wanted in the households of the West at almost any reasonable price they may choose to ask." The problem of "the overcrowded labor-market in New York" could solve "the deficit in Milwaukee and the West."[24]

The Working Women's Relief Association: The Philadelphia Variant

Other American cities replicated the general conditions in New York City, with some variations. At Philadelphia, war production more directly affected workingwomen. In August 1863, the Federal Arsenal forced a response by discharging all women employed there "other than nearest relatives of soldiers," and two hundred women protested the loss of their jobs. This brought nine hundred inexperienced seamstresses into the arsenal and left a similar number of experienced workers at the mercy of the war contractors. In these jobs, the women made the same clothing as before, but at reductions in pay of 25 percent to 40 percent. Pay in the arsenal itself fell from 1861 to 1864 for everything but cavalry pants and bed sacks, but the fall off for work done outside the arsenal was truly drastic. *Fincher's Trades' Review* urged unionization.[25]

Grievances in Philadelphia produced just as large a constituency as New York for some sort of corrective. Everyone in the needle trades had specific grievances relating to war production. Large protest meetings aired grievances, but did not look to trade unionism or other forms of self-organization as a primary means of rebuilding their lives. When one speaker tried to urge the organization of all workingwomen, the president placed it beyond the bounds. Rather, they looked to "a sound and strong public sentiment . . . *to back up* their own labor combinations, and in good time, feeling that they rest on the support of such a sentiment, they will *force* their way for themselves to the position which is theirs, compelling even Shylocks to respect what they are ready to only when there is no escape from it."[26]

The movement certainly enjoyed the same range of support it found at New York. It included Catholic-priest-turned-spiritualist Andreas Smolnikar, the New York abolitionist Theodore Tilton, and the local Quaker Alfred Henry Love, destined for international renown for his work in the Universal Peace Union. However, it also included voices such as that of Jonathan Fincher and his *Trades' Review*, which regularly wrote about the conditions of women workers, particularly those working directly in the government at the arsenal and indirectly through contractors supplying the army. The labor paper and its supporters urged the women to organize a strong union and deal with their grievances directly. With the threat of unionization in the air, a committee of concerned citizens launched the Working Women's Relief Association (WWRA). It sought only to bring together "dressmakers, milliners, Arsenal hands, and all workers on army clothing" and document the abuses. It also called protest meetings to plead with employers for better conditions.[27] A protest meeting at Sansom Street Hall was organized by these philanthropists to beg the owners for better conditions. When one speaker tried to urge the organization of all workingwomen, the president declared the subject beyond the concerns of the meeting.[28]

By the summer of 1864, the increasing cost of living and the relative stagnation of the women's wages forced the holding of more meetings. Miss Dr. Dennett spoke of "the sufferings of the sewing women of Philadelphia." "There are twenty thousand poor women in that city," she said, "who are dependent on the needle for a pittance wherewith to keep body and soul together, and many of them are literally starving." The meeting sent a petition to Secretary of War Edwin M. Stanton "imploring him to advance the price in Philadelphia Arsenal. "How long, oh, God! Will oppression and injustice bear rule and press the tears and life out of humanity?" A Mr. Darlington spoke as well, taking the independent course; Mr. Elliott "took the ground that women have too many rights now."[29]

The WWRA sponsored more meetings later in 1864. They sought to aid, in the words of Addie Hutchins, "the great army of *sewing women*, crushed and trampled to the earth, *starving* and *dying*—first enlisted their efforts in that direction." The earlier committee sent to meet Stanton reported "an earnest and sympathetic consideration and prompt action; the result of which is—*so far*—an advance of pay on the work and an increase of two thousand hands at the arsenal in this city," which represented "but a stepping-stone to what he intends to do." A later meeting reported the publication of their monthly *Woman's Journal*, which Cora Wilburn described as seeking "redress for the slavery of the whiter needle-woman." The officers, however, clarified that they did not want an effort "confined to working-women" but sought "women who can bring means, talent, eloquence and influence to the work. They also wanted a movement not "limited to women alone" but extended to male philanthropists as well. Hutchins also appealed to the middle-class ladies involved in the Christian Commission's efforts to aid the soldiers, urging them to broaden their vision to include "the relatives of those men who stand upon the battle-field." "As the interests of both sexes are involved—as they inevitably are in all things," she said, "so will both engage in the accomplishment of this great good."[30]

Through the winter, though, the contractors gained an even larger share of the production of the arsenal. A large demonstration of seamstresses protested this in January 1865. Fincher turned up and urged them, at this point, to organize a cooperative that would allow the women to be self-employed by a collective firm subcontracting from the arsenal. The movement sent at least two delegations to President Lincoln, who gave them a warm reception. As was in keeping with his policies, the president sought to encourage a strict neutrality in labor disputes. He urged the arsenal to raise the pay for women working directly for the government, to minimize reliance on subcontractors, and to expand the number of women working directly for the government. Disregarding the earlier government claim that it had no responsibility for what the contractors were doing, Lincoln suggested the War Department "hereafter manage the supplies of contract work for the Government made up by women so as to give them remunerative wages for their labor.[31]

Wartime Female Labor and the Legacy of Paternalism

What Fincher and other unionists argued was that the rights of workingwomen should not require acts of largess and philanthropy but be established and secured by the women themselves. He particularly suggested that they organize a cooperative that would allow the women to be self-employed by a collective firm subcontracting from the arsenal.[32] In the end, such advice was, of course, cheap.

Women faced a curious problem during the 1860 shoe strike that would recur through the years after. The achievement of such broad-based unity required strike leaders to avoid confronting the paternalistic assumptions of that community that precluded recognition that female workers were dependent on their own wages rather than those of male wage earners in their family.[33]

During then formative days of their union, the printers left a clear record of their horror as women began entering that holy of holies of fraternal labor. In August 1854 journeymen at the Philadelphia *Daily Register* left "in high dudgeon, because the publisher had employed two women as type-setters in a separate office." Others refused to instruct female apprentices, but none of this stopped the steady stream of women into this and other crafts. Virginia Penny, who gathered most of her information in New York City from October 1859 to February 1861, reported that the Typographical Union had "done all they could to prevent women from entering the occupation and obtaining employment." At the onset of the war, Boston women had worked in the craft for decades and "set type for nearly all the larger periodicals," while those laboring in New York and Philadelphia had also been working for years. They did so for less pay than men got, "but some earn $8 a week."[34]

Still, war had presented the old Typographical Union with a fundamentally new kind of crisis. The *Council Bluffs Nonpareil* announced, "Deserted by the printer boys, who have 'gone to the wars,' [the union] has 'enlisted' about half a dozen of the best looking girls in town, and is now 'training up' a corps of compositors not subject to the draft." One writer believed, optimistically, that the actual introduction of women into the trade meant that "the old prejudices of workingmen against the employment and competition of the other sex are rapidly disappearing." In June 1864 the Boston local, which had accorded women equal status in the shops from 1857, accepted the traveling card of Annie R. Mitchell from the Burlington local.[35] Female union membership would only increase.

Cooperation proved to be a particularly good route for workingwomen toward trade unionism. At Troy, Kate Mullaney and sister Mary, two younger sisters, and their brother Frank, as well as their mother Bridget, and Ester Keegan became mainstays of a new Collar Laundry Union. About half of the local female workforce spent twelve to fourteen hours a day washing, bleaching, and ironing the fashionable new stiff white collars, and new starching machines could take a scalding heat that human hands could not. With the active support of the local Iron Molder's Union, the laundresses went on strike against fourteen commercial laundries on February 23, 1864, for 20 percent to 25 percent increases. After five and a half days, a few of the firms gave in, and the rest did the following day, on February 29. The two unions jointly drew about four thousand workers to a picnic on July 18, attended by William H. Sylvis and reporters from as far away as New York City. There the women presented a full-color banner to the Iron Molders.[36]

In the end, women workers and issues of gender became an essential feature in the process of class formation, but rarely separate from matters of maintaining family and respecting "woman's role." Gender roles cast workingwomen in dependent conditions, and this distinguished women from male workers, even in the context of the labor movement. These women desperately needed help, and one can hardly blame them for taking it when some of their more secure sisters offered assistance. In the end, though, such women owed their elevated standing primarily to their family associations with fathers, husbands, or brothers, and to their ability to mediate with their social betters.[37] So much of the movement of workingwomen wound up centered on appeal to alleged importance of women's role as wives and mothers in establishing and maintaining middle-class standards of life and the stability of the social order.

The failure to meet "the spiritual as well as the material wants of the sewing-women, and laboring women generally" made comparisons with slavery almost unavoidable. Even some abolitionists complained that white female workers were "as wronged as masters at the South would not wrong even their slaves." *Fincher's Trades' Review* wrote of women workers of the Northern cities as "white female slaves," and Cora Wilburn discussed the problem in terms of comparative slaveries.[38]

The spiritualists' *Banner of Light* expected much from "this great labor movement—a movement which is going to lead to the final establishment of more just relations between Labor and Capital," particularly the women. The spiritualists, who generally supported a wide range of projects for the social elevation of the poor and downtrodden, editorially praised as "a move in the right direction" the initiative of some of the employers to establish what amounted to company housing for its workers. It described how "the wholesale oyster dealers of this city fitting up apartments for poor women instead of men in opening oysters." They suggested such plans could be extended to other areas, "retail dry goods stores, for instance—in which woman might be profitably employed, and herself placed above want, if some of our philanthropic merchants would bestir themselves." The fact that they did so posed problems of their own.[39]

Then, too, the rhetoric of a Northern "slavery," while apt in context, provided a powerful image to critics of the Union. Instances of labor discontent, argued the *Richmond Examiner*, proved "what we have always contended—that the poor whites at the North are far worse off than the slaves at the South; that there is a system of white slavery in the North far more exacting and inexorable than negro slavery in the South." For them "the most important thing that grew out of the movement was a most thrilling picture of white slavery at the North." "The working men and women at the North are moving," declared hopeful Confederate papers. Even in the North, the anti-Negro, anti-Lincoln Democrats such as Judge Charles P. Daly took up the cause, his wife Maria becoming WWPU's president. The *Brooklyn Daily Eagle* cast the issue as one demonstrating "the far-seeing negro-philanthropists among us who wept for the wrongs of the sleek, well-fed and contented darkey on the Southern plantation, has been entirely ignored and allowed to reap its harvest of misery and death without a word of protest."[40]

* * *

The expansion of the hired workforce stratified how workers thought they might influence power. The presence of this newly enlarging force of African American wage workers racialized perceptions of the mass, militant, and often armed general strike. It appeared as a strategy justifiable only in the most desperate layers of the workforce, more abject than most workers would ever want to admit themselves to be. The new layers of unskilled ethnic white workers functioned with more discipline on a more locally focused set of issues but still engaged in disreputably "riotous" strikes that almost always ended in violent repression. Finally, the large numbers of women driven into the workforce produced a curiously gendered strategy, whereby the vulnerable and wronged female used her condition to touch the nerve of the patriarchal society that claimed to revere them. New kinds of wage workers brought distinctive kinds of self-awareness that would inform the making of an American class sensibility and a labor movement.

While the distinctive position of women, immigrants, and African Americans created predispositions to distinctive modes of resistance, neither women, immigrants, nor African Americans—nor Anglo-Saxon Protestants—were locked into position. Under the right circumstances, of course, blacks could function in craft unions, and skilled American-born whites could riot. In September 1864, forty shop girls in Boston went on strike and kept strikebreakers away. The bosses called out the police against them.[41] One can scarcely imagine what the gentlemen benefactors of the Working Women's Relief Association might have made of this.

PART III

War, Revolution, and Labor

We're low, we're low, we're very, very low.
   And yet when the trumpets ring.
The thrust of a poor man's arm will go
   Thro' the heart of the proudest king.
We're low, we're low, and our place we know,
   We're only the rank and file;
But we're not too low to fight the foe,

—"Song of the Unenfranchised," 1865

CHAPTER 7

New Militancy across the Union

The Strike Waves and Labor Movements of 1863

Within weeks of Lincoln's Gettysburg suggestion that civil war marked "a new birth of freedom." Jonathan Fincher of the machinists' union warned workers that they, like the nation, faced a turning point in their affairs. Press accounts noted "no let-up, apparently, in the strike movement, on the part of the mechanics and workingmen." More than would later be the case, the press acknowledged that the increasing costs of living made wage increases "reasonable," though, even this early, some simply ignored the numbers and asserted that the market had already functioned to keep wages proportionate to prices. Few who earned those wages and paid those prices had the luxury of such illusions. A wave of organizations swept the major cities, particularly in the northeast. "Nearly every trade is represented in the movement for increased wages," declared the *New York Times*. An estimated four thousand workers walked off the job. Jennie Collins later traced the roots of the postwar movement to the middle of the Civil War, declaring that "from that time . . . there was little or no rest."[1]

The influx of new wage workers did not entirely alleviate the wartime labor shortages in America, which provided workers North and South a modest amount of power to protect their wages and standards of living. In the Northern cities, an almost entirely new workers' movement attained an unprecedented scale, coherence, and power. Across the northeastern United States, workers tried to build and reactivate old unions, even as they organized new ones, waging more and larger strikes and establishing a permanent labor presence in the life of cities like New York. Across the Union, new conditions gave rise to new sorts of conflicts and organizations.

The Strike Wave in Boston

By October 1863, between six thousand and ten thousand Boston workers had access to about fifty "societies for mutual protection." These included not only the old crafts but also new industrial trades and even the "clerks in retail boot and shoe, dry goods, grocery, leather, hardware and other stores." There existed "several Trades' Union Societies among the blacksmiths and machinists," but all would "hold a big influence with their organizations in all large cities and towns as regards the price of wages to be paid by employers, and also in the political movements for their interests during the next year."[2]

Wartime issues fostered a wave of labor activism particularly at the Navy Yard though also among curriers, sugar makers, polishers, varnishers, and upholsterers, as well as a "New England Dental Association." Waiters, footwear clerks, iron safe makers, cigarmakers, coopers, conductors, and drivers went on strike, as did a new Seamen's Mutual Benefit Association, professional musicians, workers at the Charlestown Water Works, trunk makers, and marble cutters.

As elsewhere, the Navy Yards proved to be the touchstone for industrial actions. In the summer, the bosses added a few blacks, and a reported 160 whites went on strike, and were discharged, the firing creating another issue. Bitterness festered until, on October 10, twelve hundred carpenters assembled in "one of the largest mechanics' meetings that has been held in Boston for years." W. A. Boardman of the Machinists' Union "and others" spoke in support of the effort, though their own leader, William F. Falls, "deprecated strikes." Despite their earlier caution, the carpenters, on November 11, "voted to unite with other workmen in the Yard in a meeting in the Monument grounds" at Bunker Hill to strike not only over pay but in protest of innovations that effectively rescinded President Martin Van Buren's 1840 order establishing a ten-hour day for government workers. Jeremiah H. Remick, "long connected with the Yard," read the "original order in regard to hours" there. Others raised strike funds in the departments dealing with gunners, provision, clothing, and ordnance. Blacksmiths, blockmakers, gun carriage makers, yard laborers, coopers, boilermakers, rope workers, plumbers, carpenters, joiners, sawyers, masons, sparmakers, painters, sailmakers, riggers, caulkers, machinists, and laborers organized. The next day, the workers voted $150 of their strike fund to send Remick to Washington. Of the thirty-five hundred workers in the yard, there remained "less than a hundred at work."[3]

The strike movement held continued rallies. When management fired some twenty-five strike leaders, the new commandant of the Navy Yard rehired them. On the third day of the strike, Senator Henry Wilson met both President Lincoln and Secretary of the Navy Gideon Welles "in behalf of the mechanics and laborers in the Boston navy yard." The movement spread into "a general strike at south Boston, and at other shops in the city" until some five thousand marched out. Meanwhile, boilermakers, iron plate makers, longshore coopers, and the mast and sparmakers walked off, the latter under the old banner "carried in the peace procession in Boston seventy-eight years ago by the North End mast and spar makers."[4]

Nailmakers at Neponset, south of the city near Dorchester, waged a bitter midwinter strike. The numbers are variously given as ranging from thirty to 140 men, small enough to be eclipsed by the larger November strikes on the waterfront. The nailmakers reportedly earned between thirty and forty dollars monthly but wanted an additional half-cent per pound of nails made at three large establishments. Remarkably, the "Neponset Nail-Makers Literary Association" called the strike. The employers complained of "riotous conduct among the workmen," and the selectmen of Dorchester sent to Boston for reinforcements to arrest the leaders. The city government there declined but gave the Chief of Police permission to send volunteers. In the end, "over forty blue-coats" turned up and "began arresting the strike leaders, who were sent to Roxbury, and then the Dedham jail." In the end, the bosses broke the strike and fired two of the strike leaders.[5]

Boston workers concluded that the only chance of success lay in concerted action. One of the Navy Yard men, A. J. Quincy, complained that in

> the unpleasant circumstance in which the yard workingmen were placed; they could not consistently present their claims as laboring men so fully now, but as soon as the rebellion was crushed there would be a mighty uprising to crush another power in the land—the rebellion against workingmen's rights. It would then be their duty to see to it that the real capital of the country, Labor, was in some degree represented in affairs of State, and that Government should not be fully monopolized by its opposing interests.

Conditions in the Navy Yard moved the machinists and blacksmiths to resolve for an eight-hour workday. By February 1864 the local Trades' Assembly had already begun to structure "a friendly discussion" of "the eight hour system" before being tabled.[6] By then, these new organizations probably gave the Boston labor movement a membership of ten thousand to fourteen thousand, while unions and strikes flared across New England.

The Strike Wave at New York

The labor upsurge in New York eclipsed that in Boston. By the fall of 1863 common experience had already moved workers organized in their crafts and industries toward common citywide organization. The press described "a very wide-spread dissatisfaction among the laboring classes, and the consequences is that 'strikes' for higher wages are being made daily." The *Scientific American* also noted the increase of strikes and unions.[7] New unions appeared among the cigarmakers, tailors, store clerks, window shade makers, lithographic printers, as well as the Tinplate, Copper and Sheet Iron Workers Protective Union. The New York Metropolitan Police also wanted a pay raise. Piano makers and carriage makers went on strike, and employers narrowly averted one among the safe makers.

In October, two thousand striking coopers paraded through the city, with large contingents from Brooklyn and Williamsburg and deputation from allied unions, such as the tailors. However, in the closed world of the workplace, disputes not only took place on the grand civic scale but became quite personal. Workers in a looking-glass manufactory on Twenty-Sixth Street walked out, but David R. Thom and another man worked under contract and stayed on the job. After work, Thom encountered a party of strikers headed by Patrick Winn, possibly the twenty-nine-year-old veteran of the Tenth New York recently discharged from the army for a disability. Thom knocked Winn down and "a general fight ensued." In the end, Thom got "stabbed in eight different places" and was "not expected to recover." Nevertheless, the strike may have expanded into the general strike movement among glasscutters who organized their own union.[8]

Setting aside the general tactic of moral appeals to the social "betters," the girls who sewed umbrellas went on strike to earn more than six to eight cents an item, earning around three to four dollars for a six-day week, laboring from 6:00 A.M. to midnight. The Workingmen's Union and the craftsmen rallied to support the new flicker of militancy by the Working Women's Protective Union, surely concerned that the movement be misdirected into purely middle-class and philanthropic channels. Papers as far away as Illinois covered the strike, but the workers faced "so much abuse from their employers" that they even offered to compromise their demands. When the bosses refused to compromise, "all were obliged to return to their work, except a few who still hold out." The *Chicago Journal* observed that striking women, "getting the merest pittance for their toil, are obliged to submit, in these high-priced times, to the low wages of former years. It is so in New York, in Chicago, and all over the country."[9]

Labor discontent invariably affected the war effort. The Starr Arms Company had the right product at the right time. It had full orders when the workforce revolted against particularly harsh work rules, published at the time in the *Yonkers Herald*. Some 360 walked out on September 8, and another eighty followed the next day, leaving only thirty-eight on the job. The strike ended on September 11.[10]

Navy Yard machinists launched what the *Fincher's* proclaimed to be "The Greatest Strike on Record!" The union spent months raising money and preparing for the July strike, and they had the resources to rent a headquarters at No.

187 Bowery, which provided a focus for plumbers and ship carpenters to established a headquarters and hold repeated mass rallies, spreading the movement into other trades. By the end of November, some seven thousand machinists from fifty shops had gone out, and the union had grown to "very formidable proportions," strengthened by fifteen thousand dollars contributed by other trades. The strike stopped work on a small fleet of ironclads, including "double enders," that could use eight guns of very heavy caliber. When the bosses sent a delegation to Washington to ask for Federal action against the strike, the machinists quickly decided to do the same.[11]

That strike sparked a contagion of solidarity. The local painters and gold beaters sent money, as did some four hundred of the estimated seven hundred Singer Sewing machine workers, who decided "to give material aid to the machinists, should they require it." Supporters met in Jersey City, Newark, and nearby communities, while those at Philadelphia and Buffalo held large rallies in support. Soon after, the carpenters sent help when the sash and blind makers struggled to organize themselves. The *New York Times* noted that "the carpenters, the wardrobe men, the gas men, the calcium light men" associated "with the principal theatrical establishments about town, following the fashion of the times, have struck for higher wages." "Perhaps," it quipped, "the actors and actresses will take it into their heads to go and do likewise." In fact, by August 1864 an Actors' Protective Union actually did exactly that.[12]

By November 12, what the press called "the striking mania" inspired three or four hundred street rail conductors and drivers who walked off the job to get more pay for their twelve- to sixteen-hour workdays. They grabbed and dunked one strikebreaker in a neighboring pond, but the strike was so well organized that even the generally hostile press commented on its lack of "rowdyism." Management tried to use unlicensed drivers, resulting in snarled traffic, arrests and fines, after which they appealed to the police. In the end, the companies caved in, the Fourth Avenue line even adding more for those on the "long route" to Harlem.[13]

The strike wave in New York City made unions more the rule than the exception in some parts of the workforce. Recalling—and surpassing—the unprecedented scale of the movement a decade earlier, unions formed among carpenters and joiners, house carpenters, confectioners, glasscutters, horse shoers, lithographers, sash- and blindmakers, cigarpackers, stagedrivers, window-shade painters, cutlers, and iron trade workers. Brooklyn had its own unions of house carpenters and house painters, the carpenters winning a short strike for more pay. Events the following spring noted organizations of plasterers, upholsterers, wheelwrights, blacksmiths, and German druggists. Some became quite large, the shoemakers' local reaching around three thousand members. For heavy lifting, workers had their Workingmen's Union, as well the trades' assembly.[14] The press accounts indicated nearly one hundred occupations on strike or organized, representing twenty-five thousand to thirty thousand workers or more, most of whom had only recently joined a union.

The wave of unionism washed over upstate New York as well. Although the Albany printers walked out at the *Standard*, unskilled laborers prevailed. On June 16 longshoremen and elevator employees took to the streets, where "a few railroad laborers" on the Central Railroad joined them, hoping for a pay raise. "About three hundred of the laborers marched to and closed the West Albany workshops. With their numbers reaching six to seven hundred, they turned to the private workshops." Both the Central and Hudson railroads agreed, and the men turned up to work the next day. However, about three hundred remained on strike, so the mayor turned up with some fifty policemen, who "drove the rioters before them. Twenty or thirty of the rioters were knocked down by the clubs of the policemen, and one was shot in the cheek," and the *Morning Express* named two strikers shot at the rally. The more persistent expected "reinforcements from Troy," but everything seems to have collapsed on the third day, June 18.[15]

Workers had gone into action across the region. Striking coopers marched through Poughkeepsie. Rochester carpenters and joiners and the Buffalo Iron Molders held elaborate "balls" around Christmas. Before the end of 1863, Rochester and Buffalo had established citywide bodies, and the Rochester printers and carpenters began discussing the prospects of a national labor convention. At the start of December, laborers on the Camden and Amboy railroad in New Jersey walked off the job to win $1.50 per day, but the sheriff deputized a posse and brought a militia company in from Trenton, dispersing the strikers and arresting many of them. Fincher hurried to Trenton when some four hundred to five hundred of the machinists and blacksmiths closed the Trenton Arms Company, addressing a mass meeting on "the Rights of Labor."[16]

Over the Rest of the Country

This unprecedented wave of organizing and strikes rippled across the country. In Philadelphia, "meetings are held daily, committees are appointed to wait on the bosses, who, in most cases, comply with the demands of their workmen, and in case of refusal, a 'strike' instantly takes place." Against a backdrop of the smoldering strike of the molders, workers sought "to institute measures in order to secure an advance of wages." He noted that Labor remained "scarce and in demand,"; "so well organized are these associations that in many cases, even when a 'strike' takes place, employers cannot induce others to take the place of the strikers."[17]

Solidarity with the New York strikers initially moved Philadelphia machinists. Three weeks into the struggle, hundreds assembled at the local National

Guards' Hall. William Sylvis of the molders joined representatives of the New York machinists to urge action. The local machinists, meanwhile, decided to demand better wages themselves in November and went on strike in December. As elsewhere, when one trade acted in the Navy Yard, other areas of the waterfront found such activities spreading there, and so sailmakers struck for twenty-five cents an hour or $2.50 per day, same as the pay in the private yards. They had offered to labor ten hours in order to get the $2.50, but authorities refused to rethink the policy until workers "demanded $2.50 per day, short or long."[18]

At Philadelphia, too, behind the newly numerous industrial workers, the traditional city crafts strove to better their lot. The city's cigarmakers, furniture workers, carpenters, and shoemakers acted to gain more wages, the last for military work done through the Federal Arsenal. Stocking makers at nearby Germantown gained higher wages. They generally fared better than the laborers, such as those on the Spruce and Pine Street railroad, who were fired for wanting a pay hike, or the striking ice gatherers on the Schuylkill arrested by the police.[19]

Still, the most historically successful craftsmen faced severe reactions. Union printers almost apologized for publishing their grievances against the *Philadelphia Age*, describing it as "unpleasant for the workingman who 'earns his bread by the sweat of his brow' to appear before the public in a card, stating private grievances, for the laborer suffers so much." The rosters of local regiments had included several of the aggrieved unionists at the *Age*, indicating that these were recently returned veterans. When the paper began trying to replace the unionists, they decided to strike over these "private grievances" on December 18. Two days before Christmas, the authorities arrested James Devine and another union member for assaulting a rat. The day after Christmas, the union named over twenty of them.[20] The strike festered into 1864.

The press surveyed two dozen strikes or organized occupations by the time the Philadelphia unions convened "a large meeting." It gathered representatives of "the machine moulders, varnishers' union, lithographic printers, spar-makers, typographical union, curriers, segar-makers, printers' union, stone and hollow-ware moulders, tinsplate and sheet-iron makers, journeymen plumbers, saddlers, upholsterers and painters." Citing the fact that their solidarity had sustained some local molders then on strike for ten months, they called for "a Grand Union of the Trades for the mutual protection of the members." Once established, the new Trades' Assembly could strengthen all participating organizations and foster organization among the unorganized.[21] The local movement likely involved at least twenty thousand workers.

In part, experience of labor in smaller cities represented similar trends. In November 1863 and April 1864, Cincinnati carpenters and Pittsburgh printers, respectively, demanded a pay increase. Cincinnati horse shoers and the city hosted a meeting of those employing molders to study union-busting techniques, which the *North American* described as "gaining liberty to manage their own property in their own way." Nevertheless, the molders struck there, and at Louisville, where the machinists and blacksmiths also walked off the job, establishing the foundations for the Louisville Trades Assembly, which went on to start a Cooperative Store. At about the same time, St. Louis workers established their new Trades' Union League.[22] Wartime Cincinnati, Louisville, or St. Louis would have supported labor movements of five thousand or more.

Organized workers had a disproportionate impact in new cities and towns where organization of any sort remained new, which is probably how wartime San Francisco experienced the first urban strike wave in the region. For several years the printers there had a small but active union, the Eureka Typographical Union, which gained considerable local prominence in a court case when a newspaper owner claimed exemption from union rules after forcing his workers to sign papers making them "partners." By April 1863, shipwrights reorganized, but the plasterers and tailors also had unions, the latter successfully striking for higher wages on the new "fancy work" being added to coats. "A quiet movement among the mechanics and laborers for an advance of wages" stirred the city a year later. Under the auspices of the first molders union on the West Coast, "two hundred and twenty-five blacksmiths, iron moulders and pattern-makers, employed in the foundries" insisted on a raise from four dollars to $4.50 per day. Local stonecutters "notified their employers that after the 1st of May their wages must be advanced from $4 to $5 per day." In May, the Milkmen's Protective Union wrote a new pay scale.[23]

Labor organizations certainly appeared in smaller manufacturing centers and industrial towns that dotted the countryside. As early as July 1862, an estimated two thousand men repairing canals near places like Easton and Mauch Chunk made a bid for higher pay in a strike reported "to be general," and boatmen on the Chesapeake and Ohio canal did the same in the fall of 1863. Morocco finishers organized at Wilmington, Delaware, as did molders at Richmond, Indiana, and Quincy, Illinois, where they waged a disastrous strike. Similar strikes swept some of the new communities of the West. The blacksmiths of Black Hawk and Central City, Colorado, walked out for five dollars a day in March 1864. The following August, Utah farmers held a convention to set their prices in something the *Vedette* called "the farmers' strike."[24]

In Kansas—which had just become a state—the *Leavenworth Daily Times* reported strikes "quite prevalent in the city; but the workmen, we believe, generally get the advanced asked for." In November 1862, it deemed "nothing more than fair" for the cabinetmakers to get the 25 percent pay hike they wanted, though the paper did belong to a union member. By the summer of 1863, Leavenworth experienced a small version of the strike wave sweeping the big cities. There, the "laborers and mechanics" held out until the employers agreed to their demands. Carpenters marched through town to the various shops and closed most of them. Citing the cost of living, the *Daily Times* thought the demands "not at all unreasonable." By March 1864 the boss tailors prepared for a strike by advertising out of town for twenty journeymen, though their workers got a 25 percent raise by the end of the year. By the fall, the local Typographical Union had "raised the price of composition to sixty cents per one thousand ems."[25]

Most dramatically, grievances erupted in the coal industry. As early as the fall of 1852, the authorities reported a "riot" of miners in Schuylkill County, Pennsylvania, that cut coal production to a third. The *Philadelphia Inquirer* reported this as a threat "to offer the government of the State either the alternative of not drafting or of remaining entirely unsupplied with coal from this region. Since the origin of the disturbance the receipts of coal in this city, from Schuylkill county, at Richmond, have been about one-third only of the usual amount was received." After winning some victories in February 1863, miners waged further strikes in April and May, inspiring the *New York Times* to complain that these did not result "from actual suffering" among miners but represented merely "an index of prosperity, not of adversity—of high wages, not of low; of independence, not of want." When the bosses and the press charged the strikers with treasonous intentions, a committee of miners wondered: "Are these people paid to vilify us? Or are they merely satisfying their aristocratic hatred of the workingman?"[26]

Similar tensions erupted in the coalfields of Illinois, from which unionism diffused to other occupations. The companies responded to the virtually universal support miners had in their communities by recruiting Belgians to break the union. The Miners Association turned them away, contributing money to send them to go elsewhere. Begun in March 1863, this particularly bitter strike continued for nine months. When the miners prevailed, their victory sparked "other strikes of coal miners in different parts of the country, all for increase of wages, and all successful." In May, John Hinchcliffe, a forty-year old Yorkshireman back from serving as a captain in Commissary Department at Cincinnati, launched the *Miner* and became the voice of the American Miners' Association.[27]

Miners' strikes early became community affairs. The *Peoria Morning Mail* reported the teamsters had joined the miners' strike in April 1863. In June, the authorities arrested ten leaders at the Kingston Mines, when men who "refused to work attempted to interfere with those who remained, got tight, threatened to burn the town, and kicked up a muss generally." By September, the authorities battled to suppress a strike of teamsters and miners. When they showed up at Kewanee, "forty or fifty of the wives and other female members of the miners' families appeared on the field armed with stones, lumps of coal, and other impromptu weapons, and with an equal or greater number of their male friends, deployed in the woods and bushes as skirmishers, marched on the bank where work was still going on, with wild shouts and threats and corresponding gesticulations." The appearance of the bosses "excited to a furious pitch of passion, appearing more like wild creatures than civilized women." They struck one of them "with sticks and clubs, three stones of coal at him, pulled his hair, and finally attempted to ride him on a rail."[28]

The scope of these activities naturally pointed toward national organization. The 1862 printers convention reinstated members in the military who had been dropped for nonpayment of dues. President of the St. Louis local, Sam Slawson, moved to seat George McK. Luken to represent Memphis on the grounds of his election the previous year, and he was sustained in refusing to recognize "a card from the 'Southern Confederacy Union No. 1,' of Nashville," while accepting the transfer of a Memphis printer with "the regular old National union card." The next convention, in May 1863 at Cleveland, resumed efforts to persuade the hitherto independent Columbia Typographical Society to join the NTU and noted the resumption of official correspondence from what had been their largest local in the South, that at New Orleans. Galvanized by the struggles at Philadelphia, the iron molders gathered for their fourth national convention at Pittsburgh in January 1863, where they elected Sylvis as president.[29]

* * *

From the fall of 1863 through the following winter, unprecedented numbers of workers across the Union realized that their wages would never catch up with the rising wartime cost of living without some action on their part. So they organized, even in those new trades and industries that developed so rapidly because of the war. The interconnected nature of those new industries meant that discontent, organization, and action spread easily from one to the other. In several cities, activities in the navy yards moved thousands in other trades along the waterfront, who, in turn, helped detonate organization and action among railroad workers. The exigencies of war and the wartime economy tended to leave the old solitary craft organizations looking increasingly quaint and inspiring a fundamentally new kind of labor movement. For Jennie Collins, this very reaction demonstrated the working class to be "naturally intelligent and able."[30]

The integral nature of these local efforts naturally produced these citywide assemblies. New York's "Central Trades Union" became part of a statewide Workingmen's Union, but a directory of *Fincher's Trades' Review* reflected the importance of local federations. Notices of the Workingmen's Assembly of Boston and vicinity and the Workingmen's Assembly of Monroe County at Rochester appeared in June, the Trades Assembly of Pittsburgh and the Trades Assembly of the City of Buffalo in September, and the Trades Assembly and League of Friendship of Louisville and vicinity in December 1863. In the following year, self-named Trades Assemblies turned up at Philadelphia in March, Troy in July, Detroit in August, and Albany and Cincinnati in September. The St. Louis Trade Union League showed up in the listings for December 1864.[31] Soon after, one formed in Brooklyn. Together, they likely represented 120,000 to 150,000 members—about half in the northeastern states.

Paradoxically, if the initial impact of the Civil War was the near destruction of labor organizations, then the conflict saw the American worker's movement march to a new high-water mark.

CHAPTER 8

Richmond, New Orleans, Nashville

The Diverse Experience of Urban Labor in the South

In April 1863 the women of Richmond seized a rare chance to express what they thought of the secessionist management of their communities. Mary Elizabeth Foy, an Irishwoman, complained that "if they didn't intend to give her something to eat why didn't they send her to the North." An Englishwoman, Isabell Hold, "wished the Yankees would come here and sweep the city." One woman simply demanded "bread or blood." With these women of the markets in the lead, "gangs of men followed them and helped them and the town was in great excitement and the shop-keepers with big stocks in much alarm." The Young Men's Christian Association distributed "some rice and other things" in an unsuccessful attempt to forestall looting. Thomas Samani, who helped them break into a store, was likely a relative of Louis Samani, a member of the local "Printers' Guards" and likely of the union. When local officials threatened to open fire, a Confederate surgeon reminded them that the people were "a power behind the throne greater than the throne."[1]

The working people of the South bore the burden of the catastrophe the owners and rulers of their society had brought down upon them. The white and black residents of the largest city in the region, New Orleans, faced an early occupation and took its own first feeble steps toward a self-reconstruction of the labor system without the masters. Occupied even earlier, Nashville faced a pragmatic Federal military transformation into a remarkably modern industrial center. Richmond became the largest, if most unplanned, city in the Confederacy, placing a large Southern workforce almost continually under the dark cloud of war. While the economy began to disintegrate across much of the Confederacy, these three communities demonstrate the kind of spectrum of possibilities Southern developments posed.

Richmond—Life under the Gun

The arrival at Richmond of the Confederate government and the armies needed to defend it required the rapid growth of its civilian population from around thirty-eight thousand to an estimated eighty thousand to ninety thousand. Demand overwhelmed the supply for all sorts of goods, including the very necessities of life. Tens of thousands of the newcomers quickly faced desperate conditions, as the amount of coffee and sugar on their tables shrank and then disappeared, with bread and meat likely to follow. Black workers had long since learned how to work around such failings of the marketplace, and their skills formed a vital matrix in which the history of Confederate labor played out, particularly in Richmond. Throughout the war, reports about blacks spying or forging passes increased, as did complaints about their fraternization and collaboration with whites.[2]

In Richmond, as across the South, immigrant workers tended to remain disproportionately hostile to the Confederacy. As the Union army first approached the capital in early 1862, the authorities renewed their efforts to suppress Unionist activities, but a portion of them, such as the Scotsman Thomas of the Unionist underground, turned toward clandestine activities. Even with the Federals on the Peninsula, the Confederate authorities at Richmond arrested "a number of Union men, principally Germans. The discovery by a detective officer, in the room of the Turners, of two National flags, and a painting of the Goddess of Liberty."[3]

The secession crisis itself goaded workers to action. Shoemakers waged a bitter strike in February 1861, and the tin-plate and sheet-iron workers organized by September. Printers had a particularly strong union, with a local at Petersburg that had seceded from the NTU, while John T. Vannerson, "Uncle Dan" Murphy, James Cowardin Jr., and Henry K. Ellyson, and other mainstays of the Richmond craft formed a powerful little local. By March 1862 a convention of newspaper publishers at Atlanta assembled to consider, in part, "the effect of a Typographical Union and its workings on the publishing interests of the Confederate States."[4]

As with fugitive slave laws, Southern bosses had no problems reconciling the rhetoric of "states rights" with an active and invasive policy on workers. After taking government printing contracts, Kentucky entrepreneur Blanton Duncan complained to the government of his "loafing" lithographers, who "deserve to be hung." With conscription, General John H. Winder responded by drafting Duncan's workers into the army, after which Duncan put Winder's image on

Confederate bonds. Duncan revived old schemes about shifting his operation to child labor and moved his project to Columbus, South Carolina, to avoid the Richmond union. Claiming an authority he did not have, he siphoned off Confederate supplies and manpower, even as he met with Union officers to smuggle needed supplies. From April 1863 Duncan got no more government contracts.[5]

In Richmond, as at Washington, printers themselves became aware that "vast quantities of printing would be required for the public service in all its departments, and that greater activity would arise in newspaper enterprise—the people to see what was being done by the army, and the soldiers to learn what was going on at home and politically." In the summer of 1862 John M. Daniel of the *Richmond Examiner* got the Hustings Court to act the union's "arbitrary regulations." On August 15, it indicted thirty-two printers for forming "an unlawful Club and combination . . . to extort great sums of money" from the bosses. When the bosses advertised for replacements, the union published their own notice, after which Daniel sued the union president "for libel" and tried to get the court to move against every member whose names they could obtain. The union got the Mayor's Court to dismiss the indictment in mid-October, but the bosses came back with a new one in November. In January 1863, the grand jury ruled against quashing "Commonwealth vs. The Richmond Typographical Society."[6] Nevertheless, Richmond printers waged a long, uphill fight with remarkable determination.

What the war brought to the honor of white Southern womanhood went far beyond what unions could remedy. According to one source, "thousands of young girls fly to the cities, and literally sell themselves for bread." Bread riots broke out at Atlanta, and six hundred Mobile women and children, families of soldiers, reportedly moved through town with clubs and hatchets, looting stores and waving banners reading "Bread or Blood" and "Bread or Peace." Salisbury, North Carolina, and Petersburg, Virginia, saw similar disorders, which broke out at the Confederate capital itself on April 2. With most of the men in the army and the city filled with refugees, Richmond business continued to charge what the market would bear, growing rich "by hoarding provisions and clothing and selling at high prices."[7]

When, in March 1863, the military tried to gain control of the available food supply, Richmond itself erupted. On Wednesday, April 1, the night of the city elections, Mary Jackson, a "huckster in the market" told John P. Tyler, a participant in the 1861 workingmen's meetings, that the women had decided to march on Capitol Square next day, after which at least some of them would "go in a body to the provision stores and demand goods at Government prices." Believing that the troops would not resist their pleas, she spoke with such desperation that the papers called her "a forty year old Amazon, with the eye of the Devil." That night, the women assembled at the Church up on Oregon Hill.[8]

Accounts vary as to what happened when as many as five thousand women turned up in the square. Although the local press generally agreed to ignore the rally, the antiunion *Examiner* blamed "concealed instigators" and "emissaries of the Federal Government" for stirring up the "prostitutes, professional thieves, Irish and Yankee hags, gallows-birds from all lands but our own." Others recognized the women as "heads of families of the working classes" and acknowledged that Confederate soldiers wanted them fed. Supporters had some ties to the earlier mechanics' movement in the city, and to the Unionist underground. One of these, Richard Frederick Walker, a typesetter and likely member of the union, held a commission in command of the printers in the home guard and had just won election to the city council. Thomas McNiven of the Unionist underground identified Walker as one of theirs and claimed that they did have a hand in the movement.[9]

When conditions failed to improve through the summer, veterans of the antebellum protests reappeared. On September 19, "a large and enthusiastic meeting of mechanics" gathered at the city hall, where members of the printers union, "Captain" E. B. Robinson, a Virginia-born refugee printer from Washington, and Thomas J. LaPrade held two of the five seats on the resolutions committee that opposed "the great and unprecedented range which speculation has taken by a combination of capital against labor." The more moderate wanted "a stringent and effective law suppressing speculation in the prime necessaries of life," while more radical participants, such as the old Unionist Samuel Huffman, had "no faith generally in legislators" and wanted collective action to "put down the prices." All of the seven-member vigilance committee had been involved in the 1861 protests, except Robinson, who had not been in Richmond at the time.[10] Conspicuous by his absence was Huffman's old ally, M. M. Lipscomb, then employed by the city to dig graves.

The vigilance committee organized a memorial and a second mass meeting on October 3 at city hall. It called for legislative action and resolved its thanks to the Common Council and to the House of Delegates, and to Mayor Joseph Mayo, who addressed them. A week later, "one of the largest and most enthusiastic meetings which has assembled in this city for a long time" took place, which the *Daily Dispatch* welcomed as "no longer . . . confined to the mechanics and working men." Still, the meeting declared it "the duty of the Government to take care of the unfortunate, and not the rich" and heard John H. Askew of the printers' union, though speeches by politicians reflected the victory of the moderates.[11]

Once the movement veered from any radicalism, the local Unionist resistance seemed to have regarded it as useless. On October 19, Walker and the other two members of the city council (said to be secretly Unionists) agreed to submit the proposed regulation of prices to voters, "believing it will be agreeable to our representatives therein to know the wishes of their constituents on that subject." In a city then approaching one hundred thousand residents, barely more than eleven hundred participated in the October 22 weekday vote, but the official count showed 867 opposed to regulation and only 249 in favor, most from the Monroe Ward, dissolving the protest into a kind of cultural suspicion of business. So the renegade newspapermen of *The Bohemian* spoofed "Gideon Grindem" of the firm "Grindem and Squeeze" and claimed motives "very patriotic—he thinks it is a shame that the currency should depreciate so much—but he never forgets to advance his prices, as gold increases in value." While professing "great sympathy for the soldier," Grindem's firm still charged him a month's pay for a pair of gloves.[12]

The coming months swept away the last vestiges of that broader movement, leaving nothing to alleviate the generally worsening conditions that winter. The authorities took some measures to ease the shortages in the spring of 1864 by turning to private contracts to increase the supply of certain commodities like beef.[13] Soon after, the Federal Armies of the James and Potomac neared Richmond, providing an attainable destination for the most discontented of Richmond, who slipped through the lines in impressive numbers.

New Orleans—Toward Reconstruction

Throughout the course of the war, New Orleans experienced as near to a Federally sponsored social revolution as any city ever has. A peculiar Southern community, the 160,000 antebellum residents made it the largest in the region, outstripping by orders of magnitude and complexity any of its rivals. Astonishingly, two successive trade unionist presidents—Stith of the printers and John T. Monroe of the screwmen—held office as mayors, the latter turning the city over to the Union forces without resistance.[14]

In New Orleans, as elsewhere, once the secessionists had their way, the rhetoric against a centralized government power shifted. At one point, a Louisianan proposed abandoning money and dividing the Confederacy "into two classes—the combatants and the produces," with government assuring "shelter, food and clothing, and nothing else." "Let all the resources and productions of every farmer or planter be put at the disposal of the Government, without pay." Government officials and none of the military would be paid. "Let every woman and every child, old enough for the purpose, be made to work without pay." Buying and selling would be criminalized, "but let food, raiment, shelter and medicine be secured to every one under a parish or county organization, controlled or supervised by the General Government." The horrified *New York Times* reported this "Communism in Dixie" as "the most gigantic scheme of practical socialism that the world ever saw" that would "furnish every man, woman and child—of both colors, we suppose—in the Confederacy with all needed food, raiment and shelter" and a "perfect equality as regards property, perfect equality as regards labor, and perfect equality as regards compensation."[15] There would, however, be no New Orleans Commune.

Yet labor discontent contributed to the failure of the secessionists to hold the city. In early 1862 the Southern military concentration at Corinth, Mississippi, had stripped the forces garrisoning New Orleans, the strategists rationalizing that the river defenses would suffice. The Department of the Navy later documented the pressures on the shipyards provoked "a general strike among all the ship carpenters," six hundred to seven hundred of whom marched along the waterfront to raise wages to four dollars or five dollars a day. Desperate to finish the defending fleet, Rafael Semmes did not have the six weeks it had taken for the bosses to break the strike two years before, so he consulted the two strike leaders he had already "imprisoned as traitors." They negotiated terms to free them and got the strikers back to work. Then, too, the Confederate authorities faced the outright mutiny of their troops at Fort Jackson (south of New Orleans), which hastened the April 25 arrival of the Federals.[16] Ironically, strikes had postponed the launching of the *Hartford*, which had led the Union ships past the forts and the ill-prepared Confederate fleet.

Considerable Unionist sentiment resurfaced as the Federals arrived. After four months of occupation, nearly twelve thousand residents had signed the loyalty oath, which permitted the reconstruction of a loyal government to proceed. Between one-tenth and one-fifth of the whites had opposed secession, and a higher proportion had never been entirely convinced of its wisdom but found acquiescence the least troublesome course. Dewitt C. Roberts singled out Northerners among the most opportunistic, such as the Pennsylvanian W. H. C. King, the foreman at the *Crescent*, who had informed on Roberts to the secessionist authorities. Roberts thought King inclined to a "spaniel-like obedience to the beck and nod" of his employer and actually suspected King head murdered one worker in the office. As the paper became rabidly secessionist, King raised a Confederate company and "managed to be chosen captain of it, flourished around largely, breathing destruction to all Yankees, (he is a native of Pennsylvania)." When the Federals turned up, King briefly went into the interior with his company before sneaking back to the city, where he claimed to be "as good a Unionist as any other man."[17]

The reappearance of the New Orleans Typographical Union did not mean it had resumed its trade-unionist function. Even more than before the war, of course, it drew much of its leadership from craftsmen such as Pennsylvania-born John Irwin "Mac" McFarland, who had come to the city from Cincinnati. McFarland was well known throughout the West as "a genial, whole-souled, and high-minded gentleman, and made a host of friends during his sojourn in

New Orleans." For the duration of the war, the union periodically published announcements for a "semi-annual" meeting, though it resumed monthly meetings by the end of the war.[18]

Under the Federal occupation, economic conditions proved generally quite grim for everything not immediately necessary to the war effort. The Federal forces held a large city, a key port, but with the hinterland still in possession of the enemy. By early May, observers wrote of "the deplorable state of destitution and hunger of the mechanics and working classes in this city." Unionists pointed out that "this hunger does not pinch the wealthy and influential, the leaders of the rebellion, who have gotten up this war, and are now endeavoring to prosecute it, without regard to the starving poor, the working man, his wife and child." "Men of Louisiana!" declared the authorities, "Workingmen, property holders, merchants, and citizens of the United Sates of whatever nation you may have had birth, how long will you uphold these flagrant wrongs, and by inaction, suffer yourselves to be made the surfs [sic] of these leaders?"[19]

In a remarkably short period, though, conditions became wonderfully confused. Radical Unionism remained anchored to appointments at the Customs House by the Department of Treasury, under Secretary Salmon P. Chase. As such, it promised limited independence and remained largely subject to the army with its strategy of keeping blacks "free" but legally bound by contracts. The army, meanwhile, had returned plantation slaves back to their work as bound, contracted labor. In short order, then, Southern whites clashed politically with the army to promote a more radical, overt, interracial political reconstruction of the state.[20]

From November 1862, the whites had organized a Republican party and were holding open meetings. The Lincoln administration appointed Thomas J. Durant attorney general for the new loyal government. The Pennsylvania-born lawyer and Fourierist socialist emerged briefly as perhaps the most strident voice of New Orleans radicalism. Though he had served in the local Confederate militia, he had opposed secession and never really abandoned his Unionism. Under the occupation, Durant was the mastermind of the Friends of Universal Suffrage. A Saint-Simonian socialist, Jean-Charles Houzeau placed his *New Orleans Tribune* in service of rational new democratic utopia. By the fall of 1864, another socialist, Sebastian Seiler, wrote to Carl Schurz of the necessity of ensuring both black suffrage and radical land reform.[21] The movement gained impressive proportions but wanted more than the military occupation wished to deliver.

All of this fundamentally reshaped the black community of New Orleans. The peculiar conditions there had allowed for the rise of a caste of *gens de couleur*, free blacks who functioned in a small subculture distinct from the enslaved African Americans. When the war began they had organized themselves to assist in the local defense of the community under the secessionists, who stupidly rejected the offer. With the Union occupation the military authorities embraced the *Corps d'Afrique*, reorganizing it into regiments of United States Colored Troops. As we have seen, the Boston trade unionist, Second Lieutenant Samuel F. H. Learned, helped officer them.[22] The war confronted black New Orleans with what could only be a common fate.

War and emancipation created a new common identity among African Americans and sanctioned the embrace of that identity by those who could not have done so earlier. One of Dewitt Roberts's fellow Typographical Unionists in New Orleans responded to the Union occupation by acknowledging his Afro-Creole origins. A worker on Houzeau's paper, John Clovis Laizer, became an important figure in the secondary leadership of the emergent black community there.[23]

Union motives, however, reflected complex and often contradictory interests. The military bureaucracy, for example, had its own agenda. It engaged in the occupation with absolutely no interest in radical social transformation, and every desire to perform only the most minimal political functions. From their perspective, the demands of organized mechanics for things like exemption from military service were simply troublesome. By the end of 1862, when General Nathaniel P. Banks—a Yankee industrialist and Democrat—took charge of the occupation, the army began moving rapidly to slow, if not stop, this dynamic; the military officials began allowing the former movers and shakers of the city to come back. In August 1863 Stith returned to the city "from Fort Pickens on parole, where he had been confined since last September as a State prisoner." In short order, he had reestablished his old base of power in the Typographical Union, which abandoned its trade-union function for the war's duration.[24]

Former Mayor Monroe had no such luck among his screwmen, workmen who would use their muscle and mechanical lifts to "screw" the cotton bales and freight into position on the steamboats. With the depleted white workforce, the new black wage earners in the city disproportionately took the fewer jobs with less regularity of work on the riverfront. Their predominance on the waterfront provided a basis comparable to the same kind of power the whites had before the war. In January 1865 a "convention of colored men" simply refused to recognize the new government. In alliance with them the *New Orleans Tribune* opposed military regulation of labor and advocated the right of all workers to make the best arrangement.[25] The war closed in New Orleans with a racially mixed strike demonstrating that a more complete reconstruction still remained possible.

Nashville—Occupation and Industrialization

The Federal occupation of another community, Nashville, transformed it completely. The census of 1860 had counted seventeen thousand residents of the Tennessee capital, but, like most Southern cities, it relied for its skilled workforce—primarily young men from the North and Europe. Antebellum printers and tailors had an early history of unions and strikes, with other occupations, such as ironworkers doing the same before as the war neared.[26] The population boomed with secession and the war, as newcomers arrived, driven or drawn there by circumstances entirely beyond their control.

In February 1862 much of the white population fled before the Union army. The Confederates "destroyed everything in the shape of machinery for manufacturing purposes, stores, etc—but most particularly did the retreating enemies employ themselves in making complete their work of destruction in the shops and manufactories attached to the Nashville and Chattanooga and the Tennessee and Alabama Railroads." By the summer, the Federals concentrated "a few locomotives and a small number of cars" and briefly opened lines into Huntsville and Stevenson in Alabama. Although the Confederate counteroffensive into Kentucky in the fall effectively demolished much of this, it also left many Southerners, white and black, seeking refuge in Nashville from the slavery or Confederate conscription. A member of the Chicago Typographical Union, Mortimer C. Misener, reporting for the *Chicago Times*, wrote that "he has never seen the like" of the numbers entering into the Union lines.[27]

Over the next year, the Federal movement into eastern Tennessee and northern Georgia required the repair and extension of the railroad grid from Nashville. By late 1863 the authorities ran a system with 271 engines with three thousand cars running over "fifteen hundred miles of converging roads in good workable condition." It employed a civilian workforce of eighteen thousand teamsters, harnessmakers, wagon builders, butchers, bakers, printers, clerks, engineers, firemen, bridge builders, car builders, carpenters, blacksmiths, stone masons, machinists, and laborers. Of these, about eight thousand lived and worked in a new community covering several miles in and around Nashville.[28]

On their way to and from the front, Whitlaw Reid of the *Cincinnati Gazette* and Benjamin Cummings Truman of the *New York Times* described the new industrial behemoth at Nashville. The massive Locomotive and Machine Department employed three thousand, and the Car Department fifteen thousand. Various foundries, blacksmith shops, and specialized workplaces to make patterns, paint, glass, and upholstery supplemented these, as did an "immense storehouse." The complex kept several thousand freight cars rolling and could perform repairs on almost three dozen locomotives at a time. They also built specialized hospital carriages, a headquarters car with a kitchen, dining saloon, sleeping apartment, wash-room, and water-closet, an office, and a "gunboat car" to carry twenty men with repeating rifles and "a six-pounder." It used five hundred carpenters and others just to build "the large lodging houses and dining halls with the attached forty barracks" and "at least a hundred negro cabins, the entire collection making quite a respectable town."[29]

An anonymous union blacksmith offered a less triumphalist view in his letters to *Fincher's Trades' Review*. He had "worked for the Government these last five or six years in several different places," most recently as a blacksmith in the Brooklyn Navy Yard. In early July 1864 he contracted "to work in the United States military railroad machine shop at Nashville, which proved to be "the meanest place I ever got into." The contractors sent agents in the North—workers called them "man catchers," like those who had seized fugitive slaves. Paid by the head, they promised high wages and never asked about the abilities of those they hired. Once they got to Tennessee, the War Department paid the men in vouchers that could be cashed for 15 percent to cash. The new arrival also had to "lend" the master mechanic fifty dollars to one hundred dollars, "and give a few glasses of rum to boot." The superintendent of one department ignored agreements on overtime wages, forced his men to work ten hours on Saturday, kept back their mail, and provided them short rations. The system "detains men here against their will, by refusing them a discharge when it is demanded."[30]

Off the job, the worker faced more disappointments. Only some lived in the barracks the officials had shown Truman, while most crowded into "mess houses—or what the men term a shebang." These lived "thick with vermin" in the upper half-story in shanties, "where you can see daylight through the seams, and be occasionally refreshed with a shower of rain and snow descending on their beds." Poor rations enabled officials to make money for "extras, to put on the table." The hospital showcased for visitors, with "accommodations for four hundred" and cost five thousand dollars monthly to operate, for which the employers deducted twenty thousand dollars monthly from workers' pay. Because the bosses had to issue a military pass for a worker to leave the city by government transport, the sick workers could have no options but "to die." Whether sick or not, workers found themselves subject to an income tax based on what they would make for a full month's labor. The blacksmith correspondent observed that three months in such conditions could reduce workers "almost to skeletons."[31]

"There is no protection for life and property in this place," complained the blacksmith. "The deaths by murder and violence average about twenty per week, and I am sorry to say that our soldiers play their part in these crimes—making victims alike of Union men and rebels." Conditions there proved so dismal that "very few workmen will stop here any length of time: for they become disgusted with the tyranny and rank injustice which prevails." By November, he had become "what they call here an 'old hand,'" he said. "Yet I have only been here four months. The faces are all new to me, with one or two exceptions." By December he hoped "to leave this God-forsaken place, where corruption, bloodshed and anarchy abound." The writer blamed "the injustice, corruption, tyranny and fraud" on "petty officials," who "would sell their God and their country for the almighty dollar." *Fincher's* called for "a prompt investigation of these charges" and deplored "such wrongs on a human being, be he white or black."[32]

Beneath the surface, though, Nashville was a company town where the employer had the power of life and death over its workers. "When they come here they find themselves under the rule of martial law," reported the trade unionist, "and if they stand up for their rights, they are given in charge of the guard, who pushes them into a guard-house at the point of the bayonet." Early on, he realized, "If we stand up to ask our rights as mechanics, we are put under military arrest and threatened with imprisonment in the State Penitentiary." For this reason, he said, the workers could not "think of a strike here, for we would be surrounded by regiments of soldiers immediately."[33]

In late September 1864 workers finally imposed some limits on the power of management. When the new master machinist scheduled an additional hour of Saturday work without overtime, he found that "the men promptly refused to work 10 hours on Saturday, preferring to [lose] the hour, rather than submit to such an unjust and arbitrary rule." At about this time, another tried to get the men working on Sunday without overtime, threatening "to put us on drill every Sunday instead of allowing us to go to church," but workers still refused, "except a few scabs." Within days, the workers did what they could, though, "warning all misguided mechanics from coming to Nashville." The individual writer acted because "Duty to my fellow mechanics urges me to warn them against the exercise of any tyrannical power or imposition on the part of the employers towards them." However, he believed that "thousands are desirous that this warning should be published." Support for *Fincher's Trades' Review* expanded into a support club of seventy-nine members in wartime Nashville.

After the first letter appeared, the local correspondent reported the reactions of his co-workers. He told the editors "your valuable paper is rightly appreciated by the mechanics of Nashville, and especially by those who work in the Military Railroad shops of the Government." "The boys all like the paper and you would have as many more subscribers, but the uncertainty of the mails, or some other cause of irregularity, discourages them." Publication of the first letter "pleased us all," he said, but "the officials did not like it very well. Some bit their lips and frowned—others read it with dismay, but not one of them had the courage or manhood to contradict a single item it contained. They dare not do it. True, there was one truckling sycophant who undertook to write an article in reply for the *Daily Press* in Nashville, but he was so ashamed of his dirty work, that he dared not put his name to it, and no notice was taken of it."[34]

In short, a labor movement stirred, even under this industrial authoritarianism. The printers' union had remarkably survived slavery, secession, Confederate martial law, and Federal martial law to send three representatives to the

May 1864 convention of the National Typographical Union. The seventy-nine workers sustained a support club for *Fincher's Trades' Review*, likely a certain core of supporters for Fincher's Machinists and Blacksmiths' Union. When the Brotherhood of Locomotive Engineers became public in 1865, it already had a division at Nashville, indicating that the secret Brotherhood of the Footboard existed there during the war. Its delegate to the 1865 convention was likely William H. Russell, a thirty-seven-year-old Indiana-born engineer at the start of the war, a family man with a wife and four daughters, who sent *Fincher's Trades' Review* money from Nashville.[35]

Many other figures from labor history passed through Nashville's brave new world without spending much time there. *Fincher's* financial contributors at Nashville included D. W. Magee, almost surely David Wood Magee, the Pennsylvania-born commander of the Eighty-Sixth Illinois from Peoria. His predecessor, Colonel David D. Irons, had been a national reformer working for the local railroad before taking the regiment into the field at Perryville. After assignment to garrison Nashville, Irons fell fatally ill, leaving Magee to take the Eighty-Sixth into the Stone's River and in the Tullahoma campaign. Magee's support for *Fincher's* did not get in the way of his ending the war a brevet brigadier general. The regimental surgeon who would have tended Irons, Dr. Marcellus M. Hooten, came from the war to help lead an independent farmers' political movement and the Greenback Party in Illinois.[36] The legacy of Union military service was clearly more complex than that shaped for it after the war.

John M. Farquhar returned to duty and a commission at Nashville, not far from where the NTU had elected him president, serving on court-martial panels. The New Hampshire–born former Methodist minister, Professor Damon Young Kilgore arrived as an army paymaster between Nashville and the outlying garrisons in northern Alabama, taking with him the Vermont-born former Universalist James Martin Peebles, both spiritualists interested in labor reform. Down the line at Chattanooga, engineers organized a division of their union, and Thomas Lloyd, the former president of the American Miners Association, organized coal production for the army.[37]

* * *

Even as secessionists warned of imminent plebeian revolution across the North, the black and white workers in the South strove to make their own conditions as tolerable as possible. The practice of trade unionism showed remarkable tenacity even in the face of massive bloodshed and siege. At the Confederate capital, the "confidential operator with General Lee" and a thrice-wounded young Mississippian, Charles A. Gaston, organized his co-workers into a "Southern Telegraphic Association," which engaged in job actions, including refusals to send messages not for military of governmental purposes.[38] Nevertheless, whatever successes workers had in the South, they struggled amidst the social disintegration of their section and experienced none of the rapid mass organization that took place in the North.

Southern workers usually got only minimal encouragement from the Federal army that occupied the South. As the war continued, slaves fleeing to freedom found the responses of Federal officers increasingly less noncommittal, but not necessarily welcoming. Union officers treated all Southerners engaged in doing something useful to Confederate arms as little more than contested resources. Most notoriously—and scandalously for Horace Greeley's *New York Tribune*—Union troops driving on Atlanta encountered a small industrial complex near Roswell, Georgia. With a disregard of civilians anticipating the conflicts of the twentieth century, they removed the men, women, and children associated with the industry to what amounted to house arrest in Kentucky. African Americans often fared little better, were themselves treated more as potential assets rather than allies.[39] Notwithstanding the rhetoric of rulers or the republicanism of their intent, war had its own hard logic that bore down most heavily on those who labored.

CHAPTER 9

The State Power

Workers and the New Authorities, North and South

Wartime spending created an economy intimately involved with government, which is how the delegation of strikers from the Navy Yard found themselves meeting with President Abraham Lincoln. They reported that "the worthy old gentleman had not left all his sympathy for laboring men with his maul and wedges in the prairie State." Being from a rural area, the president explained, "he had never participated in a strike. The only one he had ever beheld was a strike among the shoemakers of Haverhill, Massachusetts, some 12 or 15 years ago, in which the shoemakers succeeded in worsting their bosses." The president listened patiently to the strikers. After hearing them out, he replied that "he could do nothing as President, but as Abraham Lincoln his sympathies were with us." The neutrality of the administration in a strike affecting war production typified its policies.[1] Yet, North or South, workers faced the idea that government could and should be the ultimate arbiter of labor conflicts, notwithstanding a culture permeated by laissez-faire mythologies.

Just as the dynamics of the war established more centralized political power and an increasingly national market, so, too, it tended to standardize the treatment of workers' organizations. As on a battlefield, similar obstacles and problems inspired uniform responses, and employers began regularly calling upon the state power against their workers. Their newly acquired wartime power to impose the will of the owners on the workers at the point of the bayonet gave civil authorities the opportunity to make themselves even more valuable to those owners. At least given the general secessionist view of labor, official Confederate repression was more consistent with its rhetoric and proved particularly reliant on direct military measures, especially as the prospects of their war became increasingly desperate.

The National Dimension

By late 1863 the nation's capital faced "a demand from all classes of mechanics for higher wages" that moved not only women but blacks. As at Boston, New York, and Philadelphia, the waterfront became an epicenter of this new discontent. Workers organized to thwart a scheme to raise "the hours now worked in the Navy-yard" to those in the private shipyards nearby. They also won more pay "in view of the largely increased expenses of living." The riggers walked off the job to secure three dollars a day, and "most of the colored hands employed in the anchor shop struck for higher wages," demanding an increase from $1.50 to $1.75 a day. In February 1864 "about half the helpers in the blacksmith shop" at the Navy Yard were on strike.[2]

Carpenters, masons, and laborers working on the extension of the Treasury went on strike against rules to lengthen the workday. They struck over the issue, though one press account hinted that the lower-level management had fired four hundred strikers. Still, after the workers held fast for a week, Secretary of the Treasury Salmon P. Chase "expressed regret that they had quit work before waiting on him . . . and gave them assurances of a satisfactory solution of the difficulty."[3]

The "monstrous prices of food, fuel and rents" sparked a November 7 strike by about sixty bookbinders in the Government Printing Office to raise wages from sixteen to eighteen dollars a week and resurrected the idea of reducing the workday to eight hours. The walkout would also stop work for "about the same number of girls, who are to-day, however, at work as usual." By December the press reported that "the girls employed at feeding the presses at the Government Printing Office" had gone on strike themselves to win eight dollars a week. When management "engaged boys at the rate offered to the girls, and boys were found in abundance," the girls went back to work.[4]

At first, even the old Columbia Typographical Union voted to join the bookbinders with "a general strike of all the fraternity in this city." A press estimate suggested that "should the bookbinders be successful in carrying their point, there will be a general strike of all the other departments of the Government office, which now employs about 600 persons, male and female." Authorities at the Government Printing Office pointed out that law prohibited their paying more than the private establishments and actually "made strenuous efforts to induce private establishments to advance prices in accordance with the increased cost of living." Perhaps for this reason, on November 8 the union reconsidered and postponed joining the strike.[5]

The local simply could never forget its standing as the oldest and most venerable labor organization in the United States. When the new national union had not offered to give the Columbia Typographical Union the designation of Number One, the printers at the capital had chosen to remain independent of the NTU. However, the wartime expansion of business and jobs in the trade at the capital brought many into Washington from the outside. In April 1864 the Columbia Typographical Union extended a gracious olive branch to the national union with an offer to host the 1865 national convention.[6]

The NTU convened for 1864 at Louisville in May. It elected officers from twenty-one states and seated delegates from new locals at Springfield and Quincy in Illinois. The union took note of many locals that had not communicated or paid fees to the national organization in two years, revoking the charters of those locals in the north while exempting the Southern locals owing to the excuse of the war. The body also voted to recommend that to all its affiliates "the immediate initiation of such steps as will secure the formation of Trades Unions for the mutual protection and support of the working men of all trades."[7]

Always a strangely dualistic organization, the National Silk and Fur Hat Finishers' Association began coming apart, as wartime demand for fur hats increased radically. Although the union continued to recruit and charter new locals, the employers pushed the felt hat finishers—"soft hatters"—from union standards on wages and apprenticeships, but continued to organize new locals. The silk hatters appealed to the 1864 convention over the decline in union standards and their own possible loss of power within the union. The national union sustained the expulsions of those having not served a proper apprenticeship and fined the Connecticut organizations for not enforcing union standards among the silk hatters. In reality, though, the union could not prevent the employers from making the uniform price bill a dead letter.[8]

Other national unions acted as well. The Machinists and Blacksmiths convened in the fall of 1863 in the midst of the national upsurge. The National Iron Molders' Union had held its fifth annual convention at Buffalo in January 1864. Perhaps its most important achievement was the election of William H. Sylvis as president, one of those labor leaders most committed to organizing black and female workers. The Cigar Makers National Union formed in 1864 and had sufficient strength to provide the young Samuel Gompers with an education in unionism after the war.[9]

Other unions groped toward a larger scale of organization as well. Striking curriers at Salem and South Danvers anchored a national convention in mid-January 1864 where organizations in six states launched a Currier's Protective Union. Committees of coachmakers' unions from Baltimore and Washington agreed upon "articles of alliance." Baltimore lagged in their ratification owing to its preoccupation with an effort to secure a 20 percent pay increase in the city.

We know that the National Carpenters and Joiners held a national convention only because they referred to their 1869 gathering as the fifth.[10]

The New England strike wave continued into 1864. Miners at West Stockbridge, molders at Providence, mill hands at Warren, foundry workers at Stinchcomb's in Maine, and hod carriers at Rockland went on strike, as did Portland bricklayers and printers. At Lewiston, machinists and blacksmiths organized, and the carpenters tried to win a 25 percent increase and reduce their hours from ten to nine, but the local *Evening Journal* refused even to print demands.

Government and Military Power vs. Labor in the Union

In the intensified war of 1864 Federal authorities used the power of the state and the army to deal with labor demands. The policy came easy in the occupied South. Memphis had labor troubles the first summer of the war, when boss shoemakers moved to break the local union. The Memphis Typographical Union voted to tar and feather any members sympathetic to the Union, challenging other Southern labor organizations to do the same. Before the city fell on June 5, 1862, the union boasted that sixty of its ninety members had joined the Confederate defenses.[11] Even allowing for the conflation of mandatory militia service with voluntary enlistment, the claim had been exaggerated.

After the occupation, the Memphis printers sought to refocus on its original purposes. With S. P. Bassett gone, J. P. Synott told Union General Alvin P. Hovey that the union had "remained neutral during the present civil war" and asked that members not be required to take a loyalty oath. Hovey's "respectful answer" asked about the meaning of their professed neutrality in the face of vigilante violence against Unionists. "If you ask the protection of the broad wings of our old eagle, you must help to feed and support the bird," he wrote. "No class of men exercise such a vast influence over the public mind as the craft to which you belong, and you owe it to yourselves and posterity to advocate and aid the right."[12]

The government authorities never had much patience with its own workers, particularly in industries deemed war-related. In January 1864 the telegraph operators had the audacity to petition—just petition—for higher wages. The army returned the request, noting that it "can be looked upon in no other light than as a conspiracy by the parties, against the Government." They allowed that the workers could be replaced singly as other qualified people turned up, but warned that, should they try to leave as a group, they would be jailed and treated as conspirators.[13] Thus, the government's claiming to be committed to abolishing involuntary servitude created an irony lost on nobody.

On a larger scale, employers regularly called on the government to send troops against coal miners. Much of this centered in western Pennsylvania, but extended down into the area of Cumberland, Maryland, and even in Monongahela County, [West] Virginia. At Cumberland the authorities seized twenty-five of the more militant strikers and incarcerated them at Fort Delaware. By summer, the government also had a committee of striking Pennsylvania miners incarcerated at Fort Mifflin. The now-organized locomotive engineers reported that the railroads had stockpiled coal and then cut wages to provoke miners' strikes that would draw the army into the field against them.[14]

The government acted promptly when it faced a strike at Cold Springs, opposite West Point on the Hudson River. The West Point Foundry, where Robert P. Parrott produced his remarkable and innovative new heavy, rifled artillery, employed about twelve hundred laborers. About three hundred of them organized "a Laboring Men's Union," which requested an increase from one dollar or $1.25 per day to $1.50 per day. When Parrott refused the union and its supporters walked off with enough manpower to bring production to a standstill on March 10–12. Parrott remained unyielding, even when the local clergy sought to bring the two sides together and cooler heads pointed out that "injury to life and property may ensue," should the strikers be driven to desperate measures. "Delegates" came up from New York by train, and rumors spread "that military assistance will be required from West Point." In the end, the army broke the strike and imposed martial law on the town with several companies of troops. The authorities arrested four strike leaders, held them seven weeks at Fort Lafayette without a trial, though they requested one, and ultimately blacklisted three of the four.[15]

The relationship of the work to the war seems less clear in the strike wave that swept St. Louis in March and April 1864. Tailors walked out over an increase in piecework pay that would get them $2.50 a day. They also wanted union recognition and an end to wartime hiring of girls as apprentices when they received less than equal pay. After a month, the union rejected a settlement that did not meet all their demands. When the Machinists and Blacksmiths went on strike, their national president, Jonathan S. Fincher, spoke in the rotunda of the courthouse. The crowd included stove and hollowware molders, machine molders, brass finishers and molders, carpenters and joiners, ship carpenters and caulkers, brick molders, steam- and gas-pipe fitters, paper hangers, horse shoers, plasterers, painters, tinners, and printers.[16]

As in New York the previous fall, the strikes cascaded through St. Louis. The ship carpenters and caulkers went out to get a raise from five dollars to $5.50 per day, but the military turned up to protect strikebreakers, and most of the strikers had to return to work at the old rates after about a week. There were also strikes of carpenters and joiners and of the local Missouri lodges of the American Miners' Association.[17]

Most dramatically, the molders squared off once more with Giles and Oliver Filley's Excelsior Stove Works. This served to pit Republican bosses not against working-class Democratic voters but against as ardently radical Republican voters as the party's German base in the city. The union objected to replacing men who had gone to the front with boys. The employers quietly recruited twenty-five German molders to break the anticipated strike, but the union persuaded eighteen of the newcomers to go elsewhere. In retaliation, the Filleys fired Richard L. Parker, one of the strike leaders. Meanwhile, shoemakers joined the other strikes, winning a 25 percent pay hike in mid-April.[18]

On April 26, Federal General William Starke Rosecrans—a manufacturer when not in uniform—issued General Order No. 65, declaring strikes an "attack upon private rights and the military power of the nation by organizations led by bad men." Most of the text railed against the union's demand for a closed shop, the eight-hour workday, and other changes that had "no relation to the matter of wages . . . but to the internal management of such establishments." Rosecrans extended the protection of the army over employers and strikebreakers against any attempt "directly or indirectly . . . to deter or prevent any person from working" and imposed sanctions against anyone who tried to "watch or hang about such establishments" in aid of an "association or combination" of workers. It outlaws "combinations . . . to prevent journeymen mechanics, apprentices, and laborers from working in manufacturing establishments, except on terms prescribed to the proprietors thereof, by parties not interested therein." It further declared that violations would "be punished as a military offense." Worse, Rosecrans wanted "the names of all persons who have, since the 15th day of March, 1864, left their employ to engage in any such combination or association" together with their "places of residence" and "a list, by name, of all who have taken an active part in any combination to control the conduct of any such establishment."[19] Although claiming to fight against "involuntary servitude," Rosecrans at St. Louis sounded no different than his Confederate counterparts at Richmond.

The impact of Rosecrans provided yet another reason for the split that shattered the Republican coalition in the city. The German press excoriated the general for what the *Anzeiger des Westens* called its "elastic nature" and the *Neue Zeit* as "military arbitrariness." The *Westliche Post* decried it as "an attack on the freedom of labor and the right of association." The *Republican* and *Democrat* opted for the discretion of merely publishing translations of what the Germans wrote.[20]

Interestingly, the emancipationist Republican *Democrat* and the Copperhead Democratic *Republican* became beneficiaries of the order, when their printers went on strike. The defiant bosses declared "their independence of the Typographical Union." They then dishonestly reported the union "practically disbanded," leaving "each printer to make his bargain with his employer in the natural way without interference." Meanwhile, Rosecrans "detailed a number of soldiers who were printers to take the strikers places." When Lincoln found out about this, he supposedly responded: "Order those soldiers back to duty in the ranks. The servants of the Federal government shall not interfere with the legitimate demands of labor so long as I am President."[21]

On May 2, Charles L. Bernays of the Radical Republican *Anzeiger* sent a copy of the order with long protest to Lincoln. "What has happened in St Louis?" he asked. "Nothing else, but what we see every five or six years making its appearance in all the English, French, and American workshops, what we witness at this very moment in New York, in Philadelphia, in Troy, in Albany, in Cincinnati and in Pittsburgh—to wit; a strike of the tailors, shoemakers, iron-moulders, wagoners and so forth." They had not struck for "disloyal purposes or to prevent work to be done which was ordered by the Government in the different shops." "We are not half through with the destruction of slavery," wrote Bernays, "and we already begin to attack free labor." After building its armies "from the working classes" and burdening them with "the greater part of taxation," he complained, "a military commander forbids them to associate as they use to do for more than half a century in order to improve their condition and to regulate their relations between themselves and their employers."[22]

Edwin Weston wrote to Lincoln from Cincinnati, addressing himself "as a mechanic in this city interested in getting up a mass meeting of workingmen" over the issue, and he begged "to inquire if this proceeding of Major Genrl. Rosecrans is sanctioned by yourself." Weston explained that "the strikes are not confined to St. Louis" for "this great labor movement, as workingmen call it, is universal." Weston warned that "you are loosing the influence of workingmen, and should a few more mishaps occur of this kind, the next election will find the administration 'out of employment.'" Cincinnati wanted "the wages of mechanics ought to 'go up' just as much as the necessaries of life, nor do they see any difference between mechanics combining to raise their wages, and capitalists combining to 'mark up' the price of their goods. It seems to the workingmen quite as reasonable to call in the military in once, the one case as in the other." The abolitionist *Cincinnati Daily Gazette* covered the rally of about two thousand in Court Street Market, as did the *Enquirer* and *Commercial*. Fincher spoke there and found considerable interest in a General Trades Assembly of the United States.[23]

The strikes at Louisville never quite reached the scale or militancy of those in St. Louis, but the level of organization appeared to have been very comparable. It proved sufficient for General Stephen G. Burbridge, another conservative Democratic commander, to find the actions of the molders especially objectionable. On May 19 Burbridge followed Rosecrans's example with a similar order.[24]

As would later be the case, government interventions against labor organizations moved workers to take a serious look at political action.

Government and Military Power vs. Labor in the Confederacy

The Confederates had no equivalent of emancipation to resolve its labor crisis and had early turned to the conscription of white men to address the demands of war. Events pressed the Confederacy more quickly and intensely, and it responded with an expansion of involuntary servitude a year before any conscription in the Union, and the latter remained far less important numerically. Given its founding principles, the Confederacy naturally exempted from the measure anyone who owned or managed more than twenty slaves. As one Confederate soldier recalled, the measure "raised the howl of 'rich man's war, poor man's fight.'"[25] Yet anything other than a very selective, privileged exemption would have made the labor crisis even worse.

The South likely experienced many larger and more pervasive labor movements than anything earlier in its history. The largest and most obvious was that of its enslaved workforce from the plantations into refugee camps or hiding. However, more traditional labor disputes took place as well, as in September 1863, when riverboat pilots on the Alabama River "struck for higher wages, demanding $600 per month—in consequence of this there are but few boats running."[26] The outcome is unclear, but most strikes in the wartime South did not end well for the workers.

Indeed, skilled labor had been rare enough in what became the Confederacy, and drafting whites to defend slave labor at home would not resolve this particularly acute version of the Southern labor crisis. Then, too, employers and managers in the Confederacy had little enough experience addressing labor discontent in the best of times, much less in the depths of losing a war. In the sedate world of the old crafts, a number of local typographical unions continued to function. In September, the Charleston local noted "for the third time within a few short months" the death of one of its members, and February 1862 marked the passing of A. S. Willington, probably the member of the Sixth George Reserve Battalion. Although Confederate soldiers continued to officer the local, some of the members still remained concerned about regulating conditions in growing industry in the city, particularly given the state of the economy.[27] Certainly, however small, Confederate labor organizations could have an impact on the war.

War knocked the antebellum Southern workplace to pieces, sometimes literally, and DeWitt C. Roberts and his old co-workers from New Orleans witnessed much of it. When the Federal artillery first fired on Vicksburg, the printers of the *Whig* determined to remain at work: "Bomb shells fell and exploded all around it, striking several of the neighboring houses, but our office was saved from being knocked into pi—by a very few feet—for which we are very thankful." Months later, the Union Army had enveloped the city. Along with many soldiers in the besieging army—who surely had diverse and complex notions of emancipation and liberty—some members of the Typographical Union manned the city's defenses, such as Roberts's old friend Lieutenant Daniel C. Byerly of the Thirtieth Louisiana, as well as Michael Bourke of the Twenty-First.[28]

Union victories nobbled the Southern economy and, with it, any prospects of individual success for white workingmen. After the Federals began to bombard Charleston in October 1863, Evans and Cogswell decided to move to Columbia, leaving Roberts in danger of losing his exemption from the draft. He hurried to Atlanta where he "had many friends, refugees from New Orleans" and a job on the *Southern Confederacy* of Albert Roberts (no relation). There, Roberts the Illinoian met Byerly, his old foreman, on his way to the front at Chattanooga. Defeat there closed Atlanta's coal supply and shut off the gas necessary to print the morning papers, again confronting Roberts with the prospect of conscription. In December, Roberts hurried through the winter to northern Mississippi, where he found himself, like so many other Unionist refugees, dependent on the help of blacks who fed him and gave him a ride.[29]

The first days of 1864 finally brought Roberts into the Union lines just outside of Memphis. "I was a printer who had been caught in the South at the beginning of the war," he explained to a Federal officer, "and had hitherto been unable to escape; and that I was now on my way home by way of Memphis." The officer laughed and said it was his duty to stop him, "but if he were sure I was a printer he would let me pass, for there was no telling what printers would not do."[30]

Behind him, Roberts left a South of chaotic possibilities. The military drama eclipsed the circumstances of labor on its various homefronts, though they were inexorably linked. In the South, labor shortages deepened the region's reliance on black slavery and drove the Confederate authorities to ever more draconian efforts to control white workers. Though not as severe, similar shortages afflicted the Union homefront, where workers had a far deeper tradition and experience of self-organization and militant action. The expansion of war goals to include emancipation would require a broader sense of what solidarity entailed, but, most immediately, organized workers strove toward the formulation and implementation of national standards of unionism.

As the weather warmed and the armies celebrated the spring by resuming the fighting back in Georgia, Robert's brother printers back in Atlanta faced ever-worsening conditions. Under the shadow of war and martial law, the Atlanta Typographical Union voted to raise wages $1.35 to $1.87 per thousand ems. The publishers asked for a postponement, then published a card, declaring:

> We are under the necessity of suspending temporarily the publication of our journals on account of the unreasonable demand made by the Typographical Union, the printers employed in our offices in Atlanta having raised their rates upon the present prices 50 per cent. This would require a greater tax upon the public than we are willing to impose. The price of newspapers is already large enough, and we feel that the sympathies of our readers will sustain our endeavors to protect their interest as well as our own. Arrangements will be made as soon as practicable for the resumption of our issue, and in the meantime the indulgence of the public is earnestly invoked.

Ominously, reports indicated that bosses got the military authorities to rescind the exemptions of the strikers, and the conscript officer had ordered them to muster in.[31]

Confederate authorities then did what the most conservative Federal officers had only threatened. As the Federal armies pressed on in early June, Georgia officials drafted the workers and placed them under one of the bosses against whom they had gone on strike. Newly commissioned Captain Albert Roberts, the editor of the *Southern Confederacy*, took charge of a Fulton County company raised in the "present emergency" by drafting the striking printers into the military.[32]

One of the oddest Confederate military units of the war, "Roberts' Exempts" included on its roster union printers from across the South who had been driven to Atlanta as the Federal army had moved against their cities. It seems to have included First Sergeant George W. Martin, who had been a member of the St. Louis local. Memphis printers included Sergeant John L. Nelson, and Privates A. W. Eilands, William Graham, H. J. Neville, George W. Verlander from New Orleans, Thomas C. Neville of Charleston, A. P. Prince of Montgomery, J. A. Patton of Columbia, J. V. Johnston and T. B. Reynolds of Nashville, W. C. Whitmire of Atlanta, W. S. D. Wikle of Macon, as well as Charles J. White of Savannah. It also had several members of the Jackson, Mobile, and Montgomery unions, alongside a few members of unions in the North, such as Nathan S. Hales of Philadelphia, Albert Harmon of Boston, and Sylvanus D. Lines of New Haven. Some of the printers had earlier service, such as Verlander in the Sixteenth Battalion, Louisiana Infantry, and Eilands in Georgia's Third Battalion (State Guards) and the militia, in which capacity he had guarded the arsenal at Columbus. White had been among the Confederate defenders of Fort Wagner.

The continued flight of many Confederate craftsmen before the Federal advance had also allowed for the formation of new unions. In June those at Macon met "for the purpose of organizing a Printers' Union." They wrote and adopted a constitution and bylaws, taking "all measures . . . to insure a permanent organization of the Macon Typographical Union." The local continued throughout the rest of the war and beyond.[33]

As the Federal armies closed on Richmond, labor there showed a particularly reasonable desire to escape the city. On July 8, the authorities reported five operatives from the Tredegar Works "captured near Bottom's Bridge, while attempting to escape to the Yankees." They committed the runaway workers to Castle Thunder, "where it is very hot and there is no ice water." By September Confederate officials not only detained them in the act but arrested an employee at the arsenal, workers in the medical and commissary departments, a soldier, and a citizen, all "on the charge of attempting to go to the enemy's lines." In November they caught three more "workmen at the Tredegar Iron Works . . . trying to escape to the enemy's lines."[34]

Dissatisfaction among its unskilled laborers became epidemic. The "Irish grave diggers at Hollywood Cemetery" went on strike for higher wages." They were reportedly making seven dollars a day, but in Confederate money, of course. The bosses replaced them with "a lot of negroes." When the strikers attacked them "and drove them off" in early August, the authorities brought in "a force of negroes from the penitentiary," convict black labor, possibly even captured "colored volunteers."[35]

Certainly, Confederate authorities had already turned to Federal prisoners in hopes of tapping a source of more docile labor. "We want men in the field," declared the *Richmond Examiner*, "while thousands of our best troops are detailed to perform necessary labor in our workshops. Cannot the mechanics among the prisoners be put in the places of our detailed artisans in a number of trades, and the detailed men sent to the field?" The end of prisoner exchanges, it noted, condemned the workers among them to the "wearing idleness and monotony of prison life." Moreover, the forced labor of prisoners might reduce the pathetic wages of the shoemakers. This would be, of course, for the benefit of the poor, because "the rates now charged for shoes by shoemakers in this city put these absolutely necessary articles beyond the reach of the poor."[36]

In October, the press reported "another Strike among the Female Operatives at the Confederate States laboratory" on Brown's Island. While the goals of the earlier walkout remained unclear, "several hundred female employees . . . struck for an equality of wages." The bosses paid "young unmarried females, without incumbrance" five dollars a day; "those married and with families to support" got seven dollars daily. Both also got "three pounds of flour per week, at fifty cents per pound, and one pound of meat at four dollars per pound." The strikers, including those who were getting seven dollars, walked off, demanding that everyone get that rate. A committee of the strikers presented their grievances to Captain William N. Smith, superintendent of the laboratory, who favored the concession. However, Lieutenant Colonel William Leroy Broun, commanding at the arsenal, "would not yield, and yesterday an advertisement of '300 females wanted,' to take the place of the strikers, appeared in the city papers."[37]

Perhaps nothing quite revealed the desperation of Confederate labor more than their efforts to organize a telegraphers union in the army itself. In late 1863 such a Confederacy-wide effort started at Augusta, though Union military successes had fragmented communications and the prospects for such a trade organization. In May 1864 Mississippi operators attempted to anchor a new South-western Telegraphic Association. Later, in January 1865, a group based at Charleston tried to start a Confederate States Telegraphic Club.[38]

* * *

Such uses of government power provoked a natural reaction from a long artisan republican legacy stretching from Benjamin Franklin to Horace Greeley. It certainly began pushing workers and their organizations toward a new kind of labor politics. The tendency of the military to take the lead in such repressive measures forced workers to think of the problems they faced as national rather than local. As a result, the experience of workers under the Union or the Confederacy increasingly involved negotiating their way past officials who tended to equate "the cause" for which they contended with the will of the employers. Their attitudes did not necessarily regard working people as their enemies, for they accorded them insufficient power to merit such attention. Labor would emerge from the war as objects to be managed.

From the depths of the war, Doctor A. G. Parker explained the meaning of emancipation for the future of labor solidarity. "As we advance the interest of others we advance our own," he wrote. "Our armies have never been so successful as since the declaration of emancipation." Yet slavery had been "the very cap-sheaf of the bottomless pit." In getting at the truth behind "Aristocracy and Democracy," he suggested that two classes ruled on either side of the Mason-Dixon Line. "One class says, Cotton is king; the other says the mighty Dollar." God, he added, "never made kings and rulers, but men and women." "If the ability of this nation was commensurate with its avarice," he added in frustration, "they would make a ladder to heaven and tear up the golden streets to sell in Wall Street."[39]

PART IV

Shaping the Postwar Order

Come, let our voices raise
In thankful songs of praise
  For Union's might.
May we as brothers kind,
In Union strong combined,
United heart and mind,
  Uphold the right.

—IRA STEWARD, "In Union's Might"

CHAPTER 10

The Emergence of Labor Reform

Class, Citizenship, and Politics

Toward the close of 1863, some officers of the beleaguered Boston unions joined local radicals in fielding an independent "Labor Reform" ticket for the upcoming municipal elections. After having advocated class politics for thirty years through his *Boston Investigator*, Horace Seaver had organized weekly forums for years, many of which addressed labor issues. "How is it that some men receive only half allowance for doing double work," he kept asking, "while others receive double or quadruple allowance merely for looking on?" In fact, "the producers of wealth . . . always superior in numbers" permitted themselves to be victimized by elites. "If the working class had always been as enlightened as any other class of the community," wondered Seaver, "is it not certain that the institutions of society, framed and established under the influence of such enlightenment, would have been calculated to promote their interests at least equally with the interests of any other class of the community?"[1] By December, such ideas began getting a hearing, and a pattern of sporadic labor forays into independent politics began.

Contrary to the dearest national mythologies, the central role of government in economic development and the lives of American workers had already become increasingly obvious. The strike wave of late 1863 swept workers at Boston and New York into the civil life of the republic. By then, though, the idea of Labor Reform politics had flickered episodically as far as the western territories. In search of solutions, growing numbers of workers revived and revised old ideas of cooperation, communities, and land reform alongside the eight-hour day and other concerns that would preoccupy the working class thought through the rest of the century.

Working-Class Citizenship: Boston and New York

The *Boston Investigator* of Seaver and Josiah Mendum primarily promoted free thought, the idea that the superstition and religion bogged the world and human civilization from the development of a rational solution to problems. They also hosted regular Sunday meetings, Seaver having recently lectured on "Life, Revolutionary Services, and Religion of Thomas Paine." This provided a platform for other old radicals, such as the former preacher and radical abolitionist Dr. Leroy Sunderland and the veteran Chartist John C. Cluer, who had been a prominent labor agitator in the region during the 1840s but had since turned almost entirely to abolitionist work, mostly with local blacks, eventually participating in some dramatic slave rescues. His daughter Susie had just entered her teens but worked with him, doing recitations and songs, which eventually led her to a career on the stage.[2]

The troubles on the Boston waterfront later in the year moved these Boston freethinkers to schedule Sunday discussions of the labor question. Women dominated the meeting on female labor, but the strike on the docks created an immediacy that brought local union officers including William F. Falls, the machinist, to the platform. The radicals voted "for reducing the number of hours in each day's work at mechanical labor of all kinds to eight," and organized "a general protective association of trades," and discussed "a workingmen's ticket for municipal officers to be supported at the ensuing election."[3]

Despite some attrition among union officers concerned that politics might be divisive, the core of the group went forward. Andrew McCoubrey of the printers union called to order the meeting of December 10 and nominated Chester R. Merrill of Machinists and Blacksmiths to preside. Someone then handed McCoubrey a letter from Merrill declining to participate, and H. H. Boardman, another printer, warned that politicians hoped "to create disaffection." Nevertheless, the meeting nominated a ticket headed by Samuel Rogers Spinney, who hoped "to have the workman and his employer—Labor and Capital—go hand in hand, and not hostile to each other."[4]

These Labor Reformers locally faced a Republican Party so secure in power that it saw little need to make concessions to labor, and workers hoped only to register a protest. Their candidates—Spinney and Thomas C. Amory Jr.—had long been involved in city government, and the reformers made other nominations jointly with various opposition currents. In the end, Spinney won 613 votes, but the victorious candidate got 6,206 and the Democrats 2,142. Over half of Spinney's votes came from the Twelfth Ward, though workers in the First, Second, and Tenth Wards showed some support. *Fincher's Trades' Review* concluded that labor should avoid politics as divisive, and Jonathan C. Fincher himself came to the city to hammer home the point.[5]

Labor reform remained central after the election. Boston radicals continued to provide the labor movement with a weekly platform. Cluer spoke on "The Rights of Labor," and his daughter read Thomas Hood's "The Song of the Shirt." Another featured a "debate on the Labor Question before a crowded audience of ladies and gentlemen, notwithstanding the weather was unfavorable." An out-of-town speaker discussed "the particulars of the movements of the mechanics in New York City in their late attempts to increase their rates of wages." Later claimed as a pioneering anarchist, Lysander Spooner—who had argued, almost alone at first, for the constitutionality of abolitionism—spoke on January 10 about "the Wrongs of Labor and their Remedy." They urged workers to bring coal to the city cooperatively to sell it at cost.[6] In short order, these Bostonians built a new Labor Reform Association.

Political conditions differed in New York. The same sort of veteran radicals active in Boston battled to participate in the wartime Unionist coalition in New York. Ultimately, they established their own organizations that included the German Union League and representatives of trade unions. By November and December 1863, other Fourierists such as Charles Sears, with land reformers Joshua K. Ingalls and Henry Beeny, helped to raise volunteers for the army.[7]

There, too, a vicious dispute in the Navy Yard among radicalized workers was raised. One of their leaders, Moses Platt, "made an extravagant speech about capital and labor," calling on workers to throw off their yoke. At a meeting of a Brooklyn trade union meeting, one of the members rose to discuss working-class political action, adding that "the nearest approach to success was made in France during the last revolution, when the combination of labor became so strong that capitalists in all countries became alarmed and combined to put it down, and they did so through Napoleon."[8]

Employers reacted coherently when workers beyond the Navy Yard showed signs of militancy: stonecutters, blacksmiths, carpenters and laborers went on strike, as did painters and hatters, while piano makers faced a lockout, and plasterers, molders, jewelers, machinists, and musicians organized for a pay increase. A "Farmers' Protective Union of the counties of Kings, Queens, Suffolk, Westchester, Richmond and Rockland" formed. At the same time, the use of convict labor drew the molders and other trade unionists into politics, urging a bill to regulate such innovations.[9]

New York workers became increasingly concerned about politics, owing to the use of convict labor, for example. While Boston Labor Reform opted for independent nominations, New York philanthropists and gentlemen reformers launched their own "municipal reform" movement. They described it as one "entirely irrespective of party. There are no politicians in it, and no politician will find favor from it. Those who have taken hold most earnestly are the mechanics and the workingmen, who have now brought home to them, in increased rents, because of increased taxes, and in other ways, the knowledge that a reform is necessary."[10] This was not what it seemed.

As elsewhere, the reliance of the bosses on military and legislative action pushed workers toward labor-reform aspirations. At the state capital, officeholders who had balked at regulating the use of involuntary servitude by convicts proposed to regulate labor organizations by outlawing their unionist functions. In March the legislature produced the Hastings-Folger Anti-Trade Union Strike Bill. It barred labor organizations from the use of "force, menace or threat of personal or pecuniary injury" to prevent any workers from crossing a picket line.[11] In effect, the bill protected the employers' use of the threat of "pecuniary injury" to impose on their unilateral decisions about such issue. It also stripped workers of any rights to defend themselves, defining as violence even the mere verbal explanation that breaking a union would lead to a decline in wages for the strikebreaker as well as the striker.

By the end of the month the unions prepared a response, meeting at the old headquarters of the Navy Yard strikers at No. 187 Bowery. These, in turn, called "more than fifty Associations and workingmen's Unions" into an April 7 meeting in Tompkins Square. Then, "men in all parts of the City stopped work at noon and gathered in Tompkins-square, to assist at a meeting which they consider will tend to preserve their rights and liberties." By 3:00 P.M., when the rally began, there "could not have been less than ten thousand people present, which numbers was increased before the close, by fresh arrivals, to nearly twenty thousand." Some estimates ran as high as fifteen thousand. William Harding of the coach painters chaired at Stand No. 1, and there were three stands.[12]

The threats revived the issues on the waterfront and beyond. The long strike against "seven of the largest machines shops in and near New York City" had collapsed, but grievances persisted. By the time of the Hastings-Folger Bill, blacksmiths, carpenters, painters, hatters, molders, plasterers, watchmen, and others joined the lists with resolutions for more pay. Ship caulkers, meanwhile, decided to follow the workingwomen of Philadelphia and send a delegation to Washington. Ferry-boat pilots "recently organized a Protective Union and Benevolent Association." Meanwhile, the New York Journeymen Cooper's Protective Association organized on both sides of the East River and issued a blazing manifesto under the title "United We Stand, Divided We Fall." It hosted a special mass meeting on April 20 at No. 187 Bowery, the old headquarters of the machinists. It raised money and prepared for a major strike in late May.[13] The legislature had gotten its answer.

At the same time, the bill stirred considerable discussion and anger within the trades across the East River in Brooklyn. Ferryboat pilots, coopers, plumbers and others raised the issue in their meetings across Brooklyn. Indeed, the proposal essentially galvanized the local unions into a trades assembly.[14]

The Unfolding of Labor Reform Politics

Politics concerned workers least in Philadelphia. Molders supported "the most protracted and the most stubbornly contested 'strike' that has ever taken place within the history of 'Trades' Unions' on this continent," and curriers organized to support the strike in Massachusetts. In addition, brushmakers, coachmakers, harnessmakers, paperhangers, and sheet-iron workers organized. The bosses called in the police to break up the meetings of "riotous" ice gatherers on the Schuylkill. Bricklayers organized to improve pay for those five or six months of each year they could work. Coopers struck to get the first raise in five years, though one master arranged to have a journeyman arrested simply for telling an apprentice that the shop would be struck. Collarmakers secured agreements for a 30 percent pay raise, if competing employers elsewhere met the same demand, which turned the unionists to national organizations. Shoemakers became so flustered by the failures of contractors on government to keep their agreements that large numbers of them began refusing to do government work.[15]

Politics almost immediately engaged the three to four hundred miners who began to organize on May 30, 1863, at Virginia City. Often, modest stockholders' as well as workers' incomes suffered from both declining dividends and announced pay cuts. Seeking better pay and mutual aid, they resolved to form a Miner's Protective Association on June 6. They elected Robert D. Ferguson president, W. C. Bateman vice president, and B. J. Shay secretary. A branch formed at Gold Hill in August 1864. In the end, though, a workforce with such a high turnover relied heavily on the clout of their president. A Sacramento lawyer and former member of the California Assembly, Ferguson had come to Virginia City under a cloud for having assaulted the Speaker of the House. At about the time Nevada became a state in 1864, Ferguson had become a member of the bar and was destined for election to the state assembly there as well.[16]

In March 1864 the miners at Gold Hill thwarted an attempt to cut pay, but the bosses made a concerted effort to announce at making the cut effective August 1. The men at Gold Hill threatened to strike, and they marched behind a band into Virginia City, chanting, "Four dollars a day!" and "No reduction of wages!" By noon August 1, nearly two thousand miners listened to supportive addresses by politicians, including the former San Francisco Judge Frank Tilford, who suggested that whoever "in this crisis, advocates a reduction of miners' wage be girded and encircled with burning fagots, and receive the fate of the Roman felon!" Local papers, such as the *Territorial Enterprise* and the Virginia City *Union* also supported the job action as well. Within hours, the last of the owners abandoned their plans.[17]

The workers then launched the Miners' League of Storey County, celebrated with an August 6 torchlight demonstration under banners declaring "United we stand, divided we fall," and "Equal rights, laws and justice." The idea of unionizing spread to the Ormsby County mills that processed the ore; new organizations included a Miners' Leagues of Washoe County along the Truckee River, of Lander County at Austin, and protective associations at Aurora. Over time, though, the bosses tried to replace the union members and moved the press to support of their own "Citizens' Protective Association" to resist "combinations." By the end of the 1865 season, the unions were broken and miners were working for $3.50 a day.[18]

Individuals escaping the turmoil of the war turned up in such boomtowns and these new labor organizations there, such as the Washoe Typographical Union at Virginia City. Henry Trayser, a Milwaukee man, had risen from the ranks in the Fifth Wisconsin before resigning in late 1862 and, apparently, heading west, where he became the treasurer of the local. One of its members, Orion Clemens, also officered the Republicans' Union League in the territory, while Orion's brother Samuel had deserted the secessionist Missouri State Guard and gone west, where he began writing as "Mark Twain." Another veteran of the Missouri State Guard in the printers' union was the Kentucky-born "Major" John P. Bruce, who had joined at St. Joseph, Missouri; he ran for Congress in 1862, lost, and eventually opted for the newspaper business in the West. Mobility—movement from place to place—was an essential part of life in the region, so that someone like William Coyne held membership in several of the locals out west and later became an early member of the Typographical Union at Helena, the first labor organization in Montana.[19] Their organizations had unavoidable civic implications.

On one level, the refusal of the vast majority of white working-class people not to join the Democratic-fueled racist hysteria represented a clear turning point in the Civil War, as decisive in its way as what took place at Gettysburg. Such forbearance had been nothing new, though it now coincided with the implementation of emancipation. In these circumstances, organized workers—and workers generally, for the most part—chose not to be so manipulated. The old games might still work, but they need not play so easily again. Matters remained in play for years after emancipation.

Labor nationally became something of an issue in the 1864 presidential campaign. Republican leaders saw labor support as so vital that they invested continued efforts to persuade workers of the necessity of clinging to the Lincoln administration and its local representatives. Former schoolteacher William Oland Bourne resurrected his old "Iron Platform" Democrats as a "Democratic Republican Party" sustained by a "Workingmen's Democratic-Republican Association" to appeal to workers.[20]

Local issues also drew them into an alliance with the Republicans. By the fall, New York City's "Citizen's Association," promising political reform, drew some labor figures into its meetings. On September 1, the Cooper Institute "filled with the workingmen of New-York who came forward to express their dissatisfaction with the present management of our City Government, and to take management of our City Government, and to take action which would secure a reform." Peter C. Baker was the printers' leader. Speaker of the evening was Robert M. Poer, an ally of Bourne and something of a labor voice for Greeley and the Republicans.[21]

Despite the occasional flickering of the lights over these real and symbolic "workingmen," politicians quickly came to the fore to steer course. To accusations of being "antagonistic to Trades' Unions," the association adopted the rhetoric of neutrality, "saying that it desires no interference, direct or indirect, with the Trades' Unions, or with any of their regulations for the promotion of trade interests." In fact, it "appeals to the working classes, simply as citizens." Its goal seemed to be to draw thousands of otherwise loyal Republicans, particularly the Germans, into a coalition to defeat the party of Lincoln at the polls.[22] It provided another model of civic labor reform.

Cooperation, Communities, Citizenship

The working-class experience in America cultivated a social, economic, and moral critique of capitalism, albeit without any doctrinaire political blueprint. "The numerous 'strikes,' and other organized movements of the laboring classes in this country, which have taken place within the past two years, naturally attract the attention of philosophic minds to the great question involved in them," declared the spiritualist *Banner of Light*. "Monopolies of heaven and earth must be destroyed and broken down," declared one of its co-thinkers about a postwar America. "Equal rights of mankind to heaven and earth, individual sovereignty and universal equality must redeem the poor, and they only can do it. Temperance, industry and frugality cannot do it. As poverty originated in codes of Church and State, so it must end only in their abolition." "It is not money that evidences a nation's wealth, but labor."[23]

The triumph of the Republican insurgency transformed the political context of antebellum labor reform. Articulating old themes in American radicalism, Seaver insisted that the people had "*the right to good government*," which meant it should be cheap, effective, "disinterested as it regards particular class interests," "entirely elective," and "truly representative." Government, he argued, should be about "the promotion of the general welfare," securing the people "the full enjoyment of their rights," including "a good physical, mental, and moral training" and "all practicable steps which may tend to increase the production of wealth, and also to see that the wealth produced be properly distributed; in other words, that the wants of all be fully supplied." By this standard, Seaver believed that all government is "in a greater or less degree tyrannical and irresponsible" when rooted in an "*inequality of possessions*."[24]

Yet the wartime experience encouraged workers to look to some well-worn routes of attack that involved broad, concerted action without risking the treacherous game of electoral politics. The war revived a longstanding interest in cooperation, following in the wake of the earlier Protective Union Stores. The wartime papers reported on the development of new "Union stores" turning up in "some of the eastern cities," but indicate their organization stretched from Boston and New England to as far west and south as Louisville. Black Americans followed a similar, if independent, course toward these same ends, with William Craft and others in pursuit of cooperative solutions overseas.[25]

Cooperationists at Philadelphia became particularly interested in new techniques such as those formulated by the Rochdale pioneers in England. Just before the war's start, the editors of the *United States Mechanics' Own* had sought to revive the old cooperative vision of the antebellum Brotherhood of the Union, which had become increasingly identified with the *Arbeiterbund* in the local needle trades. The war years popularized the British example of the Rochdale Society of Equitable Pioneers. In 1862 Uriah Smith Stephens, James Wright, and others launched a Garment Cutters' Association of Philadelphia, a fraternal order that expanded into the Knights of Labor.[26] John Shedden, John Samuel, and Thomas Phillips, alongside contemporary labor leaders such as William H. Sylvis and Jonathon Fincher, became more prominent after the war.

Urban crowding and higher rents drove workers toward cooperative housing. "The history of building associations in this country has been rather unfavorable," noted *Scientific American*. Still, a wave of these took place in the early 1850s, including a handful of working-class colonization efforts to move west. "That such reforms as these are urgently required in New-York, no one can deny who is at all acquainted with the quarters of the City inhabited by our laboring classes. Practical philanthropy can have no better or higher object; and it is our belief that private and associated capital could find no safer or, in the end, more lucrative form of investment."[27]

At the same time, the wartime government's printing of "greenbacks" took control of the money supply out of the direct hands of the banks and seemed to jibe nicely with what reformers were discussing. Beyond a small markup to cover overhead and the clerk's time, Josiah Warren's "Time Stores" sold goods for "Labor Notes," promising the bearer a set amount of time engaged at one's own occupation. This approach eliminated the middleman and the markup, fostering a deepening equality. After time at New Harmony and Utopia near Cincinnati, he moved on to Modern Times outside New York City, where he associated with Edward N. Kellogg and Stephen Pearl Andrews. There, too, the most important American Fourierist, Albert Brisbane, took up the possibilities of a paper currency in 1863, and Cluseret's *The New Nation* took up the discussion the following year.[28]

The most obvious solution involved just moving off into your own community. After numerous communities followed the advice of Robert Owen or Charles Fourier, disaffected Americans began organizing new kinds of communities rooted in ideas like "individual sovereignty" and spiritualism, which was predicated on the idea of personal communication with the spirits of the departed. Places like Long Island's Modern Times, Utopia in Ohio or Mountain Cove in present West Virginia blurred the line between intentional communities and the surrounding society. This reflected and encouraged the desire to make socialism increasingly practical, a trend that abolitionism and the war deepened. Even against the backdrop of the war, they formed these new kinds of associations at Hammonton and Vineland, New Jersey, the Black Lake Cooperative near Crimea, Michigan, and even at Kidder, in the heart of the north Missouri guerilla war.[29]

The dislocations of war, with its massive numbers of refugees, gave new life to the communitarian idea. New York–born Benjamin N. Kinyon had fled Mississippi for Des Moines in 1862, where he practiced law and studied "the social question." In 1864 he wrote a series of neglected essays for the spiritualist *Banner of Light* on "the Poor." He estimated that "three-fourths of mankind at least, in the civilized, Christianized and governed States, are the victims of poverty. That it is not only a real evil, but the origin of the major part, at least of all evils, need not be argued." Social duty required people "to rise against a Church which shuts them out of heaven, and the State that denies their equality, and equal rights to land and all other property to supply the necessities of their organization." Neither temperance, industry, nor economy could solve the problem, which was part of the social system. "Church and State are, therefore, conceived in blasphemy against God, and are a continual warfare upon his divine laws, implanted in the constitution of his creature, man." The goal was of a world where "all would then labor to produce supplies and rejoice to see the needy appropriate them."[30]

Most clearly, the course of the war seemed to confirm the arguments of the working-class land reformers. On the eve of the battle of Shiloh, General Albert S. Johnston even offered an early Confederate contribution to the prehistory of American red-baiting, promising his men "a decisive victory over agrarian mercenaries, sent to subjugate and despoil you of your liberties, property, and honor." In fact, the Union soldiers along the Tennessee River near Pittsburg Landing included self-described "Agrarians," such as the thirty-nine-year-old William Haddock.[31]

All of this became reasonably embroiled with land reform and the growing cry for "forty acres and a mule" across the South. What made "agrarian mercenaries" particularly annoying to the slaveholders is that they had always argued not only for the abolition of slavery but also for the more equitable redistribution of land, particularly to former slaves. From 1851, when black delegates began showing up at the National Industrial Congresses, advocacy of radical democratic land reform and cooperation became increasingly interracial. John C. Cluer, the transatlantic working-class radical addressed a racially mixed public meeting of the Union Progressive Association, "a literary society of the colored men of Boston." At the height of the 1863 riots at New York, his colleague John H. Keyser organized aid for its African American victims. Their comrade William West, there retrieving the body of Ben Price from the battlefield, wrote to Wendell Phillips on the need to ensure egalitarian land reform.[32]

The mass strike in the South placed on the agenda aspects of the critique associated with the antebellum labor reformers. The former Chartist officering a black regiment, Dick Hinton wrote that "not even the bestowal of suffrage, will so materially aid [in] destroying the effects of Slavery [as] the creation of a self-reliant independent yeomanry out of the former slaves." Emancipation without land would leave the freed people to "the serfdom of capital." Even his pragmatic comrade in the Second Colorado, Major James Nelson Smith, found it the practical solution to having hundreds of black refugees on his hands involved moving them onto the deserted farms of secessionists. Already, the shoemakers' leader Alonzo G. Draper had seized two thousand acres of abandoned rebel lands in Maryland for the resettlement of the contraband and their families on what they called "Government Farms."[33] From the Maryland coast to the mountains of Arkansas, then, the pragmatic exigencies of war fostered the merits of an expropriation and redistribution of land.

Then, too, if government could intervene against the vested interest of property in people and in land, why not use it to establish rules that would gradually change the nature of the system itself? The old land reformers had raised the issue of an eight-hour day, but the best argument against any such proposals was that such a fundamental change in the rules would place the employer at a competitive disadvantage. The logical solution was a legislative mandate that all the competing businesses would have to change the rules at the same time. The various crafts and industries represented in the Boston Trade Assembly adopted this during the war as a common strategy, and, in 1863, Ira Steward launched an

Eight-Hour League there. The following year, workers in New York and Brooklyn took up the eight-hour issue.[34]

Issues of national concern also began to emerge, not the least of which was the eight-hour day. The Washington printers claimed that their early resolutions had sown the seeds that "began to take root in 1865, the movement having spread to other trades." The New York City painters, too, found themselves in the vanguard of this new movement, with "many branches" affiliated with the International Workingmen's Association and successfully winning the eight-hour day in the craft.[35]

The socialist community Modern Times (on Long Island) cradled other overarching attempts to provide a sweeping worldview that could explain social problems and their solutions. Transatlantic followers of Auguste Comte's Positivism got their start there and surely would have had a much greater influence were it not for its many competitors. An advocate of women's equality and socialism, Andrews, a Yankee abolitionist who lived in the South before fleeing a Houston mob, proved to be a lifelong radical on all other social questions and tried to combine his interests together into a philosophical "Universology" to be promoted by a "Pantarchy." Draper's mentor, Colonel William Batchelder Greene, urged a cooperative mutualism that theoretically transformed Warren's "Labor Notes" and Kellogg's paper currency into "a mutual currency" as part of a general "mutualism" that fell well within the range of how the term was used in Europe.[36] As yet, of course, greenbackism, positivism, universology, and mutualism were not seen as mutually exclusive.

Neither was spiritualism, which claimed to be both a science and religion, without fully being either. It encouraged new ways of thinking about class, race, and gender, but it also became deeply immersed in the Sanitary Commission Fairs and other events across the North to raise money for aiding wounded soldiers and looking out after their health. As the pages of their *Banner of Light* recount, spiritualists also expanded their interests to providing needed social services to the freed people and advocated a radical rethinking of Indian policy. The *Banner* also thought America to be "to-day suffering vastly more from the effects of speculation than from those of the war." Although describing this as more of a traditional financial bubble than a new trend, if encouraged "combinations everywhere would be making up to defeat the ends of grasping and unprincipled speculators."[37]

* * *

The *New York Times* acted quickly to head off this dynamic. "There would be no difficulty in establishing a Utopia if men would only behave in the way in which men ought to behave in order to make a Utopia possible," it insisted, "but as they do not and will not, people are generally agreed that Utopias are idle dreams." Only by ignoring this "perverseness of human nature" could one believe Fourierite phalansteries possible.[38]

The threat it discerned seemed so menacing because the critics of capitalism in antebellum and wartime America came from and spoke the same language of liberties and representative politics that prevailed in the wider society. Those radicals shared the general concerns of their peers about the strains of bloating budgets, massive government employment, and a growing portion of government beyond election, supervision, and accountability.[39] The war they were experiencing, however, would offer them a different set of lessons, which they would, in some ways, learn better than most.

CHAPTER 11

Toward a National Labor Presence

Exploring the Class Limits of Respectability

In September 1864 a dozen skilled white men from eight states assembled at Louisville to launch what has been (rather erroneously) called the first national labor organization in American history. They resolved: "Whereas, capital has assumed to itself the right to own and control labor for the accomplishments of its own greedy and selfish ends, regardless of the laws of nature, and of nature's God; and . . . if the dignity of labor is to be preserved, it must be done by our united actions." In fact, they had little but good intentions behind what they called the "International Industrial Assembly of North America." A third of them came from cities in slaveholding border states, and only one came from east of Ohio. Not only did they not truly represent the broadening spectrum of labor organizations springing up across the country, but they also lacked the strength and the focus to sustain any such organization.[1] In all likelihood, the founders hoped their preemptive conference might draw attention to the need for such a body and inspire efforts to build a real national convention that could move toward a vital organization.

Events through the war drove organized labor to recognize increasingly common national foundations of the problems it faced. By late 1864, circumstances incited craft organizations, including the well-practiced unionism of the printers, into militant action. Then, too, the same process spurred the unskilled, particularly associated with the railroads, into rebellious—even riotous—outbursts in pursuit of their interests. The 1864 presidential election defined the limits and vagaries of what victory for the union might mean.

Organizing the Skilled Trades: Printing

In the wake of the strike wave of late 1863 and its confrontation with the government in 1864, workers continued to attempt organization along craft lines. The press reported the organization of unions by tailors, tinsmiths, and plumbers at Brooklyn, curriers, sewing machine tailors, and dental surgeons at Boston, as well as machinists and blacksmiths at Cairo and Mound City. Clerks of various stores at New York continued to appeal for public support to get early closings, those dry-goods establishments eventually prevailing. Strikes broke out among molders at Roxbury and Elizabethport, street cleaners at Brooklyn, and the gravediggers at Calvary and Greenwood cemeteries.

None of this precluded acts of solidarity, and, in fact, virtually mandated it. New York Musical Mutual Protective Union organized benefit concerts for the workingwomen of the city. The Actors' Protective Union, led by William Davidge, a bohemian associate of labor reformers, also agreed to cooperate with the other unions, though their working hours prohibited their participation in the common evening meetings of the trade assembly.[2]

Yet the summer of 1864 brought printers to the fore across the country. Members of the craft with the oldest tradition of organization in the country had experienced the virtual collapse of many locals with the war, while others limped along without much power to do anything in terms of wages or working conditions. Late the previous year, they resisted the temptation to strike the Government Printing Office at Washington and only reluctantly took on the *Age* at Philadelphia.

Nevertheless, the larger locals had begun to recover and had positions of the union in negotiating them. And when the craft struck at Rochester, the Philadelphia local organized strike support. Moreover, printers in the capital did successfully raise the weekly pay at the *Washington Union* from eighteen dollars to twenty-one dollars weekly and piecework from fifty cents to sixty cents per one thousand ems. In November of that year, they pushed the weekly scale to twenty-four dollars.[3]

The Boston Typographical Union got a new scale in June but still found itself on strike by September, and the local press had, as usual, no qualms about maligning the strikers. In response, the printers put together their own cooperative paper, the *Daily Evening Voice*. The popular spiritualist *Banner of Light* hailed its appearance, declaring "the spirit of man rebels against his task-master . . . and the time is not distant when not only black slavery will cease to exist on this continent, but white slavery also." By November the bosses had triumphed.[4]

The New York printers also felt strong enough to start making wage demands. Union membership had fallen from more than nine hundred before the war to 254 by the fall of 1862, but it had now climbed back to about seven hundred. The union had negotiated a revised wage schedule, increasing both the piecework and the weekly rate for newspaper compositors from sixteen dollars to eighteen dollars for days and from eighteen dollars to twenty-one dollars for nights. However, the continued increases in the cost of living brought them back to ask for more on August 10. The *Tribune* declared that "it shall not accede to the Union's demand, if they can avoid it," and joined the Associated Press in a drive to break the union. On August 12, the *Tribune* night foreman passed the unionists copy for an advertisement for "twenty competent compositors," and the men refused to set the notice, walking out. "The Tribune Association have discharged all the Union men in their employ, and are now advertising for compositors from abroad," declared the *Baltimore Sun*. Soon, the small papers "in the towns up the Hudson river, are advertising for girls, who, it is contended, can set type a great deal faster and 'cleaner' than men." The *Tribune* subsequently claimed unionists "dog the homeward steps of our new journeymen in the small hours of the night."[5]

Workers now mobilized against the firm of their veteran advocate, Horace Greeley. On August 18, the Workingmen's Union called thousands into City Hall Park to hear speakers from various crafts. Perhaps nobody offered words as heartfelt as Robert M. Poer, a vital link between the labor movement and Greeley's wing of the Republican Party. "I believe Greeley's heart is yet in the right place," he said. "But as the *Tribune* is conducted by an association, I believe there is a power behind the throne greater financially than the throne itself." Two days later the strikers met at Tammany Hall, where speakers "referred to Mr. Greeley in not very complimentary language as regarded his action in the matter of the scale of prices." Supporters of the *Tribune* predictably claimed that Tammany and Democratic officials were in league against Greeley.[6]

In the end, it seemed as though the union had no powerful friends of any sort anywhere. Although the *Daily News* suggested that the craft should establish "standing committees of arbitration of employers and employees," the *Journal of Commerce* and the *Tribune* held fast against any negotiations that would recognize the union.[7] In the end, they defeated the local, the membership of which fell from about seven hundred back below three hundred.

On the heels of the New York strike came the battle with the *Chicago Times*. Rather like James Gordon Bennett and his *New York Herald*, Wilbur F. Storey and the *Chicago Times* editorialized on behalf of white labor as part of an ideological assault on the administration and emancipation. In reality, he called his employees "vermin" and used favoritism to build a network of office spies, engaging in "as spectacular a series of stratagems as ever marked management's fight against the Typographical Union." One member recalled a group from the union going to Storey over issues connected to his launching a Sunday edition, and he simply told them to "'go to hell,' or something like that." In April 1864 the printers walked out, and Storey tried to keep going on the labor of rates and his "literary" employees. Unable to entirely vanquish the union, Storey made his peace with the union but took measures "to emancipate ourselves from an obnoxious despotism." Storey, meanwhile, took measures to undermine the union by quietly acquiring a building on Randolph Street at the Chicago River, installing a composing room and training "forty young women."[8]

On the morning of September 9, the *Chicago Times* moved the women into the shop and locked out the union. The next day, the city's Trades Assembly gathered in the Courthouse Square. Speakers denounced "the Copperhead Times" and declared its editor "a traitor to his country, to his God, and to the workingmen of Chicago." Among the regular speakers at Chicago labor events like this was Elisha W. McComas, the former lieutenant governor of Virginia—an exile from the Unionist western part of the state—who had participated in an early summer meeting of the carpenters and jointers and, late in the year, lent his voice to the printers.[9] The strike established Andrew C. Cameron's *Workingman's Advocate*, which survived to give voice to postwar labor aspirations, albeit with its editor's peculiarly Democratic twist to events.

As the end of the year approached, the *Boston Post* declared its preference to follow the example of the *Chicago Times* rather than to "surrender" to the union. "The Boston newspapers, having emancipated themselves from the Printers' Union, are beginning to employ girls as compositors," interviewing one observer as "mostly set up by them" and *Traveller* "partially so." During the strike, a professional gentleman into the office declared the union "illegal and unjustifiable," as well as "an unholy combination." He favored putting down "all kinds of rebellions" to "maintain the integrity of the nation and the great business interests of the world. "Bennett's opportunistic and Copperhead *New York Herald* described the union as "a striking machine . . . smashed up by its collision with the laws of business."[10] Nevertheless, the experiment failed in Boston.

The printers had enjoyed long success as a labor organization in America and now faced seemingly unavoidable choices. Nevertheless, the NTU remained an obvious model when workers began organizing. Starting in late 1862, telegraph operators petitioned for higher wages. The following summer, this group, operating at the cutting edge of the new communications technology alongside the railroad, published a simple notice in the press: "The operators in the service of the American Telegraph company, numbering nearly five hundred persons, have established an Association similar to that of the Printers' Union, and will soon hold a Convention."[11] They would, however, face many of the same basic problems as the NTU.

Organizing the New Industries: Railroading

Contemporary accounts indicate that workers in the new industries continued to challenge their employers. Strikes broke out in the mines near Pittsburgh in September 1864. Working in the Navy Yards of New York and Philadelphia continued in flux. The machinists and shipwrights walked out at Philadelphia, urging the caulkers and boat builders to join them. In the New York area, the lightermen and longshoremen went out over pay and a shorter workday, while a police force of two hundred patrolled the area. Reflecting this, the carpenters, painters, and bricklayers of Brooklyn acted in concert over pay and union recognition.

The authorities proved particularly impatient with any interference with transportation. In June a strike broke out on the Fifteenth and Sixteenth Street lines of the Philadelphia rail lines, leading to firings and violence. At New York, the horse shoers went on strike against the use of "a shoeing machine on the omnibuses." One correspondent commented that the strike left the public "huddled into fewer cars, tortured by heat and half asphyxiated," denouncing such "gross attempts at dictation" by the workers. Violence erupted near the Sixth Avenue railroad depot when one striker allegedly used "a turning hammer" on a strikebreaker who was expected not to live. Upstate, where the previous year had seen large-scale rioting by railroad workers, saw more trouble in mid-summer 1864, when Irish laborers proved to be "more formidable than was at first anticipated," an estimated eight hundred of them chasing off German strikebreakers, leading on August 2 to "several arrests."[12]

Most important, the Brotherhood of the Footboard emerged as a secret society from discussions among railroad engineers going back to 1862. Into the winter of 1863, railroad engineer William D. Robinson worked out of Marshall on the Michigan Central to rebuild the old National Protective Association. On May 5 representatives of the Michigan railroads gathered at Detroit, and three days later a dozen of them joined hands in a circle and repeated the obligation on which they had agreed for the Brotherhood of the Footboard. By August a particularly strong "Grand Division" worked out of Detroit. By mid-November the bosses identified and discharged Robinson, and the union—what would become the Brotherhood of Locomotive Engineers—put him on the road as a full-time organizer.[13]

Fear of firings and repression motivated the secrecy. There existed, of course, a long tradition of secret societies in the working-class movement, though this had never been the preferred method of organizing a trade union, the success of which turned on its ability to recruit prospective members.[14] Discretion seemed vital to protecting members from firing and repression.

Almost immediately, the new union faced serious challenges. On January 20 the management of the Pittsburgh, Fort Wayne, and Chicago Railroad "refuses to accede to the demands of the strikers, and in view of the frequency of accidents and detentions of late, at one sweep has discharged all the employees of the road, and is determined to revolutionize the manner in which it has been operated." Unionists held a special convention at Detroit on February 23 to reorganize more tightly and turned its attention to the Chicago and Galena Railroad on March 10. The next day, the brotherhood issued a circular reporting that "the warfare opened on the Pittsburgh and Fort Wayne Road; where we are partially beaten; the contest is carried then to the Galena Road." By the spring, it had divisions organized from New England to Missouri and as far south as Nashville.[15]

On July 5, workers on the Reading Railroad struck over wages. "From the fact that no coal is arriving in the city to-day it is presumed that the strike is general along the entire length of the road, and upon all its branches." This "somewhat embarrassed the United States government in consequence of its not obtaining its usual supply of coal." "A large number of laborers employed by the Government on military railroads near Washington, were brought to Philadelphia and put to work on the Reading railroad," though strikers, on July 12, "interfered with" the strikebreakers. For this reason, "the Government, which must have coal, took charge of the road." By one account, troops temporarily replaced strikers. The "difficulties were adjusted in the course of ten days," and then the strikers returned to work.[16]

The press expressed all due shock at the existence of "a secret organization of engineers throughout the country . . . all the members of which are bound to stand by each other." It reported that "about 1,500 engineers are concerned in the movement. Their principal grievance is that they are compelled to work a greater number of hours each day than formerly." The union claimed to represent "all the engineers on the Western railroads centering in Chicago," and announced it would declare a general strike on the road March 15 unless the bosses would, among other things, reinstate those strikers fired on the Galena Railroad. "Combined railroad companies are working to crush us," the Brotherhood wrote, "and we are battling to maintain ourselves." Most of the engineers in and out of Chicago from the west "knocked off, and refused to run our trains until the difficulty on the Galena Road was adjusted." The papers called this "a general strike among the railroad engineers," but the work stoppage did not stop the Michigan Central, Northwestern, or the Burlington and Quincy, the last of which "have a separate organization, and therefore, do not come into this arrangement." Almost immediately, the Michigan Southern and the Illinois Central also declared against an agreement.[17]

Representatives from thirty-eight of the fifty-four divisions converged on Indianapolis on August 17, 1864. Citing rumors of Confederate plots to disrupt the upcoming state election, officials assigned soldiers to escort the delegates to and from their convention and guarded the hall as the representatives deliberated. The convention elected Charles Wilson of Rochester and Robert Laughlin of Hornellsville national officers and changed the name of their union to the Grand International Brotherhood of Locomotive Engineers.[18]

At the same time, a secret fraternal order, the "League of Friendship, Supreme Mechanical Order of the Sun," grew alongside the union. It involved not only union members and former strikers but also strikebreakers. An episodically self-employed North Carolinian, John Jordan Upchurch became the order's most prominent leader and shaped its increasingly conservative hostility toward trade unions. In the aftermath of the war Upchurch successfully reorganized it as the Ancient Order of United Workmen.[19] Railroad workers may have engaged in terribly militant actions, clashing with the police and authorities, but many remained unwilling to close the door on that hope that craft fraternalism might be translated into the new industries.

Legitimacy in the Context of the 1864 Elections

Throughout the course of the war, free wage workers had confronted the power structure, though often obliquely. Workers ascribed their difficulties less to systemic problems or the high-ranking elected officials than to contractors and government corruption. "We all claim to be loyal citizens," wrote the union blacksmith at Nashville, "and we think that if the actions of the Nashville officials was made known to our Government, it would not allow it." Yet even after the grievances had been publicized, officials "have even been promoted after taking from the men one-half of their rations."[20]

Through the summer of 1864 the Democratic press tried to recast labor discontent in both partisan and racial terms. It asserted "the extreme probability of a recurrence of such riots as occurred last July—aggravated in the present instance by the dearness of provisions, and the suffering endured by the workingmen of New-York from a depreciated currency." Such possibilities, of course, could justify intervention of the wartime state against workers and strikes. No such riot happened, though August saw "quite a disturbance" at Calvary Cemetery as striking gravediggers prevented strikebreakers from entering the grounds, resulting in the posting by the Brooklyn police of "a large force."[21]

The *Brooklyn Daily Eagle* repeatedly tried to link the labor troubles in the Navy Yards to Republican impositions on the workforce. It also implied that the strikes represented a disagreement within the Republican coalition, since "not of the five or six thousand employees in the Navy Yard a single man who is not a partisan of the present administration." One worker claimed he was dismissed because of politics, but this had nothing to do with the labor movement, since he "always discountenanced strikes" and never attended one union meeting. There were rumors that the yard refused to hire "a veteran who lost his arm" on the grounds that "he would not promise to vote for Lincoln in November."[22]

More tellingly, the Democratic attempts to recast themselves as friends of white labor likely backfired among many when it came to misrepresenting workers. The Democratic *New York Herald* deceptively reported on the meetings of industrialists active around the Democrat-dominated Citizens' Association as one of "iron workers." One of the ironmongers claimed that "they had been called from their workshops to consider whether the city of New York will continue being misruled in the manner in which it has been for a number of years past." Other industrialists spoke, as did "a well known speaker among the working men." The gathering opposed "the corruptions and abuses in the municipal government, which have become oppressive to the taxpayers and working classes of New York" and insisted that the city "be ruled by honest men." At its close, "A SOLDIER in the audience proposed three cheers for General McClellan, which were given with a good will." Notwithstanding the appeals to honesty, as the election approached, the same paper that had complained of the Republican exclusion of Democratic workingmen from Navy Yard employment reported that 140 of 150 participants in an informal vote there voted for McClellan. The Citizens' Association continued to orient toward labor well into the municipal elections the following year.[23] That workers got nothing out of this did not matter.

The Republican *New York News* reported what was ostensibly "the proceedings of a large and enthusiastic meeting of the working men of that city." It described its presiding officer as the "President of the Working Men's Association." Although it denounced "professional politicians, who merely pursue their selfish once [sic], regardless of their country's welfare," the meeting seems to have consisted of nothing else. It resolved that "the present party in power is revolutionary in its character and designs; that it does not aim to save the Union but to destroy it." Chauncey C. Burr, the most prominent speaker and editor of the Copperhead *Old Guard*, which had never showed any interest in the labor movement, blamed the administration for the grievances.[24] It seems likely that workers could easily resent the implication that this body represented the Workingmen's Union or a central labor body.

In a fundamental way, though, the Democrats did not speak the language of labor, if ever they had. The *Crisis* had entered the war complaining that the party of Lincoln "never tired of talking about the poor, of freedom, free labor, and free everything else. All the landless were also to be provided with free farms. What are their practices?" However, when the Republicans had given substance to their land reform rhetoric, the *Crisis* despairingly resorted to white fears of racial competition and channeled those fears into banning blacks from nonslaveholding communities or to restrict their rights there.[25] However, the tried-and-true racial appeals had already gotten all the traction they could, even when supplemented by complaints about Republican violations of constitutionally guaranteed civil liberties.

Moreover, while the Democrats complained bitterly of the militarization of politics at the expense of white Constitutional liberties, they chose as their candidate General George B. McClellan, known as "the Little Napoleon." Many, noted the *New Hampshire Sentinel*, concluded that "prosperity would never return to the land, or would return only under the rule of some military despot." The latter drew support from "a people weary of uncertainty and danger, and craving order above all things—as the French people submitted to the rule of Napoleon III, because they believed him to be the man best qualified to protect themselves and their property against the designs of the Socialists."[26] In short, McClellan loomed as the militarist option the Confederate and Copperhead press ascribed to Lincoln. However, the threat of military government rose abroad in response to the threat of plebeian revolt, and the models of Paris or Berlin in 1848 hardly suited the vast, fragmented complexities of America in the 1860s, which retained other options to the governing power.

So, too, their blind hatred of Lincoln as a rough, calloused Illinois railsplitter probably did him little harm among laboring people. Their political cartoons depicted Lincoln in 1860 as the candidate of abolitionists, blacks, temperance advocates, woman suffragists, socialists, and others whose views were rarely heard in official circles below the Mason-Dixon Line. Most interesting, perhaps, was that one of them traced the causes of the war not to secession but to Lincoln's believe in spiritualism.[27]

The 1864 combination of Republicans with War Democrats in a "Union" party also added to the national ticket of Andrew Johnson, long identified with the struggle for a Homestead Act. When the Democrats mocked the ticket of an Illinois railsplitter and a Tennessee tailor, the *New York Times* aptly replied: "Nothing is more natural than that the upholder of Slavery should taunt the Union party for naming candidates who were at one period of their lives plain working men." Such candidates were "precisely in keeping with the character of a free-labor party." In New York City, William O. Bourne's Workingmen's Democratic Republican Association had also done long and useful work as a Republican platform for addressing workers.[28]

More important, Lincoln made time to meet and respond to delegations of workers with grievances. He told striking machinists from the Brooklyn Navy Yard that he "considered the employers the first strikers, as they refused to accept the terms offered by the men, and thereby compelled the latter to cease work, or, as they term it, go on a strike; and now that both were on a strike '*the best blood would win*.'" Lincoln refused to give the bosses an extension to build the contracted ironclads, forcing a settlement. Consistent with his statements to the New York strikers, Lincoln told Philadelphia's Working Women's Relief Association that he could not interfere with private war contractors but got the local arsenal to reverse its trend toward subcontracting, to hire more women to work there directly, and to raise their pay by 20 percent. Not without reason did one historian describe the record of his presidency on labor as "unmatched in American history."[29]

In January Bourne's group began offering Lincoln and other prominent Republicans honorary membership in the group. Inequalities of property, the president lectured them, provided a "just encouragement to industry and enterprise." However, Lincoln clearly established the stakes of the war: "None are so deeply interested to resist the present rebellion as the working people. Let them beware of prejudice, working division and hostility among themselves. The most notable feature of a disturbance in your city last summer was the hanging of some working people by other working people. It should never be so. The strongest bond of human sympathy, outside of the family relation, should be one uniting all working people, of all nations, and tongues, and kindreds."[30]

The Democratic press used extracts from the president's reply to complain that it "overlooks all difference of race and regards the whites and blacks simply as laborers, and tells them that they should be bound together." "This is miscegenation and nothing else," placing the president "on precisely the same platform as Tilton, Phillips, Greeley, Parker, Pillsbury, and the rest." The appeals of Bourne's group had been that of "bogus workingmen, as it is very well known that the laboring classes of this city will vote in almost solid mass against Mr. Lincoln or any other out-and-out Republican candidate." Bourne agreed that the group "does not at present hold *public meetings*. The expense of such meetings, if they are to be of real value, is too great, and the Executive Committee believe that their work now can be accomplished in a far more effective and economical manner by correspondence with other Associations and the circulation of documents. The Association will enter the field *when its turn comes*."[31] The fact that it never did could not have been an issue in 1864.

Some radical abolitionists and European immigrants, on the other hand, seriously mistrusted the administration. As early as the outbreak of the war, some of those at New York City had urged the national formation of a distinctly radical party. Their sense of outrage deepened with administration's clash with General John Charles Fremont who had used his military authority to attempt emancipation in Missouri. By the fall of 1862, some of the German émigré organizations offered their own radical alternatives, such as Caspar Butz, running for congress from Chicago. In October 1863 they held a convention at Cleveland that reechoed the most radical of the antislavery demands, called for the demolition of the old institutions of slaveholding power, and, in essence, sought the transformation of the conflict into a revolutionary war.[32] Depending on the time and place, such sentiments expressed the views of a significant portion of the immigrant workers, but they never did so in a sustained way or in coordination with the Americans who shared their views.

Early in 1864 the willingness of the administration to tolerate slavery in the border states pitted the government against those radicals in the border eager to abolish the institution there. A range of radical émigrés tried to stir a national revolt in the party on behalf of Fremont. The former Texan Adolph Douai of the *New-Yorker Demokrat* and others heavily favored this, as did Friedrich A. Sorge, the violin master later hailed as "the Father of American Marxism." Most prominently, General Gustave Paul Cluseret, formerly of Fremont's staff, headed the effort to resurrect the antebellum internationalist coalition and rally it to the cause of Fremont.[33]

With Fremont's financial backing, Cluseret launched *The New Nation*. The cornerstone of its proposed "Ultimate Reconstruction" proved far-reaching: "Absolute and complete liberty, without distinction of race or color, and not at a future period more or less remote, but radically and at once." Claude Pelletier offered an understanding of the wartime strikes as "the preliminary skirmishes of the future war which the abolition of the wages system must infallibly bring about; a war that will be much more serious and gigantic than that which the abolition of slavery has rendered necessary." In the end, he thought, "slavery, direct and brutal, will no longer exist." The *New Nation* also published pieces by Albert Brisbane and Stephen Pearl Andrews, as well as the famous "bohemian" Edwin James, who also wrote the public press in support of the strike movement. Their meeting at the New York rooms of Women's Loyal League at the Cooper Institute brought newspapermen friendly to reform such as George Wilkes, Horace Greeley, and Kapp of the local *Kommunist* organization.[34]

Among the Americans, what was left of the land-reform movement mobilized in support of Lincoln's reelection. Lewis Masquerier—a veteran Owenite as well as a land reformer—had been writing patriotic poems and songs like "Our Second Revolution," and he turned in 1864 to Republican campaign materials. Meetings of the General Committee of the city's Union coalition included Masquerier's old friends from the National Reform organization like Frank Smith and J. K. Ingalls, as well as the Fourierist Frederick Olmstead and spiritualist and future Greenback spokesman Horace H. Day.[35]

Victory required nothing more than the reelection of Lincoln and the stubborn acceptance of the unprecedented human and material cost of the war. However, the meaning of the abolitionist victory—and what working people might be able to make of it—had yet to be resolved. In the end, though, every option the ruling elite offered the people at this point—whether Confederate or Union, and Democratic or Republican within the Union—involved a larger and more powerful national government. The scale on which workers thought of their organization would have to follow.

* * *

Beneath the turmoil of the election, though, organized labor had begun to find its own national voice. Near St. Louis, the *Weekly Miner* at Belleville, Illinois, survived from May 1863 until an 1865 libel suit forced its removal to the city, where it briefly reappeared as the *Miner and Artisan*. Strikes by desperate printers resulted in the remarkable 1864 establishment of a series of cooperative labor papers run by strikers at Chicago's *Workingman's Advocate*, St. Louis's *Daily Press*, and Boston's *Daily Evening Voice*. All espoused the cause not only of the strike that founded them but also of the labor movement in general. As well, Jonathan Fincher of the Machinists' Union launched his *Fincher's Trades' Review*, and Sylvis's union launched the *International Molders' and Foundry Workers' Journal*. In their strike, the Boston printers marched beneath "their beautiful silk banner," hopefully proclaiming "Labor conquers all things."[36]

Local movements, such as Louisville's Trades' Assembly and League of Friendship cultivated an impressive level of solidarity and a serious idea of labor reform in an effort to establish its legitimacy in the eyes of the community. Toward the end of 1864, it sponsored a Co-operative Store, but most impressive, perhaps, it decided to launch a national labor organization. Richard Trevellick of Detroit began a long career of opening, chairing, or presiding over national conventions with these "four days' harmonious sessions" from September 21 to 24 at the assembly's rooms in the Masonic Hall. They held a "Trades Assembly Soiree" for the delegates on the second day. Trevellick "and other eminent Workingmen" addressed a mass meeting of the local labor movement on the last night: "Every Workingman in the city is respectfully invited to attend, and bring his wife and ladies acquaintances with him."[37] Although no less an authority than the army and the government seemed often to challenge them, organized workers began to move inexorably to organization and a new sense of solidarity.

CHAPTER 12

A Peace of Sorts

Labor, Liberty, and Respectability

In April 1865 the masters of Richmond scurried from the city. A generation before the war, a Southern political economist had warned about the strife between principles "of property combined with sound intelligence, and of numbers, united with imperfect knowledge," of which the tendency to murder, arson, and pillage challenged the survival of civilization itself. In the end, though, the Confederates consigned the city to the flames and the looters, and order returned only on the bayonets of the blue-coated "mudsills." As their bands blared "Dixie," runaway slaves returned in uniform to claim both the song and the civilization their labors had built. As the old masters trickled back, they complained bitterly that black soldiers—such as those under former strike leader Alonzo G. Draper—were disseminating ideas of freedom, negotiating wages, and promoting land ownership to workers who had known none of these.[1] The next few weeks brought the Union a long and difficult military victory, the meaning of which remained uncertain for years.

As the conflict between the Union and Confederacy raged into its final months, the conditions that had given rise to a new, ongoing workers' movement continued to worsen. The meaning of the impendng triumph of the Union, its meaning in the working lives of Americans, remained unclear. Arguably, the question became interwoven not only with matters of gender, ethnicity, and race but with the modes of struggle with which these components of the workforces had been associated. Nevertheless, the experience of the Civil War and Reconstruction shaped the idea of an acceptably respectable and responsible labor organization, what became the cornerstone of modern American trade unionism.

The Last Wartime Labor Struggles

As the war dragged to a close, Draper—the former Yankee leader of the shoe strike—had assumed key responsibilities in the trenches. On September 29, 1864, he took his brigade against Richmond's outer defenses on New Market Heights, an action that won fourteen black soldiers the Congressional Medal of Honor, nine from Draper's brigade. Among the nearby reserves along the Darbyville Road stood Wesley W. Pasko, likely the New York printer who had slipped into Charleston to cover the bombardment of Fort Sumter. Into early 1865 Draper and his men remained within striking distance of the city, he taking periodic charge of his entire division, gaining a promotion to general in March. By then, growing numbers of runaway slaves, Confederate deserters, and even the relatives and friends of high-ranking secessionists passed through their lines and the Union command notified the ranks nearest the capital that matters were approaching a crisis. Draper's men kept their fires, tents, parades, and drills as conspicuous as possible to magnify their numbers.[2]

Early April brought news of Union victories to the southwest beyond Petersburg near Five Forks. Among the mortally wounded there, Garrick F. Moore of the Boston Typographical Union had returned to the field from serious wounds at Gettysburg. The successes to which he contributed threatened to close the last road west from Richmond and Petersburg, and notification to Union troops to expect an enemy evacuation of those cities. In the predawn hours of April 3, the Federals near Richmond saw flames, indicating the Confederates had abandoned their capital. Although a detachment of black cavalry had ridden ahead, protocol awarded provostal duties to the first infantry to secure the occupation, and Draper's column hurried north along the James toward Richmond. When ordered to yield the road to white troops, Draper complied but sent his men through the adjacent field "on a double-quick." To the cheers of slaves, free blacks, and some whites, their band struck up "Dixie" and other tunes as they filed through the eastern part of town, quickly intermingling with the civilians, sharing rations, and helping to organize efforts to fight the fires.[3]

Over the next few days the better parts of the three Union armies converged on the disintegrating remnants of what remained of the Confederate Army of Northern Virginia, which found itself bottled near Appomattox Court House and forced to surrender on April 9. Also wounded at Gettysburg, Thomas M. Golden of the Savannah Typographical Union and the Second Georgia Battalion witnessed the collapse of the rebellion, as did union brothers on both sides.

Other Confederate armies remained in the field, but the surrender of Lee's forces and the loss of Richmond made it just a matter of time before they, too, would capitulate.

Through the closing months of the war employers and workers faced labor disputes with new strategies, tactics, and weapons, though without often resorting to them. Government authority loomed over every possible dispute, and both sides battled over that intangible notion of public opinion said to control government authority. Everywhere, growing numbers of workers became aware of its importance and the potential of solidarity.

The old crafts closed the war with several strikes. Molders walked off the job at Indianapolis, Detroit, and Chicago, as did the nailmakers of Wareham, Massachusetts, and the carpenters and joiners of St. Louis. Galvanized partly by the presence of that broad movement in the Navy Yard, Brooklyn bricklayers, plumbers, plasterers, and others contributed to the growing movement in the building trades that erupted into an April strike wave. This inspired plans for "all societies to unite with us in forming a Workingmen's Union in this city, for without union we are powerless in defence of our rights to raise us to that dignity which our importance to the community entitles us." Among others, William Sylvis and Jonathan C. Fincher spoke.[4] By February 1865 the assemblies in the state combined to launch the Workingmen's Assembly of the State of New York.

Workers in the new industries strove to find their own way to legitimacy. One association of miners in western Pennsylvania sought incorporation by the state, but strikes continued in the area, even spilling over into the Mahoning Valley of Ohio. February 1865 saw a strike among the miners and railroad workers on the Delaware, Lackawanna, and Western Railroad and the Delaware and Hudson Canal Company, as did laborers at the Downer oil works in Pennsylvania that March. Workers on the Milwaukee and LaCrosse Railroad went out early in the year. Mule spinners lost a strike in the Chicopee textile mills but shortened their workday to eleven hours at Pittsfield, Southbridge, and elsewhere, including the Lonsdale Company in Rhode Island. At Lewiston, Maine, where they already had eleven hours, they tried to get ten. Workers also went on strike in a New York cotton factory and a window glass factory at Glassboro, New Jersey. Pennsylvania strikes became "frequent" in 1865, "chiefly against a reduction of wages, but generally ended by the submission of the employees." During these weeks, the first strikes hit the iron-mining regions on Lake Superior Mines, to which the authorities responded with a U.S. gunboat and troops from Detroit.[5]

Workers certainly learned that either party—or both of them—could oppose them. In New York their ballots had helped elect the largely Democratic "Citizens Association," which got the legislature in late 1864 to cap at $300,000 what could be used for "keeping the streets clean." Street sweepers had gotten one dollar and $1.25 daily "from time immemorial before the war." Two years earlier, the sweepers and dirt cartmen won big increases respectively to two dollars and to fifty cents. "At the eleventh hour," the mayor's office declared the wages "altogether illegal, and has determined to sign no more requisitions for these claims." As a result, "street-cleaning is entirely suspended, the laborers are in a distressed state for want of their wages." Quipped the *New York Times*, "unless the matter is settled soon, the city is likely to meet the fate of the ancient towns of Herculaneum and Pompeii."[6]

A few weeks later, the Republicans in Portland, Maine, set aside the vote of a town meeting to "offer bounties to prevent a draft" and soon after reneged on their promise to replace the most objectionable candidates on its ticket. Local workers formed a "Labor Reform Association" that had only 125 members and had existed for two weeks before proposing a modification of the ticket on the Saturday before the Monday election. Significantly, the movement had the support of the *Daily Evening Courier* and its conductor, Joseph Blake Hall, then Maine's Secretary of State. He had published an interesting succession of newspapers before becoming one of the state's leading Republicans. In part, the municipal election shaping up in Portland represented a clash over the Republican commitment to its reforms rhetoric. Hall, who also dabbled in spiritualism remained an old-line reformer, not entirely comfortable with the business interests muscling their way into power within the party.[7]

One of the Portland labor reformers responded when *Fincher's Trades' Review* sounded a skeptical note about the effort. With the campaign, he argued, "we have compelled the newspapers to discuss our claims as 'a moral and political reform party.'" Although "the subsistence, the war material and clothing for the army and navy are the produce of labor," the capitalist support for war turned on their privilege, which "enslaved the government, and threw the whole burden of its support upon labor." Although workers suffered "a kind of legislation intended to throw the burdens of sustaining the government upon the labor of the country," the Portland movement thought "the wealth, the capital, the property of the nation, all the accumulated result of labor, ought to be taxed for the protection and perpetuity of the nation."[8]

As expected, though, the Republicans swept the local elections on March 6. Their candidate won reelection with 1,735 votes, while the Democrat got 674; and Albert H. Waite on the Labor Reform ticket got 498 votes. Given the results of the previous election, its seemed as though the Labor Reformers had drawn about the same numbers of voters from both parties. Wrote one of them, "[We] did not expect to cast over 300 votes, yet we actually cast 500 votes."[9]

As the molders finished their sixth national convention at Chicago in January 1865, Sylvis explained carefully how only the workers themselves could keep the union afloat despite several disastrous local strikes the employers had imposed on it. On February 21, prominent union officers from locals at Boston, Philadelphia, Baltimore, "and other cities" met at New York's Cooper Institute. Although their purposes were vaguely described as "to advance the interests of the laboring classes," the composition indicated that unions on the East Coast were as interested a national labor body as were the handful of mostly western men that had met the previous fall in Louisville.[10]

Staking its claim to respectability in the face of all of this, laudatory and fulsome newspaper accounts met the fiftieth anniversary celebration of the Columbia Typographical Society. John C. C. Whaley of the union had presided over a banquet of roughly 150 members and their guests at the Seaton House, and a union member led the Finley Hospital Band, which provided the music. George S. Gideon, one of the old-timers in the union, presented the old composing stone on which its founders had drafted their constitution in the waning days of the War of 1812. In addition to prominent members of the press and authors, the union had hosted the mayor and various Federal officials and Congressmen, including Speaker of the U.S. House Schuyler Colfax, with John G. Nicolay attending on behalf of President Lincoln, whom the union happily toasted, along with the army and the navy.[11]

Only weeks later—just days after the surrender at Appomattox—assassins attacked the president and other officials in Washington. The printers voted to accord the honors of membership to "the noble, the artless, the generous, and the philanthropic spirit of Abraham Lincoln," agreeing to "attend the funeral in a body, and wear the usual badge of mourning for thirty days." Locals at Philadelphia, Boston, Baltimore, Troy, and elsewhere did likewise.[12]

At New York City's funeral parade, the Workingmen's Union sponsored a general contingent estimated at five thousand, along with many individual unions that participated on their own. A thousand members of the Caulker's Association carried "a handsome obelisk, elaborately draped in mourning, with a dial on either side, stopped at twenty-two minutes past seven, with suitable inscriptions." Another thousand marched with the Steam Boiler Makers' Association, more than eight hundred with the dry goods clerks, and six hundred from the New York and Brooklyn Sawyer's Association. The Waiter's Protective Benevolent Association turned out "in strong force," as did the house carpenters, the Cooper's Benevolent Society, and the Longshoremen's Union Protective Association. In addition, the Turners, the Social Reform societies, and three hundred members of the Arbeiterbund marched, as did the cigarmakers, the German carvers, and others.[13] For many of these unions, the war of 1861–65 represented part of a triumphalist pageant of an expanding freedom measurable, in part, by acceptability and respectability of their union.

Redrawing the Margins of Liberty

Peace brought changes as wrenching, in their way, as the war had been. Some of the strongest parts of the wartime labor movement dissolved with the wartime economy. The on-and-off strikes at the Brooklyn Navy Yards subsided as the ship joiners and painters went back. The ship carpenters held off, waiting to hear from Secretary Gideon Welles. He had promised to meet with the men, but he had gone to Fort Sumter for the anniversary celebrations and returned to the news of the president's murder. Therefore, "not over seventy-five or a hundred workmen" lingered around the meeting hall, discussing the false rumor that one of them had refused to work and "been Court-martialed." In the end, the ship carpenters decided to stay out for $4.50 per day, and the caulkers, first-class joiners, riggers, and sparmakers also wanted a raise, but they were also angry over the blacklisting of union members. In the end, though, peace left the bosses free to slash pay and jobs, leaving one observer reporting that "hundreds of workmen of all classes were about the gate and in the different saloons in that neighborhood."[14] Respectability proved elusive for some.

Indeed, those workers who had taken it on their own to force emancipationist policies on the government had a different fate. Federal officials had charge of an area, and they were as likely as the Confederate to fret that "the agrarian mania has taken a strong hold of a certain class, and the cry of contrast between rich and poor is loudly raised. Every city and town that we hear from is effervescing." At Richmond, Draper's victorious black soldiers naturally contributed to what another Union officer described as "a disposition everywhere on the part of the poor people and the poorer class of returned soldiers toward agrarian riots." At the behest of the old city fathers, the army ordered all of them out. Within days of the war's end, a white Virginian rightly described this as a surrender to the aristocracy that had tried to destroy the nation.[15]

At the same time, emancipation reflected military necessity and left the government the arbiter of liberty. Yet victory freed the authorities of the need to placate irksome plebeian allies, and the regime that came to power with Lincoln's assassination saw little from which they sought to free the nation.

By the year's close, native peoples got a bitter foretaste of the dynamics of postwar society. The Lincoln administration had persistently stood by the legitimacy of the Unionist governments of the nations in the Indian Territory, insisting that neither Confederate military occupation nor its threat had legitimately negated the antebellum treaties that established and respected native sovereignty in their designated lands. In September 1865 the U.S. government officially reversed this, setting aside the legitimacy of the pro-Unionist governments in favor of the secessionist bodies, which dissolved the prewar treaties and opened the way to their renegotiation. The result redrew the allocated territories for each of the nations, allowing western states and territories to remove their unwanted native residents to the Indian Territory and delivering remarkably generous land grants to the railroads.[16]

Civil War abolished "involuntary servitude," as it had been institutionalized in the South, but not the premises of white supremacy. It emancipated race from slavery, starkly making it an issue in itself. War freed Americans from the weight of slavery but not the burden of race.

War over the future nature of labor in America had demonstrated the different ways of being a worker in America. The hired workforce included distinctive components with very different experiences—and local conditions would surely permit distinguishing within these broad groupings of formerly enslaved African Americans, the more recently arrived unskilled immigrant, and the women heading off to work. These experiences naturally shaped predispositions to peculiar modes of formulating and expressing their interests. The extent to which a labor movement would reflect a generalized, common identity as a "working class" would turn not simply on some psychological identity but the concrete assimilation of these different experiences.

Philanthropists on the East Coast had hurried into position to establish the most coherent attempt to secure the rights of vulnerable and downtrodden female labor. In lieu of unionism, they offered a line from job services that would lead ultimately to the settlement house. By mid-1865 promoters touted the philanthropy of the Working Women's Protective Union as an "excellent institution" that not only assisted working women in the formulation of contracts with their employers but started a new "Working Women's Library." Certainly, at least some of the women decided that being culturally improved to middle class standards did not represent their most immediate concerns. Anna Tobitt, Elizabeth C. Browne and others launched their own Working Women's Association, organized September 17, 1865.[17] In offering what assistance it could, organized labor had reached the point of going beyond good advice.

Organized labor formulated new approaches to female labor in the aftermath of the war. The printers had earlier moved from what amounted to barring women, to acceptance without encouragement. By 1871 the NTU instructed its locals to organize women in the trade.[18] Unions had begun an often-glacial shift toward making the labor movement a movement of the entire workforce in terms of gender, though the sufficiency of that remained fluid.

Race claimed much more immediacy. African Americans in the South, however, had instigated the largest and most dramatic labor movement in American history in the decentralized, bottom-up rolling strike for self-emancipation. These methods grew from the situation of Southern black labor and owed nothing to the earlier labor organizations among white craftsmen, who made little effort to learn anything from the great wartime slave strike and its successes.

Black workers themselves quickly challenged the limits of what government sanctioned. Many tried, at least, to redefine that sense of class. They organized and led strikes of their own, from the plantations of Louisiana to the docks at Savannah and Charleston. Black tailors also went out in this last town.[19] The histories and outcomes of these endeavors are unclear, but the authorities had many well-developed means for crushing black labor.

This provided a great challenge to white workers, particularly in the South. The few Southern unions resurfacing after the war often had little continuity from their antebellum predecessors, though they maintained the same composition, as though the war never took place. By the close of 1865 white screwmen had returned to work in New Orleans, and a racially mixed strike sought to raise the pay to seven dollars for foremen and six dollars [per week? day?] for gang members. "They marched up the levee in a long procession, whites and blacks together." Still, not that much later, racial violence became part of this struggle. Far to the north, at Baltimore, Confederate veterans among the ship caulkers returned and drove blacks out of the waterfront shipyards.[20]

Yet even Confederate veterans did not initially share a common vision of how to deal with race. The Pennsylvania-born Confederate officer Daniel C. Byerly of the New Orleans Typographical Union became a rabidly unreconstructed rebel and lost his life when he assaulted former Reconstruction governor of Louisiana and Union veteran Henry C. Warmouth. Yet Virginia-born Samuel W. Grubb of the Atlanta local became a Radical Republican in city's government in 1871, and made enough enemies to leave the area for Illinois the following year.[21] Still, in the absence of radical policies imposed from without, the politics of the white Redeemer South would resolve these tension, leaving little doubt.

This sort of thing had national implications. At Washington, D.C., the venerable old Columbia Typographical Union faced the application for membership of Lewis H. Douglass.[22] The son of Frederick Douglass and a veteran of the famed Fifty-Fourth Massachusetts had grown up in and around the newspaper trade and took a job in the Government Printing Office. The union divided over the extent to which they were willing to defy or defer to the prejudices of returning former Confederates who refused to work with any African Americans. Other blacks—William A. Lavelette, Frederick Douglass Jr., Keith Smith—became part of the controversy as well. Despite a spirited and inspiring effort by a large and very articulate minority of white unionists who fought for racial equality, the majority of the oldest labor organization in the United States brought lasting shame upon itself by deferring to its most bigoted members.

The issue landed in the NTU convention, where there actually existed considerable sympathy for admitting Douglass. After all, locals in the North had black members, and Daniel W. Flynn of Washington, who had been fighting the issue for a long time within his local, delivered "a well-written address . . . extending the right hand of fellowship to the negro." The documentation of Douglass's qualifications demonstrated "that the only objection that could be made against his admission was his color." One of the Canadians, Stephen C. Kyte, told the convention that excluding Douglass would be "a blot upon the character of any enlightened organization." However, the long effort of many in the NTU to get the Washington union to admit blacks found much of the union predisposed to duck the issue by deferring the questions to the locals and agreeing to exclude blacks from any national deliberations that might affect that policy. In a shameful reflection of the Reconstruction generally, racial exclusion became the price of reconstructing a national union.

In reality, perceptions of a uniform idea of "whiteness" explain less about the dynamics of race than an acknowledgement of that racial identity and the importance ascribed to it proved to be uneven. Clearly, printers did not realistically expect the cotton fields to empty qualified typesetters and pressmen into the labor markets of the craft. Although members of the NTU did not elect delegates to their national convention based on their views on race, those delegates did vote to permit exclusion, and they did so for different reasons. Clearly, they did not share a belief in equality deeply enough to impose common standards on those locals that sought to maintain the forms of white supremacism that had become commonplace in the wider society. And members within those locals adopted the policies they had simply because it seemed the easiest course to defer to the most vocally racist of the members. In the end, enough workers thought it best to defer to the most reactionary of their numbers as a pragmatic accommodation of a color bar they believed immovable.

Other unions may have experienced similar turmoil within their ranks, with sometimes even more deplorable outcomes. The coopers in New York, sailors out of Baltimore, and bricklayers in Washington passed resolutions barring African Americans. A convention of the National Carpenters and Joiners—actually one of several competing bodies—also adopted a national bar on black members.[23] These racial exclusions, of course, had implications far beyond race, providing a clear measure of the quality of worker self-perceptions and defined the practical limits of any operative institutional measure of the class solidarity that emerged from the war.

The Margins of Respectability

Americans coming out of the Civil War confronted the staggering price of having tampered with basic social structures. Estimates of the dead and maimed have long been underestimated, but the current numbers suggest about eight hundred thousand dead and more than a million, wounded or broken in health, who hobbled on among their countrymen, though the meaning of the economic figures are less obvious. In 1860 the receipts and expenditures of the Federal government came to, respectively, $56,054,000 and $63,201,000, while the numbers for 1865 were $322,000,000 and $1,295,100,000. These show that only part of the states that spent the lesser amount wracked up a nearly twenty-one-fold increase in expenditures. About 11.3 percent the Federal spending in 1860 had to be borrowed against the future, while more than 75 percent of the spending in 1865 represented debt, so the 1865 deficit of $973,100,000 was about 136 times that of 1860. Overall, the land and naval operations had cost more than $3 billion. By 1879 pensions and financing of the debt more than doubled that amount.[24] Finance capital boomed into its Gilded Age and an upward spiral that did not, nevertheless, bring along much of the nation.

This newly empowered capital saw a new future for itself. Wartime commentators had pointed to Nashville—that almost Orwellian industrialization—as a microcosm of the nation's future. They suggested that "the organization, the skill, the capital, and the enterprise which now finds scope at the national railroad headquarters of Tennessee, under Government direction, will find an open highway and a field of operation in the innermost heart of the South before many more months have elapsed." "What has befallen Tennessee will come to the lot of the whole producing regions of the South," they declared, calling it "The March of Progress."[25] Where workers could gain and maintain respectability in all of this remained unclear.

In the end, Horace Greeley's *New York Tribune* translated a kind of residual Fourierism into an idea that fostering capitalist development actually hastened new communitarian and democratic standards. It found it shocking that the top owners and managers of corporations were excluding shareholders from democratic control over the business. "The theory of a corporation is, or should be, that every stockholder shall be entitled to a voice in its management, which shall be potential in proportion to the amount of his tock," it editorialized. "Nothing but pure democracy should preside in the annual meetings."[26] That this internal collective democracy of the corporation had not yet transformed it into a cooperative did not mean that they might not eventually prove to be their antithesis.

Broader Republican rhetoric remained mixed, but similar themes predominated. The party and its leaders had long talked of the unity of interests between capitalists and laborers, which again echoed an old Fourierist argument about capital and labor, which proposed to extend the protection accorded one to the other. "Labor is capital," as Jennie Collins insisted. "The capital of the working men and women does not receive its just portion of the profits when united with the capital of the wealthy." Yet publications such as the *Scientific American* could agree that the worker's "capital is his hands and skill" and still oppose strikes because the "bad feeling" they generated could be "generally antagonistic to the best interests of the men themselves."[27]

During the war, even those who accepted the legitimacy of workers' grievances, the need for organization, and the justice of a strike could still call for their selective repression. Regardless of what the employers did, striking had forced bosses "who are under contract to the Government, to lie idle, they are directly hindering the operations of the Government itself, and at a time when it needs the whole service of all its men, to put to death this wicked rebellion." In taking action, workers striving for the just ends could transgress the "rational limit even to the demands for justice."[28]

The old Republican spokesman of the New York workers, William Oland Bourne, still spoke of a mutuality of interests between employers and employees, but he practically dismissed demands of the latter "for eight hours a day, or six hours a day, with pay equivalent to ten hours for the shorter period of labor." Once ruled by King Cotton, "*the world is governed by the laws of trade*" and only "selfish and ill-informed men" caused "discords among the industrial classes." Bourne added that the unions had never issued "one sentiment to condemn the usurpation which held four million of black laborers as property, nor one resolution of sympathy with the same four million that had been invested with self-ownership."[29]

In fact, Bourne was being less than honest. He certainly knew that unions focusing on local concerns had seen no reason to address slavery directly, and that labor generally left a complex, contradictory, and dynamic record on slavery. He was also aware that trade unionists had volunteered to fight over this particular question, including the leader of the largest antebellum strike, and had been waging a direct war on slaveholding alongside black soldiers on the battlefield. Then, too, appeals to Newtonian "laws of trade" willfully ignored the fact that the parameters had always been negotiable, and unionism's effort to shape wages and hours grew from long practice, not some alchemical scheme to reverse gravity. In the end, Bourne translated the utopian idea that workers had "capital" in their labor power into a view of trade unions as unjust "combinations" if they engaged in strikes.

Some unions thrived by courting such an idea of respectability. In June 1865 a reunited NTU convened at the Academy of Music, expecting the return of several Southern locals. By the war's end, the thirteen founding locals of 1853 had reached eighty-five, not counting Washington and Toronto. Of the eighty reporting through *The Printer*, some fifty-four, representing the largest and most active locals, functioned in states and territories that had no slavery.[30]

The largest and most secure of their locals—that at New York—came out of the war a radically different organization. Although the union had entered the Panic of 1857 with 917 members, it fell in 1858 to only 318. It built itself up a second time, reaching nearly six hundred before the war had collapsed membership again to 254 by the fall of 1862. For a third time, it recruited itself up to 677, before its wartime strike against the *Tribune* reduced membership back down to 299. Returning from the battlefields, the former Hawkins Zouave (9th New York) member Robert McKechnie and others led the union into a three-year recovery from 1865 to 1868 that saw membership growth from 299 to 1,226, reaching 2,106 at the start of 1869 with McKechnie's three-month "general amnesty" for those who had been members but were expelled or left at any point. By 1876, the local attained 2,644.[31] This represented ten times the number it had eighteen years before, and those few members around from 1862 must have been lost in a sea of new faces.

Institutionally stable unions avoided strikes, modes of struggle suited to the desperate circumstances of unskilled immigrant laborers in wartime. Strikes could be even more risky with legions of workingmen in uniform returning home. Sylvis and other leaders of the molders had already decided that the employers had hoped to goad the union into a general strike so as to bring to bear forces that could crush the union.[32] The survival of unionism, then, would require alternate avenues of change.

The Boston Labor Reform Association pointed toward efforts to gain workers' rights through government action. On April 28, 1865, a joint legislative committee on the apprenticeship system returned to the Massachusetts assembly requesting information that led to the appointment of "an unpaid commission of five to collect information and statistics in regard to the hours of labor and the condition and prospects of the industrial class." It proposed some tax relief for mechanics and "authorizing the formation of co-operative associations."[33]

Interestingly, Major John W. Mahan, a member of house from Boston, pressed the matter. A young attorney, he had risen in the ranks under the late Captain William Madigan's company of the Ninth Massachusetts. He persuaded the Judiciary committee to agree as to the constitutionality of "regulating and limiting the number of hours constituting a day's labor." The proposed bill would penalize anyone requiring more hours than the law permitted and included a clause against combinations by businessmen to increase the price of the necessities. The committee—which did not report until February 1866—included such prolabor figures as Edward H. Rogers and strongly recommended legal action for the eight-hour day, though Rogers pressed for the regulation of hours for adults as well as child labor. The following year, the state appointed "General" Henry K. Oliver, a veteran of the war and the Boston Typographical Union, as special state constable to enforce the provisions.[34]

Labor also wanted the repeal of conspiracy laws, the abolition of contract labor in the prisons, and the prohibition of child labor. They imposed on government a certain ownership of the social problem by demanding the establishment of a bureau of labor statistics. Massachusetts established its Bureaus of Labor Statistics in 1869. Pennsylvania (in 1872) and Connecticut (by 1873) organized bureaus of their own: Ohio, New Jersey, Indiana, Missouri, and Illinois by 1880, and another twenty-two states by 1900. Some Civil War veterans among the trade unionists, such as Oliver in Massachusetts and Aaron K. Dunkle in Pennsylvania, took charge of them. Put in a more formulaic fashion: "On account of the war, labor was scarce and wages high, and the labor organizations of the time were concerned less with bettering their industrial condition, and more with politics."[35]

Some union leaders had already begun to formulate a strategy of avoiding strikes. "The word arbitration was as yet unspoken," recalled Terence V. Powderly. While workers at first had to strike "in order to get a hearing," he complained that it became "the recognized weapon of defense with organized and unorganized workmen whenever a dispute arose between the employers and workmen." Workers lacked the patience to heed advice from their leaders to moderate the struggle.[36]

Based on the earliest of these victories in Massachusetts, *Fincher's Trades' Review* suggested: "Let the workmen of that State exact of every aspirant for nomination a pledge, that, if nominated, he will go for the proposed measure; and any aspirant to nomination refusing to give such a pledge, let him be defeated, by all means." Mass meetings, torchlight parades and other means of mobilizing the workers carried the day. Labor memorialized the Congress, which on June 24, 1868, passed a national eight-hour law. The following May, President Ulysses S. Grant issued a presidential statement that the law did not intend to reduce wages proportionate to the reduction of hours.[37]

* * *

The end of the Civil War also fostered a promise of social peace that inspired faith in respectable and responsible unionism. Many workers carried into the war the hope that it would establish a system of free labor and the dignity of the worker. Its outcome, though, left each American "in an antagonistic position to his fellow beings," making it "necessary to secure for his own use as much property as he can procure." Horace Seaver pointed out that "the poor are obliged to compete with each other; not with respect to the outlay of their moneyed capital, of which they are *minus*, but with respect to their labor, the only capital they have at their disposal." This meant that most people had to live "without ever making any use of their reason, beyond the best method of getting money and how to enjoy it, leaving all the rest unknown or unheeded." Indeed, under this system, most "think it is enough to do as they are ordered."[38]

More than this, the progress of a political alliance of union leaders and sympathetic politicians raised the possibility of moving labor reform through a government that had ended slavery. In particular, it created a situation in which the leaders of the most successful and secure unions could become as invested as the employers in avoiding conflicts that might lead to strikes. Paradoxically, union officials might naturally see an institutional security by not mobilizing workers in the numbers needed to bring new social weight to bear on the questins they face. For the wider society, this new approach also promised to preclude the necessity for troublesome and often unmanageable movements, the diverse constituencies and individuals of which might have their own concerns and agenda.

Though the elements of this may be evident in hindsight, none of this simply fell into place at the war's end. Rather, a new idea of class would have to be reconstructed with the nation.

EPILOGUE

1877

Reconstructions of Class

As of July 27, 1877, nearly thirteen years had passed since Union General Andrew Jackson Smith scrambled to protect St. Louis from Confederate forces that included those under General John S. Marmaduke. On this later day, the two generals cooperated to take the city from its people. At Lafayette Square on the south side, they and other former officers of both sides gathered a small force of well-armed regulars and militia to the cheers of the businessmen and their retainers. From there they marched north into the center city to seize the headquarters of the general strike waged by other Civil War veterans. The workers had not only brought industry to a standstill, but they had chased the police and city government from their offices and largely took control of the community. That Friday, though, many of them remembered the war as they watched the armed, uniformed ranks moving against them, while others recalled the bloodbath that had crushed the Paris Commune a few years earlier.[1]

That same year officially brought an end to the last contemporary hope for a real Federal Reconstruction of the South. Many had anticipated the triumph of a "free labor" ethos that precluded "wages slavery." The war had not precluded such an outcome, though its reconstruction of the American class formation went far beyond the radical expansion of wage labor to shape how workers needed to see themselves in their civilization. Workers, too, reconstructed their movement as the International Industrial Assembly of North America gave rise to a National Labor Union in 1866. The NLU embarked on a winding course that led through the Knights of Labor to the American Federation of Labor, which Samuel Gompers took into the next century.

Solidarity's Legacy: Labor Radicalism

The Civil War had indisputably been a conflict around the issue of "free labor." Before his battlefield death, trade unionist Joseph Moreau found that war contains "no glory, except in the glory of the cause he defended." That cause for which he found and died had been "all rights for all people," but the dominant educational, political, ecclesiastical, and intellectual mores of American life had a different perspective.[2] Moreau's movement emerged from the war badly wounded and scarred, to face larger and more impersonal new companies and industries that cared little for intellectual or moral suasion about a cause.

Some workers had gone into the war with a certain sense of class solidarity—with questions about the meaning of liberty and economic privilege, of war and peace, and of the nature of America—that had long predated the war, and they resurfaced repeatedly. The personnel reflected this as well. Ideas of "liberty" and aspirations of mobility may remain just as important to people who find themselves frustrated in their realization by social and cultural standards unaddressed in a democratic civilization. In the United States, too, insistence that a representative system of government reflect the will of its majority of laboring people gave rise to talk of the "Social Republic," or what critics called a "Red Republican" or "Black Republican." The wartime and postwar documents on the movement reflected great continuity between antebellum radicals into the war and beyond. Local circles of old land reformers, unrepentant Fourierists, old cooperationists, and émigré radicals continued to meet and to try to influence the course of the broader movement in Boston, New York, Philadelphia, and virtually every city of any size. David Montgomery's *Beyond Equality* correctly pointed to vital connections between them and Radical Republicanism.[3]

With the significant exception of the land reformers, antebellum social critics had generally tended to rest their hopes for building a better, freer America on moral appeals and reasoned arguments, to which they believed their rulers not to be entirely immune. The major organizations of women workers during the Civil War had tested the strength of any paternalistic sense of fair play and found it severely compromised. As the role of women in American society changed after the war, this approach became less and less a gendered response. The experience of the war dealt a severe blow to older utopian ideas of "moral suasion."

Conversely, the triumph of emancipation demonstrated the power of government to foster change. Reaching beyond reforms such as a bureau of labor statistics, this included a lien law to protect wages and the regulation of working conditions, including child labor. Increasingly, workers turned to solutions such as Ira Stewart's new eight-hour philosophy. The postwar workers' movement proposed fundamental social change through government action.

Workers and reformers of all sort seized upon the Boston idea of 1863 and the Portland model of 1865 to launch an independent Labor Reform Party in New Hampshire in 1868. They expressed their historic debt to the Republicans for having led the nation through the war but determined to make possible an independent working-class expression at the polls. They would "coalesce with no other organization" and hoped to be "not the party of a day."[4] The idea spread back into Massachusetts and beyond. What would be left of the National Labor Union resolved itself in 1872 into a National Labor Reform Party.

Their preoccupations centered on a politicized version of currency reform that rallied discontented workers and farmers through the rest of the century. The National Labor Union took up the issue quickly, and the language used on its behalf increasingly recalled that which had urged abolitionism, partly because its spokesmen, from Wendell Phillips to James B. Weaver, had come out of the antislavery tradition. Weaver headed the presidential ticket of the Greenbackers in 1880 and the Populists in 1892.[5]

While the land question had lost none of its old appeal, solutions even more centered on government emerged. At the height of the war, in August 1864, young Henry George joined the Eureka Typographical Union and began his attempt to understand his own poverty amid the wealth of California. His *Progress and Poverty* provides an analysis of the relationship between economic development and the degradation of the laboring classes. His move to New York City framed a mass rediscovery of radical "free soil" politics in the Gilded Age. In the 1880s George represented a renewal of the land reform struggles to which some of the old-timers had devoted their lives, so, too, had younger protégés, such as William Hansen, John A. Lant, and Charles Commerford, a former baseball star and the son of the late John Commerford.[6] George's 1886 mayoral campaign offered a seemingly scientific yardstick for social ills, with a simple "single tax" on underutilized land that would keep more of it in circulation and available to maintain a middle class.

Through such agencies, even fraternalism and cooperation became more politicized. Even the broader quasi-fraternal associations of the postwar labor movement—from the Knights of St. Crispin to the Knights of Labor—grew from deeply rooted antebellum precedents and from widespread norms among the Freemasons and Odd Fellows across the society.[7] By the late 1870s, a newly politicized socialism appeared, advocating government support and funding of workers' cooperatives.

To a great extent, American socialism grew directly from the experience of the Civil War. The first presidential candidate to run as a socialist, Simon Wing, had been too old to go to war but had been active in the antislavery movement and other antebellum reforms. From Dr. George C. Stiebling in the 1870s through the rest of the century, veterans played a key role in efforts to establish a party. These included prominent figures such as William P. Rogers, former commander of the *Merrimack*, and General Arthur F. Devereux, who had held the line at Gettysburg on the third day of the Confederate assaults. John H. Dennis of Michigan left the Republican Party for the Greenbackers before coming to socialism, and Lafayette Crum participated in every third party to sweep upstate New York, before joining the socialists thirty-one years after being wounded at Gettysburg.[8]

Rejected for military service, Cyrenus Osborne Ward entered the Brooklyn Navy Yard, working there through the worst of its wartime struggles. Born upstate and raised in Illinois, he had already become a brilliant autodidact and polyglot, as well as an accomplished musician. His play, "The Great Rebellion: Reminiscences of the Struggle that Cost a Million Lives," embraced the stereotype of Lincoln as the railsplitter recounting homespun stories, but it placed abolitionism, the struggle for emancipation, and the arming of blacks at the center of the conflict. After the war, he went overseas, where he visited Karl Marx, Charles Darwin, and other luminaries of the new sciences of change inspiring his own work, particularly his *Ancient Lowly: A History of the Ancient Working People*.[9] His wartime experience was as deep (in its own way) as that of his thrice-wounded brother, the sociologist Frank Lester Ward.

The Civil War also informed the course of the two first socialist presidential candidates. Simon Wing's running mate in 1892—and himself the 1896 presidential candidate—Charles H. Matchett had gone to war, he said, "simply because I was a young man and wasn't contented to stay where I was. In those days I used to love the Star-Spangled Banner, and even cried about it, and sometimes the thought of it brings tears to my eyes yet." He spent a year on the *USS North Carolina* watching the army and navy fail to take Charleston, an experience that left him "disgusted [such that he] didn't re-enlist." Returning home, he shipped out on the Great Lakes, just at the time the Seamen's Union organized out of Buffalo and waged a series of strikes. As with Ward, Matchett's socialism grew from his wartime experience.[10]

Certainly, many such figures drew conclusions about race that belie the simplistic assumptions. Some white and black radicals had collaborated for years before the war. In the wake of the war, Peter H. Clark, the first prominent African American socialist and the schoolteacher who had organized Cincinnati "black brigade" when the Confederates in 1862 had deep ties with local radical currents through William Haller and other whites, made a valuable contribution as these currents coalesced after the war. His Brooklyn comrade, Caleb Pink, also made the transition from land reform to socialism, carrying its message to "the colored citizens of Williamsburg" and other black audiences. William H. Sylvis—head of the molders' union and later the National Labor Union—always remained adamant on the necessity of accepting blacks into the workforce and into the unions.[11]

Hopes for a substantive egalitarian change in American life cultivated a deep hope among workers. In the first year's after the war, advocates of everything from cooperation through land reform to socialism hoped to achieve pervasive changes in the economic and social system without civil strife. Wartime trade unionists easily expropriated the terminology of the "Irrepressible Conflict" to describe the relations of capital and labor.[12] At the same time, using the same terminology would not substitute for a movement that assimilated the range of ways in which workers had resisted their exploitation.

Yet the fact that ethical arguments had failed to change even such an obvious injustice as slavery must surely have dampened hopes. The reality of the American Civil War—and the later brutal repression of the Paris Commune in 1871—did not, however, entirely disabuse workers of the general faith that the lessons of the Civil War would convince the ruling elites to accept that the abolition of wage slavery would not require the bloodshed needed to wash away chattel slavery.

Then came 1877.

Another Civil War?

Republican President Rutherford B. Hayes dealt a final blow to Reconstruction in 1877, after winning his office in one of the most bitter and questionable national elections in U.S. history. Both parties avoided addressing the issue, though the Democrats campaigned for reform and against corruption, while Hayes offered an alternate vision that opposed corruption and favored reform. Democrats determined to restore the former Confederate states, confident that they would support their party, while the Republicans lacked the will to push an agenda of Reconstruction any further than they had.

Perhaps no industry more favored an end to Reconstruction and the restoration of national order on whatever grounds it might be had than the railroads. The largest and most central industry to the country had ties to virtually everything. It and the forces that had financed it had corrupted and discredited the outgoing administration of President U.S. Grant. As of 1877, the incoming president, his vice president William A. Wheeler, and their secretaries of state, war, and the navy had direct ties to the railroads, as did the attorney general.

The railroads, having already earned a long list of enemies, responded to the Panic of 1873 by continuing to pay dividends while slashing wages for its workers. By May and June 1877, several of the unions on the railroads planned a job action over the series of pay cuts imposed to sustain ongoing dividends for the stockholders. However, they kept postponing action in hopes that a strike might be averted. Prepared to strike, the workers held back a few more weeks.

On Monday, July 16, news that the Baltimore & Ohio Railroad would cut yet another 10 percent of their pay reached the workers in the rail yard at Martinsburg,

West Virginia. Already prepared for a strike, they walked off the job en masse but returned with arms and occupied the roundhouse. Governor Henry Matthews, a former Confederate officer, arranged to send troops in cooperation with others. The next day, the strike spread to Cumberland, Maryland, and Newark, Ohio.[13]

Shooting between the strikers and those the authorities had sent against them had already begun by the time the movement reached Pittsburgh on Thursday. On Friday, armed troops opened fire on strikers at Baltimore, in a sad reprise of the 1861 riot. The government arranged for General Winfield S. Hancock, the hero of Gettysburg, to move on the city. Over the weekend, the strike reached the St. Louis area, and Monday carried it to Rochester, Terre Haute, Indianapolis, Chicago, San Francisco, and Kansas City.

Everywhere, legions of other workers joined those on the railroads. The violence at Pittsburgh, Baltimore, and Chicago demonstrated a discontent that reached far beyond that industry. As of July 24 the walkout had grown into a general strike at St. Louis and soon after took a similar course on a smaller scale in Toledo. Not until August 1, when the holdouts at Scranton caved, did the government restore order and force the workers back to their jobs.

Immigrants had provided disproportionate numbers of those vast armies of unskilled labor. Even at the time, observers chose to see the strike not as the result of productive, industrious, sober sons of Franklin and the founders but of the disreputable, lazy, and destructive tramps, street urchins, aliens, and others of various types. Jane Swisshelm, the feminist writer, warned of the strikers in her native Pittsburgh as "an Irish Catholic mob," and others called them "half-grown boys" and blacks.[14]

Significantly, one of the most salient features of the strike movement was the active participation, prominence, and leadership of African Americans. Although many may have been relative newcomers to wage labor, they took up the rhetoric by which wage workers had always expressed their interests and entered the fray on their behalf. Peter H. Clark, one of the most prominent African Americans in the Midwest, also became one of the strike's most visible public defenders.[15]

Blacks established a clear presence in all of the cities, but those on the waterfront at St. Louis, Louisville, New Orleans, and Galveston clearly formed an important vanguard of the movement. At one point, a black striker in St. Louis took the platform and asked the predominantly white crowd if they would stand behind the effort of African Americans on the waterfront to win wage concessions. "We will," thundered the crowd, and stormed off to the docks.[16]

Regardless of their race or craft identities, those workers of 1877 who took to the streets in a mass strike may well have seen themselves as "white," but they had actually adopted the behaviors and practices associated with African Americans. Conditions had finally reached the point where they drew upon the one weapon they had for making their interests felt: their numbers. Simply put, this is why the 1877 strike threw the authorities for a loop.

For their part, African Americans tended to understand that the government would not hesitate to drown the strike in blood, a truth to which the whites seemed to be oblivious. At St. Louis, black strikers in 1877 concentrated near the headquarters, expecting the socialists running the movement to provide them the means needed to defend the headquarters, but that never happened. Other African American strikers hedged their bets as to whether many of the whites would stand by them. At Galveston, Norris Wright Cuney, a black Republican recently defeated for mayor, reminded the several hundred African American strikers there "that there were over seven hundred armed men trained [as] soldiers in the city, who could annihilate them all in an hour; and if they could not, he said, that in the city of Houston there were 1,000 men under arms who could be brought to this city within two hours to accomplish that bloody work."[17] Those willing to meet the bosses and the government on their own terms would not be numerous enough to prevail.

With the collapse of the strike, even some of the more radical whites were quoted as blaming the "niggers" for having carried the action far beyond what they had intended. Certainly, the existing unions scrambled after the strike to disclaim any responsibility for the action. The head of the Brotherhood of Locomotive Engineers, whose locals had clearly been involved in organizing and leading the strike in places, disowned any responsibility for it, claiming that his union had nothing to do with it. This established the foundations for a misleading idea that one hundred thousand workers had engaged in a "spontaneous" strike.[18] This very tangible measure of "whiteness" did not simply have to do with race but with the racialization of militant mass actions.

Class never superseded race because emancipation was never abolition under another name, as contemporary politicians and generals—and many later historians—pretended. Abolition proposed to end the inequality that slavery had created because it envisioned a society based on the imperative of human equality, whatever its internal ambiguities about how that could and should play out. In contrast, emancipation represented a legal change aimed at weakening the enemy's prospect for success. Once secession had been defeated, the Federal authorities had no compelling interest in pursuing the egalitarian logic, in which few had actually been interested. "Free labor" would never work out to mean the same for African Americans as for whites. Indeed, emancipation left them with what remained the vague and tentative status of "free blacks" before the war.

Even some of the best allies of the black victims of slavery expressed a remarkable contempt for African American workers. Allan Pinkerton, who had helped runaway slaves, now distinguished between what he saw as legitimate or respectable labor activities and those more questionable and illegal activities characteristic of the "Sambos." "Any one understanding the mercurial nature of that childish and ignorant race," he wrote of blacks, "would readily know that it requires but the veriest trifle to stimulate them into making a show of themselves."[19] Bringing one's numbers to bear recalled the bullying of the "childish and ignorant."

The results of Reconstruction, then, did not represent some anomalous betrayals of the freed people by the shortcomings of national policy. Rather, what happened to blacks came from the same institutional process that warred on Indians, the humanity of women, and the innately democratic character of the mass strike. Reconstruction did not fail; it succeeded as its real movers and shakers determined it should.

As part of this, the experience of Civil War and Reconstruction cultivated an essential myth of progress, or an "irrepressible" expansion of equality and justice along with the extension of market capitalism, as it exists in practical terms. Organized workers in America had already cultivated assumptions fundamentally compatible with these myths (or a consensus to act as though they did). They assumed that, while employers may have an interest distinct form their workers, there still existed broad fundamentals, such as the commitment to the health and well-being of the business, the industry, and the society. Over time, labor organizations came to see a role for government, though primarily as an arbitrator and regulator to help employers recognize and act on concerns shared with their workers.

These kinds of trade unionists behaved accordingly. They sought to avoid wielding a shillelagh or rummage through a city looking for firearms to force the authorities to stand down. Responsible self-organization seemed to promise the possibility of worker self-improvement, albeit in a piecemeal and individual fashion, industry by industry and workplace by workplace. They balked at mobilizing their numbers, which the press almost invariably reported as bullying and brutalization or the threat of such things. That kind of advocacy for the employers obviously resurrected the slaveholder's claims to their possible victimization based on their fears of being murdered in their beds by the overwhelming numbers of machete-wielding slave rebels.

The Price of Respectability

The myths associated with the Civil War and Reconstruction contributed to the idea of American exceptionalism. Any civilization (or even locality) has important peculiarities in its experience, but, in practical terms, the idea of American exceptionalism extracts the United States from the same kinds of historical and institutional processes that shape other peoples. Strangely enough, the crushing of the 1877 strike becomes part of what allegedly distinguishes America from societies that experienced decades of persistent class discontent. However tenuous and gradual, the innately progressive and ultimately egalitarian nature of American civilization precluded the need for Irish Republicans, French Communards, German Social Democrats, or Russian Nihilists. Over time, they placed anything smacking of anarchism, socialism, or communism as foreign and "un-American."

Their faith is rooted in an obliviousness to what actually happened abroad. Eighteen seventy-seven came only a few years after the suppression of the Paris Commune and kindred movements in France with the subsequent cantonal revolts in Spain. Only a few years later, the newly unified German government officially outlawed the social democracy there. Class consciousness abroad mandated neither a Russian Revolution nor a German Social Democracy, nor even a British Labour Party. The reality of class consciousness kept it always in flux. E. P. Thompson's massive tome *The Making of the English Working Class*, for example, wisely keeps its focus on the English, explicitly setting aside the peculiar discussion of the Scottish, Irish, and Welsh experience of class.

The 1877 strike provides the first of several dramatic chapters in postwar labor history. These included a series of localized mass strikes and riotous outbreaks, such as Haymarket, Homestead, Pullman, and similar episodic outbursts into the 1930s. As with 1877, labor organizations that waged a mass militant strike risked finding themselves largely on their own, facing the power of the state, and burying their dead. Post–Civil War authorities came down on such actions as consistently as antebellum authorities had upon slave rebellions, albeit certainly with less generalized brutality.

Strikes and organizing continued, of course, but rarely through an attempt to mobilize and bring to bear the numbers needed to bring about a rapid conclusion favorable to the workers. More often than not, it would be a measure of last resort, forced upon employees by the employers and permissible only in a responsible and orderly fashion, as a structured ritual conducted in a well-regulated scale with a very well-considered impact on society.

Labor organizations gained what they did by shying away from the mobilization of numbers. The power structure, the media, and the school system all combined to anathematize bringing the largest numbers to bear on a question. They recast such a fundamental expression of the democratic will as somehow unfair, bullying, and not quite "respectable" and "white." It establishes a taboo that fundamentally precludes the essence of solidarity and an assertion of the democratic will. This vital difference in the way in which workers needed to relate to the dominant institutions underlay the later long-standing tensions between craft and industrial unionism or even over the acknowledgement of race as an issue.

Toward the end of the century, American civilization put a brake on the Robber Barons only when they had become dangerous to themselves. Its solution was to rely directly on the force that had prevailed through the Civil War, the government. Based on a series of experiments at the state and local levels, going back to the efforts inspired by the Labor Reformers in Massachusetts, the authorities made themselves the arbiter of all things bright and beautiful. And, if they did it right, there would be no need for shillelaghs. In short order, it would begin acknowledging unions as respectable bodies (and women as citizens), once they had behaved respectably and obediently in the World War.

Despite the racialized nature of their origins, the distinctive modes of labor resistance did not determine anything immutable about the composition or nature of the movement. While radicals agitated for generations on behalf of "industrial unionism," their success ultimately involved merely extending that same business unionism characteristic of the crafts to new groups of workers. So, too, women, African Americans, or any members of any other minority have played major roles in the labor movement, though their "success" came to be measured by the yardstick of a respectability shaped by white craftsmen. Indeed, on the eve of the Haymarket affair of 1886, ethnic anarchists complained when an African American protested the lack of access to the ballot, while foreign-born "dregs and scum" could vote.[20] In the end, though, the black writer simply made his bid to demonstrate the same kind of respectability that formed the core of a labor strategy among the whites.

With the adoption of the National Labor Relations Board during the Great Depression, politicians, judges, lawyers, and bureaucrats came to have a far greater role, directly or indirectly, in shaping the course of a lawful strike than the democratic will of the workers likely to be affected by the outcome. The mere acknowledgement of the latter challenged the monopoly of capital over government of the workplace. The same consideration doomed the persistent historic efforts to democratize land ownership or to reform currency or change any of the essential institutions and structures that maintain the status quo. This codified the deeply rooted sense that the legitimacy of labor organizations rests on governmental approval rather than the will of the workers themselves.

The twentieth century also expanded a fundamental aspect of those myths about the Civil War, equating military power with liberation and shaping a martial tradition fueled by class identities. Before his death on the battlefields of the Civil War, Joseph N. Moreau talked of the glory of war in terms of what it materially created. In his pioneering 1886 history of American labor, Richard T. Ely wrote that "the universal freedom of the laboring classes from the yoke of slavery could not fail to have an elevating influence on those engaged in manual toil."[21] One need not dispute his observation to note that his equation of emancipation with "universal freedom" remains rather undeveloped.

Certainly, never before or since had so many figures associated with labor and labor reform became general officers. European revolutionaries such as Fritz Anneke, August Moor, and Joseph Weydemeyer attained such rank, as did trade unionists such as Alonzo G. Draper and Edward F. Schneider, a Kansas member of the NTU. Politicians such as John Cochrane and Benjamin F. Butler identified with the movement, and a number, including Butler, James B. Weaver, and Arthur F. Devereux became closely involved after the war in the Greenback-Labor and Populist causes or in the socialism of Edward Bellamy's *Looking Backward*.[22] The numbers increased, of course, as one looked into lower ranks.

Military service permitted workers to step out of a position defined by labor into one defined by serving the power structure. From the printers' union, John M. Farquhar, Amos J. Cummings, and John M. Tobin earned Congressional Medals of Honor for their bravery in battle. Farquhar and Cummings also later won election to the U.S. House of Representatives. In Farquhar's case, he put in his day's work at the case before heading off for the congressional nominating meeting, where he "won the nomination by defeating the proprietor of the paper he was working on."[23] Participation in the war not only expressed a class identity but could provide a mechanism for the kind of personal mobility that mediated any such identity.

Even in the Civil War, members of the Denver printers' union—disproportionately from the *Rocky Mountain News*—had been in "the Bloodless Third," which perpetrated one of the worst racial massacres of the age against a peaceful encampment of Indians along Sand Creek. After his service elsewhere, William Allen Heaton stayed in the army "to chase recalcitrant plains Indian wards to where they were ordered to be." The authorities who stole the land of the Shivwits Indians named Howland Butte and Sumner Point for two union printers in the 1869 expedition through the Grand Canyon. A charter member of two western locals, Hugh McQuaid broke the story of the 1876 massacre of the Seventh Cavalry at Little Big Horn to the outside world. After the Indian Wars, the U.S. found larger fish to fry. In 1918, the *Typographical Journal* reported several grandsons of one Civil War veteran off to the war in Europe. The president of the Baltimore local during the Civil War had been the son of a Mexican War soldier, and his own descendants fought Spain and joined the marines to fight on the western front.[24] Increasingly, history divided Moreau's idea of the honor of war from its actual outcome, which has, in modern times, never entered into the institutionalized faith that the fighting, death, and slaughter had been honorable, respectable, and responsible.

Later, when government action got around to dismantling the color bar that it had itself promulgated, it urged organized labor to address the discriminations of race and gender that their employers had authored. In part, it did so in the hope of enlisting unions to encourage women and African Americans to behave in a more "respectable" way. By this time, American unions had already surrendered themselves to cooperation with the government in its efforts to domesticate workers and their organizations abroad. For this reason, the political meaning of calls to erase the distinctions of "whiteness" retains more than a hint of ambiguity, particularly when embraced and defined by the same elite institutions that invented and promulgated the concept and legal definitions of race in the first place and proposed to address race without addressing the social and institutional structure of class power.

Here, then, lay the real, if unconscious context of Samuel Gompers's dismissiveness of *Klassen Bewustzein*—an awareness of class—and what he called a *Klassengefühl*, which he suggested made the AFL so successful. The earlier emphasis on thought and discussion became a simple reliance on unexamined "feeling." We can call it by any label, but it will not naturally be a class sense, in any meaningful sense. In fact, that "class" feeling would not necessarily reach beyond the industry or even the workplace. For very sound reasons rooted in a collective history and individual experience, the fellow "feeling" that developed among Americans workers often tended to be implicitly racial. Whether intentional or not, Gompers's *Klassengefühl* among the unions implicitly embraced the limits imposed upon it by the dominant institutions.[25] The issue was a question of feelings rather than practical knowledge and the related action.

In short, American institutions shaped the kind of labor organizations that could behave in such a way as to cooperate in their own marginalization in the lives of the nation and of its workers. Unwilling to rely on their strength of numbers, they became unconcerned about the vital need to continue organizing more and larger unions. Without a strategy centered on the strength of numbers, acting on their own would never become a permanent feature of their political universe, which left them restricted to lesser-evil politics and lobbying. If organized workers cannot overcome this legacy of "whiteness," it is difficult to see how they have any future of their own in shaping American life.

Even to the present day, the pundits, lobbyists, and politicians hostile to worker self-organization talk of "union thugs," not as a seriously descriptive term, but because of its impact. It not only flusters representatives and supporters of organized labor, but it also provides an ongoing reminder to stay without the bounds of what their social betters and economic superiors will regard as respectable. It helps to trigger the systemic default rejection of anything smacking of militancy or relying on the force of numbers to "bully" opponents. In short, it tends to leave organized labor with no options but the least effective and most likely to result in the loss of membership and power.

* * *

If the Civil War remains unfinished—as has often been said—the task remains largely in the hands of American working people. In lieu of anything substantive that might threaten the structures of power or wealth, we have a range of official rituals fostering the fiction that racial injustices are fundamentally declining or even that racism is dead. There is no basis to believe that structures and practices that have grown from past injustices and have failed to address the issue will do so in the future. Conversely, workers will never supersede race while they have anathematized those modes of struggle pioneered by the most exploited and oppressed of their number, including the mass strike of the slaves. Certainly, that process would cultivate a more complete construction of workers' self-awareness as a *class*.

Skepticism about such a future would be easy, were it not for the memory of experiences such as the Civil War. The outbreak of the conflict demonstrated just how remarkably brittle even the oldest institutionalized injustices can be. Only two years after securing a virtually unchallenged white voter consensus not to interfere with black slavery, hundreds of thousands of Americans were in motion, most seeing themselves engaged in an overt war for slave liberation. The president who had advocated thinking anew did not himself survive to address many of those cumbersome old institutions and values in which profits had priority over people. But in the fields and factories, working people came to realize that the allegedly immutable and natural structures of power and wealth proved no match for history's fateful lightening.

Notes

Abbreviations

ADC	*Augusta Daily Constitutionalist*
BDE	*Brooklyn Daily Eagle*
BET	*Boston Evening Traveller*
BH	*Boston Herald*
BI	*Boston Investigator*
BoL	*Banner of Light*
BS	Baltimore *Sun*
CG	*Columbus Gazette*
CJ	*Chicago Journal*
CL	*Cleveland Leader*
CM	*Charleston Mercury*
DP	*Daily Picayune*
FTR	*Fincher's Trades' Review*
GWT	Georgia *Weekly Telegraph*
HoP	*Herald of Progress*
HDT	*Houston Daily Telegraph*
HT-WT	Houston *The Tri-Weekly Telegraph*
HW	*Harper's Weekly*
IPE	*The Iron Platform. Extra*
ISZ	*Illinois Staats-Zeitung*
LDJ	*Louisville Daily Journal*
LDT	Leavenworth *Daily Times*

LH	*Labor History*
MDA	*Memphis Daily Appeal*
MDAv	*Memphis Daily Avalanche*
MDT	Macon *Daily Telegraph*
NN	*The New Nation*
NODD	New Orleans *Daily Delta*
NODP	New Orleans *Daily Picayune*
NYDT	*New York Daily Times*
NYDTrib	*New York Daily Tribune*
NYH	*New York Herald*
NYT	*New York Times*
NYTrib	*New York Tribune*
Pr	*The Printer*
PrC	*The Printers' Circular*
PA	*Philadelphia Age*
PP	*Philadelphia Press*
PtsS	*Pittsfield Sun*
PI	*The Philadelphia Inquirer*
QDWR	Quincy *Daily Whig and Republican*
RE	*Richmond Examiner*
RDD	*Richmond Daily Dispatch*
RS	*Richmond Sentinel*
RT	*Railway Times*
RW	*Richmond Whig*
SA	*Scientific American*
SFEB	*San Francisco Evening Bulletin*
SLCDN	Salt Lake City *The Deseret News*
StMD	*St. Louis Missouri Democrat*
StR	*St. Louis Republican*
USMO	*United States Mechanics' Own*
WmA	*Workingman's Advocate*

Acknowledgments

1. American Civil War Research Database, Historical Data Systems, available at http://www.civilwardata.com; Betts's site is http://www.uttyler.edu/vbetts/newspaper_titles.htm.

Introduction

1. E. F. Ware, "The Lyon Campaign in Missouri: Being a History of the First Iowa Infantry and of the Causes which Led Up to Its Organization and How It Earned the Thanks of Congress, which It Got; Together with a Birdseye View of the Conditions in Iowa Preceding the great Civil War of 1861," (Topeka, 1907), 62, and also 34, 38, 42; Friedrich A.

Sorge's *Labor Movement in the United States: A History of the American Working Class from Colonial Times to 1890* (ed. Philip S. Foner, Brewster Chamberlin, Angela Chamberlin [Westport, Conn.: Greenwood, 1977]) devotes a mere two pages to the war years, padded by short sketches of William Sylvis and Ira Stewart, with a merely encyclopedic recitation on emancipation. David Roediger's *Seizing Freedom: Slave Emancipation and Liberty for All* (London: Verso, 2014) was released as this book goes to press and will hopefully be a major contribution to this sparsely covered subject of the process of slave self-emancipation.

2. For an overview of these issues of class formation, see Jacqueline Jones, *A Social History of the Laboring Classes: From Colonial Times to the Present* (Malden, Mass.: Blackwell, 1999), 92–116; Martin J. Burke, *The Conundrum of Class: Public Discourse on the Social Order in America* (Chicago: University of Chicago Press, 1994). See Robert J. Steinfeld, *Coercion, Contract, and Free Labor in the Nineteenth Century* (Cambridge: Cambridge University Press, 2001).

3. Russell Lee Johnson, *Warriors into Workers: The Civil War and the Formation of Urban-Industrial Society in a Northern City* (New York: Fordham University Press, 2003).

4. Iver Bernstein, *The New York City Draft Riots: Their Significance for American Society and Politics in the Age of the Civil War* (New York: Oxford University Press, 1990); Grace Palladino, *Another Civil War: Labor, Capital, and the State in the Anthracite Regions of Pennsylvania, 1840–68* (Urbana: University of Illinois Press, 1990). The only book-length study on the labor movement per se in this period remains Jonathan P. Grossman's *William Sylvis: Pioneer of American Labor* (New York: Columbia University Press, 1945).

5. See Bruce Laurie, *The Working People of Philadelphia, 1800–1850* (Philadelphia: Temple University Press, 1980) and his *Artisans into Workers: Labor in Nineteenth-Century America* (Urbana: University of Illinois Press, 1989).

6. David R. Roediger's *The Wages of Whiteness: Race and the Making of the American Working Class* (London: Verso, 1991) merits close study. On the surface, for example, Noel Ignatiev's *How the Irish Became White* (New York: Routledge, 1995) or Matthew Frye Jacobson's *Whiteness of a Different Color: European Immigrants and the Alchemy of Race* (Cambridge, Mass.: Harvard University Press, 1998) makes an interesting point that also smudges contemporaries understood to be "white." See also Alexander Saxton, *The Rise and Fall of the White Republic: Class Politics and Mass Culture in Nineteenth-Century America*, 2nd ed. (London: Verso, 2003). Politically, the broad political assumption is that, in America at least, results reflect some democratic consensus among whites, treating policies as rather straightforward translations of human wishes, values, and aspirations.

7. Eric Williams, *Capitalism and Slavery* (Chapel Hill: University of North Carolina Press, 1944); Bill Cecil-Fronsman's review of John Ashworth's *Slavery, Capitalism, and Politics in the Antebellum Republic, Vol. 1: Commerce and Compromise, 1820–1850* (Cambridge: Cambridge University Press, 1995). See also Ashworth's *Slavery, Capitalism and Politics in the Antebellum Republic, Vol. 2: The Coming of the Civil War, 1850–1861* (Cambridge: Cambridge University Press, 1996). Editors of the journal *Historical Materialism* marked the 2011 sesquicentennial with a symposium that "brought together some of the most significant Marxist scholars working in this area to debate the issues," with the following contributions to the journal (vol. 19, no. 4 [2011]): Steve Edwards, "A Symposium on the

American Civil War and Slavery"; Neil Davidson, "The American Civil War Considered as a Bourgeois Revolution"; Charles Post, "Social-Property Relations, Class-Conflict and the Origins of the US Civil War: Towards a New Social Interpretation"; John Ashworth, "Towards a Bourgeois Revolution? Explaining the American Civil War"; Charles Post, "Social-Property Relations, Class-Conflict and the Origins of the U.S. Civil War: Towards a New Social Interpretation"; Robin Blackburn, "Karl Marx and Abraham Lincoln: A Curious Convergence"; August H. Nimtz, "Marx and Engels on the U.S. Civil War: The 'Materialist Conception of History' in Action."

8. Caitlin C. Rosenthal's "From Memory to Mastery: Accounting for Control in America, 1750–1880," *Enterprise and Society* (December 2013), and her "Slavery's Scientific Management: Accounting for Mastery," in *Slavery's Capitalism*, ed. Seth Rockman, Sven Beckert, and David Waldstreicher (Philadelphia: University of Pennsylvania Press [forthcoming]). See also: Katie Johnston, "The Messy Link between Slave Owners and Modern Management," *Working Knowledge: The Thinking that Leads*, available at http://hbswk.hbs.edu/item/7182.html (accessed September 20, 2014).

9. Bell I. Wiley, *The Life of Billy Yank: The Common Soldier of the Union*, 2nd ed. (1952; Baton Rouge: Louisiana State University Press, 1971); Reid Mitchell, *Civil War Soldiers: Their Expectations and their Experiences* (New York: Viking, 1988); James I. Robertson, *Soldiers: Blue and Gray*, American Military History (Columbia, S.C.: University of South Carolina Press, 1988); James M. McPherson, *For Cause and Comrades: Why Men Fought in the Civil War* (New York: Oxford University Press, 1997); Phillip S. Paludan, *"A People's Contest": The Union and the Civil War* (New York: Harper and Row, 1988).

10. "The Late Dr. Francis," *NYDT*, February 11, 1861; "The Funerals Yesterday," *NYH*, February 11, 1861. On Mather, see "Our New York Letter," *PI*, July 17, 1861; Reins, "the oldest printer in New York," died March 23 at West Farms, Westchester County, in his eightieth year. "Death of David H. Reins," *Pr* 4 (July 1862): 55; and "Affairs in New York," *BS*, March 25, 1863, 4. Also noted, "Affairs in New York," *BS*, July 18, 1861, and "Letter from New York from Our Own Correspondent," *SFEB*, August 2, 1861. See also Mark Lause, *Some Degree of Power: From Hired Hand to Union Craftsman in the Preindustrial American Printing Trades, 1778–1815* (Fayetteville: University of Arkansas Press, 1991). For Gideon, see "Correspondence of the Baltimore Sun," *BS*, February 26, 1864. For the invitation, see "Correspondence of the Baltimore Sun," Washington, April 7, *BS*, April 8, 1864. George G. Seibold, comp., *Historical Sketch of Columbia Typographical Union. Number One Hundred and One (Known as Columbia Typographical Society from 1815 to 1867)* (Washington, D.C.: National Capital Press, 1915), 17–18, also noting the death of John C. Rives in April 1864.

11. *New York American Citizen*, April 10, 1809, cited in Lause, *Some Degree of Power*, 121–22. See also, for this early period, Howard B. Rock, *Artisans of the New Republic: The Tradesmen of New York City in the Age of Jefferson* (New York: New York University Press, 1979) and Charles G. Steffen, *The Mechanics of Baltimore: Workers and Politics in the Age of Revolution, 1763–1812* (Urbana: University of Illinois Press, 1984). See also: David Montgomery, *Beyond Equality: Labor and the Radical Republicans, 1862–1872* (New York: Knopf, 1967); Walter Hugins, *Jacksonian Democracy and the Working Class* (Stanford, Calif.: Stanford University Press, 1960); Edward Pessen, *Most Uncommon Jacksonians:*

the Radical Leaders of the Early Labor Movement (Albany: SUNY Press, 1967); Bruce Laurie, *Working People of Philadelphia, 1800–1850* (Philadelphia: Temple University Press, 1980); Sean Wilentz, *Chants Democratic: New York City and the Rise of the Working Class, 1788–1859* (New York: Oxford University Press, 1984). For the economic ideas and social values commonplace in the period, see Paul K. Conkin, *Prophets of Prosperity: America's First Political Economists* (Bloomington: Indiana University Press, 1980), and Martin J. Burke, *The Conundrum of Class: Public Discourse on the Social Order in America* (Chicago: University of Chicago Press, 1995).

12. John C. Fincher, "Early History of Our Organization," *Machinists and Blacksmiths Journal* (February 1872): 520–21, in Commons et al., *History of Labour in the United States*, vol. 2 (New York: Macmillan, 1918), 8; and Alice R. Prutton Matej, *From Socialism to Solidarity: The Politics of District 54 International Association of Machinists and Aerospace Workers*, PhD diss., Kent State University, 1999.

13. Eric Foner, *Free Soil, Free Labor, Free Men: The Ideology of the Republican Party before the Civil War* (New York: Oxford University Press, 1970). See, for example: Jonathan A. Glickstein, *Concepts of Free Labor in Antebellum America* (New Haven, Conn.: Yale University Press, 1991); Jonathan A. Glickstein, *American Exceptionalism, American Anxiety: Wages, Competition, and Degraded Labor in the Antebellum United States* (Charlottesville: University of Virginia Press, 2002); and Amy Dru Stanley, *From Bondage to Contract: Wage Labor, Marriage and the Market in the Age of Slave Emancipation* (Cambridge: Cambridge University Press, 1998).

14. James W. Russell, *Class and Race Formation in North America* (Toronto: University of Toronto Press, 2009); Ira Berlin, Steven F. Miller, Joseph P. Reidy, and Leslie S. Rowland, eds., *The Wartime Genesis of Free Labor: The Upper South*, series 1, vol. 2 of *Freedom: A Documentary History of Emancipation 1861–1867, selected from the Holdings of the National Archives of the United States* (Cambridge: Cambridge University Press, 1993), 15; Junius P. Rodriguez, ed., *Encyclopedia of Slave Resistance and Rebellion* (Westport, Conn.: Greenwood, 2007); Eugene D. Genovese, *From Rebellion to Revolution: Afro-American Slave Revolts in the Making of the Modern World* (Baton Rouge: Louisiana State University Press, 1980); Cyril Lionel Robert James, *A History of Negro Revolt* (New York: Haskell, 1969); Joao Jose Reis, *Slave Rebellion in Brazil: The Muslim Uprising of 1835 in Bahia* (Baltimore, Md.: Johns Hopkins University Press, 1993); Matt D. Childs, *The 1812 Aponte Rebellion in Cuba and the Struggle against African Slavery* (Chapel Hill: University of North Carolina Press, 2006); David P. Geggus, ed., *The Impact of the Haitian Revolution in the Atlantic World* (Columbia: University of South Carolina Press, 2001); Robin Blackburn, *The Overthrow of Colonial Slavery, 1776–1848* (London: Verso, 1988); Herbert Aptheker, "Resistance and Afro-American History: Some Notes on Contemporary Historiography and Suggestions for Further Research," in *Resistance: Studies in African, Caribbean, and Afro-American History*, ed. Gary Y. Okihiro (Amherst: University of Massachusetts Press, 1986); Carroll, Joseph Cephas, *Slave Insurrections in the United States, 1800–1865* (New York: Negro Universities Press, 1968); Nicholas Halasz, *The Rattling Chains: Slave Unrest and Revolt in the Antebellum South* (New York: McKay, 1966); Junius P. Rodriguez, ed., *Slavery in the United States: A Social, Political, and Historical Encyclopedia* (Santa Barbara, Calif.: ABC-CLIO,

2007); Thomas J. A. Davis, *Rumor of Revolt: The "Great Negro Plot" in Colonial New York* (New York: Free Press, 1985); Jeffrey J. Crow, "Slave Rebelliousness and Social Conflict in North Carolina, 1775–1802," *William and Mary Quarterly* 37, no. 1 (1980): 79–102; Donald D. Wax, "'The Great Risque We Run': The Aftermath of Slave Rebellion at Stono, South Carolina, 1739–1745," *Journal of Negro History* 67, no. 2 (1982): 1–47; Norrece T. Jones Jr., *Born a Child of Freedom, Yet a Slave: Mechanisms of Control and Strategies of Resistance in Antebellum South Carolina* (Hanover, Conn.: University Press of New England, 1990); Philip J. Schwarz, "Gabriel's Challenge: Slaves and Crime in Late-Eighteenth-Century Virginia." *Virginia Magazine of History and Biography* 90, no. 3 (1982): 283–309; Philip D. Morgan and George D. Terry, "Slavery in Microcosm: A Conspiracy Scare in Colonial South Carolina," *Southern Studies* 21, no. 2 (1982): 121–45; James Sidbury, *Ploughshares into Swords: Race, Rebellion and Identity In Gabriel's Virginia, 1730–1810* (New York: Cambridge University Press, 1997).

15. Samuel Gompers, *Seventy Years of Life and Labor: An Autobiography*, 2 vols. (New York: Dutton, 1925), 1:383. Morris Gompers, a thirty-nine-year-old Dutchman, arrived July 30, 1863, on the "London." *Passenger Lists of Vessels Arriving at New York, New York, 1820–1897*, from the National Archives Microfilm Publication M237, Records of the U.S. Customs Service, Record Group 36; National Archives, Washington, D.C., posted online at Ancestry.com, *New York Passenger Lists, 1820–1957*.

16. Jennie Collins, *Nature's Aristocracy; or, Battles and Wounds in Time of Peace: A Plea for the Oppressed*, ed. Russell H. Conwell (Boston: Lee, Shepard, and Dillingham, 1871), 284. For a more explicitly Christian appeal, see Mary Bayly, *Workmen and Their Difficulties* (New York: R. Carter, 1861).

17. Focused on those results, economist Jeffrey Rogers Hummel's *Emancipating Slaves, Enslaving Free Men: A History of the American Civil War* (Chicago: Open Court, 1996) offers a paradoxical reappraisal of nationalist war goals in light of the war's results.

Prologue

1. March 5 statement, *The Collected Works of Abraham Lincoln,* 9 vols., ed. Roy P. Basler (New Brunswick N.J.: Rutgers University Press, 1953–55), 4:7; "The Massachusetts Strikes," "The Strikes: Progress of the Labor Movement in New England," *NYH*, March 7 and 12, 1860.

2. Standard histories of American labor in this period are John R. Commons et al., *History of Labour in the United States*, 2nd ed., 4 vols. (1947); and Philip S. Foner, *History of the Labor Movement in the United States: From Colonial Times to the Founding of the American Federation of Labor* (1972). For some fine local studies, see Susan E. Hirsh, *Roots of the American Working Class: the Industrialization of the Crafts in Newark, 1800–1860* (1978) and Steven J. Ross, *Workers on the Edge: Work, Leisure, and Politics in Industrializing Cincinnati, 1788–1890* (1985).

3. Ethelbert Stewart, *A Documentary History of Early Organizations of Printers* published as U.S. Government, Department of Commerce and Labor, *Bulletin of the Bureau of Labor* 11, no. 61 (November 1905): 931–32; George A. Stevens, *New York Typographical*

Union No. 6: Study of a Modern Trade Union and Its Predecessors (Albany: Lyon, 1913), 104–13, 195–200, 201–06; and Mark A. Lause, *Some Degree of Power: From Hired Hand to Union Craftsman in the Preindustrial American Printing Trades, 1778–1815* (Fayetteville: University of Arkansas Press, 1991). See also, *100 Years as a Chartered Union 1852–1952: History of Pittsburgh Typographical Union No. 7* (Pittsburgh: Typographical Union No. 7, 1952), 33–34.

4. George E. McNeil, *The Labor Movement: The Problem of To-day; The History, Purpose and Possibilities of Labor Organizations* (Boston: Bridgman; New York: Hazen, 1887), 388–89, 393, 394; David Bensman, *The Practice of Solidarity: American Hat Finishers in the Nineteenth Century* (Urbana: University of Illinois Press, 1985), 8–10, 22–23. See also John Cameron Simonds, *The Story of Manual Labor in All Lands and Ages* (Chicago: Peale, 1887); Journeyman Stonecutters Association, available at http://www.stonecarver.com/union.html (accessed September 20, 2014); "City Intelligence," *NYT*, September 17, 1859. They have since merged with the Laborers International Union of North America (LIUNA). "The Stone-Cutter's Strike," *USMO*, April 7, 1860, 2. Courtesy of the Rare Collections Library of the State Library of Pennsylvania, Harrisburg.

5. Commons et al., *History of Labour*, 1:622; "New-York City: National Convention of Cigar-makers," *NYT*, July 3, 1856; P. M. Arthur, "The Rise of Railroad Organization," in McNeil, *Labor Movement*, 312–13, 314, Arthur's full piece being on 312–30; "Movements of the Engineers: New-York City; The Erie Railroad and Its Employees—Trouble Again with the Engineers," *NYT*, October 4, 1856.

6. Frank K. Foster, "Shoemakers in the Movement," McNeil, *Labor Movement*, 192–213; "Shoemakers' Meeting—A Trade-Union Resolved On," *NYT*, June 1, 1858; McNeil, *Labor Movement*, 386, 387, 389, 394; "The House Painters," *USMO*, March 17, 1860, 2; Robert Howard, "Progress in the Textile Trades," 216, the entire article running 214–40; Grace Palladino, *Another Civil War: Labor, Capital, and the State in the Anthracite Regions of Pennsylvania 1840–68* (Urbana: University of Illinois Press, 1990), 58, 59; Edward A. Wieck, *The American Miners' Association: A Record of the Origin of Coal Miners' Unions in the United States* (New York: Sage, 1940), 26, 28, 114, 143, 190, 191–92, 193, 194, 195; Daniel Weaver, "Forty Years a Miner and Men I Have Known," in *United Mine Workers' Journal*, August 13, 1908. For an alternative Philadelphia claim among the painters, see *Historical Sketches of the Oldest Painter's Association in America* (n.p, 1898) and *Constitution and By-laws of the Amalgamated Journeymen House Painters' Beneficial Association of Philadelphia and Vicinity* (n.p., 1900).

7. For the Machinists and Blacksmiths, see Commons et al., *History of Labour*, 2:8, 9. "Labor Troubles in Pennsylvania," 278–79; "Strikes and Lockouts Occurring in the United States Prior to 1881," *Third Annual Report of the Commissioner of Labor, 1887: Strikes and Lockouts* (Washington: Government Printing Office, 1888), 1046. On the Amalgamated: Angela Tuckett, *The Blacksmiths' History: What Smithy Workers Gave Trade Unionism* (London: Lawrence and Wishart, 1974), 54–67; and "Amalgamated Society of Great Britain," *FTR*, December 12, 1863, 6. For the molders: Jonathan Grossman, *William Sylvis, Pioneer of American Labor: A Study of the Labor Movement during the Era of the Civil War* (New York: Columbia University Press, 1944), 84, 87, 181, 184; *Proceedings of the Annual*

Session of the Iron Molders' Union of America, in Convention Assembled at Cincinnati, Ohio, Jan. 8th, 1861 (New York: Cassin and Fincher, at the Office of the U.S. Mechanics' Own, printer, 1861), 13–14; and, from the *USMO* in 1860: "Another Strike in Albany," January 28; "Moulders' Strike in St. Louis," March 24; "The Moulders' Strike in Buffalo—the Immaculate Press," April 21; "Letter from St. Louis," May 19; "The Strike at Zanesville" May 26; with a list of expelled members at Albany, and "Workingmen of St. Louis up and in Arms!" June 2; and (on the Baldwin strike, 1860) "The Strike in Philadelphia," March 17; "Latest from the Strike at Baldwin" and "Third Week of the Strike," March 24; "The Strike at Baldwin," April 21; "Letter from the Strike at Baldwin," May 12; "More about Baldwin," May 26; with "Letter from England" by "International," June 2, 1860.

8. James C. Sylvis, *The Life, Speeches, Labors, and Essay of William H. Sylvis* (Philadelphia: Claxton, Remsen, and Hafffelfinger, 1872), 13–90; Charlotte Todes, *William H. Sylvis and the National Labor Union* (New York: International Publishers, 1942), as well as Grossman, William Sylvis. From the *USMO*, see "Letter from Wm. H. Sylvis," May 12, May 19, and May 26, 1860; and "Isaac J. Neal Letter," "Letter from the President of the Moulders' Union," and Will Horan, "Letter from the Vice-President of the Iron Moulder's Union," April 14, April 21, and May 26, 1860.

9. Bruce Laurie, *Working People of Philadelphia, 1800–1850* (Philadelphia: Temple University Press, 1983), but see, too, his *Artisans into Workers: Labor in Nineteenth-Century America* (New York: Noonday, 1989).

10. Robert L. Perkin, *The First Hundred Years: An Informal History of Denver and the* Rocky Mountain News (Garden City, N.Y.: Doubleday, 1959), 31–34, 124, 198; *Reminiscences of General William Larimer and of his Son William H. H. Larimer, Two of the Founders of Denver City* (Pittsburgh: Mellon, 1918), 143.

11. For the dispute, Stevens, *New York Typographical Union No. 6*, 258–66, 266–69, 275, 276–77; "Proposed Consolidation of the 'Printer's Cooperative Union' and the 'Typographical Union,'" *NYDT*, November 29, 1853. See also "Printers' Festival," *NYDT*, January 18, 1854.

12. Commons et al., *History of Labour*, 1:552–54, 554–55, 557, 560–61 and note, citing coverage by both the *NYH* and the *NYDT*. On Franks, see *NYDT*, January 27 and February 14, 1851, and John Humphrey Noyes, *History of American Socialisms* (Philadelphia: Lippincott, 1870), 92. From the *USMO*: on New York, "The Bricklayers," March 17, and two under "Our New York Correspondence," May 19 and June 2, 1860; on Philadelphia: "Meeting of Trade Delegation," September 24, 1859; "Anniversary Supper of the Philadelphia Bookbinders Union," and "Ship Carpenters," March 10, and "The Ball," March 31, 1860. See: Edwin C. Rozwenc, *Cooperatives Come to America: The History of the Protective Union Store Movement, 1845–1867*, 2nd ed. (Philadelphia: Porcupine, 1975), 65. "German Meeting in the Park" *NYDT*, August 14, 1850; Commons et al., *History of Labour*, 555–56; on William B. Greene, see: Josiah Warren's *Equitable Commerce*, William B. Greene's *Mutual Banking*, Edward Kellogg's *Labor and Other Capital*, and Stephen Pearl Andrews's "Declaration of Fundamental Principles."

13. J. R. Y. "The Private Soldier," *Philadelphia Press*, May 18, 1863; Seaver, *Occasional Thoughts*, 16, 37, 154, 49–50.

14. The original was serialized in 1802 issues of the *Temple of Reason*, but it remained in

circulation among radical secularists for generations: *Equality; or, A History of Lithconia*, 2nd ed. (Philadelphia: Liberal Union, 1837), 96, 97, 101, 102, 104; "Equality; or The History of Litchonia," *Boston Investigator* 32 (March 25; and April 1, 8, 15, 22, and 29, 1863) pp. 23, 375, 381, 389, 397, 405, 409; *Boston Investigator* 33 (May 13, 20, and 27, 1863), pp. 7, 15, 23; *Equality; or, A History of Lithconia*, 3rd ed. (Boston: Mundum, 1863). For a corrective to the longstanding misattribution of the work to Dr. James Reynolds, see Michael Durey's "John Lithgow's Lithconia: The Making and Meaning of America's First 'Utopian Socialist' Tract," *William and Mary Quarterly*, third ser., vol. 49 (October 1992): 675–94.

15. Ronald G. Walters, *American Reformers, 1815–1860* (New York: Hill and Wang, 1978), and on this particular subject, see Helene Zahler's *Eastern Workingmen and National Land Policy*, Columbia University Studies in the History of American Agriculture (New York: Columbia University, 1941), and Jamie L. Bronstein, *Land Reform and Working-Class Experience in Britain and the United States, 1800–1862* (Stanford: Stanford University Press, 1999). The prominence of a radical critique of early capitalism is discussed in Eric Foner, *Tom Paine and Revolutionary America* (New York: Oxford University Press, 1976); Arthur E. Bestor, *Backwoods Utopias: The Sectarian Origins and the Owenite Phase of Communitarian Socialism in America, 1663–1829* (Philadelphia: University of Pennsylvania Press, 1950); David Harris, *Socialist Origins in the United States: American Forerunners of Marx, 1817–1832* (The Netherlands: Assen, 1968); and, particularly for the 1840s, Carl J. Guarneri, *The Utopian Alternative: Fourierism in Nineteenth-Century America* (Ithaca, N.Y.: Cornell University Press, 1991). Two key works on the role of immigrant workers are Clifton K. Yearley Jr., *Britons in American Labor: A History of the Influence of United Kingdom Immigrants on American Labor, 1820–1914* (Baltimore, Md.: Johns Hopkins University Press 1957), and Bruce Levine, *The Spirit of 1848: German Immigrants, Labor Conflicts, and the Coming of the Civil War* (Urbana: University of Illinois Press, 1992).

16. Seaver, *Occasional Thoughts*, 164; Warren Chase, *The American Crisis: or, Trial and Triumph of Democracy* (Boston: Marsh, 1862).

17. Bruce Laurie, *Beyond Garrison: Antislavery and Social Reform* (New York: Cambridge University Press, 2007); Aileen S. Kraiditor, *Means and Ends in American Abolitionism: Garrison and His Critics on Strategy and Tactics, 1834–1850*, 2nd ed. (New York: Vintage, 1969); Lewis Perry, *Radical Abolitionism: Anarchy and the Government of God in Antislavery Thought* (Ithaca, N.Y.: Cornell University Press, 1973); James Brewer Stewart, *Holy Warriors: the Abolitionists and American Slavery* (New York: Hill and Wang, 1976); Richard H. Sewell, *Ballots for Freedom: Antislavery Politics in the United States, 1837–1860* (New York: Oxford University Press, 1976); and Ronald G. Walters, *The Antislavery Appeal: American Abolitionists After 1830* (Baltimore, Md.: Johns Hopkins University Press, 1976).

18. *USMO*, May 19, 1860. Also from *USMO*: "Mr. Oberkline's Lecture," February 4, 1860, and "Oberkline," May 19, 1860 (Oberkline spoke); "Workingmen of St. Louis up and in Arms! A Great Mass Meeting of the Workingmen," June 2, 1860; "Another Strike of the Tunnel Men," March 17, 1860; "Letter from Cincinnati," March 24, 1860; "Letter from Wilmington, Del.," March 24, 1860; "Meeting of the Workingmen in Baltimore," March 31, 1860; "Baltimore Letter," May 19, 1860; "The Strike at Zanesville," May 26, 1860; "Pittsburgh Letter," May 19, 1860; "Pittsburgh Letter," June 2, 1860.

19. William Hardinge, Coach Painters' Association, quoted in George A. Stevens, *New York Typographical Union No. 6: Study of a Modern Trade Union and Its Predecessors* (Albany, 1913), 588. From the *USMO*, see: "Trades Unions," October 22, 1859; "Harmony among Mechanics," January 28, 1860; "Employment of Mechanics and their Wages," February 25, 1860; "United Labor" with "Less Work and More Pay," May 26, 1860; "Workingmen—Their Condition and Prospects," March 24, 1860; "Land for the Landless," October 15, 1859; and two pieces titled "The Homestead Bill," February 11 and June 2, 1860; "Distribution of Wealth," May 12, 1860; re: eight hours, untitled item, May 26, 1860; "Co-Operational and Mutual Assurance," April 28, 1860; "Co-operation and Mutual Assurance," May 26, 1860. See also Stewart, *Documentary History*, 982, and Stevens, *New York Typographical Union No. 6*, 592. "The Philadelphia Savings Store on the Rochdale Plan," *USMO*, March 3, 1860.

20. See also the Slave Rebellion Web site, http://slaverebellion.org/index.php?page=guide. Theodore W. Allen, *The Invention of the White Race*, 2 vols., exp. ed. (London: Verso, 2012), consisting of volumes on *Racial Oppression and Social Control* and *The Invention of the White Race*. David R. Roediger, *The Wages of Whiteness: Race and the Making of the American Working Class*, rev. ed. (London: Verso, 1999), elaborated on by David R. Roediger, *Towards the Abolition of Whiteness: Essays on Race, Class and Politics* (London: Verso, 1994); David R. Roediger, *Colored White: Transcending the Racial Past* (Berkeley: University of California Press, 2002); Anthony Gronowicz, *Race and Class Politics in New York City before the Civil War* (Boston: Northeastern University Press, 1998). See also: Roediger, "Accounting for the Wages of Whiteness: U.S. Marxism and the Critical History of Race," in *Wages of Whiteness and Racist Symbolic Capital Racism Analysis—Series B: Yearbooks*, ed. Wulf D. Hund, Jeremy Krikler, David Roediger (Berlin: Verlag, 2010), 9–36; Matthew Frye Jacobson, *Whiteness of a Different Color: European Immigrants and the Alchemy of Race* (Cambridge, Mass.: Harvard University Press, 1998); and Edward Ball, *Slaves in the Family* (New York: Farrar, Straus, and Giroux, 1998).

21. Betsy Fancher, *The Lost Legacy of Georgia's Golden Isles* (Garden City, N.Y.: Doubleday, 1971); Gwendolyn Midlo Hall, *Africans in Colonial Louisiana: The Development of Afro-Creole Culture in the Eighteenth Century* (Baton Rouge: Louisiana State University Press, 1992); *Africanisms in American Culture*, ed. Joseph E. Holloway (Bloomington: Indiana University Press, 1990); James Oakes, *Slavery and Freedom: An Interpretation of the Old South* (New York: Knopf, 1990); Philip D. Morgan, *Slave Counterpoint: Black in the Eighteenth-Century Chesapeake and Low Country* (Chapel Hill: University of North Carolina Press, 1998); Gwendolyn Midlo Hall, *Africans in Colonial Louisiana: The Development of Afro-Creole Culture in the Eighteenth Century* (Baton Rouge: Louisiana State University Press, 1992); Ira Berlin, *Many Thousand Gone: The First Two Centuries of Slavery in North America* (Cambridge, Mass.: Belknap, 1998); *Masters and Slaves in the House of the Lord: Race and Religion in the American South, 1740–1870*, ed. John B. Boles (Lexington: University Press of Kentucky, 1988); Margaret Washington Creel, *"A Peculiar People": Slave Religion and Community Culture Among the Gullahs* (New York: New York University Press, 1988); Charles Joyner, *Down by the Riverside: A South Carolina Slave Community* (Urbana: University of Illinois Press, 1984); Richard Price, *First Time: The*

Historical Vision of an Afro-American People (Baltimore, Md.: Johns Hopkins University Press, 1983).

22. *NYH*, April 16, 1853, in *The Black Worker: A Documentary History from Colonial Times to the Present, Vol. 1: The Black Worker to 1869*, ed. Philip S. Foner, and Ronald L. Lewis (Philadelphia: Temple University Press, 1978), 191–93, 193–96, 239, 240–41, 366–68. In Foner's vast contribution to labor history, he frequently contradicted himself, documenting a black participation in the labor movement in one place while simply denying it happened in another. See also, James Macune Smith, 1851 report on "The Social Conditions of the Negro Race," 246–47. See also Steven Hahn, *A Nation under Our Feet: Black Political Struggles in the Rural South from Slavery to the Great Migration* (Cambridge, Mass.: Harvard University Press, 2003). See, in general: Larry Koger, *Black Slaveowners: Free Black Slave Masters in South Carolina, 1790–1860* (Jefferson, N.C.: McFarland, 1985); Peter Kolchin, *American Slavery, 1619–1877* (New York: Hill and Wang, 1993); Leland Ferguson, *Uncommon Ground: Archaeology and Early African American, 1650- 1800* (Washington, D.C.: Smithsonian Institution Press, 1992); Loren Schweninger, *Black Property Owners in the South, 1790—1915* (Urbana: University of Illinois Press, 1990); Richard C. Wade, *Slavery in the Cities: The South 1820–1860* (Oxford: Oxford University Press, 1967); W. Jeffrey Bolster, *Black Jacks: African American Seamen in the Age of Sail* (Cambridge, Mass.: Harvard University Press, 1997); Allan Austin, *African Muslims in Antebellum America: Transatlantic Stories and Spiritual Struggles* (New York: Garland, 1984).

23. One of the least appealing attributes of "whiteness studies," as adherents prefer to self-specialize themselves, is the unwillingness to recognize that there were many different ways to be "white." This blind spot has led to some terribly unfortunate conclusions. David R. Roediger, *Working toward Whiteness: How America's Immigrants Became White; The Strange Journey from Ellis Island to the Suburbs* (New York: Basic, 2005).

24. Role of Know-Nothings in defining Irishness (alleged one million members). Jay P. Dolan, *The Irish Americans: A History* (London: Bloomsbury, 2008), 96–98. For comparisons of the black and Irish experiences, see *The Black and Green Atlantic: Cross-Currents of the African and Irish Diasporas*, ed. Peter D. O'Neill and David Lloyd (London: Palgrave Macmillan, 2009) and *Critical White Studies: Looking behind the Mirror*, ed. Richard Delgado and Jean Stefancic (Philadelphia: Temple University Press, 1997), 327–28; for the Germans, see untitled letter by "Brick Oven," *USMO*, April 21, 1860.

25. Of 1.8 million landing in New York during famine years, 848,000 were Irish, the rest mostly German, but only 134,000 Irish were born residents in New York City, according to the 1850 census. The conclusion is that 85 percent of Irish used New York City as a steppingstone. Reginald Byron, *Irish America* (Oxford: Clarendon, 1999), 54–55.

26. "Female Labor," *New Republic*, October 4, 1862, 389.

27. Christopher L. Tomlins, *Law, Labor, and Ideology in the Early American Republic* (Cambridge: Cambridge University Press, 1993). As Seaver described it, "The poor are obliged to compete with each other; not with respect to the outlay of their moneyed capital, of which they are *minus*, but with respect to their labor, the only capital they have at their disposal" (*Occasional Thoughts*, 167).

28. See also: Jennie Collins *Nature's Aristocracy*, 294; Horace Seaver, *Occasional Thoughts*, 167.

Chapter 1. Workers and the Crisis of Nationhood

1. Stevens, *New York Typographical Union No. 6*, 658–60. The *Tribune* also sent bohemian playwright Frank Wood to cover events "for one of our dailies during the hottest of the early secession fury." See also Fitzhugh Ludlow, "Frank Wood," *New Nation*, April 2, 1864, 12–13.

2. On Macon, Georgia, see "A New Acquisition" and "A Mechanic" letter from Vicksburg, *USMO*, February 25 and April 7, 1860.

3. See Lynn as a microcosm of the social process of industrialization, see Norman Ware's *The Industrial Worker, 1840–1860* (Boston: Houghton Mifflin, 1924), 34–35, 39–44, and Alan Dawley's *Class and Community: The Industrial Revolution in Lynn* (Cambridge, Mass.: Harvard University Press, 1976). See also Paul G. Falen, *Mechanics and Manufacturers in the Early Industrial Revolution: Lynn, Massachusetts, 1780–1860* (Albany: State University of New York Press, 1981), as well as James L. Huston, *The Panic of 1857 and The Coming of the Civil War* (Baton Rouge: Louisiana State University Press, 1987), 224–30. Citing all of these, see Lause, "'Turning the World Upside Down': A Portrait of Labor and Military Leader, Alonzo Granville Draper," *Labor History* 44 (May 2003), 189–204.

4. The New England shoe strike "subsequently extended to Natick, Marblehead, Newburyport, Milford, Haverhill, Saugus, Grafton, South Reading, Salem, Stonham, Sutton, Waltham, [and] Woburn [Mass.]; Dover, Farmington, Sebrook, Northwood, Great Falls, Salmon Falls, [and] Hamilton, N.H.; Portland [Maine] . . . [and] was estimated at about twenty thousand." "1860 Leading Events in the United States," *NYH*, January 1, 1861. See, too, Massachusetts Bureau of Statistics of Labor, "Part I: Strikes in Massachusetts," *Eleventh Annual Report of the Bureau of Statistics of Labor of Massachusetts. January 1880* (Boston: Rand, Avery, 1880), 17–18, cited "Strikes and Lockouts . . . in the United States," 1046.

5. Untitled item, *RDD*, March 13, 1860; "Northern White Slaves and Southern Black Ones," [West Baton Rouge] *Sugar Planter*, March 24, 1860, 2; and *The Collected Works of Abraham Lincoln*, ed. Roy P. Basler, 9 vols. (New Brunswick, N.J.: Rutgers University Press, 1953–55), iv, 7. See also: Greeley in Kansas, called on by Leavenworth Typographical Union, in Wilder, *Annals of Kansas*, 255; Martha B. Caldwell, "When Horace Greeley Visited Kansas in 1859," *Kansas Historical Quarterly* 9 (May 1940): 123–24.

6. Andrew W. Freeman, *Abraham Lincoln Goes to New York* (New York: Coward-McCann, 1960), 88. Born Conkling, Broome County, May 15, 1841, *Biographical Directory of Congress*; Henry B. Rankin, *Intimate Sketches of Abraham Lincoln* (Philadelphia: Lippincott, 1924), 190–91, in Freeman, *Abraham Lincoln Goes to New York*, 92–93, 152; Stevens, *New York Typographical Union*, 651–54.

7. "Official Report of the Ninth Annual Session of the National Typographical Union," *Pr* 3 (June 1860): 6; Tracy, *History of the Typographical Union*, 185–95.

8. Louise Roberts Anaya, *Book of Memorial Memberships: Centennial Edition, 1829–1929* (Jacksonville: Illinois College Alumni Fund Association, 1929), 62; D. C. Roberts, *South-*

ern Sketches; or, Eleven Years Down South, Including Three Years in Dixie (Jacksonville; Roberts, 1865), 9–12, 13–15, 19, 20, 34, 50. "Montgomery, Ala." *Pr* 3 (February 1860): 209, which also mentioned correspondence from Wilcox "County, Alabama" in the "Official Report of the Ninth Annual Session of the National Typographical Union," and J. Nathan Ells's account of the "Augusta Union," June 1860, 3, and July 15, 1860, 29.

9. "Serious Affray," *Pr* 2 (July 1859): 54. Also: Perkin, *First Hundred Years*, 180–81. Lorien Foote, *The Gentlemen and the Roughs: Violence, Honor, and Manhood in the Union Army* (New York: New York University Press, 2013) and similar studies of gender and masculinity run the risk of oversimplification and generalizations that preclude recognizing of this kind of journeyman's abhorrence of violence.

10. "Official Report of the Ninth Annual Session of the National Typographical Union," *Pr* 3 (June 1860): 4–5, 3. See also: "National Typographical Union," *BS*, May 9, 1860; "National Typographical Union; Nashville, Tenn; New York," *BS*, May 17, 1860; "National Typographical Union," [Stockton, Calif.] *Weekly San Joaquin Republican*, May 26, 1860. The sickly Patterson died in Nashville within weeks of the convention. "Death of a Printer," *Pr* (July 1860): 35.

11. On Harsha, *Compendium of History and Biography of the City of Detroit and Wayne County, Michigan* (Chicago: Taylor, 1909), 505–6; "The Originator of the National Typographical Union in Congress," *BH*, February 12, 1861; Mark A. Lause, *Young America: Land, Labor, And The Republican Community* (Urbana: University of Illinois Press, 2005), 81, 114, 119, 120, 122–23, 129, 135–36.

12. James L. Huston, *The Panic of 1857 and the Coming of the Civil War* (Baton Rouge: Louisiana State University Press, 1987).

13. William A. Phillips of Kansas; Henderson, then holding credentials from Oregon; William E. Stevenson of Virginia; and veteran Ohio freethinker, Owenite, and Fourierist, John Harmon. The influence of the *Tribune* group garnered Horace Greeley credentials for Oregon, D. C. Henderson for Texas. William B. Hesseltine, ed., *Three against Lincoln: Murat Halstead Reports the Caucuses of 1860* (Baton Rouge: Louisiana State University Press, 1960), 285–86, 290–92, 295–300. Roy P. Basler, ed., *Collected Works of Abraham Lincoln*, 9 vols. (New Brunswick, N.J.: Rutgers University Press, 1953–1955), 3:236; Roy P. Basler, "Introduction" to Scripps, *Life of Abraham Lincoln*, 16–17, 18–19; Grace Lock Scripps Dyche, "John Lock Scripps, Lincoln's Campaign Biographer, a Sketch Compiled from his Letters, by His Daughter, Grace Locke Scripps Dyche," in *Transactions of the Illinois State Historical Society for the Year 1924, Publication Number Thirty-one of the Illinois State Historical Library*, ca. p. 109; "Printers in Luck," *Pr* 3 (April 1861): 250. In general, see Hermann Schlüter, *Lincoln, Labor, and Slavery: A Chapter from the Social History of America* (New York: Scholastic, 1913).

14. "Meeting of Public Bodies," and "Meeting of the South Brooklyn Union League," *BDE*, September 7, 1860.

15. Katherine Harry, "The Civil War and the Maryland Coal Trade," *Maryland Historical Magazine* 62 (December 1967): 363–64. When Lincoln took office and Bittenger was appointed postmaster at St. Joseph: "Printers in Luck," *Pr* 3 (April 1861): 250. Conversely, the Federal postal service under the Democrats tried to block unionist publications as well

as abolitionist work, declaring the NTU's official organ not to be a newspaper for mailing purposes. "The Question Settled," *Pr* 4 (May 1859): 6.

16. Lause, *Young America*, 12–14, 26–28, 76–77, 97, 108–9, 119–20, 127; and Mark A. Lause, *A Secret Society History of the Civil War* (Urbana: University of Illinois Press, 2011), 41–44, 81–85, 101–2, 135–36, 146–47.

17. *NYDTrib*, October 5, 11, 12, 13, 17, 18, 19, 20, 23, 26, and 27, 1860; and November 2, 3, 6, 8, and 20, 1860; *The Tribune Almanac for 1860*, 19; and for the returns, see *The Tribune Almanac for 1861*, 40, both in *The Tribune Almanac for the Years 1838 to 1868; Inclusive: Comprehending the Political Register with the Whig Almanac . . .*, 2 vols. (New York: Tribune, 1868), vol. 2. On Poer: Stevens, *New York Typographical Union No. 6*, 289–90; Commerford to Johnson, *Papers of Andrew Johnson*, 3:358.

18. "The Industrial Congress," *HoP*, November 17, 1860, and December 1, 1860; "The Industrial Congress," *BS*, November 22, 1860; "The Industrial Congress of Workingmen's Commonwealth," *NYH*, November 21, 1860. See also the notice of the Industrial Congress in *BoL*, November 10, 1860, 7. See also: "Letter from New York," *PP*, November 23, 1860. For the evolution of such a group among the spiritualists, see "Social Equality," *HoP*, July 7, 1860.

19. "The Industrial Congress," *HoP*, December 22, 1860; "The Industrial Congress," *NYH*, November 24, 1860.

20. Falen, *Mechanics and Manufacturers*, 255n14; "Lynn Municipal Elections," *BH*, December 11, 1860; "Presentation to a Mayor Elect," *BH*, December 17, 1860. Printers planning to vote against City Controller George W. Hufty: "Communications Relative to the Hufty Excitement," *USMO*, April 21, 1860. "The Present Dominant Party," professing friendship; advertisement, "The Professions of the People's Party to the Workingmen," *USMO*, April 21, 1860.

21. *The Papers of Andrew Johnson*, 4:493, 593; and, "Our New York Correspondence," *CM*, January 5, 1861.

22. "To the Men Who Work, in the North and South," *Quaker City*, March 9, 1850. Three pieces on the "Brotherhood of the Union," *USMO*, March 10, April 7, May 26, 1860. See also Lippard's work, "Quaker City," *USMO*, May 12, 1860. "The Impending Crisis," *USMO*, December 24, 1859. "The Army and Navy," *USMO*, January 7, 1860. Resistance to the rhetoric: "Disunion," *USMO*, June 2, 1860. See also coverage of the Order of United American Mechanics: "The United Mechanics Association," *USMO*, April 14, 1860. From the UMA to be sent to *Independent Press* and *Workingman's Advocate* along with the *Mechanics' Own*. "Resolutions," *USMO*, April 21, 1860. "Officers of the Grand National Council of United Mechanics," *USMO*, April 21, 1860; "Address to the Mechanics and Workingmen, Farmers and Merchants of the United States," *LDJ*, January 7, 1861; "To the Mechanics and Workingmen, Farmers and Merchants of the United States," *BH*, January 12, 1861; "Workingmen for the Union in Cincinnati," *NYDT*, January 7, 1861; and "The Workingmen of Cincinnati on the National Troubles," *BH*, January 5, 1861; By "Pontiac" under "From Kentucky," *NYDT*, January 11, 1861; Z. F. Smith, *The History of Kentucky* (Louisville: Courier-Journal, 1886), 596. Kentucky Secretary of State Joshua F. Bell addressed the third Louisville meeting on January 10. See also: Foner, *History of the Labor*

Movement, 298–306; Montgomery, *Beyond Equality*, 92; *Philadelphia Enquirer*, February 18, 1861; J. Matthew Gallman, *Mastering Wartime: A Social History of Philadelphia during the Civil War* (Philadelphia: University of Pennsylvania Press, 2000), 218.

23. Francis Fisher Browne, *The Every-Day Life of Abraham Lincoln*, 2nd ed. (Lincoln: University of Nebraska Press, 1995), 384. Browne used the account of William Henry Smith, which is tainted by his belief that Oberkline and the labor delegation visiting Lincoln was manipulated. Noteworthy for associating Lincoln with another Ohio reformer is Freda Postle Koch, *Colonel Coggeshall: The Man Who Saved Lincoln* (Columbus, Ohio: PoKo, 1985).

24. "Workingmen's Convention at Pittsburgh," *PI*, January 12, 1861; also as "Telegraphic News," "Working Men's Convention at Pittsburgh," *RDD*, January 14, 1861; and, "Union Mass Convention of the Workingmen of Pittsburgh," *BH*, January 12, 1861. Henry B. McCarty "President of the Trades' Assembly" chaired by Wm. H. Moody of Typographical Union, secretary: "The Working-Men in Council" [From *Evansville Journal*], *BH*, January 12, 1861. See also Terence V. Powderly, *Thirty Years of Labor 1859–1889* (New York: Kelley, 1967, repr. from the rev. ed., Philadelphia: n.p., 1890), 29–30; "The Workingmen in Faneuil Hall: Mass Meeting for the Union," *BH*, February 21, 1861; Notice of Reading attempt, *NYDT*, January 18, 1861.

25. "Workingmen's Mass Meeting at Newark," under "The Disunion Movement," *NYDT*, January 10, 1861; "Anti-Coercion Mass Meeting" [from *NYH*], *MDA*, January 23, 1861; "Working Men's Meeting in New York," *BH*, January 16, 1861; "Sympathy for Secession," *NYDT*, January 11, 1861; "Another Union Demonstration Coming," *NYH*, January 26, 1861. P. K. to editor, "Mass Meeting of Workingmen," and "The Late Union Meeting," *BDE*, January 17 and January 30, 1861; Charles Commerford to Andrew Johnson, *The Papers of Andrew Johnson*, 4:493, 593.

26. "Workingmen of Philadelphia in Council," *PI*, January 17, 1861; "Union Workingmen's Meeting in Philadelphia," *NYDT*, January 28, 1861; "Great Union Meeting of Workingmen in Philadelphia," *BH*, January 28, 1861; Sylvis, *Life, Speeches and Essays*, 42–46; Commons et al., *History of Labour in the United States*, 4 vols. (New York, 1918–35), 2:10–11; Grossman, *William Sylvis*, 45–47.

27. "Mechanics and Workingmen's Meeting," "Meeting of the Workingmen's Association," and "The Workingmen of Memphis," *MDA*, January 26 and February 3, 1861.

28. "Commissioned" under "Local Matters," "Extract of a letter dated Trenton, N. J., December, 5th, 1860" with "Wednesday morning . . . Dec. 12, 1860," "Meeting of Citizens" under "Local Matters," "Invasion of a Hen-House," three items as "Meeting at the African Church," and "Attention, Richmond Invincible" in "Military Notices," *RDD*, November 1 and December 12, 1860; January 12, 21, 23, 24, and 25, 1861, and April 20, 1861. "Meeting at the African Church" under "Local Matters," *RDD*, January 25, 1861.

29. *Proceedings of the Annual Session of the Iron Moulder's Union of America, in Convention Assembled, at Cincinnati, Ohio, Jan. 8th, 1861* (New York, 1861), 4, 6, 21–22, 24–25, 26, 30.

30. United correspondent from Indianapolis, February 20, and "Convention of Workingmen and Citizens' Union Association," *Louisville Daily Journal*, February 23 and March 2, 1861.

31. Gallman, *Mastering Wartime*, 218.

32. "Washington's Birthday in Philadelphia Parade, etc.," and "Washington's Birthday," *NYH*, February 23, 1861; "Parade of the Workingmen," *NYDT*, February 23, 1861.

33. Ellis P. Oberholtzer, *Philadelphia: A History of the City and Its People*, 4 vols. (Philadelphia: Clarke, 1912), 2:359; Journeyman Stonecutters Association, posted at http://www.stonecarver.com/union.html. They have since merged with the Laborers International Union of North America (LIUNA).

34. Joe Gray Taylor, *Louisiana Reconstructed, 1863–1877* (Baton Rouge: Louisiana State University Press, 1974). Beauregard ran for mayor as a Democrat, defeated by Gerard Stith. Roberts, *Southern Sketches*, 87; Eric Arnesen, *Waterfront Workers of New Orleans: Race, Class and Politics, 1863–1923* (New York: Oxford University Press, 1991), 21.

35. "New Orleans Typographical Union," *DP*, April 21 and 22, 1861. S. A. Gray, president, and Tim H. Draper secretary.

36. "The Times Are out of Joint," *Pr* 3 (May 1861): 273.

37. James B. Jones to Abraham Lincoln, January 24, 1864, including extensive headers from Confederate newspapers expressing the secessionist view of labor. See also *White Slaves: It is of the greatest importance to the workingmen of the United States to understand the true sentiments and objects of the leading traitors of the South. Their opinions of workingmen—who earn their support by their daily labor—are clearly set forth in the following extract from the speech of Mr. Hammond, of South Carolina, in the Senate of the United States, on the 4th of March, 1858. . . .* (New York: Sold by Sinclair Tousey, 1863); "The Rebellion against Democracy" and "The Great Questions of the Rebellion," *The Iron Platform. Extra.—No. 26* (January 1863), 1, 1–2.

Chapter 2. Continuities of Class

1. "From New York," *PI*, July 26, 1861; "The Shadow on the Wall" [from the *Courier des Etats Unis*], *BDE*, August 16, 1861. See also McKay, *Civil War and New York City*, 97; "German Socialism and the War," *NYDT*, August 12, 1861.

2. "Meetings, etc." *CM*, February 2, 1861. A letter dated at Charleston, February 13, says: "The Typographical Union here has dissolved its connection with the national body." "Quick Passage," *RDD*, February 28, 1861. See also: untitled item, *CM*, March 2, 1861; "News Items," *Saturday Evening Post*, March 9, 1861, 7; and Yates Snowden, *Notes on Labor Organizations in South Carolina, 1742–1861* (Columbia: University of South Carolina, 1914).

3. "Various Matters," and "Boston Printers' Union," *BH*, April 9, 15, 1861; "Delegate to the National Convention," *SFEB*, April 1, 1861; "Postponement of the National Typographical Convention," *NYDT*, April 23, 1861, and, under the same heading, in *Pr* 3 (April 1861): 249; "National Union Delegates," *Pr* 3 (April 1861): 249; Tracy, *History of the Typographical Union*, 195, 197–98; Stevens, *New York Typographical Union*, 577–78; *Leaves of History from the Archives of Boston Typographical Union No. 13: From the Foundation of the Boston Typographcial Society to the Diamond Jubilee of its Successor* (Boston: BTU, 1923), 13. At the start of April, the Eureka Typographical Union at San Francisco sent its delegate east

to reach New York in time. "Eureka Typographical Union," "Ball of the Typographical Union," and "Typographical," [Stockton, Calif.] *Weekly San Joaquin Republican*, May 12, August 25, and September 15, 1860; "The Typographical Union," *DP*, April 25, 1861.

4. Massachusetts, Wisconsin, Missouri, and Kentucky sent representatives to the Machinists' 1861 convention. Commons et al., *History of Labour*, 2:9–10. On the molders: *Proceedings of the Annual Session of the Iron Moulder's Union of America, in Convention Assembled, at Cincinnati, Ohio, Jan. 8th, 1861* (New York: Cassin and Fincher, at the Office of the "U.S. Mechanics' Own," 1861), 4, 6, 21–22, 24–25, 26, 30; and *Proceedings of the Fourth Annual Session of the Iron Moulder's International Union, in Convention Assembled, at Pittsburgh, Pa., January 6th, 1863* (Philadelphia: Pile, 1863).

5. Seibold, *Historical Sketch*, 18; and, Gallman, *Mastering Wartime*, 232; "Meeting of the Pattern Makers," *BH*, December 9, 1861.

6. Thomas H. O'Connor, *Civil War Boston: Home Front and Battlefield* (Boston: Northeastern University Press, 1997), 160–61. See also Stanley L. Engerman and J. Matthew Gallman, "The Civil War Economy: a Modern View," in *On the Road to Total War: the American Civil War and the German Wars of Unification*, ed. Stig Förster and Jorg Nagler (Washington: German Historical Institute; Cambridge: Cambridge University Press, 1997), 222–23.

7. O'Connor, *Civil War Boston*, 161–62.

8. Louisa Vaira, "Some Aspects of Pittsburgh's Industrial Contributions to the Civil War," in *Industry and Infantry: The Civil War in Western Pennsylvania*, ed. Brian Butko and Nicholas P. Ciotola (Pittsburgh: Historical Society of Western Pennsylvania, 2003), 61–69.

9. "Labor and Prices," *BoL*, January 17, 1863, 4; "Low Rents for Cities," *BoL*, March 29, 1862, 4; "Homes for the Laboring Class," *BoL*, December 17, 1864, 4.

10. "Distress among the Working Classes" [from *Traveller*] under "Affairs about Home," *BH*, July 9, 1861; and "The Wants of the Working Classes: Efforts Made on Their Behalf," *NYDT*, July 13, 1861; James M. Morris, "The Road to Trade Unionism: Organized Labor in Cincinnati to 1893," PhD diss., University of Cincinnati, 1969.

11. "From New York," *PI*, July 26, 1861; "The Shadow on the Wall" [from the *Courier des Etats Unis*], *BDE*, August 16, 1861. See also McKay, *Civil War and New York City*, 97; "German Socialism and the War," *NYDT*, August 12, 1861. "Mass Meeting in Worker's Hall," "Mass Meeting at North Market Hall," *Illinois Staats-Zeitung*, May 25 and November 11, 1861, available on the Newberry Library Foreign Language Press Survey, posted from http://flps.newberry.org.

12. "Fallacies of the Workingmen," *NYH*, August 24, 1861; "From New York," *PI*, July 26, 1861; "By Argus," "Our New York Letter," *PI*, July 29, 1861.

13. "Meeting of Workingmen—Destitution—Demand for Work—An Appeal to the Declaration of Independence" [from *New York Day Book*], *MDA*, August 3, 1861, and from New York Express as "Remarkable Demonstration of German Workingmen," *MDA*, August 4, 1861; "The German Workingmen in New York," *RDD*, August 26, 1861; "Yankee Civilization," *HT-WT*, August 1, 1862; Quote from correspondence, August 1861, "The Last of L. L. D. Russell, the Prophet," *HW*, February 15, 1862, 112.

14. *HT-WT*, June 27, 1862; "High Prices," *HT-WT*, December 1, 1862.

15. Gallman, *Mastering Wartime*, 242–43.

16. Letter from "A Workingman," "The Strike in the Navy Yard—The Other Side of the Question," *BDE*, January 3, 1862; "The Navy Yard Difficulties Here and Elsewhere," *BDE*, January 22, 1862.

17. "General Notes," *NYDT*, January 1, 1862; *Eastern Argus*, January 17, 1862, cited Charles A. Scontras, *Collective Efforts among Maine Workers: Beginnings and Foundations, 1820–1880* (Orono: University of Maine, Bureau of Labor Education, 1994), 329. See *Fifth Annual Levee of the Journeymen Shipwrights . . . Union Hall, Boston . . . January 25th, 1865* (Boston: n.p. 1865).

18. "Affairs at the Philadelphia Navy-Yard," *NYDT*, January 22, 1862; "Strike at the Navy Yard," *PI*, January 17, 1862, then also "Strike at the Philadelphia Navy-yard" [from *PI*, January 17], *NYT*, January 18, 1862; "Local Intelligence," *PI*, January 18, 1862. (John Crosland enlisted in U.S. Army Ordinance Dept.) "Meeting of Ship Joiners," *PI*, January 18, 1862; "The Navy Yard," *PI*, January 20, 1862, first paragraph of which is "Affairs in Philadelphia," *BS*, January 21, 1862; "Ordered Away," *PI*, January 20, 1862; Gallman, *Mastering Wartime*, 241; "The Navy Yard Difficulties Here and Elsewhere," *BDE*, January 22, 1862.

19. Wieck, *The American Miners' Association*, 22–28, 29, 46n, 72, 86, 97, 100–101, 188; "Miscellaneous," *RDD*, August 29, 1861. The city's labor movement had a long history before the arrival of émigré radicals like Col. Joseph Weydemeyer.

Russell M. Nolen, "The Labor Movement in St. Louis Prior to the Civil War," *Missouri Historical Review* 34 (October 1939): 18–37; and Walter R. Houf, "Organized Labor in Missouri Politics before the Civil War," *Missouri Historical Review* 56 (April 1962): 244–54.

20. "The Riots at Pottsville," *NYT*, May 9, 1862; "The Riots in Schuylkill County: The Departure of the Grey Reserves—Their Arrival in Minersville—A Night March," *PI*, May 8, 1862; "The War at the Coal Mines: The Miners Strike in Schuylkill County—Forced March of the Grey Reserves—Attack on a Collier Guard," *PI*, May 9, 1862; "Latest from the Seat of War," *PI*, May 9, 1862; "The Pottsville Strike," *PI*, May 9, 1862; "End of the Miners' Strike," *PI*, May 10, 1862; "Another 'Rebellion' in Yankee Land," *Richmond Daily Dispatch*, May 26, 1862. See also Grace Palladino, *Another Civil War: Labor, Capital, and the State in the Anthracite Regions of Pennsylvania 1840–68* (Urbana: University of Illinois Press, 1990), 124–26, 127–28.

21. "The Laborers Forming a Protective Union," *SFEB*, May 7, 1861; "What a 'Rat' Office Is," *SFEB*, August 21, 1861; "Amusements," *SFEB*, August 6, 1861. Also, this evening, music by Andrews's band. "Anniversary Ball of the Typographical Union," *EB*, August 27, 1861; "Typographical Union," *SFEB*, October 28, 1861; and, "The Laborer's Strike," *PI*, November 5, 1861.

22. "Strikes in Massachusetts," 19, cited "Strikes and Lockouts . . . in the United States," 1047; "The Perils of Fire," *FTR* 1 (August 29, 1863), 50; "Strike at Cohoes," *FTR*, April 9, 1864, 74. From the *Troy Whig*, August 18, 1863: "Monday morning fire in jacket and shoddy manufactory at Cohoes, spread fast, three killed and nineteen injured." "The Catastrophe at Cohoes," *NYDT*, August 23, 1863.

23. Collins, *Nature's Aristocracy*, 284; Catherine H. Vanderslice, *The Civil War Letters*

of George Washington Beidelman (New York: Vantage, 1978), quoting G. W. Beidelman to Jacob Beidelman, September 13, 1863, at 184–85, with other information from 1, 3–5, 10–11, 14–16, 19; *History of Pennsylvania Volunteers, 1861–65*.

24. For *Our Daily Fare*, nos. 1–12, issued June 8–21, 1864, see U.S. War Department, *Bibliography of State Participation in the Civil War 1861–1866*, 3rd ed. (Washington, 1913), 41. Frank Moore, ed., *The Rebellion Record: A Diary of American Events*, 12 vols. (New York 1861–66[?]), vol.2, "Diary of Events," p. 9, citing *NYTrib* of June 30, and, on Virginia, vol. 4, "Poetry and Incidents," p. 104; Richard Moe, *The Last Full Measure: The Life and Death of the First Minnesota Volunteers*, 2nd ed. (New York; Avon, 1994), 115; spoof notice of slave advertising for runaway master. *BoL*, December 28, 1861, 8. Apparently, this was Daniel Leasure's 100th Pennsylvania.

25. On Kinkead, *History of Pennsylvania Volunteers, 1861–65*. U.S. War Department, *Official Army Register of the Volunteer Force of the United States Army for the Years 1861, '62, '63, '64, '65*, 8 vols. (Washington, 1865), 3:933 (hereinafter *OAR*); and, "Affairs at Martinsburg," *RDD*, July 12, 1861; and, on Creighton's unit, *The Rebellion Record*, vol. 2, "Poetry and Incidents," p. 99, citing *NYH* of July 11, 1861. A New York paper reported that they worked under the supervision of two lieutenants with some editorial experience. "Our War Roster," *BoL*, December 13, 1862, 8; "Our War Roster," *BoL*, December 20, 1862, 4. Robinson brought back newspapers from the South. "Relics from Virginia," *BoL*, September 20, 1862, 4. Typographical union members are reported by local in *The Printer*.

26. "Correspondence," Springfield *Illinois Daily State Journal*, September 11, 1861; "The News" *NYH*, September 28, 1861. *Soldier's News-Letter* 1, no. 14 (June 14, 1862), number on Ship Island, Mississippi.

27. For *Our Regiment*, see "The Typo Warriors," *Pr* 4 (November 1861): 19; "Our Regiment Is Published by the Typos of the 13th: Now and Then," Camp Rolla *Our Regiment*, July 22, 1861, 1; At Lexington, *The First Kansas*, January 18, 1862; "To Our Patrons," Rolla *Camp Sweeny Spy*, July 4, 1861, 1; William Cam, "Rules and Regulations: Fourteenth Illinois Infantry," under Otterville *The First Division Proclamation*, February 1, 1862, 4; Otterville *War Eagle and Camp Journal of the Army of the West*, January 11, 1862, 1.

28. "The Civil War Diary of John Howard Kitts," *Kansas State Historical Society Collections*, 14 (1915–18): 321, 322, 323; Kim Allen Scott, "The Fighting Printers of Company E, Eleventh Kansas Volunteer Infantry," *Arkansas Historical Quarterly* 46 (Autumn 1987): 271–73, 273–74, 279–80. The *Van Buren Press* had ceased publication in January 1862; Thomas O'Bryan, proprietor. Fort Gibson, *Cherokee Tomahawk*, March 13, 1865.

29. *Historical Encyclopedia of Illinois and History of Tazewell County*, 975; Albert D. Richardson, *The Secret Service, the Field, the Dungeon, and the Escape* (Hartford, Conn.: American, 1866), 154 and, reprinting the printers' "Valedictory" to the unfortunate Johnson, on 154–55. See also *The Rebellion Record*, 2, "Poetry and Incidents," 43, citing *Boston Transcript* of June 25.

30. "From Jefferson City," *PI*, September 28, 1861; "The News," *NYH*, September 28, 1861, and repeated under "Various Matters," *BH*, October 1, 1861.

31. On Jackson, see "Secession among the Typos," *PI*, March 9, 1861, and *BS*, March 13, 1861. "Meetings, etc.," *CM*, May 4, 1861; and "More Secession," *MDT*, July 20, 1861. For

New Orleans, *Pr* 4 (July 1861): 9, with membership figures from vol. 3 (November 1860), 128. For Petersburg, "Tuesday Morning June 4, 1861," "Typographical," *RDD*, June 4, 1861.

32. "Miscellaneous War Items," *MDA*, June 7, 1861; "Typographical," *MDA*, June 8, 1861; and, "A Printers' Union Secedes," *BS*, September 21, 1861; "A Printers' Union Secedes," *BH*, September 26, 1861.

33. Nashville letter of March 16 in *Pr* 3 (March 1861): 225; that of July 9, 1865, from the Mobile local in "Our Correspondence," 4 (July 1865): 88.

34. On the persistence of Southern Unionism: "Southern Unionists," *The Iron Platform. Extra.—No. 39* (February 1864): 8; "New-York Workingmen's Association," *NYDT*, August 20, 1864. For the Union Leagues, see Lause, *Secret Society History*, 130, 132, 137, 146, 186, 193. Mentioned the clandestine copperhead organizations, listing: the "Circle" or "Knights of the Mighty Host," "Southern League," "Order of the Sons of Liberty," "Order of the American Knights" and, most famously, Beckley's "Knights of the Golden Circle," *The Iron Platform. Extra.—No. 39* (February 1864): 7.

35. Ingalls's "Land Reform in 1848 and 1888: George Henry Evans and Henry George," *Truth Seeker* 15 (April 28, 1888): 258. The old National Reformers played little role in such locally elite associations. Henry W. Bellows, *Historical Sketch of the Union League Club of New York: Its Origins, Organization and Work, 1863–1879* (New York: Putnam's, 1879) on Cooper, 46; Goodwin 46, 83; on Kapp and Skidmore, 47. *Proceedings of the Organization of the Loyal National League at the Cooper Institute, Friday Evening, March 20th, 1863* (New York: Putnam's, 1863) on Goodwin, Hunt, and Bryant, 48, and Minturn, 5. See also, "The Loyal Meeting," *NYDT*, July 16, 1862; Union League, Oberholtzer, *Philadelphia*, 2:372–73.

36. "The Militia Law and the Newspapers," *CM*, December 6, 1861, reprinted, citing *Exchange* in *RDD*, December 11, 1861. *Nashville Evening Bulletin. Tenn.: An Association of Journeymen Printers* vol. 1, no. 1 (March 26, 1862) through vol. 1, no. 4 (March 29, 1862); John W. Barry, of Nashville union, May 2, untitled notice, *Pr* 3 (May 1861): 274.

37. "Monday Morning . . . Nov. 11, 1861," *RDD*, November 11, 1861; "No Pay for the Eight-Hour Printers," untitled item, *RDD*, December 10 and December 17, 1861.

38. Confederate Bond Engravers, see http://www.Confederatebonds.com/printers.htm.

Chapter 3. Organized Labor Goes to War

1. George L. Wood, *The Seventh Regiment: A Record* (New York: Miller, 1865), 235–36, 260–61, 261–62, 263–64; *Roster of . . . Ohio*, 1:133, 1:134, 2:201. "A Word to the Working Classes," *Columbus Gazette*, March 1, 1861; reprinted with attribution to George W. Bungay, "A Word to the Working Classes," *LDJ*, March 9, 1861. "The Union of Printers for the Sake of the Union." Benjamin Pearley Poore, "Boston Printers' Banquet," *Pr* 3 (June 1859): 27.

2. Powderly, *Thirty Years of Labor*, 35. See also Samuel Walker, "Terence V. Powderly, Machinist: 1866–1877," *Labor History* 19 (Spring 1978): 165–84.

3. Comparison of membership lists in *The Printer* to the Combined Military Service Records; "Shooting Sticks in the Field," *BoL*, April 27, 1861, 5; *Pr* 3 (May 1861): 274; *Pr* 4 (July 1861): 8; "Printers Volunteering," *SFEB*, June 3, 1861; for Charles L. Dearborn, see also untitled, "Young Dearborn," which one of the printers wrote from the front. *BoL*,

October 4, 1862, 5; *Leaves of History*, 13. "In Memoriam," *Transactions of the Kansas State Historical Society: First and Second Biennial Reports*, 1 and 2 (Topeka: Kansas Publishing House, 1881), 168, 181.

4. Lause, "'Turning the World Upside Down': A Portrait of Labor and Military Leader, Alonzo Granville Draper," *Labor History* 44 (May 2003): 189–204. Alfred S. Roe and Charles Nutt, *History of the First Regiment of Heavy Artillery Massachusetts Volunteers, Formerly the Fourteenth Regiment of Infantry, 1861–1865* (Worcester: Regimental Assoc., 1917), 20.

5. Wieck, *American Miners' Association*, 113; "Engineer Regiment—Major Edward W. Serrell" under "Latest Mail Gleanings," *PI*, July 27, 1861; "Latest Mail Gleanings," *PI*, Monday, July 29, 1861.

6. "Patriotism at the Navy-Yard," *NYDT*, May 13, 1861. Benjamin F. Delano appointed treasurer and committee of three: Faron, John Fox, and Romeo Friganzo, with George H. Myers as secretary. The gathering also voted to present "a suitable emblem . . . as a token of their esteem and appreciation" to the thirty-eight-year-old caulker, David Hogg, who had quit to join the Empire City regiment, the Forty-Second New York. "Local Intelligence," *PI*, May 6, 1861. It specified also Lafayette Wilder, William R. Wells, Joseph B. Fuller, Denison Card, and Henry M. Bilden. "Condensed Report of the Proceedings of the National Typographical Union—Tenth Session," *Pr* 4 (July 1862): 53.

7. "To Our Readers," *ADC*, March 13, 1862; "Ourself," [West Baton Rouge] *Sugar Planter*, May 11, 1861.

8. Estill's letter to *The Printer*, March 1861; [Obediah Hicks], *Life of Richard F. Trevellick, the Labor Orator; or, The Harbinger of the Eight-Hour System* (Joliet, Ill.: Williams, 1896), 9, 22–23, (Australia) 23, 25–32, (New Zealand) 24, 35, 35–36, 38–39. For press notices of Southern printers, see *Rebellion Record*, 4; "Poetry and Incidents," 26, 38; and "Diary of Events," 98; as well as William H. H. Parry, "Obituaries," *RDD*, September 25, 1861.

9. Roberts, *Southern Sketches*, 27–28, 29, 35–36, 37–38, 39–40, 42, 59–60, 64, 65–66; "A Printer Hung," *PI*, July 3, 1861. See also: "Local Military Items," *BDE*, August 18, 1862.

10. "From the West," "Movements of Federal Troops," *RDD*, October 18, 1861.

11. *Roster of Confederate Soldiers of Georgia 1861–1865*; "Oglethorpe Light Infantry," *MDT*, July 27, 1861; combined service records on these individuals, as well as "Typos in the Kansas Regiments," *Clinton Journal*, July 4, 1861.

12. Masquerier, *Sociology*, 137; "Death of Joseph N. Moreau," *PR* 4 (July 1863): 182; and *PR* 5 (September 1863): 8. J. R. Y., "The Private Soldier," *PP*, May 18, 1863; "Minutes of the Proceedings of the Infidel Convention," *BI*, October 26, 1859. Cummings, "Our Gun Was Kept in Motion," in *Deeds of Valor . . . How American Heroes Won the Medal of Honor*, eds. Walter F. Beyer and O. F. Keydel, 2 vols. (Detroit: Perrien-Keydel, 1907), 1:166–68. George D. Moreau, also of the 119th Pennsylvania, was likely his brother.

13. U.S. War Department, *OAR*, 111, 884 and 8:43. The most accessible source of service records is the American Civil War Database of the Historical Data Systems (http://www.civilwardata.com).

14. T. M. Acton (Atlanta); Thomas M. Golden (Savannah); William H. McFarland and N. T. Powers (Richmond); and Jordan Stone (Petersburg).

15. *The Martyrs and Heroes of Illinois in the Great Rebellion: Biographical Sketches*, ed.

James Barnet (Chicago: Barnet, 1865), 57–59, 73, 78. The other member was Corporal A. Wayne Sefton.

16. On the Second Wisconsin, "A Good Regiment," *HW*, July 13, 1861, 435; On O'Donnell, see Donald L. Smith, *The Twenty-Fourth Michigan of the Iron Brigade* (Harrisburg, Pa: Stackpole, 1962), 76, 135, 145. See also Orson B. Curtis, *History of the Twenty-Fourth Michigan of the Iron Brigade, Known as the Detroit and Wayne County Regiment* (Detroit: Winn and Hammond, 1891), 39. Local members John J. Duryea and Robert Gibbons remained in the regiment, and those already gone were Sydney P. Bennett, Dewitt C. Butterfield, First Sergeant Barrett B. Halstead, and Sergeant Timothy Finn.

17. Privates Edward Y. Allen, Spencer K. Doan, William G. Magonigle (W. B. Magonigle in the Printers' Circular lists, which often lacked consistency and erred in middle initials), John T. Ryan, George G. St. John, William B. Warren. Elias Diffenbaugh (Philadelphia) had been in the 121st.

18. Abner Ralph Small, *The Road to Richmond: The Civil War Memoirs of Major Abner R. Small of the 16th Maine Volunteers*, ed. Harold Adams Small (New York: Fordham University Press, 2000), 100.

19. Walter S. Robertson and Whitmore R. Whidby in the Thirty-Eighth; Thomas E. Brady and James P. Floyd in the Twelfth. The Third Alabama had Bennett B. Brown, Halsted Bullis, John J. Cotlin, and John L. Lavalette from Mobile, and James S. Jacobs and Mathew T. Lama of Montgomery. Members of the Fourteenth North Carolina also included Private Joseph H. Alford and local members who had been in the regiment, Sergeant William H. Moore and Private Sidney R. Taylor.

20. Other members of the Thirty-Third: Charles F. Richards, then absent with wounds from Chancellorsville and Amos C. Clapp, recently discharged for disability. James B. McAlister of the New York local and David Crampton of Troy may have been in the Hundred Nineteenth New York, but both were gone by Gettysburg, the latter having been killed at Chancellorsville. From the same local, Lieutenant Charles Ashby of the Fifty-Fourth had gone home only weeks before.

21. David G. Stein (Seventh Ohio) was a possible former member of the unit. *CL*, September 29, 1862. See also the biography of Creighton in Major George L. Wood, *The Seventh Regiment: A Record* (New York: Miller, 1865), 235–91.

22. *The Martyrs and Heroes of Illinois in the Great Rebellion: Biographical Sketches*, ed. James Barnet (Chicago: Barnet, 1865), 74–77; "Brig. Gen.—-supplementing report," March 2, 1864, in "CMSR Return of Casualties in the Union Forces at Wapping Heights, Manassas Gap, Va., July 23, 1863," *The War of the Rebellion: A Compendium of the Official Records of the Union and Confederate Armies, Published under the direction of the . . . Secretary of War*, 70 vols. (Washington: GPO, 1880–1901) (hereinafter cited as *O.R.*), series 1, vol. 22, pt.1, p. 192 (in the same volume, see "Report of Maj. William H. Hugo," Seventieth New York Infantry, 564); Masquerier, *Sociology*, 126, and his "In Memorium" to Price's memory, 165–67, 195, also 167–75; "An Action at Manassas Gap," *FTR* 1 (August 1, 1863): 35. Captain Samuel F. Norton in the Second U.S. Sharpshooters, surely "Colonel" Norton, the Union veteran prominent as a postwar Illinois insurgent and Nationalist. Captain James C. Whal-

ley, who had just left the Seventy-First, may have been J. C. C. Whalley, a labor leader back in the city.

23. The most significant engagement near where I grew up was at Pilot Knob, Missouri, where the Federal numbers were not too small to spare a union member, John R. Cummins of the Davenport Typographical Union, serving in a detachment of the Fourteenth Iowa.

24. *O.R.*, series 1, vol. 34, pt. 4, p. 188; Sylvis, *Life, Speeches, Labors*, 49–50. When the war came, Sylvis went to work as a teamster in Washington, D.C., and raised troops. Sylvis, *Life, Speeches, Labors*, 47. On Brown, see *Roster of the Soldiers of the State of Ohio*, 8:671, but also "A Letter from an Old Reformer," *Freedom* 1 (undated, no page, No. 5 [1891]); and *Remarks of Aaron V. Lane at the Funeral of Joel Brown, Mt. Healthy, Ohio, November 21, 1900* (n.p.; n.p., [1900]), 16–17. William P. Leonard, *History and Directory of Posey County* (Evansville, 1882), 40; *History of Posey County, Indiana* (Chicago, 1886), 445; *OAR*, 6:70—New Harmony Free Land Association, Ms Mins. Workingmen's Institute, New Harmony, which also has a painting of Bennet in a Union officer's uniform.

25. J. R. Y., "The Private Soldier," *PP*, May 18, 1863; Horace Seaver, *Occasional Thoughts of Horace Seaver: From Fifty Years of Free Thinking; Selected from the Boston Investigator* (Boston: Mendum, 1888), 16.

26. *Pr* 4 (September 1862): 88. All these figures are based on the reports in the contemporary directories in *The Printer* and do not reflect the numbers given in Stevens, *New York Typographical Union No. 6*, 415; *Proceedings of the Franklin Typographical Society, at the Observance of the Semi-Centennial*, 13–14; "A Commendable Movement among the Printers," *PI*, August 18, 1862; "The Great Union Demonstration Yesterday Afternoon," *BH*, August 28, 1862. See, also: "Philadelphia Typographical Society," *PI*, January 5, 1863, and the notice of the "Cooper Shop Soldiers' Home," *FTR* 2 (December 19, 1863): 11. On Chicago: untitled item, *LDJ*, November 3, 1862. The directory of the New Haven local lists Stephen S. Taylor and Hervey L. Smith as dead or killed by November 1862. *Pr* 4 (November 1862): 104–5. Harvey M. in East Orrington, Me., Brotherhood of the Union, reported as having gone to California ca. 1854. For Harrisburg, George A. Brooks was dead by January 1863. *Pr* 4 (January 1863): 119–20. Of the Chicago local, see J. H. Rumer, W. D. Williams, and M. Wellis, dead by November 1863 (*Pr* 4 [November 1862]: 104–5); *Pr* 5 (November 1863): 25–26; *Leaves of History*, 13.

27. Commons, et al., *History of Labour*, 2:9. Massachusetts, Wisconsin, Missouri, and Kentucky sent representatives to the Machinists' 1861 convention. *Proceedings of the Annual Session of the Iron Moulder's Union of America, in Convention Assembled, at Cincinnati, Ohio, Jan. 8th, 1861* (New York, 1861), 4, 6, 21–22, 24–25, 26, 30; Robert Howard, "Progress in the Textile Trades," in McNeil, *Labor Movement*, 216–17, entire article on 214–40.

28. "Our War Correspondence," *PR* 4 (November 1862): 105. Farquhar had worked at Petersburg earlier and was well known enough to merit mention in the Richmond press. Untitled item, *DD*, August 16, 1862.

29. *The Printer*; *OAR*, 6:351; *Biographical Directory of Congress*; Illinois Adjutant General, *Report of the Adjutant General of the State of Illinois 1861–1866: Roster of Officers and Enlisted Men*, 9 vols. (Springfield, 1900), 5:287–88; Sylvis, *Life, Speeches, Labors*,

47–49. Farquhar resigned, letter of December 1862 from Nashville. Tracy, *History of the Typographical Union*, 200–201. Lt. Col. Charles T. Hotchkiss, Eighty-Ninth Illinois Infantry, Camp near Murfreesborough, Tenn., January 7, 1863, *O.A.R.*, ser.1, vol. 20, pt. 1, pp. 309–10, 310–11. History of the Eighty-Ninth Infantry, from *Report of the Adjutant General of the State of Illinois 1861–1866*, 5:287–288. See also James Lee McDonough, *Stones River: Bloody River in Tennessee* (Knoxville: University of Tennessee Press, 1980), 86–90. The Moulders' leader Henry J. Eisenach, Residence Wayne County, Michigan, twenty-two years old, enlisted on March 3, 1862 at Detroit as a private, on which day he mustered into "G" Company, Michigan 1st Infantry. He re-enlisted on March 4, 1864, and was killed on May 5, 1864, at Wilderness, Virginia. *Record of Service of Michigan Volunteers 1861–65*; Report of Maj. Gen. William S. Rosecrans and List of Mentions, Cincinnati, Ohio, January 7, 1864, *O. A. R.*, series 1, vol. 30, pt. 1, pp. 80, 91; Illinois Adjutant General, *Roster of Officers and Enlisted Men* 9 vols. (Springfield, 1900); History of the Eighty-Ninth Infantry, from *Report of the Adjutant General of the State of Illinois 1861–1866*, 5:287–88; "Special Order in Combined Military Service Records." Later orders dated the promotion to February 24, coupling it to a command of Company B; "Civil War Medal of Honor Recipients Citations."

30. Stevens, *New York Typographical Union*, (Ottarson) 646–47, (Peck) 660–61; *How Private Geo. W. Peck Put Down the Rebellion; or, The Funny Experiences of a Raw Recruit* (Chicago: Conkey, 1900); Theodore C. Tracie, *Annals of the Nineteenth Ohio Battery Volunteers Artillery: Including an Outline of the Second Division, Twenty-Third Army Corps; Lights and Shadows of Army Life, as Seen on the March, Bivouac and Battle-Field* (Cleveland: J. B. Savage for the Battery Committee, 1878); Lause, *The Antebellum Crisis and America's First Bohemians* (Kent, Ohio: Kent State University Press, 2009). George F. Williams, "Lights and Shadows of Army Life," *Century Magazine* 28 (October 1884): 803–19; *The Memorial War Book as Drawn from the Historical Records and Personal Narratives of the Men who Served in the Great Struggle* (New York: Dreyfus, 1894); *Bullet and Shell: War as the Soldier Saw It; Camp, March, and Picket; Battlefield and Bivouac; Prison and Hospital.* (New York: Fords, Howard, and Hulbert, 1883); "Major G. F. Williams, Journalist, is Dead; Veteran of 83 Was Managing Editor of the *New York Times* from 1870 to 1873," *NYT*, January 1, 1921.

31. "Necrology," *Missouri Historical Review* 5 (January 1911): 122–23.

32. April 8, 1864, entry. John Ransom, *Andersonville Diary: Life Inside the Civil War's Most Infamous Prison* (Baton Rouge; Louisiana State University Press, 1984), 63; Stevens, *New York Typographical Union,* 654–55.

33. "A Memorial Address, giving a sketch of his life and extracts from his letters, was delivered before the Union by Mr. Thomas Gliddon, on Saturday evening, June 7, 1862, which has since been published in an elegant pamphlet form, and a copy set to this office." "Death of William Randle Wells," *Pr* 4 (January 1863): 118. On Madigan: *Proceedings of the Franklin Typographical Society, at the Observance of the Semi-Centennial of Its Institution, January 17, 1874: With a Brief Historical Sketch* (Boston: Franklin Typographical Society, 1875), 14; "Death of Ex-Vice-President Madigan," *Pr* 4 (July 1862): 55, and the resolutions (August 1862): 71; Daniel G. Macnamara, *History of the Ninth Regiment Mas-*

sachusetts Volunteer Infantry, June 1861–June 1864 (New York: Fordham University Press, 2000), 119–20, 128; "Death of Ex-Pres't Madigan," *Pr* 4 (July 1862): 55. The commander of the Ninth took the sword from the field and returned it to the union, who presented it to Madigan's father. *Leaves of History*, 13; "William Madigan," *BoL*, August 16, 1862, 6. Also. "Typographical," *CG*, December 11, 1863; "In Memoriam," *Pr* 4 (February 1864): 56; "Typographical Union," *CG*, June 10, 1864; and untitled item, *CG*, December 9, 1864; untitled item, *CG*, January 15, 1864.

34. Dayton Kelley, "L. A. Hine, Prophet of the Rights of Man," unpublished paper, Baylor University (available at the Ohio Historical Society, Columbus), 18–19. A copy of this unpublished 1969 paper from Baylor University at Waco, Texas, is at the Ohio Historical Society, Columbus.

35. *CL*, December 1, December 3, December 5, December 17, 1863.

Chapter 4. The Great Slave Strike

1. "The Strike in the Washington Navy Yard" under "Strikes in Other Cities" [from *Washington Evening Star*] under "The Labor Movement," *NYH*, November 14, 1863.

2. In a recent discussion on H-Net (Humanities and Social Sciences Online, http://www.h-net.org) labor historians discussed the largest and most important strikes in American history. The introduction of the wartime slave strike fell with a great thud. Apparently, they did not strike if they did not have dues cards. See also Eric Foner, "The Civil War and Slavery: A Response," *Historical Materialism* 19, no. 4 (2011): 92–98. Eric Foner, *Free Soil, Free Labor, Free Men: The Ideology of the Republican Party before the Civil War* (New York: Oxford University Press, 1970) and Eric Foner, *Politics and Ideology in the Age of the Civil War* (New York: Oxford University Press, 1980).

3. Herbert Aptheker, *American Negro Slave Revolts* (1943; New York: International, 1969), 360, 94, 362, 364, 365–66, 366n.

4. Ibid., 364, 364n, 365n, 94, 362, 364, 364–65, 365, 365n.

5. Ibid., 366.

6. "War Recollections," *The Alarm*, July 7, 1888; Allan Pinkerton, *The Spy of the Rebellion* (New York: Dillingham, 1883), 354–57. See also the chapter on African American organizations in Lause, *Secret Society History*.

7. "House of Representatives," *RDD*, March 1, 1865.

8. Midori Takagi, *"Rearing Wolves to Our Own Destruction": Slavery in Richmond* (Charlottesville: University Press of Virginia, 1999), 131–32, 133–34; Aptheker, *American Negro Slave Revolts*, 366, 95, 367.

9. Aptheker, *American Negro Slave Revolts*, 361–62, 95, 367, 361.

10. Most recently, see Victoria E. Bynum, *The Free State of Jones: Mississippi's Longest Civil War* (Chapel Hill: University of North Carolina Press, 2003); and Sally Jenkins and John Stauffer, *The State of Jones* (New York: Doubleday, 2009).

11. Ira Berlin, ed., *The Destruction of Slavery* (Cambridge: Cambridge University Press, 1985); Mary Frances Berry, *Military Necessity and Civil Rights Policy: Black Citizenship and the Constitution, 1861–1868* (Port Washington, N.Y.: Kennikat, 1977).

12. James D. Schmidt, *Free to Work: Labor Law, Emancipation and Reconstruction, 1815–1880* (Athens: the University of Georgia Press, 1998).

13. Ira Berlin, Steven F. Miller, Joseph P. Reidy, and Leslie S. Rowland, eds., *The Wartime Genesis of Free Labor: the Upper South*, series 1, vol. 2 of *Freedom: A Documentary History of Emancipation 1861–1867, Selected from the Holdings of the National Archives of the United States, ed. Ira Berlin* (Cambridge: Cambridge University Press, 1993), 381, 608n.

14. Steven Hahn, Steven P. Miller, Susan E. O'Donovan, John C. Rodrigue, and Leslie S. Rowland, eds., *Land and Labor*, series 3, vol. 1 of Berlin, *Freedom*, 39, 59–60, 751–56; noting black referee, 753n; see also 788, 789–90.

15. Ibid., 509.

16. Ibid., 603, 636–37, 677–78.

17. "Affairs about Home: Emancipation Celebration at Tremont Temple," *BH*, January 2, 1863.

18. Ira Berlin, Thavolia Glymph, Steven F. Miller, Joseph P. Reidy, Leslie S. Rowland, and Julie Saville, eds., *The Wartime Genesis of Free Labor: The Lower South*, series 1, vol. 3 of *Freedom: A Documentary History of Emancipation, 1861–1867* (New Haven: Yale University Press, 1991), 26; Berlin et al., *Free Labor: Upper South*, 15–16, 247, 248–49, 261–62, 357–58. Colored Union Benevolent Association, Gurden Snowden, Charles H. Brown, James H. Wright, Sandy Alexander, Henry Loggens, Charles Wilson, Henry Brooks, John Shorter, Joseph Shorter.

19. Classified advertisement, *BDE*, December 24, 1863. Charles W. Worster, resident, Grant County, Indiana, twenty-one years old, enlisted on May 15, 1861, as a corporal and mustered into "H" Company, Indiana 12th Infantry the same day. He died of disease on December 7, 1861, at Sharpsburg, Maryland, and was buried at Antietam National Cemetery, Sharpsburg, gravesite no. 3444.

20. Notice in *New South*, August 8, 1863; *Rebellion Record*, 4, "Poetry and Incidents," 104; "A Strike," *NYDT*, August 14, 1863, reprinted "From Port Royal—Contrabands Must Work," *RDD*, August 20, 1863. Presidents of Free Labor Associations of Craven, Cartenet, Hyde, and Beaufort Counties organizing. "The Free-Labor Movement—Ten Loyal Regiments to be Organized—Feeling against Gov. Stanly," *NYDT*, January 27, 1863. John Johnson Elwell was the "Chief Q. M. Dep't of the South."

21. G. W. Beidelman to Jacob Beidelman, September 13, 1863, in Vanderslice, *Civil War Letters*, 184.

22. Lowry, *Tarnished Eagles*, 211.

23. *The Lesson of St. Domingo: How to Make the War Short and the Peace Righteous, from the "New York Tribune" of May 27, 1861* (Boston: Williams, 1861); and, *Leaves of History*, 15.

24. Peter H. Clark, *The Black Brigade of Cincinnati, Being a Report of Its Labors and a Muster Roll of Its Members; Together with Various Orders, Speeches, Etc. Relating to It* (Cincinnati: Boyd, 1864); Herbert G. Gutman, "Peter Clark: Pioneer Negro Socialist, 1877," *Journal of Negro Education* 34 (Autumn 1865): 413–18; Nikki M. Taylor, *America's First Black Socialist: The Radical Life of Peter H. Clark* (Lexington: University Press of Kentucky, 2012). See also Ira Berlin et al., eds., *The Black Military Experience*, series 2, vol. 1 of

Freedom: A Documentary History of Emancipation 1861–1867, Selected from the Holdings of the National Archives of the United States (Cambridge: Cambridge University Press, 1982). Thomas Henry Tibbles, the future vice presidential candidate of the Populists, had a long association with the Indians. *Buckskin and Blanket Days: Memoirs of a Friend of the Indian* (1905; Chicago: Donnelley, 1985).

25. In general, see Lause, "Turning the World Upside Down," 189–204.

26. Ibid., 196–97.

27. Ibid., 197–98.

28. *OAR*, 7:354, 8:181, 8:294.

29. Lause, *Race and Radicalism in the Union Army* (Urbana: University of Illinois Press, 2009).

30. Webb B. Garrison, *Mutiny in the Civil War* (Shippensburg, Penn.: White Mane, 2001), 75–83.

31. Eric Foner, *Nothing but Freedom: Emancipation and Its Legacy* (Baton Rouge: Louisiana State University Press, 1983).

32. "The Ordeal of Free Black Labor," *NYDT*, February 21, 1864; "Brick Oven," *USMO*, April 21, 1860.

33. "Regular lies about Democratic parades being fired on, babes in arms being wounded, flags shot up," *Cleveland Leader*, September 17, 1863; "Free Negroes—Foresight of the Convention," *Jonesboro* [Illinois] *Gazette*, April 12, 1862; and, on violence in Detroit, *Cleveland Leader*, May 9 and 11, 1863. See also Leonard L. Richards, *"Gentlemen of Property and Standing": Anti-Abolition Mobs in Jacksonian America* (Oxford: Oxford University Press, 1971), and David Grimsted, *American Mobbing, 1828–1861: Toward Civil War* (Oxford: Oxford University Press, 2003). The primary appeal of Democratic white supremacists, though, aimed at employers, warning about the unreliability and disloyalty of African American labor. The Civil War did not change this. Secessionist papers issued indirect warnings to Northern employers in reporting from Nassau, Bahamas, that "negroes here struck for higher wages. It creased great excitement, and 'twas thought they would rise; it was settled, however, and they went to work again at the old prices." "Nassau items" (from the *Savannah Republican*), *RDD*, July 13, 1864.

34. Editorial, "The Industrial Congress," *NYH*, November 23, 1860; "Promoting Amalgamation" (from *NYH*), *DP*, December 16, 1863.

35. "From New York Fools Day—Practical Manifestations and Personal Illustrations," *PI*, April 2, 1861.

36. Roberts, *Southern Sketches*, 76–78, 84, 93–95. Members of the Savannah Typographical Union found that their involvement in local defense measures drew them into the Sixty-Third Georgia, their part of which occupied some of the defenses around Charleston. Company B included Sergeant David M. Middleton and Privates Michael J. Divine, John M. Harrison, Robert P. Sabate (or Sabatta or Sabatty), Charles J. White, as well James Gow, a member of the Augusta local. Company F added Captain John H. Lopez and Wm. R. Evans, John L. Grayson, Martin Kelahan, Edward R. Law, and George C. Ulmer. Roberts, *Southern Sketches*, 101, 102, 103.

37. Ibid., 136–40.

38. A. J. H. Duganne, *Camps and Prisons: Twenty Months in the Department of the Gulf* (New York: Robens, 1865), 99–100, 100–101.

39. G. W. Beidelman to Jacob Beidelman, September 13, October 18, 1863, and letter to the editor of the *Press*, November 24, 1863, in Vanderslice, *Civil War Letters*, 184–85, 187–88, 190–91. When his father asked whether his messmates were "whites, or blacks, or a mixture of both," Beidelman managed to answer without answering. "The mess is composed of all the commissioned officers (whites) in the camp, who choose to board there and pay for their board. The non-commissioned staff of the Post (of which I am one) also board there, but do not pay."

40. James M. McPherson, *The Struggle for Equality: Abolitionists and the Negro in the Civil War and Reconstruction* (Princeton, N.J.: Princeton University Press, 1964); George R. Bentley, *A History of the Freedmen's Bureau* (New York: Octagon, 1974); E. Merton Coulter, *The South during Reconstruction, 1865–1877* (Baton Rouge: Louisiana State University Press, 1947); Eric Foner, *Nothing But Freedom*. See also Robert Dale Owen, *The Wrong of Slavery, the Right of Emancipation, and the Future of the African Race in the United States* (Philadelphia: Lippincott, 1864).

41. "Labor in the Interior," *Leavenworth Daily Conservative*, May 6, 1864; "The Late Discussion on the War," *BS*, January 17, 1863.

42. Allan Pinkerton, *Strikers, Communists, Tramps and Detectives* (New York: Carleton, 1878), 381.

Chapter 5. The Alienation of Militancy

1. "Brooklyn News," *NYT*, April 2, 1861; "From New York Fools Day-Practical Manifestations and Personal Illustrations," *PI*, April 2, 1861; "Central Trades Union," *NYDT*, March 25, 1863. For more than thirty years Mayor Fernando Wood's Democratic Party had professed to speak for the enfranchised white labor men. See also Eugene E. Leach, "Changing the Tiger: The Mob Stigma and the Working Class, 1863–1894," *Labor History* 35 (Spring 1994): 187–215.

2. *OAR*, 4:250, 4:341, 7:167, 7:201. Phillip Shaw Paludan, "*A People's Contest*."

3. *Pr* 3 (May 1861): 274; *OAR*, 1:159; *Leaves of History*, 13, 5–7, 9–10, 11; Macnamara, *History of the Ninth Regiment*, 9, 10, 18, 19, 29. For Treanor, see the *Cincinnati Daily Nonpareil*, June 12, 1850.

4. Robert P. Sutton, *Les Icariens: The Utopian Dream in Europe and America* (Urbana: University of Illinois Press, 1994), 113–14; "Patriotic Socialists," *PI*, May 17, 1861.

5. "Interesting View of Things at Washington," *RDD*, August 19, 1861; Foner and Lewis, *Black Worker to 1869*, 274–75, 276–77, 306; "A Struggle between the Races" and "A White Man Shot by a Negro," *FTR* 1 (July 11 and 18, 1863): 22, 27; On Buffalo, "The Strike among Laborers," *NYDT*, May 16, 1863.

6. "Labor Troubles in Pennsylvania," 280, cited in "Strikes and Lockouts . . . in the United States," 1048; Gallman, *Mastering Wartime*, 234, 235–36, 237, 238, 239; on Arch Street "Strikes," with "W.H.S., letter of June 8," "The Moulders on Strike," "Stove and Hollow-War

Molders," "One Year Ago To-Day," Sylvis letter, February 11, 1864, *FTR* 1 (June 13, 1863): 6; (June 20, 1863): 10; (July 11, 1863): 22; and vol. 2 (December 19, 1863): 11; (February 20, 1864): 47; also, *Proceedings of the Fifth Annual Session of the Iron Molders' International Union, in Convention Assembled, at Buffalo, N.Y., January 6, 1864* (Philadelphia: *FTR*, 1864), 8.

7. "Boston Letter," *Christian Inquirer*, January 17, 1863; Massachusetts Bureau of Statistics of Labor, *Eleventh Annual Report of the Bureau of Statistics of Labor of Massachusetts*, 19, 20, cited "Strikes and Lockouts . . . in the United States," 1047; *Lewiston Falls Journal*, April 16, 1863; May 11, 1860, cited Scontras, *Collective Efforts Among Maine Workers*, 333.

8. "The Grain-Shovelers' Strike," *NYT*, July 9, 1862; "Brooklyn News," *NYT*, July 17, 1862; *New York Evangelist*, July 17, 1862; "Labor vs. Machinery—The Grain Shovellers' Strike," *NYDT*, July 9, 1862; "Our New York Letter," *PI*, July 14, 1862; "Affairs in New York. New York, July 11," *BS*, July 14, 1862.

9. "General City News," *NYT*, October 11, 1862; and "Our New York Letter: Thurlow Weed Certainly Going to Europe," *PI*, November 19, 1862.

10. McKay, *Civil War and New York City*, 163; "General City News," *NYDT*, October 29, 1862; "A Strike among the Employees of the Gas Companies," with "General City News," *NYDT*, November 13, 1862; "The Late Strike at the Manhattan Gas Works—An Action for False Imprisonment," *NYDT*, December 17, 1862.

11. "Thurlow Weed," *PI*.

12. McKay, *Civil War and New York City*, 163. In *BDE:* "Local Military Items" (August 18, 1862); "Anticipated Strike in the Navy Yard" (November 22, 1862); "The Navy Yard 'Strike'" with "Another Meeting this Morning" (December 22, 1862); "The Strike at the Navy Yard" (December 23, 1862); and "Strike of Shipwrights in Navy Yard" (December 24, 1862). In *NYDT*: "Navy-Yard Politics" (July 17, 1857); "Meeting of Journeymen House Painters" (November 14, 1862); "The Wages of Labor" (November 22, 1862); "Affairs at the Brooklyn Navy-Yard" (December 23, 1862). "City Intelligence" (from *New Orleans Delta*, July 6), *NYH*, November 4, 1862; "Affairs in New York," *BS*, November 13, 1862.

13. "Facts and Fiction," *SLCDN*, December 31, 1862; "Meeting of Mechanics in Tammany Hall," *NYDT*, February 8, 1863; and "Central Trades Union," *NYDT*, March 25, 1863.

14. "Strike of the Laborers at the New Court House," *BDE*, May 19, 1862; classified advertisements, *BDE*, April 29, 1863; McNeil, *Labor Movement*, 394, cited "Strikes and Lockouts . . . in the United States," 1048; "Our New York Letter," *PI*, December 9, 1862; "Trade Movements: Meetings of the Piano Makers, Painters, Tailors, Bakers and Coopers," *NYDT*, March 30, 1862; "New-Jersey," *NYDT*, May 3, 1863; "Strike among the Harness-makers at Newark," *NYT*, September 7, 1862.

15. "Meeting of Mechancis in Tammany Hall," *NYTrib*, February 7, 1863.

16. "Camden Matters," *PI*, March 31, 1862; "The Strikes," *NYT*, March 24, 1863.

17. "The Labor Movement: Formidable Strike of the Dock Laborers on the Erie Railroad Piers," *NYH*, March 24, 1863; "The Strikes" with "Strike of Employees of the Erie Railroad Company," *NYT*, March 24, 1863."Strikes and Lockouts," 1048. Also see Eric Arnesen, *Waterfront Workers of New Orleans: Race, Class and Politics, 1863–1923* (New York: Oxford University Press, 1991), 20; "Amalgamation Existent in Acquackanonk, New Jersey," *FTR* 1 (August 22, 1863): 46.

18. "Central Trades Union," *NYDT*, March 25, 1863.

19. "Strike of the Journeymen Tailors," *NYDT*, March 24, 1863; "Trade Movements: Meetings of the Piano Makers, Painters, Tailors, Bakers and Coopers," *NYDT*, March 30, 1863; "The Strikes," *NYT*, March 24, 1863; and, "Our New York Letter," *PI*, April 3, 1863.

20. "Our New York Letter," *PI*, April 3, 1863; "The Trades' Movement: Mass Meeting of the Working Men of Brooklyn," *BDE*, April 24, 1863.

21. Various reports under "Our New York Letter," *PI*, June 9, 10, 12, 1863; "Strikes," *FTR* 1 (June 13, 1863): 6; "The Struggle for Bread!" *FTR* 1 (June 20, 1863): 10; "The N.Y. Trades Movement," *FTR* 1 (June 27, 1863): 44; "Strike among the Longshoremen," *NYDT*, June 9, 1863; McKay, *Civil War and New York City*, 197.

22. "The N.Y. Trades Movement," *FTR* 1 (June 27, 1863): 14; and "The Police among the Strikers," *NYT*, June 20, 1863.

23. "Our New York Letter," *PI*, June 12, 1863; "Trade Movements: Meetings of the Piano Makers, Painters, Tailors, Bakers and Coopers," *NYDT*, March 30, 1863; "Local Intelligence," *NYDT*, June 2, 1863.

24. "The Germans and the Democracy," *PtsS*, June 25, 1863; "Quarterly Report of the President of the Chicago *Arbeiter-Verein*," *Illinois Staats-Zeitung*, May 26, 1862; and "German Citizens of Chicago Hold Emancipation Meeting," *Illinois Staats-Zeitung*, January 13, 1863, available on the Newberry Library Foreign Language Press Survey, http://flps.newberry.org. See also Mischa Honeck, *We Are the Revolutionists: German-Speaking Immigrants and American Abolitionists after 1848* (Athens: University of Georgia Press, 2011).

25. Julián Marías offered his own very-well-considered summary of earlier interpretations of this matter in his *Generations: A Historical Method*, translated Harold C. Raley (Birmingham: University of Alabama Press, 1967), particularly 170–88 for an informative discussion of generational series.

26. Roberts, *Southern Sketches*, 48–49, 62, 66, 68–69, 73–74.

27. David M. Barnes, *The Draft Riots in New York, July 1863: The Metropolitan Police, Their Services during Riot* (New York: Baker and Godwin, 1863); Iver Bernstein, *The New York City Draft Riots: Their Significance for American Society and Politics in the Age of the Civil War* (Oxford: Oxford University Press, 1999); Adrian Cook, *The Armies of the Streets: The New York City Draft Riots of 1863* (Lexington: University Press of Kentucky, 1974); James Barnet Fry, *New York and the Conscription of 1863* (New York: Putnam's, 1885); James Dabney McCabe, *The Life and Public Services of Horatio Seymour* (Oxford: Oxford University Press, 1868); Barnet Schecter, *The Devil's Own Work: The Civil War Draft Riots and the Fight to Reconstruct America* (New York: Walker, 2005); also Foner and Lewis, *Black Worker to 1869*, 287.

28. "Words to Workingmen," *NYDT*, July 16, 1863.

29. "Excitement in Brooklyn," *BDE*, July 16, 1863.

30. James R. Gilmore, "The New York 'Tribune' in the Draft Riots: The Story of a Member of the Staff who Assisted in Arming the 'Tribune' Office," *McClure's Magazine* 5 (October 1895), 445–54. Cummings's comrades were Patrick O'Rouke and Thomas N. Rooker.

31. "More Particulars of the N.Y. Riot," *QDWR*, July 16, 1863; "Telegraphic," [Springfield] *Daily Illinois State Journal*, July 17, 1863.

32. "Sound Doctrine from a Workingman," *NYDT*, July 19, 1863. See the broadsides: *To the Laboring Men of New York* (New York: n.p., July 18, 1863); *Don't Unchain the Tiger!* (New York: n.p., July 24, 1863); *A Challenge* (New York: n.p., Aug. 25, 1863); "A Few Thoughts on Mobs," *FTR* 1 (July 25, 1863): 30. See also, their earlier open letter to Mayor Fernando Wood on "The Future of the Democratic Republican Party," *IPE* 24 (November 1862): 1–4.

33. "Special Notice," *IPE* 39 (February 1864): 4.

34. "The Chicago *Arbetier-Verein* and as German Volunteer Defense Corps President Speaks for the Society," *Illinois Staats-Zeitung*, July 30, 1863, available on the Newberry Library Foreign Language Press Survey, posted from http://flps.newberry.org.

35. H. M. Failing, president, and R. S. Hill, rec. secretary, notice "To the Printers of the United States," *NYDT*, May 22, 1863. Old scale, eleven dollars per week or thirty-two and thirty-four cents per one thousand ems; new scale, eighteen dollars per week and thirty-seven cents per one thousand ems. "Meeting of the New York Compositors," under "New York City News," *BDE*, September 24, 1863; Stevens, *New York Typographical Union No. 6*, 276–77.

36. Joel T. Headly, *The Great Riots of New York, 1712–1873* (New York: Thunder's Mouth, 2004), 219–20.

37. "The True Character of the New York Riots," (quoting the *Le Siècle*), *London Daily News*, August 1, 1863. Cluseret documented "the hatred against the blacks," noting that black sailors on English schooners from the Bahamas had to take refuge on a French frigate.

38. August 1863, New York, last meeting—elected the following officers: president, E. P. McDermott (plasterers); vice president, J. J. Blair (machinists); 1st secretary, E. Kerr (Brooklyn plasterers); 2nd secretary, J. J. Burby (carpenters); treasurer, W. McClure (machinists); seargent-at-arms, Lemuel Powell (carpenters). "Workingmen's Union," *NYDT*, August 2, 1863.

39. "The Strikes," *NYT*, March 24, 1863.

40. "The Origins of the Troubles Yesterday," *BH*, July 16, 1863.

41. Roberts, *Southern Sketches*, 128–29, 135.

Chapter 6. The Survival of Moral Suasion

1. "A Library for Working Women," *NYDT*, October 27, 1863; "The Widow's Mite," *BoL*, October 17, 1863.

2. Seaver, *Occasional Thoughts*, 17, 19.

3. "Additional from the North," "The Condition of Affairs in New York," *RDD*, April 5, 1864.

4. "A Plea for the Working Women: An Address by Miss Lizzie Doten, at Lyceum Hall, Sunday Evening, April 27th 1862," *BoL*, May 10, 1862, 4; "The Laboring Women," *BoL*, April 23, 1864, 4.

5. McKay, *Civil War and New York City*, 197; "Women and Work," *BoL*, December 5, 1863,

4; "A Labor movement in the Right Direction—The Working Women's Protective Union," *BDE*, March 22, 1864; "Dietary of the Working Classes," *SA* 10 (April 2, 1864): 210. See Mary E. Massey's *Women in the Civil War* (Lincoln: University of Nebraska Press, 1994), originally published ca. 1965 as *Bonnet Brigades*; Edwin G. Burrows, *Gotham: A History of New York City to 1898* (Oxford: Oxford University Press, 1999).

6. "Dietary of the Working Classes," *SA* 10 (April 2, 1864): 210; Stevens, *New York Typographical Union No. 6*, 284–85.

7. "A Subject of Much Concern: The Increased Rent of Dwelling-Houses—Causes of the Rise—What Can be Done to Provide Homes for the People," *NYDT*, February 18, 1865; "The True Mission of the Trades' Unions," *BDE*, March 23, 1865.

8. "A Plea for the Working Women: An Address by Miss Lizzie Doten, at Lyceum Hall, Sunday Evening, April 27th 1862," *BoL*, May 10, 1862, 4; "Women and Work," *BoL*, December 5, 1863, 4; and "The Working Women's Relief Association," *BoL*, September 17, 1864, 4.

9. "The Laboring Women," *BoL*, June 18, 1864, 4.

10. "Injustice to Woman in the 'Daily Whig and Republican'" [from *CJ*], *QDWR*, October 23, 1863. "We estimate the forwardness of our civilization by the position of woman. Where she is compelled to labor as the beasts of the field, it is impossible that she should be other than degraded and down-trodden." Strikes "taking place in the chief cities of the country, for higher prices of labor, bring this topic before the public mind with more force and minuteness than ever before, and offer suggestions for the improvement of woman's condition that might not otherwise occur to the general mind." "Women and Work," *BoL*, December 5, 1863, 4.

11. "A Plea for the Working Women: An Address by Miss Lizzie Doten, at Lyceum Hall, Sunday Evening, April 27th 1862," *BoL*, May 10, 1862, 4.

12. "Miss Hardinge's Enterprise in behalf of Homeless and Outcast Females," "The Lost Ones of the Cities," *BoL*, April 13, 1861, and March 8, 1862; "Affairs about Home," *BH*, March 27, 1861; "The Lost Ones of the Cities," *NYDT*, February 25, 1862.

13. "Emma Hardinge, to Her Friends in America," *BoL*, September 19, 1863, 8.

14. Collins, *Nature's Aristocracy*, 314; "A Plea for the Working Women: An Address by Miss Lizzie Doten, at Lyceum Hall, Sunday Evening, April 27th 1862," *BoL*, May 10, 1862, 4.

15. "Plea for the Working Women." See also: "Women's Work and Women's Wages," *USMO*, May 19, 1860, and "A Laborer for Equal Rights" *USMO*, June 2, 1860; Bella Bush, "A Song for the Army of Knitters," poem, *BoL*, December 20, 1862, 4.

16. "Right Kind of Woman's Rights," *USMO*, March 17, 1860; "School Teachers," and Sarah Parkes's "A Sketch from Real Life," *FTR* 1 (July 4, 1863): 18; and *FTR* 4 (January 28, 1865): 33.

17. "Women and Work," *BoL*, December 5, 1863, 4, and "The Laboring Women," and *BoL*, April 23, 1864, 4; "True Gallantry," *FTR* 1 (November 28, 1863): 103. Brooklyn, "The Sewing Women," *FTR* 2 (December 12, 1863): 7. *Appleton's Dictionary of New York and Its Vicinity* (New York: Appleton, 1892), 29. Working Woman's Protective Union, organized 1863, incorporated 1868; *Cleveland Leader*, December 8, 1863; McKay, *Civil War and New*

York City, 197. See also the account of William O. Bourne's "Workingwomen's Protective Union," in *The Soldier's Friend* (February 1867): 4.

18. "The Widow's Mite," *BoL*, October 17, 1863, 4. From *NYDT*: "A Library for Working Women" (October 27, 1863); "Strike among Female Employees" (November 11, 1863); "Women's Work and Their Struggle for Better Compensation" (November 15, 1863); Letter of Mme. Demorest on "The Question of Labor: Women's Work and Wages" (November 18, 1863); and a response under "The Question of Woman's Work and Wages" (November 22, 1863). "Strike by Hair Cloth Weavers" under "City Items," *NYTrib*, November 11, 1863; "The Females on Strike" under "The Labor Movements in New York: The Various Branches of Trade Affected: The Principal Passenger Railways in New York Stopped Running," *PI*, November 14, 1863; McKay, *Civil War and New York City*, 197; "Women and Work," *BoL*, December 5, 1863. Fincher's labor paper reprinted the spiritualist poem by W. M. Fernald, "The Working Girls," *FTR* 2 (December 19, 1863): 9.

19. "Aid for the Working Women," classified advertisement, *BDE*, March 19, 1864, and "A Labor Movement in the Right Direction—The Working Women's Protective Union," *BDE*, March 22, 1864. Southern papers picked up the press as well: see "White Slavery in the North" [from the *RE*, based on the account in the *New York News*], *ADC*, April 28, 1864; "Women's Work and Wages," dated New York, March 26, in "Letters from the People," *NYDT*, April 2, 1864. See also "Women's Labor," *FTR* 2 (April 16, 1864): 78, and "The Working Women's Movement," *FTR* 2 (April 30, 1864): 86. At the conclusion of the proceedings, Miss Teresa Esmonde, the well-known dramatic reader, read the "Song of the Working-Women," attributed to Mrs. Ann S. Stephens. "White Slavery in the North" [from the *RE*, based on the account in the *New York News*], *ADC*, April 28, 1864.

20. Two items under "The Laboring Women," *BoL*, April 23 and June 18, 1864. See also: "Women's Work and Wages," dated New York, March 26, in "Letters from the People," *NYDT*, April 2, 1864; "Women's Labor," *FTR* 2 (April 16, 1864): 78.

21. "Houses for Workingmen New-York and Paris Contrasted," *NYDT*, September 13, 1864.

22. McKay, *Civil War and New York City*, 197, 160; "Board of Education," *BDE*, December 7, 1864; "Women's Protective Union," *NYH*, December 18, 1864; Henry Morford noted in "Appeal for the Workingwoman," *FTR* 4 (January 7, 1865): 21; David N. Camp, ed., *The American Year-Book and National Register for 1869* (Hartford: Case, 1869), 1:224.

23. Cora Wilburn, "The Wrongs of Needle Women," *BoL*, December 24, 1864, 3.

24. "The Sewing Women," *BoL*, January 30, 1864, 4.

25. Gallman, *Mastering Wartime*, 243–44; "White Female Slaves," *FTR* 1 (August 1, 1863): 34; "Who Pockets the Difference?" *FTR* 1 (September 5, 1863): 54; "Frauds in Leather Contracts," (September 12, 1863): 58; "Working Women," *FTR* 1 (September 26, 1863): 66.

26. "Women and Work," *BoL*, December 5, 1863, 4; McKay, *Civil War and New York City*, 197; Gallman, *Mastering Wartime*, 244–45.

27. "Women and Work," *BoL*, December 5, 1863, 4; "The Sewing Women," *BoL*, December 12, 1863, 4; "Affairs About Home," *BoL*, February 26, 1864, 4; "Proceedings of the Yearly Meeting of Progressive Friends," *BoL*, July 9, 1864, 4. See also sources cited in note 25 in this chapter.

28. Gallman, *Mastering Wartime*, 244–45; Rachel Filene Seidman, "Beyond Sacrifice: Women and Politics on the Pennsylvania Homefront," PhD diss., Yale University, New Haven, Conn., 1995.

29. "Proceedings of the Yearly Meeting of Progressive Friends," Chester County, Pennsylvania, June 2–5, 1864, *BoL*, July 9, 1864, 3.

30. "The Working Women's Relief Association," *BoL*, September 17, 1864, 4; "The Working Women's Relief Association: An Acknowledgement," *BoL*, November 5, 1864, 4; Cora Wilburn, "The Wrongs of Needle Women," *BoL*, December 24, 1864, 3.

31. Gallman, *Mastering Wartime*, 239–40, 245–46. Also, "Seamstresses Strive for Increase in Wages," *Illinois Staats-Zeitung*, April 23, 1864, available on the Newberry Library Foreign Language Press Survey, posted from http://flps.newberry.org.

32. Gallman, *Mastering Wartime*, 239–40, 245–46.

33. Blewett discusses some of the internal friction in the strike movement that resulted; see Mary H. Blewett, *We Will Rise in Our Might: Workingwomen's Voices from Nineteenth-Century New England* (Ithaca: Cornell University Press, 1991), 77–78, 81. "The Great Shoemakers Strike," *USMO*, March 3, 1860; "Latest from the Seat of War," *USMO*, March 10, 1860; and "The Strike among the Cordwainers of Massachusetts," *USMO*, March 17, 1860.

34. Caroline H. Dall, *The College, the Market, and the Court; or, Woman's Relation to Education, Labor, and Law* (Boston: Lee and Shepard, 1867), 183–84; Virginia Penny, *The Employments of Women: A Cyclopaedia of Woman's Work* (Boston: Walker, Wise, 1862), 380–81, 382, with overview of women working in different shops on 384–85. See also "Women Printers," *USMO*, November 26, 1859. Tracy dated the appearance of women in composing rooms to 1854. *History of the Typographical Union*, 153–54.

35. "Summary of News," *PI*, August 29, 1864; and, "Female Labor," *BDE*, July 28, 1864; *Leaves of History*, 10. Debate over charters to Women's Typographical Union No. 1 of New York, "Proceedings of the Seventeenth Session of the National Typographical Union. Albany, N.Y., June 1869," *PrC* 4 (July 1869): 169.

36. *Kate Mullaney: A True Labor Pioneer* (Albany: New York State Public Employees Federation, AFL-CIO, 1998); continued into 1866, women donated a thousand to moulders' Great Lock-Out; "Co-operation in Troy," *FTR* 4 (January 7, 1865): 22.

37. Michael D. Pierson, *Free Hearts, Free Homes: Gender and American Antislavery Politics* (Chapel Hill: University of North Carolina Press, 2003), 120–22.

38. Cora Wilburn, "The Wrongs of Needle Women," *BoL*, December 24, 1864, 3; "White Female Slaves," *FTR* 1 (August 1, 1863): 34; McKay, *Civil War and New York City*, 160; Camp, *American Year-Book*, 1:224.

39. "Women and Work," *BoL*, December 5, 1863, 4; "A Move in the Right Direction," *BoL*, September 17, 1864.

40. "White Slavery in the North" [from the *RE*, based on the account in the *New York News*], *ADC*, April 28, 1864; "The Laboring Women," *BoL*, April 23, 1864, 4; "A Labor Movement in the Right Direction—The Working Women's Protective Union," *BDE*, March 22, 1864.

41. O'Connor, *Civil War Boston*, 210.

Chapter 7. New Militancy across the Union

1. "Our New York," *PI*, October 29, 1863; "General City News," *NYDT*, November 12, 1863; Collins, *Nature's Aristocracy; or, Battles and Wounds in Time of Peace: A Plea for the Oppressed* (Boston: Lee and Shepard, 1871), 287; "Immense Profits," *RDD*, November 11, 1863; Fincher urged workers Summer 1863 to concerted action, *FTR* 1 (July 11, 1863).

2. From *BH*: "Meeting of the Tin Plate Workers" (July 2, 1863); "Tin Plate Workers' Association" (July 13, 1863); "The Great Labor Movement," (October 13, 1863); and untitled notice on the funeral of James C. Baker of the machinists and blacksmiths (January 4, 1864). Letter from Charleston in "An Appeal to the Shoemakers Working in the Factories on Ladies' Work," *FTR* 1 (November 21, 1863): 99.

3. From *BH*: "Large Meeting of the Journeymen House Carpenters at Williams Hall" (October 10, 1863); other items variously from November 11–12, 1863, include "To the People of Boston and Vicinity," "Prices Paid in the Charlestown Navy Yard," "The Hours of Labor at the Charlestown Navy Yard," "The Charlestown Navy Yard Strike," "Affairs about Home," "The Movement of Navy Yard Workmen in regard to Hours of Labor," "The Navy Yard Meetings"; and untitled item on the first annual Ball of Boston Caulkers' Association (January 4, 1864). "The Strike in the Charlestown Navy-yard," *NYDT*, November 11, 1863; "The Strikes in Boston," *NYDT*, November 12, 1863; "Great Demonstration of the Boston Carpenters," *FTR* 1 (October 17, 1863): 78; "The Charlestown Navy Yard Strike," *FTR* 1 (November 21, 1863): 98; "Mean Proscription," *FTR* 2 (December 5, 1863): 2; "Mechanics Ball at Boston" on painters, letter on painters, another on carpenters and joiners, and "Staples" on "A True History of the Charlestown Navy Yard Strikes," *FTR* 2 (December 26, 1863): 14, 15, 35; McNeil, *Labor Movement*, 125; "Strikes in Massachusetts," 20, cited "Strikes and Lockouts," 1048; and Foner and Lewis, *Black Worker to 1869*, 285.

4. "The Charlestown Navy Yard Movement," *BH*, November 14, 1863, and "The New Commandant of the Charlestown Navy Yard," *BH*, December 10, 1863; "Strikes and Lockouts," 1048; "Strikes and Mobs," *PI*, November 14, 1863; "The Boston Strikers," *BS*, November 14, 1863; "Strikes in Other Cities," *NYH*, November 14, 1863. "The Boiler Makers' Strike" and "The Labor Movement—The Strike of the Boiler and Plate Iron Workers of East Boston," *BH*, November 10, 1863; "Affairs about Home," *BH*, December 1, 1863; "The Strikes in Boston," *NYDT*, November 12, 1863; "The Uprising in Boston" with "The Charlestown Navy Yard Strike," *FTR* 1 (November 21, 1863): 98; "Mean Proscription," *FTR* 2 (December 5, 1863): 2; "Staples" wrote "A True History of the Charlestown Navy Yard Strikes," *FTR* 2 (January 30, 1864): 35; "Strikes at the Boston Navy Yard: Combination of Workmen—Strike among the Boiler and Plate Iron Workers of East Boston—Stoppage of Work on the Monitors," *BDE*, November 10, 1863; "Strikes in Massachusetts," 19; "Strikes and Lockouts," 1047.

5. "Excitement at Neponset: Strike among the Nail-Makers," *BH*, December 21, 1863; "Affairs about Home," *BH*, December 22, 1863; "A Riotous Strike Suppressed," *BS*, December 21, 1863; "Riotous Demonstrations of Strikers," *BS*, December 22, 1863; "The Labor 'Strikes,'" *RT* 16 (January 16, 1864): 22; and, "Strikes in Massachusetts," 20, cited "Strikes and Lockouts," 1048.

6. "The Hours of Labor at the Charlestown Navy Yard," *BH*, November 11, 1863; "Meeting of the Trades' Assembly," *BH*, February 13, 1864. See also David Roediger, "Ira Steward and the Anti-slavery Origins of American Eight-Hour Theory," *LH* 27 (Summer 1986): 410—26.

7. "The Labor Movements in New York," *PI*, November 14, 1863; "Strikes," *SA* 8 (February 21, 1863): 121.

8. "Trade Movements in New York," *FTR* 1 (October 10, 1863): 74; "Coopers' Demonstration in New York," *FTR* 1 (October 24, 1863): 86; and "The Revolution in New York," *FTR* 1 (November 21, 1863): 98; "The Wages Movement," *NYTrib*, November 14, 1863; "The Labor Movements in New York," *PI*, November 14, 1863; "Another Man Brutally Stabbed," *NYT*, October 28, 1863.

9. "'Injustice to Woman' in the 'Daily Whig and Republican" [from *CJ*], *QDWR*, October 23, 1863. From NYDT: "The Working Women's Union: Preliminary Meeting of Female Operatives to Form a Protective Association," (November 19, 1863); "The Labor Movement," (November 22, 1863); "General News," (November 25, 1863); "The Work of Women: A Suggestion for their Benefit," (November 26, 1863); "Women and their Employers," (December 6, 1863). "The Wages Movement," *NYTrib*, November 14, 1863; "Umbrella Sewers on Strike," *FTR* 1 (October 17, 1863): 78. See also "The Working-Women of New York," *FTR* 1 (November 21): 98; "The Revolution Progressing," *FTR* 1 (November 28): 102; "Uncalled Officiousness," *FTR* 2 (December 12, 1863): 6; "Trade Movement in New York," *FTR* 2 (December 14, 1863): 14.

10. Work rules from *Yonkers Herald*. "White Slavery," *FTR* 1 (September 12, 1863): 58; two letters under "Communications," *FTR* 1 (September 19, 1863): 59 and 63.

11. From *NYTrib*: "Machinists' Strike" (November 10, 1863); "City Items" (November 11, 1863); "The Wages Movement" (November 14, 1863). "The Machinists' Strike," *NYH* (December 19, 1863). From *NYDT*: "The Strike of the Machinists" (November 11, 1863); "Naval Movements"(November 12, 1863); "The Strike of the Railroad Employees" (November 13, 1863); "The Strikes. Mr. Lincoln on the Strikes [from *Fincher's*]" (December 5, 1863). Two pieces on "The Machinists Strike," *SA* (December 12 and 19, 1863); "Cessation of Work on the War Steamers," *BH*, December 7, 1863; "General News," *PI*, November 13, 1863; "The Labor Movements in New York," November 14, 1863; "State Legislature," *BDE*, March 20, 1863; "'The Navy Yard is Ours,'" *BDE*, October 22, 1863; "Post Election Discharges," *BDE*, November 9, 1863. "Another Strike in the Navy Yard," *FTR* 1 (July 11, 1863): 23; "The Revolution in New York" with "The Machinist's Appeal," *FTR* 1 (November 21, 1863): 98; account of nonmembers of the Machinists Protective Union participating in the strike with "The Greatest Strike on Record!" *FTR* 1 (November 28, 1863): 102, 103; and "The New York Strike" with letter on the subject, *FTR* 2 (December 19, 1863): 10, 11. Gallman, *Mastering Wartime*, 235; "The labor strikes are spreading over the North. In New York, Boston, and Philadelphia, the mechanics have struck for higher wages. The Government hands are also striking." "Miscellaneous," *RDD*, November 16, 1863.

12. "Trade Movements in New York," *FTR* 1 (October 10, 1863): 74; "House Painters Meeting," *FTR* 1 (November 28, 1863): 102; "The Campaign," *FTR* 2 (December 5, 1863): 3; "Equitable Society of Journeymen Curriers of Newark," *FTR* 2 (December 12, 1863): 6;

"Disappointment" with letter of support from Newark, "Mass Meeting of Workingmen," *FTR* 2 (December 12, 1863): 14, 15; letters to editor, *FTR* 2 (January 23, 1864): 31. "The Labor Movements in New York," *PI*, November 14, 1863; "City Intelligence," *PI*, November 28, 1863; "The Machinists Strike," *SA* 9 (December 12, 1863): 377. From *NYDT*: "Naval Movements" (November 12, 1863); "A Struggle among the Employees of the Gas Companies" (November 13, 1863); "Actors' Protective Union" (August 5, 1864); and "Meeting of the Actors' Protective Union" (August 19, 1864). "The Gas Question" for the formation of a "Gas Consumers Protective Union" by "gas consumers," "The New Gas Company," *BDE*, January 28, 1864, and classified advertisements, *BDE*, February 4 and 5, 1864; Gallman, *Mastering Wartime*, 234.

13. "General City News," *NYDT*, November 12, 1863; "Strikes on the City Railroads" and "The Strike of the Railroad Employees," *NYDT*, November 13, 1863; "The Labor Movements in New York," *PI*, November 13 and 14, 1863; "The Wages Movement," *NYTrib*, November 11 and 14, 1863.

14. "The Revolution in New York" (on house carpenters, confectioners, glasscutters, horse shoers, lithographers, sash- and blindmakers, cigarpackers, stagedrivers, window-shade painters, ironworkers, as well as the Brooklyn housepainters), *FTR* 1 (November 21, 1863): 98; "An Irrepressible Conflict" (on plasterers), *FTR* 2 (February 20, 1864): 47; "Labor and Wages" (on upholsterers, wheelwrights, blacksmiths, German druggists), *FTR* 2 (March 26, 1864): 66; "The Trades' Movement: Mass Meeting of the Working Men of Brooklyn," *BDE*, April 24, 1863; on the three thousand shoemakers, "A Successful Strike," and on carpenters, *BDE*, November 9, 1863. "The Wages Movement," *NYTrib*, November 14, 1863.

15. "Exciting Times!" *FTR* 1 (June 27, 1863): 15; letter from Troy, *FTR* 2 (December 12, 1863): 7; "Strike," *NYDT*, June 16, 1863; "From Albany," *NYDT*, June 17, 1863; McNeil, *Labor Movement*, 125, 136, cited in, cited "Strikes and Lockouts" 1048; "Strike of the Railroad Laborers," *BH*, June 17, 1863; "Railroad Strikers Resuming Work," *BH*, June 19, 1863; "Strikers' Riot in Albany," *NYT*, June 18, 1863; "The Railroad Strike," *PI*, June 19, 1863. "The laborers on the New York Central Railroad have had a strike for higher wages, and had a riot at Albany, N. Y., on the 17th." "Miscellaneous," *RDD*, June 22, 1863.

16. "Communications" on Buffalo, *FTR* 1 (July 11, 1863): 23; "?," *FTR* 1 (October 10, 1863): 75; "Movement in the Right Direction," *FTR* 1 (October 17, 1863): 78; "Iron Moulders' Ball Buffalo," *FTR* 2 (December 19, 1863): 10; "Carpenters and Joiners Ball," *FTR* 2 (December 26, 1863): 14; and "Mass Meeting of Workingmen," *FTR* 2 (December 26, 1863): 15; "Trades Assembly Mass Meeting," *FTR* 2 (January 23, 1864): 30; as well as "The M. and B. of Trenton, N.J.," *FTR* 1 (November 28, 1863): 103; letter by J. C. Fincher "Rights of Labor" from *Trenton True American*, reprinted "Mass Meeting in Trenton,"*FTR* 2 (December 5, 1863): 3; "The Strike at Amboy," *FTR* 2 (December 12, 1863): 6. See also the editorial on "Co-operation of Labor—A Practical Solution," *NYDT*, December 26, 1863. On Poughkeepsie, "Strike of Coopers—The Strikers on Parade," *BH*, October 13, 1863; "Mob Law in New Jersey: Serious Disturbance at South, Amboy-the Rioters Suppressed," *PI*, December 5, 1863, also printed as "Railroad Strikers at South Amboy," *BS*, December 5, 1863; "Serious Disturbance on the Camden and Amboy Railroads," *NYDT*, December 7, 1863; and untitled item in *HT-WT*, December 25, 1863.

17. "The Strike in Philadelphia" [from *PA*], *SLCDN*, December 2, 1863.

18. "City Intelligence," *PI*, November 28, 1863; "The Machinists Strike," *SA* 9 (December 12, 1863): 377; Gallman, *Mastering Wartime*, 234. Local machinists mentioned in "The Revolution Progressing," *FTR* 1 (November 7, 1863): 90; "Meeting of Workingmen," *FTR* 2 (December 5, 1863): 2; and "The Sail Makers,"(December 19, 1863): 10. "Labor Troubles in Pennsylvania," 280; "Address delivered at Buffalo, N.Y., January 1864," in Sylvis, *Life, Speeches, Labors*, 90–127.

19. "Strike last Monday, Proprietors Called 'Police! Police!'" *FTR* 2 (January 23, 1864): 30; Gallman, *Mastering Wartime*, 234, 235, 237.

20. "The Printers' Ball," *FTR* 1 (November 28, 1863): 103; "Strike on 'The Age,'" *FTR* 2 (December 26, 1863): 14; and "By Order of the Union to the Public," *FTR* 2 (December 26, 1863): 15. In *PI*: "The Printers' Union" (August 10, 1863); "Special Notices: By Order of the Typographical Union to the Public" (December 21, 1863); "Philadelphia Typographical Society" (January 4, 1864); "Annual Meeting of the Nonpareil Typographical Society" (January 18, 1864); "Died," regarding funeral of Stephen D. Bennett (February 2, 1864). Gallman, *Mastering Wartime*, 232, 233. Devine may have been the sergeant of the 178th Pennsylvania mustered out that summer.

21. "Meeting of Delegates of Different Trades," *PI*, November 25, 1863; "Communications" on housepainters, *FTR* 1 (October 24, 1863): 83; "The Revolution Progressing" (on machinists, carpenters, machinery moulders, sparmakers, oak coopers, painters, cigarmakers), *FTR* 1 (November 7, 1863): 90; "The Trade Movement in Philadelphia" and "Notice—to the Organized Trades of the City of Philadelphia," *FTR* 1 (November 21, 1863): 98; "Meeting of Workingmen," *FTR* 2 (December 5, 1863): 3; "Amalgamated Society of Great Britain" on the presence of that society in the American workforce, *FTR* 2 (December 12, 1863): 6; "Ball of the Journeymen Tailors Protective Union" with "Meeting of the Trades Assembly," *FTR* 2 (December 19, 1863): 10; "Stove and Hollow-Ware Moulders," *FTR* 2 (December 26, 1863): 15; "Trades Assembly of Philadelphia," *FTR* 2 (February 27, 1864): 51. The same source acknowledges among its "agents" a members of the Amalgamated Society at Susquehanna Depot. "The Police," *FTR* 1 (November 28, 1863): 103; "Police! Police!" *FTR* 2 (January 23, 1864): 30.

22. "Mechanics, Attention," *LDJ*, May 3, 1864; untitled item, *LDJ*, May 13, 1864; *The Constitution of the Cincinnati Journeymen Horseshoer's Society, Organized June 13, 1863* (Cincinnati: Donnelly, 1863), Cincinnati Historical Society Library; *Constitution and By-laws of the Carpenters and Joiners' Union of the City of Cincinnati, O., Organized April 1, 1864* (Cincinnati: Donnelly, 1864). See also "Workingmen?" *FTR* 1 (November 7, 1863): 90; "Our Peregrination," *FTR* 1 (November 28, 1863): 102; and "Trades' Union League," *FTR* 1 (November 28, 1863): 103; various letters, *FTR* 2 (January 23, 1864): 31; "Labor and Wages," *FTR* 2 (March 26, 1864): 66. See also, *Bill of Prices and Mode of Measurement of the Association of Master Stone-cutters of Cincinnati, Adopted January 11, 1864* (Cincinnati: Donnelly, 1864).

23. From *SFEB*: "Typographical Union Election" (April 28, 1862); "The Plasterers' Union" (May 12, 1862); "Another Benefit Performance at the Circus" (May 14, 1862); "Handsome Benefit" (May 23, 1862); "The Patriotic Fund" with "Eureka Typographical Union Election" (October 27, 1862); "The End of the First 'Rat' Libel Case" (November 4, 1862);

"A Few Words on the 'Rat' Libel Cases," (October 27, 1862); "Special Notices" (May 25, 1864). "Strikers in California," *BS*, April 5, 1864; McNeil, *Labor Movement*, 596; "Strikes and Lockouts," 1047; *Proceedings of the Sixth Annual Session of the Iron Molders' International Union*, 8; *The Constitution and By-laws of the Journeymen Shipwrights' Association of the Port of San Francisco* (San Francisco: Women's Union Printers, 1869) dated the organization from April 1, 1857, and its reorganization to April 23, 1863. Also frequent references to a "California Protective Union."

24. "From Great Salt Lake City," *NYDT*, October 2, 1864.

25. "Strikes," *LDT*, November 5, 1862, as well as notices in *LDT*, July 10, 1863; July 16, 1863; March 20, 1864; and September 8, 1864. See also Martha B. Caldwell, "When Horace Greeley Visited Kansas in 1859," *Kansas Historical Quarterly* (May 1940): 123–24; *Smoky Hill and Republican Union*, September 17, 1864, 3.

26. Qtd. Palladino, *Another Civil War*, 128, also 30, 141, 158–59; "Resistance to the Draft in Pennsylvania," *PI*, October 25, 1862; "The Coal Miners," *NYDT*, April 26, 1863; "The Schuylkill Coal Region," *NYDT*, June 21, 1863.

27. McNeil, *Labor Movement*, 258, cited in cited "Strikes and Lockouts," 1047; Wieck, *American Miners' Association*, 114, 116, 118, 120–28, 143, 188, 195. This accounts for the scarcity of the article in the city. *LDT*, November 29, 1862.

28. "Double Strike," *Peoria Morning Mail*, April 1, 1863; "A Riot Squelched," *Peoria Morning Mail*, June 10, 1863; "Women on a Strike" [from *Chicago Tribune*], *BH*, September 10, 1863.

29. *Proceedings of the Fourth Annual Session of the Iron Moulder's Union of America, in Convention Assembled, at Pittsburgh, Pa., January 6, 1863* (Philadelphia, 1863); "Condensed Report of the Proceedings of the National Typographical Union—Tenth Session," *Pr* 4 (July 1862): 52, 53; "Encouraging for Union," *Pr* 4 (November 1862): 104; "Iron Moulders' Convention," *BS*, January 10, 1863; various notices on the NTU convention, *BS*, April 3, 1863; "National Typographical Union," *BS*, April 10, 1863; as well as two other pieces under "National Typographical Union," *BS*, May 6, 1863, and May 8, 1863; "Delegates to the National Convention," *PI*, April 13, 1863; "Typographical," *CG*, April 10, 1863; "Items," *LDJ*, April 14, 1863, and "Telegraphic News," *LDJ*, May 5, 1863; "Meeting of the National Typographical Union," and "The National Typographical Union," *BH*, May 5, 1863, and May 8, 1863; "Meeting of the National Typographical Union," *NYH*, May 5, 1863; Seibold, *Historical Sketch of Columbia Typographical Union*, 18; "The Late Discussion on the War," *BS*, January 17, 1863; Tracy, *History of the Typographical Union*, 195–99, 200–205, with New Orleans on 201–2; NTU convention: *CL*, May 4–6, 1863. The NTU welcomed George M. Luken, elected a delegate from Memphis for the previous year's cancelled convention, but it sustained the decision of Samuel Slawson, a St. Louis officer, in refusing to accept a card of transfer signed "Southern Confederacy Union, No. 1" at Nashville. "The Typographical Union," *PI*, April 14, 1862; Stevens, *New York Typographical Union*, 578.

30. Collins, *Nature's Aristocracy*, 172–73.

31. The directories in *FTR* document the appearance of the following: June 20, 1863 (Workingmen's Assembly of Boston and vicinity); June 27, 1863 (Workingmen's Assembly of Monroe County); September 5, 1863 (Trades' Assembly of Pittsburgh); September 19, 1863 (Trades' Assembly of the City of Buffalo); December 5, 1863 (Trades' Assembly and League

of Friendship of Louisville and vicinity); March 26, 1864 (Trades' Assembly of Philadelphia); July 30, 1864 (Trades' Assembly of the City of Troy); August 20, 1864 (Trades' Assembly of Detroit); September 10, 1864 (Trades' Assembly of the City of Albany); September 17, 1864 (Trades' Assembly of Cincinnati); December 3, 1864 (St. Louis Trade Union League). On New York, see "Meeting of Mechanics in Tammany Hall," *NYDT*, February 8, 1863; "Central Trades Union," *NYDT*, March 25, 1863. Leaders of the unions met monthly at Buffalo, twice monthly at Boston, Rochester, Troy, Philadelphia, Pittsburgh, St. Louis, and Louisville, and weekly at Albany, Detroit, and Cincinnati.

Chapter 8. Richmond, New Orleans, Nashville

1. "Bread Riot of 1863: Reminiscences of a Memorable Period of Our War History," *RDD*, December 30, 1888; *RE*, April 4 and 7, 1863. Many of these sources are posted at "Civil War Richmond" at http://www.mdgorman.com.

2. Midori Takagi, *"Rearing Wolves to Our Own Destruction": Slavery in Richmond* (Charlottesville: University Press of Virginia, 1999), 140–45.

3. "Reign of Terror at Richmond," *HW*, March 22, 1862, 179.

4. Notices in Petersburg *Daily Express*, May 9, 13, and 14, 1857; June 29, 1858; January 9, 1860; January 7 and June 4, 1861. "Minor Items," *NYDT*, February 25, 1861; "Richmond, Va.," *Typographical Journal* 53 (November 1918): 459. In *RDD*: "Wanted," February 21, 1861; "Card" with "Wanted," February 23, 1861; "Very High Law Which We Will Not Submit To," February 26, 1861; "To Alex, Hill & Co." February, 27, 1861; "Wanted," March 11, 1861; "Typographical," June 4, 1861; "Notice," September 20, 1861; "Special Notice.—To the Journeymen Tin-Plate and Sheet Iron Workers' Society of the City of Richmond," November 7, 1861; "Richmond Typographical Society," February 3, 1862; "The Southern Editorial Convention," March 14, 1862. *Constitution and By-Laws of the Richmond Typographical Society: With the Rules of Order and List of Prices. Adopted, with Amendments, January 18, 1862* (Richmond: Wynne, 1862).

5. "Local Matters," *RDD*, April 11, 1862, and "Would Not Work?" *RDD*, April 12, 1862; for Confederate Bond Engravers, see http://www.Confederatebonds.com/printers.htm; William S. Pretzer, "'The British, Duff Green, the Rats and the Devil': Custom, Capitalism, and Conflict in the Washington Printing Trade, 1834—36," *LH* 27 (1985): 5–30; "Colonel Blanton Duncan's Lithographic Establishment in Columbia," *CM*, August 1, 1862. See also: W. Stephen Belko, *The Invincible Duff Green: Whig of the West* (Columbia: University of Missouri Press, 2006).

6. A. T. Cavis and E. MacMurray, "History of the Columbia Typographical Society of Washington, D.C.," *PrC* 6 (May 1871): 105. In *RDD*, see the announcements, "Richmond Typographical Society," February 3, April 5, May 3, July 5, 19, August 2, 1862; see also in *RDD*: "Local Matters," August 14, 1862; "Grand Jury," August 15, 1862; "Hustings Court, Aug. 15," August 16, 1862; *Richmond City Business Directory, 1860—Printers*: Goode, J. C., 180 Main, Aurora Lodge, No. 116, meets at the room over Goode's printing office, Main Street, between 10th and 11th, every Friday night. *The Stranger's Guide and Official Directory for the City of Richmond* (Richmond: Evans, 1863); "A Strike in Richmond," *NYDT*, August 17, 1862; "Letter from Richmond," *MDA*, August 22, 1862; "Indictment of 'The Richmond

Typographical Society,'" *MDT*, August 22, 1862, and *GWT*, August 22, 1862, and same statement without heading in *NODD*, August 27, 1862. In *RDD*: "Hustings Court" (September 11, 1862); two items entitled "Proceedings in the Courts" (October 17 and 18, 1862); "Court Proceedings" (November 14, 1862, and January 17, 1863); and regarding the union's survival, the announcements under "Richmond Typographical Society" (November 1, 1862; February 7, 1863; March 7, 1863; March 24, 1863; April 4, 1863). For the persistence of the union, even into 1863 and after, see "Southern Literary Messenger," *RDD*, April 7, 1863.

7. Roberts, *Southern Sketches*, 127; "Bread Riot in Mobile, Alabama," *FTR*, September 19, 1863, 63; "Bread Riot of 1863: Reminiscences of a Memorable Period of Our War History," *RDD*, December 30, 1888; "Bread Riot, Again: Further Reminiscences of the Sacking of Stores by a Mob of Women in 1863; A Memorable Event in the City's War History—Recollections of a Number of Well-Known Citizens," *RDD*, January 20, 1889; Bessie Martin, *A Rich Man's War, A Poor Man's Fight: Desertion of Alabama Troops from the Confederate Army*, 2nd ed. (Tuscaloosa: University of Alabama Press, 2003), 132–33.

8. *RE*, April 4 and April 8, 1863.

9. "The Bread Riot in Richmond," *BH*, April 14, 1863; "Bread Riot of 1863," *RDD*, December 30, 1888; and, *RE*, April 4, 1863; Markle, *Spies and Spymasters*, 141; Ernest, *Urban Leaders and Social Change*, 166–67; Alfred H. Bill, *The Beleaguered City: Richmond, 1861–1865* (New York: Knopf, 1946),163–64, 165–66; *RE*, April 8, 1863; Ernest B. Furgurson, *Ashes of Glory: Richmond at War*, 193–98; Marie Tyler-McGraw, *At the Falls: Richmond, Virginia, and Its People* (Chapel Hill: University of North Carolina Press, 1994), 150–56; "Recollections of Thomas McNiven," http://www.mdgorman.com/Other_Sites/mcniven_recollections.htm (accessed September 20, 2014).

10. Ernest, *Urban Leaders*, 166–67; Kimball, *American City, Southern Place*, 227–28. Alexander B. Wells wished to make Confederate money equal as well to "Yankee greenbacks." "Local matters," *RDD*, September 21, 1863.

11. Notices under "Local matters," *RDD*, October 5 and October 12, 1863. Also Bill, *Beleaguered City*, 202; Ernest, *Urban Leaders*, 191–92, 192–93, 193n.

12. "Bohemiana," *Bohemian* 1 (Christmas 1863): 39; Minutes of the Richmond Council and Henrico Court Proceedings, posted on Richmond at War. Ernest, *Urban Leaders*, 194–95.

13. Bill, *Beleaguered City*; Ernest, *Urban Leaders*, 195–199, 200–203, with 199 on Walker.

14. Useful for some developments in the hinterland, but more so for what it suggests to future researchers, is Roger Wallace Shugg, *Origins of Class Struggle in Louisiana: A Social History of White Farmers and Laborers during Slavery and after, 1840–1875* (Baton Rouge: Louisiana State University Press, 1966). See also Michael D. Pierson, *Mutiny at Fort Jackson: The Untold Story of the Fall of New Orleans* (Chapel Hill: University of North Carolina Press, 2008), which makes an argument that will only be strengthened over time by casting an eye to the internal class questions in the city.

15. "Communism in Dixie," *NYT*, September 20, 1863.

16. "Investigation of Navy Department" in *Official Records of the Union and Confederate Navies in the War of the Rebellion*, series 2, vol. 1, pp. 755–56, 770–71. See also on this, Pierson, *Mutiny at Fort Jackson*, 41.

17. Joe Gray Taylor, *Louisiana Reconstructed, 1863–1877* (Baton Rouge: Louisiana State

University Press, 1974), 14–16; Roberts, *Southern Sketches*, 33–34. See also Lawrence N. Powell, ed., *Reconstructing Louisiana* (Lafayette: Center for Louisiana Studies, University of Louisiana at Lafayette, 2001); Peyton McCrary, *Abraham Lincoln and Reconstruction: The Louisiana Experiment* (Princeton, N.J.: Princeton University Press, 1978); Ted Tunnell, *Crucible of Reconstruction: War, Radicalism, and Race in Louisiana, 1862–1877* (1984; Baton Rouge: Louisiana State University Press, 1992).

18. The New Orleans Typographical Union claimed to have formed May 1835 and "re-organized under the National charter," claiming "one of the most flourishing Unions in the country," with a membership of "about 350." See also *Visitor's Guide to New Orleans. November, 1875* (New Orleans: Waldo, 1875), 126—27. "Death of a Printer," *LDJ*, April 6, 1863. See also items under "The City," under "New Orleans Typographical Union," *DP*, January 23, 1863, January 5, 1864, January 13, 1865, March 5, 1865; "Typographical Union" [from *NODD*, July 6], *NYH*, July 21, 1862.

19. "General Orders—No. 25," *LDJ*, May 30, 1862.

20. "Our New Orleans Correspondence," *NYDT*, October 2, 1862; Jacob Barker, *The Ballot Box, the Palladium of Our Liberties New Orleans, July, 1863* (New Orleans: Printed for the compiler, 1863).

21. "How the Meeting Was Got Up," *BDE*, November 1, 1862; "The City," *DP*, July 12, 1863, and February 17, 1864; "A Distinguished Radical in Danger for 'Free Speech,'" *NN*, April 9, 1864. Consulting with Houston: Stephen Pearl Andrews, "A Private Chapter of the Origin of the War: Second Paper," *NN*, April 9, 1864; Taylor, *Louisiana Reconstructed*, 25–26, 27–28, 31, 43, 134, 150, 160; Seiler to Schurz, September 14, 1864, in Foner and Lewis, *Black Worker to 1869*, 327, but see also 337–38; Jean-Charles Houzeau, *My Passage at the New Orleans Tribune: A Memoir of the Civil War Era*, ed. David C. Rankin, trans. Gerard F. Denault (Baton Rouge: Louisiana State University Press, 1984). Also, for the Workingmen's National Union League of New Orleans, see "Address to Southern Workingmen," *IPE* 39 (February 1864): 3–4.

22. Eric Arnesen, *Waterfront Workers of New Orleans: Race, Class and Politics, 1863–1923* (New York: Oxford University Press, 1991), 19; Taylor, *Louisiana Reconstructed*, 10–11.

23. Laizer, J. Clovis (NTU 17), New Orleans. J. C. Laizer, *Pr* 2 (July 1859): 55, and *Pr* 2 (February 1860): 208.

24. "The Draft in Louisiana: First District of New Orleans; Names of the Drafted—Tuesday, March 7, 1865," *DP*, March 8, 1865; "The City," *DP*, February 17, 1864; "Interesting from New Orleans," *NYH*, August 8, 1863; "The City," *DP*, February 17, 1864; Arnesen, *Waterfront Workers*, 21; "Free Labor in Louisiana," *Liberator*, April 21, 1865, 61.

25. Berlin et al., *Wartime Genesis of Free Labor: The Lower South*, 373–74.

26. Anita S. Goodstein, *Nashville, 1780–1860* (Gainesville: University of Florida Press, 1989), 127–28, 130–31; "Labor" in "The Tennessee Encyclopedia of History and Culture," available at http://tennesseeencyclopedia.net/entry.php?rec=757 (accessed September 20, 2014).

27. Benjamin C. Truman, "War Pictures—No. 1: The Military Railroad System," November 15, 1864, in *NYT*, November 22, 1864; "Affairs in the Southwest: Rebels Anxious to Avail Themselves of the Proclamation," *NYT*, December, 16, 1863. The report was ascribed to a "Col. Misener," but there was no Col. Misener.

28. "The March of Progress in the Wake of Ruin—Industrial Amelioration in the South," *NYT*, November 22, 1864; George Edgar Turner, *Victory Rode the Rails: The Strategic Place of the Railroads in the Civil War* (1953; Lincoln: University of Nebraska Press, 1992), 287–88, 288–89, 290–93; and Benjamin C. Truman, "War Pictures: The Military Railroad System." This piece would be largely reprinted as "The Military Railway System of the United States," *RT* 16 (December 10, 1864): 394. On Truman's other papers, see J. Cutler Andrews, *The North Reports the Civil War* (Pittsburgh: University of Pittsburgh Press, 1955), 758; and Gerald M. Capers, *Occupied City: New Orleans under the Federals, 1862–1865* (Lexington: University of Kentucky Press, 1965), 62. See also Truman's "The Completeness of Reconstruction," *Civil War Papers: California Commandery/Oregon Commandery*, published by the Commandery, vol. 2 (Milwaukee: Burdick, Armitage, and Allen, 1896). Chattanooga rolls of participation name Thomas E. Champion, Owen Stuart, August Willich.

29. Truman, "War Pictures: Military Railroad System" and "March of Progress," *NYT*, November 22, 1864; "Military Railway System," *RT* 16 (December 10, 1864): 394; "Exodus of Carpenters," *BH*, August 29, 1864. Truman had been a member of the Typographical Union and may have been listed in the New York local as "Benjamin F. Truman." *Pr* 2 (May 1859): 7.

30. Letters in "Communications," *FTR* 3 (October 15, 1864): 79; *FTR* 4 (December 10, 1864): 7; *FTR* 4 (January 7, 1865): 23.

31. "A Blacksmith," *FTR* 3 (October 15, 1864): 79; "Employee," *FTR* 4 (December 10, 1864): 7; "An Employee," *FTR* 4 (January 7, 1865): 23, all under "Communications." Truman, "War Pictures: Military Railroad System"; Letter of "Employee," *FTR* 4 (December 10, 1864): 7, and "An Employee," *FTR* 4 (January 7, 1865): 23, both under "Communications," 7.

32. The October 3 letter says he went to Nashville in July, and the last letter, in early December, stated that he had been "working the last five months in the U.S. Military Railroad Machine Shops for the Government." "Something the Government Should Look To," *FTR* 3 (October 15, 1864): 78, and "Government Employees," *FTR* 3 (November 26, 1864): 102.

33. "Communications," *FTR* 3 (October 15, 1864): 79, and *FTR* 4 (January 7, 1865): 23.

34. Letter of "Employee," dated November 22, 1864, in "Communications," *FTR* 4 (December 10, 1864): 7. See also, "Before the Battle," *LDJ*, December 25, 1864.

35. "Condensed Report of the Proceedings of the National Typographical Union, Twelfth Session," *Pr* 5 (June 1864): 88. For contributors see *FTR* 3 (October 15, 1864): 7, and *FTR* 3 (November 5, 1864): 90, as well as "An Item for our Readers," *FTR* 4 (February 18, 1865): 46, and "Annual Convention of the Brotherhood of Locomotive Engineers," *FTR* 4 (September 23, 1865): 136. After the war, he turned up as an official of the Louisville division. See the directories in the *Locomotive Engineers' Monthly Journal* 3 (December 1869): 575, and 4 (April 1870): 191. Orlando Edward Parsons went to Nashville in 1863 as conductor. "Probably no man in Missouri has done more than he for the advancement of the cause of labor." Howard L. Conard, ed., *Encyclopedia of the History of Missouri: A Compendium of History and Biography for Ready Reference*, 6 vols. (New York: Southern History, 1901), 5:68.

36. *FTR* 4 (December 10, 1864): 6; on Hooten, *OAR*, 6:348.

37. "Reform Convention at Evansville, Rock Co. Wisconsin," *BoL*, September 19, 1863, 8; Joseph Osgood Barrett, *The Spiritual Pilgrim: a Biography of James M. Peebles* (Boston: White, 1872), 88–89; Wieck, *American Miners' Association*, 26, 28, 193.

38. Plum, *Military Telegraph*, 2:118–19.

39. Michael D. Hitt, *Charged with Treason: Ordeal of 400 Mill Workers during Military Operations in Roswell, Georgia, 1864–1865* (Monroe N.Y.: Library Research, 1992). Notwithstanding the title, the book documents no charge of treason but only the fully modern policy of removing workers to where their skills and labor would no longer be a potential menace to the Federal cause.

Chapter 9. The State Power

1. "The Strikes. Mr. Lincoln on the Strikes," *NYDT*, December 5, 1863. Also, "The President's Message," *FTR* 2 (December 19, 1863). David Montgomery, *Citizen Worker: The Experience of Workers in the United States with Democracy and the Free Market During the Nineteenth Century* (Cambridge: Cambridge University Press, 1993).

2. "Movement among the Government Bookbinders," *PI*, November 4, 1863. "General City News," *NYDT*, November 1, 1863; "Dispatch to the Associated Press," *NYDT*, November 7, 1863; "A Strike at Washington," *FTR* 1 (November 7, 1863): 90; "The Washington Strike," *FTR* 1 (November 14, 1863): 94; "Book-Binders, Be on Your Guard!" *FTR* 1 (November 21, 1863): 98; with "The Uprising in Boston," letter on the aftermath, *FTR* 4 (January 14, 1865): 27. "The Strike in the Washington Navy Yard" under "Strikes in Other Cities" [from *Washington Evening Star*] under "The Labor Movement," *NYH*, November 14, 1863; "The Labor Movement in the Washington Navy Yard," *BH*, December 9, 1863; "Correspondence of the *Baltimore Sun*," Washington, February 16, *BS*, February 17, 1864 "Strikes and Mobs," *PI*, November 14, 1863. See also "Miscellaneous," *RDD*, November 16, 1863.

3. "A Strike at Washington," *FTR* 1 (November 7, 1863): 90; "The Washington Strike," *FTR* 1 (November 14, 1863): 94; "News from Washington," *NYDT*, November 4, 1863; "Dispatch to the Associated Press," *NYDT*, November 7, 1863; "News from Washington," subheading "Secretary Chase and the Treasury Workmen," *NYDT*, November 9, 1863; "Labor Movement in "Washington—Captain Black, of the 9th Mass. Regiment, Reinstated in the Service," *BH*, November 5, 1863; "Interesting from Washington," *PI*, November 4, 1863.

4. "The Washington Strike," *FTR* 1 (November 14, 1863): 94; "The Female Strikers at Work Again!" *FTR* 2 (December 26, 1863): 15. From *NYDT*: "News from Washington" (November 4, 1863); "Dispatch to the Associated Press" (November 7, 1863); "News from Washington," subheading "Secretary Chase and the Treasury Workmen" (November 9, 1863). "Labor Movement in Washington—Captain Black," *BH*, November 5, 1863; "Movement among the Government Bookbinders," *PI*, November 4, 1863; "The Female Strikers at Work Again" under "Interesting from Washington," *PI*, December 19, 1863.

5. "News from Washington," *NYDT*, November 4, 1863, and "News from Washington," subheading "Secretary Chase and the Treasury Workmen," *NYDT*, November 9, 1863;

"News from Washington," *NYH*, November 8, 1863, and notice [from *Washington Chronicle*] in "The Strikes in Other Cities" under "The Labor Movement," *NYH*, November 2, 1863; "The Washington Strike," *FTR* 1 (November 14, 1863): 94; "The Female Strikers at Work Again!"; *FTR* 2 (December 26, 1863): 15.

6. "Washington printers: John C. Rives funeral to take place Wednesday, Columbia Typographical Society to attend printer of the debates in both houses of Congress, House adjourning over to allow members to attend. Another, William A. Kennedy, printer and had several position in the municipal government, died after nine months illness, this morning." From Potomac, "Correspondence of the Baltimore Sun," Washington, April 11, 1864, in *BS*, April 12, 1864. Washington printers got scale up from $18 a week to $21 and piecework from fifty to sixty cents per thousand ems. November 1864, weekly scale increased to $24." Seibold, *Historical Sketch of Columbia Typographical Union*, 19.

7. "The National Typographical Union," *FTR* 2 (April 30, 1864): 86; "National Typographical Union," *LDJ*, May 3, 1864; untitled item, *G*, May 13, 1864; "Typographical Union," *BS*, May 4, 1864. See also, "From Philadelphia," *NYDT*, April 11, 1864; Tracy, *History of the Typographical Union*, 205–11.

8. Bensman, *Practice of Solidarity*, 23–24.

9. "Session of the International Union of Machinists and Blacksmiths of N.A.," *FTR* 1 (September 26, 1863): 66, and "Proceedings of the International Union of Machinists and Blacksmiths of North America," *FTR* 1 (October 3, 1863): 70; "Fifth Annual Session of the Iron Moulders' International Union," and the letter from Sylvis, *FTR* 2 (January 23 and 30, 1864): 30, 38; "The Iron Moulders' Union," *BS*, January 9, 1864; "Iron Molders" under "The Wages Movement," *NYTrib*, November 14, 1863; *Proceedings of the Fifth Annual Session of the Iron Moulder's Union of America, in Convention Assembled, at Buffalo, N.Y., January 6, 1864* (Philadelphia, 1864). See also Richard T. Ely, *The Labor Movement in America* (New York: Crowell, 1886), 62–63.

10. Untitled item, *BH*, December 23, 1863; from Potomac, "Correspondence of the Baltimore Sun," Washington, April 7, *BS*, April 8, 1864. "The Final Meeting? For the Purpose," six states represented. "National Convention of Journeymen Curriers," *FTR* 2 (January 23, 1864): 30. "Proceedings of the Fifth Annual Session of the Carpenters and Joiners," *WmA*, October 2, 1869, cited in Foner and Lewis, *Black Worker to 1869*, 385.

11. *MDA*, July 30, 1861; "Southern Mothers," *MDA*, August 8, 1861; "Latest News from the South," *BS*, April 28, 1862; "Printers Scarce," *BH*, April 29, 1862. From what can be reconstructed of its membership rolls and local enlistments, the claims were grossly exaggerated.

12. "Latest News from the South," *BS*, April 28, 1862; "Printers Scarce," *BH*, April 29, 1862; "The Memphis Typographical Union," *NYDT*, July 28, 1862. "Memphis Typographical Society," *MDA*, December 29, 1863. Well into late 1863, its ranks included some Confederate soldiers.

13. William R. Plum, *The Military Telegraph during the Civil War in the United States*, 2 vols. (Chicago: Jansen, McClurg, 1882), 2: 115–16.

14. Wieck, *American Miners' Association*, 107–11, 142, 146, 149–50, 154–56; Palladino, *Another Civil War*, 158–59, 160–61; Gallman, *Mastering Wartime*, 235. Also see "Labor

and Wages," *FTR* 2 (March 26, 1864): 66; for government use of troops against the miners, see "Address Delivered by William H. Sylvis," *FTR* 4 (January 14, 1865): 25.

15. "Labor and Wages," *FTR* 2 (March 26, 1864): 66; "Address Delivered by William H. Sylvis," *FTR* 4 (January 14, 1865): 25; "Parrott Guns—Modern Artillery" with "Why the Shelling of Charleston was discontinued" [from *Boston Journal*], *NYDT*, September 17, 1863, "Excitement at the West Point Foundry: Workmen on a Strike," *NYDT*, March 14, 1864. Minister of St. Mary's given as Rev. Father Caro, but rector of St. Mary's at the time was Rev. Father Charles W. Morrill.

16. *StR*, April 3, 1864, and *StMD*, April 3, 26, 1864, cited in Gerteis, *Civil War St. Louis*, 254–55; and, "Address Delivered by William H. Sylvis," *FTR* 4 (January 14, 1865): 25; "The Tailors of St. Louis," *FTR* 2 (April 16, 1864): 78; "Proceedings, Machinists and Blacksmiths of North America," *FTR* 1 (October 3, 1863): 70; *StMD*, April 8 and 16, 1864, cited in Gerteis, *Civil War St. Louis*, 254–55; "Carpenters and Joiners in Council," *FTR* 4 (April 8, 1865): 75, 79, and "St. Louis Carpenters and Joiners," *FTR* 4 (April 15, 1865): 79.

17. *Tenth U.S. Census*, 20: 499, cited in "Strikes and Lockouts," 1048–49; "St. Louis Carpenters and Joiners," *FTR* 4 (April 15, 1865): 79; Wieck, *American Miners' Association*, 114.

18. *Proceedings of the Sixth Annual Session of the Iron Molders' International Union*, 7–8; *StMD*, April 3, 8, and 18, 1864, and *StR*, April 16 and 18, 1864, cited in Gerteis, *Civil War St. Louis*, 255–56nn39–41, 367. *StR*, April 3 and 14, 1864, and *StMD*, April 3 and 15, 1864, cited in Louis S. Gerteis, *Civil War St. Louis*, 254–56. For general mentions of the St. Louis strike wave, see "Letter from St. Louis," *FTR* 2 (April 9, 1864): 74; "The National Land Transfer Association," *FTR* 2 (April 9, 1864): 4; and "Address Delivered by William H. Sylvis," *FTR* 2 (January 14, 1865): 25.

19. For this and the next paragraph, see Gen. Orders No. 65, April 29, 1864, in *O.A.R.*, ser. 1, vol. 34, pt. 3, pp. 345–46. See also, Sylvis, *Life, Speeches and Essays*, 135, cited in Gerteis, *Civil War St. Louis,* 257n43, 367. "Official Tyranny," *FTR* 2 (May 14, 1864): 95.

20. Gabor S. Boritt, *Lincoln and the Economics of the American Dream* (Memphis, Tenn.: Memphis State University Press, 1978), 220–21; *StMD*, April 15, 19, and 26, and May 3, 4, 22, and 31, 1864; *StR*, May 5, 1864, cited in Gerteis, *Civil War St. Louis*, 257–58; Foner, *History of the Labor Movement*, 1:331–33, 354–55; Montgomery, *Beyond Equality*, 100; Sylvis, *Life, Speeches and Essays*, 133–35, cited in "Strikes in St. Louis," *NYDT*, May 8, 1864; "Official Tyranny," *FTR* (May 14, 1864): 95; "Address Delivered by William H. Sylvis," *FTR* (January 14, 1865): 25.

21. "A Printers' Union Dissolved," [Boise] *Idaho Tri-Weekly Statesman*, November 29, 1864; *New Orleans Times*, January 7 and 16, 1865; "President Lincoln and Labor," *Monthly Journal of the International Association of Machinists, Published in the Interest of the Machinists' Trade* 5 (July 1893): 244. The account names M. H. Madden and Thomas Gaule as having reported this. Michael H. Madden of Pekin, enlisted September 17, 1864, as private, Co. K, 146th Illinois, mustered out July 8, 1865. Probably Thomas Gault of the Eighth Missouri, Co. A.

22. Charles L. Bernays to Abraham Lincoln, May 2, 1864, Abraham Lincoln Papers. Bernays enclosed a copy of Rosecrans's General Orders No. 65, issued on April 29, 1864, which prohibited the formation of labor unions in St. Louis. See also Lincoln to Oliver

D. Filley, December 22, 1863. Note also the editorial "General Rosenkranz' Order against Strikes," *Illinois Staats-Zeitung*, May 4, 1864, available on the Newberry Library Foreign Language Press Survey, posted from http://flps.newberry.org.

23. Edwin Weston to Abraham Lincoln, Monday, May 2, 1864, in Abraham Lincoln Papers at the Library of Congress. Transcribed and annotated by the Lincoln Studies Center, Knox College, Galesburg, Illinois; "Working Men's Mass Meeting," *FTR* 2 (May 21, 1864): 98.

24. Discussed in "Address Delivered by William H. Sylvis," *FTR* 4 (January 14, 1865): 25.

25. Sam R. Watkins, *"Co. Aytch," Maury Grays, First Tennessee Regiment; or, A Side Show of the Big Show*, 2nd ed. (Chattanooga: Times, 1900), 37.

26. "A Modest Demand," *RDD*, September 14, 1863.

27. From *CM*: "Meetings, etc." (August 17, 1861); "Tributes of Respect" (September 2, 1861); "Southern Typographical Union" (September 14, 1861); "Charleston Typographical Society" (January 2, 1862); "Charleston Typographical Society" (February 4, 1862).

28. [From the *Vicksburg Whig*] *RDD*, August 16, 1862. Another unionist P. Richardson may have been either Perry Richardson of Miles Legion, captured at Port Hudson, or Peter Richardson of the Twenty-Eighth Louisiana.

29. Roberts, *Southern Sketches*, 39, 83, 111–12, 114–16, 118, 119, 124–25, 128–29, 135, 136–40. In August 1863 Roberts wrote to his father that he was not in the army but an exempt, and that he hoped to remain one. Again he was locked up, his letter seized and read; he was sent to the house of corrections rather than prison. His friendship with one of General P. G. T. Beauregard's relatives may have contributed to Roberts's release by the mayor. *Southern Sketches*, 78–80, 83.

30. Roberts, *Southern Sketches*, 140. Other members of the NTU went north earlier and joined the Union Army. Several members of the Montgomery and Mobile locals fought in the First Alabama Cavalry—the Federal First Alabama Cavalry.

31. "By Telegraph" and "Printers on a Strike," *RDD*, April 13, 1864; "Letter from Shreveport, May 2d, 1864," *HDT*, May 6, 1864. See also Wallace P. Reed, ed., *History of Atlanta, Georgia* (Syracuse N.Y.: Mason, 1889), 102.

32. Summerville's "[Captain] Albert Roberts, Journalist of the New South, Part II," *Tennessee Historical Quarterly* 42 (1983): 179–202; Thomas E. Lyle, Larry O. Blair, and Debra S. Lyle, eds., *Organization Summary of Military Organizations from Georgia in the Confederate States of America* (Louisville, Tenn: Byrons, 1999), 312, with the roster identified in Janet B. Hewett, ed., *Confederate State Roster Georgia Confederate Soldiers Unit Roster*, arr. Joyce Lawrence (Wilmington, N.C.: Broadfoot, 1995), 4:876–77. Roberts wrote of Mill Springs in January 1862 as "John Hapley," "Battle of Fishing Creek," *MDAv*, January 31, 1862.

33. "Printers' Union," *MDT*, June 29, 1864; "New Advertisements," *MDT*, January 7, 1865. In January 1865 at Augusta, Georgia, industrialists plead for exemptions of employees; see "Meeting of Mechanics, Artizans, Officers C.S.A., etc.," *Southern Cultivator* 23 (January 1865): 11.

34. "T. Evans, Tom Jones, John Paul, Geo. Smith, and F. A. Howell; Caught Going to

the Yankees," *RW*, July 9, 1864. "J. Evans, Thomas Jones, John Paul, George Smith and T. A. Howall," from *RS*, July 9, 1864. "On Saturday J. F. Taylor, employee in the Arsenal, C. Algin, of the Medical Department, M. Ryan, of the Commissary Department, J. Head, of Captain English's local company, and M. Dunnivant, citizen . . .," "Charged with Attempting to Go to the Enemy," *RS*, September 19, 1864. "Lazarus Long, Elijah Person, and J. Phillips 'Going North,'" *RS*, November 14, 1864; "Running the Blockade," *RW*, November 14, 1864.

35. "Strike Among the Grave-Diggers," *RDD*, August 5, 1864.

36. "Making Yankee Prisoners Useful" [From *RE*], *CM*, September 20, 1864.

37. "Another Strike among the Female Operatives at the Confederate States Laboratory" [*RE*], *NODP*, October 28, 1864. Sergeant William N. Smith, in both the Third Arkansas and the Sixth Virginia Cavalry, both Army of Northern Virginia. "Further Southern News," *NODP*, October 28. "Another Strike among the Female Operatives" [from the *RE*], *PI*, October 20, 1864. Also as excerpt from *RE*: untitled, *HT-WT*, November 16, 1864.

38. Plum, *Military Telegraph* 2: 119–20.

39. "Reform Convention at Evansville, Rock Co. Wisconsin," *BoL*, September 19, 1863, 8.

Chapter 10. The Emergence of Labor Reform

1. Seaver, *Occasional Thoughts*, 17, 47–48. For Seaver's background as a Baptist minister, see Cyrus Eaton, *History of Thomaston, Rockland, and South Thomaston, Maine*, 2 vols. (n.p.: Hallowell, 1865), 1:455–56.

2. See "Things in General," *BI*, January 13, 20, and 27, 1864; "Thomas Paine" in Seaver, *Occasional Thoughts*, 43–44. De Robigne Mortimer Bennett, *World's Sages, Infidels and Thinkers* (New York: Truth Seeker, 1876), 856–57; for Seaver, 858–59; for Mendum, 1030–31; for Lant, 872–73. For Masquerier, see George E. MacDonald, *The Fifty Years of Freethought, Being the Story of the Truth Seeker, with the Natural History of Its Third Editor*, 2 vols. (New York: Truth Seeker, 1929). Untitled item [from *Boston Journal*], *BI*, December 9, 1863. "Mechanics' Mass Meeting," *BH*, December 3, 1863; "Meeting of Mechanics," *BI*, December 23, 1863; "The Labor Question," *BI*, December 23, 1863; "The Labor Question," *BI*, December 30, 1863; "The Labor Question," *BI*, January 13, 1864; and, "The Labor Question," *BI*, January 20, 1864. Participation noted under "Things in General," *BI*, December 9, 16, 23, and 30, 1863, and January 6, 13, 20, and 27, 1864. "J. C. Clure," letter, *FTR* 2 (December 12, 1863): 7.

3. "Things in General," *BI*, December 2, 1863; untitled item [from *Boston Journal*], *BI*, December 9, 1863; "Mechanics' Mass Meeting," *BH*, December 3, 1863; "Municipal Affairs," *BH*, December 8, 1863.

4. "Working Men's Meeting at Faneuil Hall" and "The Protective Union Association," *BH*, December 11, 1863; "Affairs About Home" and "The Municipal Election," *BH*, December 14, 1863. See also: "Politics," *FTR* 1 (November 28, 1863).

5. "The City Election: The Republican Ticket Elected; Mayor Lincoln's Plurality 4064," *BH*, December 11 and 15, 1863; On Spinney and Amory, see: William Schouler, *A History*

of Massachusetts in the Civil War, 2 vols. (Boston: Author, 1868, 1871), 2:582; "The Shoals of Politics," *FTR* 2 (December 26, 1863); "A Lesson to Workingmen," and "What I Have Noticed," all *FTR* 2 (December 26, 1863). Ward 1 also elected John Turner, formerly identified with the Workingmen's Party supporting the workingmen. "Address to Workingmen" under "Affairs about Home," *BH*, October 31, 1864; O'Connor, *Civil War Boston*, 209.

6. All items under "Things in General," *BI*, December 9, 16, 23, and 30, 1863, and January 6, 1864; see also "The Labor Question," *BI*, December 23, 1863. On Kaulbach, see *Voice of Industry*, January 9, 1846, and *Young America*, February 28, 1846. Thomas Hood, "The Song of the Shirt" from *Punch; or, the London Charivari*, December 19, 1843, in *Adventures in English Literature*, ed. R. B. Inglis et al. (Toronto: Gage, 1952), 436–37. Addressed meeting: see "The Labor Question," *BI*, January 13, 1864; "Things in General," *BI*, January 6, 13, 1864. Workingmen's Charitable Cooperative Association of Charlestown(?) and Vicinity: John M. Swaine and George H. Spaulding, letter. *FTR* 4 (January 14, 1865): 27.

7. *Independent Beacon* 1:8–10, 135, 136–38. G. B. Clark, Oliver Hull, Jonathan Adams, and William M. Allen played active roles in the organization. *BI*, February 14, 1849; Albert Post, *Popular Freethought in America, 1825–1850* (New York: Octagon, 1974), 108–9. "Minutes of the Proceedings of the Infidel Convention," *BI*, October 26, 1859; "Tax-Payers' Union Party," *NYT*, October 4, 1861; "Workingmen's League," *NYT*, October 20, 1861; and Ingalls, "Land Reform in 1848 and 1888: George Henry Evans and Henry George," *Truth Seeker* 15 (April 28, 1888): 258. Henry W. Bellows, *Historical Sketch of the Union League Club of New York: Its Origins, Organization and Work, 1863–1879* (New York: Club House, 1879), 46; on Goodwin, pp. 46, 83; on Kapp and Skidmore, p. 47. *Proceedings of the Organization of the Loyal National League at the Cooper Institute, Friday Evening, March 20th 1863* (New York: Westcott, 1863); on Goodwin, Hunt, and Bryant, p. 48; on Minturn, p. 5. "The Union. Monster Mass Meeting of the Loyal Citizens of New York," *NYT*, March 7, 1863. "Tremendous Union and War Meeting in New York," *Farmer's Cabinet*, March 12, 1863, 2; untitled item, *Farmer's Cabinet*, March 19, 1863, 2; "The Union Mass Meeting," *Farmer's Cabinet*, June 25, 1863, 2. "A Call for Volunteering," *NYDT*, November 15, 1863, and "Grand War Meeting," *NYDT*, November 30, 1863.

8. "The Trades' Movement: Mass Meeting of the Working Men of Brooklyn," *BDE*, April 24, 1863.

9. On the Farmers Protective Union, see "Laws of New York—By Authority," *BDE*, June 29, 1864.

10. "The Municipal Reform Movement," *NYDT*, March 31, 1864. On convict labor, see *Proceedings of the Seventh Annual Session of the Iron Molders' International Union, in Convention Assembled, at New York City, January 3, 1866* (Philadelphia: Selheimer, 1866).

11. Stevens, *New York Typographical Union No. 6*, 586–87.

12. "Mass Meeting of Workingmen: Twenty Thousand People Assembled—The Workingmen Protest against the Bill Now Pending in the Legislature, in Relation to Strikes" and "General News," *NYDT*, April 8, 1864; "The New York Workingmen" under "The Trades Movements: Opposition to Senator Hastings's Bill—A Trades Convention," *BDE*, April 1, 1864; "The Hastings Proscription Bill of New York," *FTR* 2 (April 9, 1864).

13. "The Labor 'Strikes,'" *RT* 16 (January 16, 1864): 22; "Extensive Labor Movement

at the Navy-Yard" under "Local Intelligence," *NYDT*, March 9, 1864; and, "Carpenters and Ship Joiners," *FTR* 2 (April 16, 1864): 78. "Commandants have no secretaries but are allowed two clerks and as many assistants or writers as may be actually necessary to carry on the duties of their offices." Letter on "Officials in the Navy Yard" under "Views of Correspondents," *BDE*, April 26, 1864. On coopers, hatters, moulders, and plasterers, "Strikes in New York," *BS*, July 20, 1864; McKay, *Civil War and New York City*, 198; "The Labor Movement: The Coopers—Strike for $3 a Day," under "Views of Correspondents," *BDE*, April 26, 1864, and "Meeting of the Coopers," *BDE*, June 23, 1864, 3.

14. "Meeting of the Coopers' Society," "The Plumbers of Brooklyn," and "The Carpenters Society" under "The Trades Movements: Opposition to Senator Hastings's Bill—A Trades Convention," *BDE*, March 30, 1864; "Workingmen's Convention: Meeting to Protest against the Bill to Prevent 'Strikes'—What the Workingmen Have to Say—Speeches, Resolutions, &c.," *BDE*, April 1, 1864, with "The Labor Movement: The Coopers—Strike for $3 a Day," *BDE*, April 6, 1864; and "The Pilot's Protection Union," *BDE*, April 26, 1864.

15. "From Philadelphia" on printers, *NYDT*, April 11, 1864; and, "Police! Police!" on ice gatherers, *FTR* 2 (January 23, 1864): 30; and Sylvis, "One Year Ago To-Day," *FTR* 2 (February 20, 1864): 47; and, Gallman, *Mastering Wartime*, 234, 235, 236, 237, 241, 144–45, 234, 235.

16. Richard E. Lingenfelter, *The Hardrock Miners: A History of the Mining Labor Movement in the American West, 1863–1893* (Berkeley: University of California Press, 1974), 32–33. See also Ronald C. Brown, *Hard-Rock Miners: The Intermountain West, 1860–1920* (College Station: Texas A&M University, 1979), 145–60. See *The Works of Hubert Howe Bancroft*, vol. 25 of the *History of Nevada, Colorado, and Wyoming, 1540–1888* (San Francisco: History Company, 1890), 304; Sam P. Davis, ed., *The History of Nevada* (Reno: Elms, 1913), 1:313; J. P. O'Brien, ed., *History of the Bench and Bar of Nevada* (San Francisco: Bench and Bar, 1913), 57 and 44 (lawyer made speaker of the assembly); "Reception of Ferguson's Body," *Sacramento Daily Bee*, September 15, 1858.

17. Lingenfelter, *Hardrock Miners*, 33, 34–37; Thomas J. Dimsdale, *The Vigilantes of Montana; or, Popular Justice in the Rocky Mountains*, 3rd ed. (Helena, Mont.: State Publishing, 1915), 239, and 145–46 (on involvement in law enforcement).

18. Lingenfelter, *Hardrock Miners*, 37–38, 38–39, 39–42. See also Rodman W. Paul, *Mining Frontiers of the Far West 1848–1880*, 2nd ed. (Albuquerque: University of New Mexico Press, 2001), 69.

19. Thomas Baker, "Major John P. Bruce," in James H. Mills, "Reminiscences of an Editor," *Contributions to the Historical Society of Montana, with Its Transactions, Officers and Members* 5 (Helena, Mont.: Independent Pub. Co., 1904), 279n–81n, 286, and 286n; *The Forgotten Men: Missouri State Guard*, comp. Carolyn M. Bartels (Independence, Mo.: Two Trails, 1995), 38; Preston Filbert, *The Half Not Told: The Civil War in a Frontier Town* (Mechanicsburg, Pa.: Stackpole, 2001), 78–80.

20. "Democratic Republican Letter to Fernando Wood," *IPE.—No. 24* (November 1862), 1–4; "The Future of the Democratic Republican Party," *IPE.—No. 26* (January 1863), 7; "The Democratic League," *IPE.—No. 39* (February 1864), 3; and "Workingmen's Correspondence. Letter to the Workingmen of Chicago" with "Special Notice," *IPE.—No. 39*

(February 1864), 3. See also his broadsides: *To the Laboring Men of New York* (New York: n.p., July 18, 1863); *Don't Unchain the Tiger!* (New York: n.p., July 24, 1863); *A Challenge* (New York: n.p., August 25, 1863); *An Abolition Traitor* (New York: n.p., August 29, 1863); *Dan'l O'Connell on Democracy!* (New York: n.p., October 13, 1863); *A Traitor's Peace* (New York: n.p., October 30, 1863); and *White Slaves* (New York: Sinclair Tousey, 1863).

21. "Workers in Wood: Mass Meeting at the Cooper Institute; Municipal Reform Demanded," *NYDT*, September 2, 1864, and "Reform Mass Meeting," *NYDT*, September 4, 1864. On Baker, see "New York Typographical Society," *BH*, January 12, 1861.

22. "The Syracuse Convention," *NYDT*, September 11, 1864; "Stand Number One," continued by "The Union Demonstration," *NYDT*, September 28, 1864, and "No interference with Trades' Unions," *NYDT*, September 29, 1864. The Citizens' Association included such prominent Democrats as August Belmont and Charles O'Conor. "Municipal Affairs: City, Governmental, and Sanitary Reform," Washington, March 22, *NN*, March 26, 1864.

23. "The Labor Question," *BoL*, April 2, 1864, 4; "Reconstruction—Religious, Political and Social: A Lecture Delivered through and by L. Judd Pardee, at Lyceum Hall, Boston, Sunday Evening, July 17th, 1864," *BoL*, August 6, 1864, 2; and "Wealth and Riches," *BoL*, December 31, 1864, 4.

24. Seaver, *Occasional Thoughts*, 14–15, 168–69, 169–70.

25. John Samuels, "Societies for Mutual Improvement," *FTR* 1 (July 18, 1863): 25; "Combination for Mutual Aid," *FTR* 1 (August 22, 1863): 46; "Co-operation: Self-Help by the People," *FTR* 1 (November 28, 1863): 104; "A Mutual Coal Association," *FTR* 2 (December 19, 1863): 10; "Co-operative Stores," *FTR* 2 (January 9, 1864): 23; "Brooklyn: Self-Help," *FTR* 2 (April 16, 1864): 4; "Co-operation in our City: An Appeal to the Employers, Both Male and Female of the City of Philadelphia," *FTR* 4 (January 14, 1865): 27; Hammonton, "The Settlement at Hammonton, N.J.," *BoL*, June 22, 1861; "The Hammonton Settlement," *BoL*, September 28), 1861, 3; "The French Co-operative Societies," *NYDT*, May 8, 1864; "Co-Operative Societies," *SA* 10 (May 7, 1864): 297; Foner and Lewis, *Black Worker to 1869*, 336–37.

26. The three items on the "Brotherhood of the Union," Philadelphia *USMO*, March 10, April 7, and May 26, 1860; McNeil, *Labor Movement*, 397, 399, 610; and, "A Distinguished Radical in Danger for 'Free Speech,'" *NN*, April 9, 1864, 12. See also on Sylvis, his "Address Delivered at Chicago, January 9, 1865," Sylvis, *Life, Speeches, Labors*, 127–72. See also Steve Leikin, *The Practical Utopians: American Workers and the Cooperative Movement in the Gilded Age* (Detroit: Wayne State University Press, 2005), 1–5, 9–10, 12–19.

27. "Houses for Workingmen New-York and Paris Contrasted," *NYDT*, September 13, 1864; "Social Condition of Working-men," *SA* 10 (April 30, 1864): 281.

28. Josiah Warren material includes "Banking and Currency" by "W.," *BoL*, December 4, 1858, 5; "True Civilization," *FTR* 1 (July 4, 1863): 19. See also Progressive Annual for 1862, Progressive Annual for 1863, Progressive Annual for 1864; Brisbane, *The Philosophy of Money* (n.p.: n.p., 1863) and "The Philosophy of Money," *NN*, June 25, 1864, but also "Finance and the Finances," *NN*, March 12, 1864; "Finance and the Finances," *NN*, March 12, 1864. He explained his plan in his *Equitable Commerce* (later *True Civilization*).

29. Hammonton, N.J., settlement, *BoL*, September 28, 1861, 3; Note on Black Lake Cooperative Association (Alcander Longley), Crimea, Michigan, *BoL*, January 11, 1864, 5.

30. *The History of Polk County, Iowa* (Union Historical Company, Birdsall, Williams, 1880), 967; "The Poor," *BoL*, July 16, 1864, 2, and "The Poor: Number Two," *BoL*, November 12, 1864, 2. See also the pieces by D. H. Hamilton, starting with "'The Spirit of Reformers,'" *BoL*, October 1, 1859, 7.

31. Johnston's proclamation of April 3, 1862, is appended to Report of General P. G. T. Beauregard, C.S. Army, April 21, 1862, *War of the Rebellion O.R.*, ser. 1, vol. 10, pt. 1, p. 396; pt. 2, p. 389. On Haddock, see *WmA*, 1844 issues: July 13, July 20, August 3, September 7, September 14, September 21, September 28, October 26, November 2, November 6, November 23, December 7, December 14, December 21, 1844; and 1845 issues: January 18, January 25, March 22; *Young America*, September 27 and December 20, 1845; *NYDTrib*, June 4, 1851; *OAR*, 7:265 and 242; J. K. Ingalls, *Reminiscences of an Octogenarian in the Field of Industrial and Social Reform* (New York: Holbrook, 1897), 37–38, 35, 38. For his assembly nomination, *Workingman's Advocate*, September 9, 1844; his singing, *Workingman's Advocate*, November 16 through December 21, 1844, and February 15, 1845; and his "Circular to the Trades," *Workingman's Advocate*, March 1, 8, 15, and 22, 1845; his songbook, Masquerier's *Sociology*, 126. See also Dyer, *Compendium of the War of the Rebellion*, 3:1163, 1170. On the Western Farm and Village Association, see: "Early Days in Winona," *Winona Daily Republican*, January 4, 1901; "These Pioneer Men and Women Stayed to Brave Hardships of Early Days at Minnesota City," *Winona Republican-Herald*, February 22, 1929.

32. "Affairs about Home: Emancipation Celebration at Tremont Temple," *BH*, January 2, 1863; Joel T. Headly, *The Great Riots of New York, 1712–1873* (New York: Thunder's Mouth, 2004), 219–20. *Cleveland Leader*, July 20, 27, and 30, 1863; "The Colored Labor Convention: Second Day's Session—Resolutions and Committees," *NYTrib*, January 11, 1871. See also "Proceedings of the Yearly Meeting of Progressive Friends," Chester Co. Pennsylvania, June 2–5, 1864, *BoL*, July 9, 1864, 3. For the persistence of land reform in politics: "From New Jersey: Legislative Proceedings," *Philadelphia Evening Telegraph*, February 23, 1871; "A petition from the National Land Reform Association, asking the Legislature to protest against land grants," "Pennsylvania Legislature," *Philadelphia Evening Telegraph*, February 24, 1871; West to Phillips, December 29, 1863, in Phillips Papers, Cambridge, cited Timothy Messer-Kruse, *The Yankee International: Marxism and the American Reform Tradition, 1848–1876* (Chapel Hill: University of North Carolina Press, 1998), 28.

33. Berlin et al., *Wartime Genesis of Free Labor: The Upper South*, 81, 589–90. Another consequence of this process predisposed the labor movement to a new kind of bifurcation between the trade unionists and those David Montgomery called "sentimental labor reformers" looking back to some golden age of class harmony.

34. Seibold, *Historical Sketch of Columbia Typographical Union*, 17, 18, 24; "Eight Hours Per Day," *FTR* 1 (October 3, 1863): 70; and "The Eight-Hour System," *FTR* 1 (October 1, 1863): 86; "Brooklyn Boss Baker's Association" and "A Proposition to Reduce the Hours of Labor," under "The Trades Movement," *BDE*, July 14, 1864.

35. Seibold, *Historical Sketch of Columbia Typographical Union*, 24; On painters, see McNeil, *Labor Movement*, 386, 387, 389, 394.

36. Madeleine B. Stern, *The Pantarch: A Biography of Stephen Pearl Andrews* (Austin: University of Texas Press, 1968).

37. "Sanitary Spiritualist Convention," *NYDT*, April 3, 1865; "The New Mania," *BoL*, October 17, 1863; "No Speculation," *BoL*, October 1, 1864.

38. "Slavery and Union," *NYT*, July 29, 1863.

39. Michael Thomas Smith, *The Enemy Within: Fears of Corruption in the Civil War North* (Charlottesville: University of Virginia Press, 2011).

Chapter 11. Toward a National Labor Presence

1. John R. Commons, Ulrich B. Phillips, Eugene A. Gilmore, Helen L. Sumner, and John B. Andrews, eds., *A Documentary History of American Industrial Society*, 10 vols., reprinted (New York: Russell and Russell, 1958), 9:123; "Louisville Convention: A Full Report of the Proceedings," *FTR* (October 15, 1864): 80. "The Industrial Congress," *PI*, September 26, 1864.

2. Classified advertisements, *BDE*, May 3 and December 22, 1864; untitled item, *BH*, June 28, 1864; and "Amusements," *NYDT*, September 21, 1864; *BS*, July 15, 1863; "Can the Actors Strike?" *PI*, July 21, 1864, and "The Thespian 'Strikers,'" *PI*, July 23, 1864; "The Actors' Protective Union," *NYDT*, August 5, 1864, and "Meeting of the Actors' Protective Union," *NYDT*, August 19, 1864.

3. Seibold, *Historical Sketch of Columbia Typographical Union*, 19.

4. Rev. E. H. Chapin, "Affairs about Home," *BH*, July 25, 1864; "The Daily Evening Voice," *BoL*, Dec. 17, 1864, 4; O'Connor, *Civil War Boston*, 211; *Leaves of History*, 17–18, 19–20, 18–19. Lt. Co. John G. Chambers of 23rd Massachusetts buried in Medford yesterday. Member of Masonic Order, Franklin Typographical Society; see also Boston clubs, "The Uprising in Boston," *FTR* 1 (November 21, 1863): 98.

5. Stevens, *New York Typographical Union No. 6*, 278–86, 286n, 287–88, 291–93. *PI* and some of the other papers complained that this did not reflect the will of the workers but "the dictates of the Typographical Union." The *Tribune* declared that "it shall not accede to the Union's demand, if they can avoid it." "Our New York Correspondence: The Printers Strike; The Typographical Union Overdoing the Thing—Probable Results," and notice of "Journeyman Printer" writing to the *Tribune* "a well considered protest against the schedule of prices demanded by the Printer's union of New York," *PI*, August 11 and 13, 1864. New York City printers announced arrangement "for a meeting of workingmen and others, to memorialize the President" over draft and the war: "Affirs [*sic*] in New York," *BS*, August 17, 1864.

6. "The Printers' Strike" and "Demonstration of the Printers in the City Hall Park," *NYDT*, August 19, 1864; Stevens, *New York Typographical Union No. 6*, 289; "The Strike among Compositors," *NYH*, August 14, 1864; "The Printers' Strike," *NYH*, August 21, 1864. On Poer, see "The Workingmen of New York: Workingmen's Democratic Republican Association," and "Officers of the Workingmen's Democratic Republican Association," *IPE.—No. 39* (February 1864), 1–3, 4.

7. Stevens, *New York Typographical Union No. 6*, 293–94. The *New York Journal of Commerce* noted the demise of the Typographical Union, quoted as saying that "a monument of folly, arrogance and extortion, and its fate is a warning to all who conspire to destroy others in hope of benefiting themselves—'Rest in peace.'" "Miscellaneous," *MDT*, October 4, 1864.

8. Justin E. Walsh, *To Print the News and Raise Hell: A Biography of Wilbur F. Storey* (Chapel Hill: University of North Carolina, Press, 1968), 121+n, 123, 224+n, 225+n. Storey was one of those colorfully nasty and opportunistic nineteenth-century editors who would print anything to sell papers, mostly attacks on those he regarded as vulnerable. He "never seemed willing to admit that a man had done a good thing," and he would probably be most remembered in Chicago for having been beaten in the street by a troupe of dancers for having referred to them as bawd (120, 121).

9. Walsh, *To Print the News*, 224+n–25+n; Bessie Louise Pierce, *A History of Chicago*, 3 vols. (New York: Knopf, 1940), 2:162–64, 500–503; *FTR* (June 11, 1864): 7.

10. Untitled item, *LDJ*, December 22, 1864; "A Professional Man on the Strikers," *BH*, December 5, 1864; Editorial, "Printers' Strikes," *NYH*, December 4, 1864, reprinted as "Printers' Strikes" in *BH*, December 6, 1864; O'Connor, *Civil War Boston*, 210, 211.

11. "Miscellaneous" [from Northern press], *RDD*, August 11, 1863; on late 1862, see William R. Plum, *The Military Telegraph during the Civil War in the United States, with an Exposition of Ancient and Modern Means of Communication, and of the Federal and Confederate Cipher Systems; Also a Running Account of the War between the States*, 2 vols. (Chicago: Jansen, McClurg, 1882), 2:113–14.

12. On Philadelphia, see "Discharged from Service," *PI*, June 22, 1864; Gallman, *Mastering Wartime*, 236. On New York, see from 1864 issues of *NYDT*: "Great Conflagration in Saratoga," July 6; G.W.B. on "Strikes and Strikers—The Horse-Shoers," August 5; "Strike among Blacksmiths—A Man Fatally Injured," and "Strike of the Horse-Shoers," August 5; "Strike on the Adirondack Railroad," August 10; "The Late Strike among Horse-Shoers—The Injured Man Examined by the Coroner," August 11; G. W. E., letter on "Strikes and Strikers—The Horse-Shoers," August 28; "The Horseshoers and the City Railroads," *NYH*, August 20, 1864. For upstate, see *NYDT*, August 3, 1864; and, Gallman, *Mastering Wartime*, 235.

13. McNeil, *Labor Movement*, 314, 315, 316–17.

14. This tradition is discussed in Lause, *Secret Society History*.

15. "Affairs at the West," *NYDT*, March 20, 1864; "The Strike on the Fort Wayne Railroad," *PI*, January 21, 1864. Also, "Strike on the Fort Wayne Railroad," *BS*, January 22, 1864; McNeil, *Labor Movement*, 317, 318, 319. See also John Wallace from Galesburg, "Temperance," *FTR* 3 (October 29, 1864): 87.

16. "Labor Troubles in Pennsylvania," 280; Gallman, *Mastering Wartime*, 236, 242n; "Strike on the Reading Railroad," *NYDT*, July 6, 1864; "Money, Stocks, Markets, &c." *PI*, July 13, 1864. See John L. Blackman Jr., "Seizure of the Reading Railroad in 1864," *Pennsylvania Magazine of History and Biography* 111 (January 1987): 49–60. Government use of troops against the strikers on the Reading Railroad in "Address Delivered by William H. Sylvis," *FTR* 4 (January 14, 1865): 25.

17. "Combined Movements of Engineers on Western Railroads to Aid Strikers," *BH*,

March 15, 1864; "The Strike on the Western Railroads," *NYT*, March 15, 1864; "Affairs at the West," *NYT*, March 20, 1864; "Strike on the Western Railroads," *BS*, March 16, 1864; "Engineers' Strike at Chicago," *FTR* 3 (March 26, 1864): 66.

18. McNeil, *Labor Movement*, 317, 318, 319; and "Locomotive Engineers," *FTR* 4 (April 1, 1865): 71.

19. Kevin Warneke, "Father of Fraternalism: A Working Man with a Plan," *American Heritage*, January–February 2003; excerpt from *Gazetteer and Business Directory of Montgomery County, N.Y., 1869–70* (Syracuse: Hamilton Child, 1869); J. P. Ashcom, M.D., from 1871 "Renovo Record"; *The Life, Labors and Travels of Father J. J. Upchurch, Founder of the Ancient Order of United Workmen: Written by Himself*, rev. and ed. Sam Booth (San Francisco: Dewey, 1887), 20–22; McNeil, *Labor Movement,* 12.

20. Letter of "A Blacksmith," October 3, and "Employee," November 22, both under "Communications," *FTR* 3 (October 15, 1864): 79, and *FTR* 4 (December 10, 1864): 7.

21. "Strikes in New York," *BS*, July 20, 1864; "Mayor Gunther on the Emergency," *NYDT*, July 12, 1864, and "Mayor Gunther and the Workingmen of New-York," *NYDT*, July 16, 1864; "Trouble at Calvary Cemetery," *BDE*, August 18, 1864. See also G. W. E., letter on "Strikes and Strikers—The Horse-shoers," *NYT*, August 28, 1864, and "The Influence of Political Mobs," *Independent*, August 25, 1864.

22. In *BDE*: "The Strike in the Navy Yard" (June 23, 1864); "The Way Union Sentiment Is Fostered in the Navy Yard: A Gross Outrage" (July 23, 1864); "Conditional Exemptions" (July 27, 1864); "Curious Political Revelations—the Aldermanship of the 20th Ward" under "Views of Correspondents" (September 10, 1864).

23. "Municipal Reform: Mass Meeting of the Iron Workers of New York; The Cooper Institute Fitted with Mechanics in Favor of a Reform in the City Government—Governor Seymour Requested to Remove City Inspector Bouir," *NYH*, July 29, 1864; "Signs of the Times," *BDE*, September 10, 1864. Names of prominent Democratic politicians are mentioned in "Citizens Association of New-York," *NYT*, November 16, 1865; also, "John Hecker for Mayor," *NYT*, December 2, 1865.

24. "Peace Meeting in New York," *RDD*, March 21, 1864.

25. "The Republican Party and Their Professions for the Poor," *The Crisis*, April 4, 1861, 5, and the editorial comment of May 28, 1862, 139, 140. For samples of these, see Foner and Lewis, *Black Worker to 1869*, 270–71, 271–73, 279–81.

26. "The Presidential Election," [Keene] *New Hampshire Sentinel*, May 26, 1864.

27. *Interior Causes of the War: The Nation Demonized, and Its President a Spirit-Rapper, by a Citizen of Ohio* (New York: Doolady, 1863), 1; "Much more of misery than happiness has followed its advent"; "Spiritualism," *FTR* 1 (August 18, 1863): 38.

28. "Our Candidate for the Vice-Presidency: Popularity of the Nomination," *NYDT*, June 22, 1864. See also: "Francis W. Hughes," *IPE.—No. 26* (January 1863): 8; broadside, *Dan'l O'Connell on Democracy!* (New York: n.p., October 13, 1863); broadside, *A Traitor's Peace* (New York: n.p., October 30, 1863); "The Democratic League," *IPE.—No. 26* (January 1863): 7; "The Workingmen of New York: Workingmen's Democratic Republican Association," *IPE.—No. 39* (February 1864): 1–3; "Southern Promises: King Cotton," *IPE.—No. 40* (March 1864).

29. "The Strikes: Mr. Lincoln on the Strikes," *NYDT*, December 5, 1863; Gallman, *Mastering Wartime*, 239–40; Gabor S. Boritt, *Lincoln and the Economics of the American Dream*, 227.

30. "Reply of President Lincoln," *IPE.—No. 40* (March 1864): 1–2. Other letters of reply in *IPE.—No. 40* (March 1864) from Major General A. E. Burnside, Hiram Walbriudge, Henry Winter Davis, Frank Blair, Marcus L. Ward, Erastus Brooks, S. I. Prime, Hogart Ford, J. Butler Wright, and Charles Gould. From William O. Bourne et al., to Abraham Lincoln, January 5, 1864; New York City Workingmen's Association to Abraham Lincoln, January 1, 27, 1864; "From Washington," *NYDT*, March 22, 1864; response to the NY Democratic Republican Workingmen's Association: "President Lincoln on the Rights of Labor," *HW* (April 2, 1864), 211. See also *Dan'l O'Connell on Democracy!* and *A Traitor's Peace*.

31. "President Lincoln and the Workingmen" [from the *New York World*], and "The President—the Workingmen—and 'the Nigger' of the 'World,'" *IPE.—No. 40* (March 1864): 4–5, 6–7; "Special Notice," *IPE.—No. 39* (February 1864): 4. See also "New-York Workingmen's Association," *NYDT*, August 20, 1864.

32. "The Convention of Radical Germans," *CL*, October 22, 1863, and "German Radical Convention," *CL*, October 26, 1863; "Radical German Convention at Cleveland," *PP*, October 29, 1863; "The Candidacy of Caspar Butz," *Illinois Staats-Zeitung*, September 18, 1862; Philip S. Foner, "Friedrich Adolph Sorge: 'Father of Modern Socialism in America,'" in Sorge, *Labor Movement*, 7–8.

33. "Mass Meeting of Foreign-Born Citizens," *NYDTrib*, April 1, 1863; Justine Davis Randers-Pehrson, *Adolf Douai, 1819–1888: The Turbulent Life of a German Forty-Eighter in the Homeland and in the United States* (New York: Lang, 2000). In the *New Nation*, 1864: "Candidates for the Presidency" (March 5); "Political: The Fremont Movement" (March 12); "Radicalism in the Senate" with "The Missouri Radical Convention" under "Political: General National Convention" (March 19); "The New Nation," "Correspondence: The Presidential Nomination" with "Political: Formation of a Fremont Campaign Club," "Municipal Affairs: City, Governmental, and Sanitary Reform," (March 26); and "Political: The Pomeroy-Chase" (April 2), along with reprints of the Cleveland convention in the issue of May 28.

34. "Ultimate Reconstruction," and "What We Are and What We Want," *NN*, March 5, 1864; "Platform of the Fremont Campaign Club," under "Political: Formation of a Fremont Campaign Club," *NN*, March 26, 1864. Claude Pelletier, "Communications: Philosophy of Strikes," *NN*, March 5, 1864; "Political: Formation of a Fremont Campaign Club," Washington, March 22, *NN*, March 26, 1864. McCurdy and Manierre had earlier shared the platform with land reformer Henry Beeny and other radicals to encourage recruitment. "Meetings: Grand War Meeting," *NYT*, November 30, 1863; "A Private Chapter of the Origin of the War," *NN*, April 9, 1864. "The Rights of Labor," *NYTrib*, November 16, 1863. For a valuable corrective, see Mischa Honeck, *We Are the Revolutionists: German-Speaking Immigrants and American Abolitionists after 1848* (Athens: University of Georgia Press, 2011).

35. For Masquerier's songs and poems, see Masquerier, *Sociology*, 165–75, 195; and letter of S. W. Tabor to Masquerier in the Lant Papers; "Union General Committee Nominations," *NYT*, September 28, 1864.

36. *St. Louis Daily Press* mentioned "Gleanings from Our Co-laborers," *FTR* 4 (January 28, 1865): 34; from *St. Louis Democrat*: "Plan to crush the union, which is on strike there." *White Cloud Kansas Chief*, December 22, 1864. See also "The Great Union Demonstration Yesterday Afternoon," *BH*, August 28, 1862; Rev. E. H. Chapin, "Affairs about Home," *BH*, July 25, 1864; "The Daily Evening Voice," *BoL*, December 17, 1864, 4; O'Connor, *Civil War Boston*, 211; *Leaves of History*, 17–18. "Lt. Col. John G. Chambers of 23rd Massachusetts buried in Medford yesterday. Member of Masonic order, Franklin Typographical Society."

37. Classified ads, *LDJ*, September 24, 1864; "Notices of the Day," *LDJ*, September 23, 1864. See also, "Louisville Convention," *FTR* (October 15, 1864): 80. "Notices of the Day," *LDJ*, December 22, 1864.

Chapter 12. A Peace of Sorts

1. Qtd. in Melvin M. Leiman, *Jacob N. Cardozo: Economic Thought in the Antebellum South* (New York: Columbia University Press, 1966), 211. See also Nelson Lankford, *Richmond Burning: the Last Days of the Confederate Capital* (New York: Viking, 2002), and Furgurson, *Ashes of Glory*, 327–57.

2. Lause, "'Turning the World Upside-Down': A Portrait of Labor and Military Leader, Alonzo Granville Draper," *LH* 44 (May 2003): 189–204. Same age as the Wesley Washington Pasko who covered Fort Sumter.

3. From the *Whig* "Latest News from Richmond," *FTR* 4 (April 22, 1865), 92.

4. "Brooklyn (?) Strikes," *FTR* 4 (April 22, 1865): 92; "Brooklyn News," *NYDT*, May 3, 1865; classified advertisement. "To the Workingmen of Brooklyn," *BDE*, April 14, 1865; "The Workingmen: Atheneum Mass Meeting," *BDE*, May 9, 1865; "The Late Workingmen's Convention," *BDE*, May 10, 1865; "Meeting of Workingmen," *BDE*, May 19, 1865.

5. Several hundred miners demanding a pay increase from $1.75 to $2 per day marched from Negaunee to Marquette, where they "compelled the stoppage of all work in shipping gore from the docks there." Untitled item [from *CT*], *Black Hawk* [Gilpin County, Colo.] *Daily Mining Journal*, August 21, 1865.

6. "The Street-Sweepers on a Strike," *NYDT*, December 31, 1864.

7. "The Portland Election: Working Reform Matters in That City," *FTR* 4 (April 1, 1865): 71; Joseph Griffin, ed., *History of the Press of Maine* (Brunswick, 1872), 209–10, 212, 63. Also Edward H. Elwell, *Portland and Vicinity, with a Sketch of Old Orchard Beach and Other Maine Resorts*, rev. ed. (Portland: Loring, Short and Harmon, 1881), 33; Joseph Williamson, *A Bibliography of the State of Maine from the Earliest Period to 1891*, 2 vols. (Portland: Thurston, 1896), 1:534; Joseph Williamson, "Spirit Photographs," *The Photographic News: A Weekly Record of the Progress of Photography*, January 9, 1863, 20; "The Allen Boy Medium," *BoL*, April 1, 1865, 4.

8. Portland letter from "L.P.P.," "The Portland Election: Working Reform Matters in that City," *FTR* 4 (April 1, 1865): 71. Joseph B. Hall. Also mentioned were R. B. Bean and L. P. Ingree, as well as candidate Albert H. Waite.

9. "Charter Elections," *NYDT*, March 8, 1865; "The Portland Election: Working Reform Matters in that City," *FTR* 4 (April 1, 1865): 71.

10. *Proceedings of the Sixth Annual Session of the Iron Molders' International Union, in Convention Assembled, at Chicago, Ill., January 4, 1865*, (Philadelphia: *FTR*, 1865); "General News," *NYDT*, February 22, 1865.

11. Seibold, *Historical Sketch of Columbia Typographical Union*, 19–23, 23–24; "Philadelphia Typographical Union," *PI*, April 22, 1865; "Common Branch," *PI*, May 5, 1865; "Telegraph to the Herald: From Washington," *BH*, January 9, 1865; A. T. Cavis and E. MacMurray, "History of the Columbia Typographical Society of Washington, D.C.," *PrC* 6 (August 1871): 250–51.

12. *A Tribute of Respect by the Citizens of Troy, to the Memory of Abraham Lincoln* (Albany: Munsell, 1865), 251; "Honors to Mr. Lincoln's Remains in Baltimore," and "In Memoriam!" *BS*, April 21, 1865; *Leaves of History*, 20. See also "The Death of President Lincoln," *Soldier's Friend* 1 (May 1865): 2, and "A Soldier's Tribute," *Soldier's Friend* 1 (June 1865): 4.

13. *The Lincoln Memorial* (New York: Bunce and Huntington, 1865), 194, 195. See also "The Funeral of President Lincoln," *FTR* 4 (May 13, 1865): 94.

14. From *BDE*: "Arrested" (December 24, 1864); "The Navy Yard Strike: Excitement Subsiding—Many of the Men Return to Work" (April 14, 1865); "Affairs at the Navy Yard" (April 21, 1865); "The Strike in the Navy Yard" (April 27, 1865); "Address Delivered by William H. Sylvis," *FTR* 4 (January 14, 1865): 25; "Brooklyn Strike," *FTR* 4 (May 6, 1865): 91. The Democratic *Daily Eagle* had alternatively claimed that the Navy Yard hadn't hired Democrats and that its most hard-working employees were Democrats, yet a Republican official claimed that the Navy Yard retained Democrats in preference to Republicans, particularly the Germans. "Local Politics," *BDE*, June 7, 1865.

15. Edward S. Sanford, "U. S. Military Telegraph Service to Secretary Stanton, July 16, 1863," in O.A.R., ser.1, vol. 27, pt. 2, p. 890; Lause, "Turning the World Upside Down," 189–204.

16. Lause, *Race and Radicalism*, 126, 132.

17. "Working Women's Protective Union," *BDE*, June 21, 1865; Working Women's Association, organized September 17, 1865, listed in *The American Year-Book and National Register for 1869*, ed. David N. Camp (Hartford; O.D., Case, 1869), 1:224.

18. William Lyon Mackenzie King, "The International Typographical Union," *Journal of Political Economy* 5 (September 1897): 460–63.

19. Foner and Lewis, *Black Worker to 1869*, 229–40, 352, 357–58, 359. Certainly old habits die hard, and we can see the persistence of race and bound labor in Moon-Ho Jung, *Coolies and Cane: Race, Labor, and Sugar in the Age of Emancipation* (Baltimore, Md.: Johns Hopkins University Press, 2006). See also Sylvis's warning about "The Bogus Indenture," *FTR* 2 (January 9, 1864): 23; on the government use of convict labor, see "Address Delivered by William H. Sylvis," *FTR* 4 (January 14, 1865): 25.

20. Eric Arnesen, *Waterfront Workers of New Orleans: Race, Class and Politics, 1863–1923* (New York: Oxford University Press, 1991), 20, 21–22; Foner and Lewis, *Black Worker to 1869*, 352; "Colonization of the Rebel States" *NYTrib*, February 7, 1863. By late 1865, Mobile, Savannah, and Atlanta had 109 members, of which only twenty-seven had been members in 1861. Some twenty of Nashville's members in 1861 were among the eighty-eight members of 1865.

21. Grubb's election in 1871: see Wallace P. Reed, ed., *History of Atlanta, Georgia* (Syracuse N.Y.: Mason, 1889), 257; Roberts, *Southern Sketches*, 37–38, 39–40, 42, 59–60, 64, 65–66; *Historical Encyclopedia of Illinois and Knox County* (Chicago: 1899); Sarah Blackwell Gober Temple, *The First Hundred Years: A Short History of Cobb County, in Georgia*, 6th ed. (Athens: Agee, 1989), 595; Dawne Temple's summary of the obituary in the *Indiana Democrat*, January 28, 1875, posted at http://listsearches.rootsweb.com/th/read/PAWESTMO/2009-01/1231718479 (accessed October 8, 2014).

22. William Lyon Mackenzie King, "The International Typographical Union," *Journal of Political Economy* 5 (September 1897): 464–65; "Proceedings of the Seventeenth Session of the National Typographical Union, Albany, N.Y., June 1869," *PrC* 4 (July 1869): 170–71; Foner and Lewis, *Black Worker to 1869*, 374–83.

23. Foner and Lewis, *Black Worker to 1869*, 426–468, 356–57, 371–72, 384, 385. See also Herman D. Bloch, "Labor and the Negro 1866–1910," *Journal of Negro History* 50 (July 1965): 163–84, and Sumner Eliot Matison, "The Labor Movement and the Negro during Reconstruction," *Journal of Negro History* 33 (October 1948).

24. U.S. Census 1860; *National Almanac 1863*, 322–25. See also Stanley L. Engerman and J. Matthew Gallman, "The Civil War Economy: A Modern View," in *On the Road to Total War: The American Civil War and the German Wars of Unification*, ed. Stig Förster and Jorg Nagler (Washington: German Historical Institute; Cambridge: Cambridge University Press, 1997), 222–23.

25. "The March of Progress in the Wake of Ruin: Industrial Amelioration in the South," *NYT*, November 22, 1864.

26. "Manufacturing Mismanagement," *NYTrib*, April 3, 1863.

27. Collins, *Nature's Aristocracy*, 294; "'Bosses' and Workmen," *SA* 10 (January 2, 1864): 9.

28. "Strikes," *BoL*, November 21, 1863, 4.

29. "Workingmen's Correspondence: Letter to the Workingmen of Chicago," IPE.—No. 39 (February 1864): 3; "Workingmen's Reforms," *Soldier's Friend* 1 (August 1865): 4; "Bricklayers and Strikes," *Soldier's Friend* 4 (August 1868): 4. "Property is the fruit of labor—property is desirable—is a positive good in the world. That some should be rich, shows that others may become rich, and hence is just encouragement to industry and enterprize. Let not him who is houseless pull down the house of another; but let him labor diligently and build one for himself, thus by example assuring that his own shall be safe from violence when built." "Reply of President Lincoln," along with other letters of reply from: Major General A. E. Burnside, Hiram Walbriudge, Henry Winter Davis, Frank Blair, Marcus L. Ward, Erastus Brooks, S. I. Prime, Hogart Ford, J. Butler Wright, and Charles Gould, *IPE* 40 (March 1864): 1–4; Abraham Lincoln to the Workingmen's Democratic Republican Association, March 21, 1864.

30. "Meeting of the National Typographical Union," *PI*, April 17, 1865; "City Intelligence," *PI*, June 5, 1865; and "Fourteenth Annual Session of the National Typographical Union," *PI*, June 6, 1865; Tracy, *History of the Typographical Union*, 211–15. These included: eleven in New York, five each in Ohio and Illinois; four in California; three each in Indiana, Pennsylvania, Iowa and Kansas; two each in Michigan, Connecticut, Wisconsin, Minnesota,

and Canada; and one each in Massachusetts, Maine, Rhode Island, Oregon, as well as the territories of Nebraska, Nevada, and Colorado.

31. Stevens, *New York Typographical Union No. 6*, 416, with a membership chart on 415–16 and McKechnie's biography on 648–51.

32. *Proceedings of the Seventh Annual Session of the Iron Molders' International Union, in Convention Assembled, at New York City, January 3, 1866* (Philadelphia: Selheimer, 1866), 7, 9.

33. Charles F. Pidgin, *History of the Bureau of Statistics of Labor of Massachusetts, and of Labor Legislation in that State From 1833 to 1876* (Boston: Wright and Potter, 1876), 13; "The First Step," *FTR* 4 (May 13, 1865): 94.

34. Macnamara, *History of the Ninth Regiment*, 9, 18; Pidgin, *History of the Bureau of Statistics*, 15, 16, 17–19, 21.

35. Fred Rogers Fairchild, *The Factory Legislation of the State of New York* (New York: Macmillan and American Economic Assoc., 1906), 28, or *Publications of the American Economic Association*, series 3, vol. 6 (November 1905): 764; William F. Willoughby, *State Activities in Relation to Labor in the United States*, published as *The Johns Hopkins University Studies in Historical and Political Science*, series 19, nos. 4–5 (April–May 1901), 187, 189; *Leaves of History*, 15–16.

36. Terence V. Powderly, *Thirty Years of Labor, 1859–1889: In Which the History of the Attempts to Form Organizations of Workingmen for the Discussion of Political, Social, and Economic Questions Is Traced* (Columbus: Excelsior, 1889), 55.

37. "Political Action," *FTR* 4 (May 20, 1865): 98; Seibold, *Historical Sketch*, 24.

38. Seaver, *Occasional Thoughts*, 164, 167, 36.

Epilogue

1. David T. Burbank, *Reign of the Rabble: The St. Louis General Strike of 1877* (New York: Kelley, 1966), 45, 51, 103, 139.

2. J.R.Y., "The Private Soldier," *PP*, May 18, 1863.

3. "Death of Lambert A. Willmer," *FTR* 2 (January 2, 1864): 18. William Hawes, "one of the old abolitionists and a land reformer," reciting poem "Eternal Justice" by Charles Mackay, *Voices from the Mountains and from the Crowd* (Boston: Ticknor, Reed, and Fields, 1853), 22–23, 24. M. Hanley, "Old John Brown," *The Alarm*, November 8, 1884, 1. Member "delivered a biographical lecture on the old hero, in which he was held up as a model for men to copy. The lecturer claimed that John Brown was a complete man, and showed that he had varied talents of a truly high order. One expression appeared, however, to strike the audience with incredulity; it was when he placed John Brown among those men who had poetic gift and power." Recited poem also ascribed to Brown by James Redpath, *The Public Life of Capt. John Brown . . . with an Auto-Biography of his Childhood and Youth* (Boston: Thayer and Eldridge, 1860), 155–56; Samuel Phillips Day, *Down South, or, an Englishman's Experience at the Seat of the American War*, 2 vols. (London: Hurst and Blackett, 1862).

4. "To the Voters of New Hampshire: Reasons for Organizing a New Party," and "An

Entirely Independent Ticket," [Concord] *Labor Reform Dispatch*, February 11, 1870, p. 2. Copy at the American Antiquarian Society, Worcester, Mass.

5. "The officers of the National Labor union have issued an address to their organization heartily endorsing the financial platform of *The Herald*, particularly the anti-national bank portion." *Opinions of Our National Banks, and the Practice of Selling U.S. Bonds on Commission* (Washington: United Press, 1868), 18. On Underwood, "Minutes of the Proceedings of the Infidel Convention," *BI*, October 26, 1859.

6. *Pr* 5 (August 1864): 122; these connections are discussed in Lause, "Origin of Henry George's Single Tax," *Historian* 52 (May, 1990): 394–410. For this critical period, see also Leon Fink, *Workingmen's Democracy: The Knights of Labor and American Politics* (Urbana: University of Illinois Press, 1985).

7. Officers were Newell Daniels (formerly of Milford, Mass.), Samuel Wilson, W. C. Haynes, Albert Jenkins, Thomas Houren, F. W. Wallace, Henry Palmer. McNeil, *Labor Movement*, 198.

8. Record of Service of Michigan Volunteers 1861–65; *Who's Who in Socialist America* (Appeal to Reason, 1914), 26, 29, Crum having also turned up in various other third parties upstate. Enlistments "a larger number of men on the North Carolina at the present time than were ever on that vessel before, notwithstanding the large number of men who are being daily shipped on board vessels leaving the Yard," and doubled the guard of Marines on the recruits. Captain Meade of the North Carolina resigning. "Affairs at the Navy Yard. Vessels Fitting Out for Service: Activity in the Various Departments—Vessels Ordered Off," *BDE*, April 27, 1864.

9. C. Osborne Ward, *The Great Rebellion: Reminiscences of the Struggle that Cost a Million Lives; A Drama in Five Acts* (New York: n.p., 1881). Sergeant Lester F. Ward of the Hundred Forty-First Pennsylvania needed opportunities to begin pondering the realities of social life, and this started him toward becoming the iconoclastic sociologist as well as a follower of Edward Bellamy's Nationalist movement. Clifford H. Scott, *Lester Frank Ward* (New York: Twayne, 1976), 19, 20.

10. "Socialists May Name Him," *NYTrib*, March 16, 1896. See also: "The Ticket: Socialist Presidential Nominees; For President Simon Wing of Massachusetts, for Vice President Charles H. Matchett of New York," *Weekly People*, September 4, 1892. "Wants to Be President," *NYTrib*, July 11, 1896; "Matchett, America's Socialist Pioneer, Dies after Long Sickness," *New York Evening Call*, October 25, 1919; and, "Charles H. Matchett, Socialist," *NYDT*, October 26, 1919; "Wants to Meet Bryan," *NYDTrib*, July 23, 1896. At this time, Boston had a union that looked out for "Sailors' Wages," *BH*, December 4, 1863, but a Buffalo Seamen's Union likely covered the Great Lakes; see Receipts, *FTR* 4 (March 12, 1864): 58.

11. Foner and Lewis, *Black Worker to 1869*, 335–36; "An Enthusaistic Meeting of Colored Citizens: Grant and Wilson Indorsed," *NYT*, July 24, 1872. Vital, too, is Taylor, *America's First Black Socialist*, superseding earlier work, such as Gutman's "Peter Clark: Pioneer Negro Socialist, 1877."

12. "An Irrepressible Conflict," *FTR* 2 (February 20, 1864): 47. "An Irrepressible Conflict," *FTR* 2 (February 27, 1864): 51

13. James D McCabe, *The History of the Great Riots: Being a Full and Authentic Account of the Strikes and Riots on the Various Railroads of the United States and in the Mining Regions; Embracing Brilliant and Graphic Pen-Pictures of the Reign of Terror in Pittsburgh, Baltimore, Chicago, and Other Cities: The Conflicts between the Troops and the Mob; Terrible Conflagrations and Destruction of Property—Thrilling Scenes and Incidents, etc., etc., Together with a Full History of the Mollie Maguires* (Philadelphia: National Pub. Co., 1877); J. A. Dacus, *Annals of the Great Strikes in the United States: A Reliable History and Graphic Description of the Causes and Thrilling Events of the Labor Strikes and Riots of 1877* (St. Louis: Scammell, 1877); Pinkerton, *Strikers*.

14. Robert V. Bruce, *1877: Year of Violence* (Indianapolis: Bobbs-Merrill, 1959), 181, 187. See also Sylvia D. Hoffert, *Jane Grey Swisshelm: An Unconventional Life* (Chapel Hill: University of North Carolina Press, 2004). As significant exceptions, the bosses brought blacks from Kentucky and West Virginia against the miners in Illinois, which fanned the fires of all the wartime racial fears of racial competition. Too, the strike in San Francisco and on the West Coast proved to be easily turned against the Chinese.

15. Taylor, *America's First Black Socialist*; Philip S. Foner, *The Great Labor Uprising of 1877* (New York: Monad, 1977), 125; Bruce, *1877*, 293. Yet this was a very peculiar role for an African American. So, too, was the recruitment of black strikebreakers from Kentucky and West Virginia to break the strike of the miners around Braidwood, Illinois.

16. Qtd. from Foner, *Great Labor Uprising*, 181. In addition to the works of Bruce and Foner, see: Jeremy Brecher, *Strike!* (Boston: South End, 1997); David O. Stowell, *Streets, Railroads, and the Great Strike of 1877* (Chicago: University of Chicago Press, 1999); Brian Luskey, "Riot and Respectability: The Shifting Terrain of Class Language and Status in Baltimore during the Great Strike of 1877," *American Nineteenth Century History* 4, no. 3 (2003): 61–96; Drew E. VandeCreek, *The Great Strike of 1877 and the Labor Question* [e-book] (Alexandria, Va.: Alexander Street, 2007); Michael A. Bellesiles, *1877: America's Year of Living Violently* (New York: New Press, 2010), as well as the fictionalized account in Lucia Dailey, *Mine Seed* (2002). See also Richard Slotkin, *The Fatal Environment: The Myth of the Frontier in the Age of Industrialization, 1800–1890* (New York: Atheneum, 1985).

17. Foner, *Great Labor Uprising*, 169–70, 197–99; Bruce, *1877*, 263. See also: Maud Cuney Hare, *Norris Wright Cuney: A Tribune of the Black People* (New York: Crisis, 1913); Ernest Obadele-Starks, *Black Unionism in the Industrial South* (College Station: Texas A&M University Press, 2001); Douglas Hales, *A Southern Family in White and Black: The Cuneys of Texas* (College Station: Texas A&M University Press, 2003).

18. Foner, *Great Labor Uprising*, 169–70, 181–83, 184–85. See, for example, the prominence of the engineers in organizing the strike at Galesburg in Lause, "'The Cruel Striker War': Rail Labor and the Broken Symmetry of Galesburg Civic Culture, 1877–1888," *Journal of the Illinois State Historical Society* 91 (Autumn 1998): 89–93.

19. Pinkerton, *Strikers*, 381.

20. "The Negro," *The Alarm*, April 4, 1885, 2.

21. Ely, *Labor Movement in America*, 615. See John T. McEnnis, *The White Slaves of Free America: Being an Account of the Sufferings, Privations and Hardships of the Weary Toil-*

ers in Our Great Cities as Recently Exposed by Neil Nelson, of the Chicago Times; Female Labor, Child Labor, Contract and Prison Labor: With Special Contributions by Judge T. M. Cooley, T. V. Powderly, and Others (Chicago, Peale, 1888).

22. *O.A.R* 1:130 (Draper); 6:80 (Willich); 6:358 (Champion); 7:210 (Anneke); 7:370 (Lynde); 1:721 (Moor); 1:295 (Champion); 1:975 (Ullman). Frederick Phisterer, *Statistical Record of the Armies of the United States* (New York, 1883): 439, 259 (Ullman); 501, 260 (Willich); 1041, 277 (Cochrane); 1046, 277 (Willich); 1058, 277 (Hovey); 1183, 283 (Ullman); 1415, 291 (Walker); 2256, 310 (Champion); 2348, 312 (Weaver); 2484, 315 (Draper); 2647, 322 (Draper). *Who Was Who in the Union*, 81 (Cochrane); 422 (Ullman); 457 (Willich); *Pr* V (November 1863): 26 (Schneider). *Roster of . . . Ohio*, 3:303 (Moor). *NYDTrib,* October 18, 1851 (Ullman). *Cincinnati Daily Nonpareil*, March 11, 1851 (Moor).

23. "Buffalo, N.Y.," *Typographical Journal* 53 (July 1918): 44; *Biographical Directory of Congress*.

24. The Third included officers of the Union: Ambrose W. Barnard, David G. Cobbs, William G. Creighton, Charley French; Company A Sergeants W. Bird Johnson and Warren W. Whipple; in Company B, Simeon Whitely, "honorary member." Whitely had been the U.S. Indian agent for the Utes in the territory until 1865. Untitled item, [Denver] *Rocky Mountain News Weekly*, June 7, 1865; untitled item, *Black Hawk* [Gilpin County, Colo.] *Daily Mining Journal*, June 6, 1865; Notice in *Typographical Journal* 53 (September 1918): 296; "I.O.O.F. Visitors from Wyoming and Colorado Cantons in Cheyenne," *Cheyenne Daily Leader*, April 28, 1891; "Personal Paragraphs," *Omaha Daily Bee*, December 30, 1892; Perkin, *The First Hundred Years*, 197; for Jack Sumner and Oramel G. Howland, see Donald Worster, *A River Running West: The Life of John Wesley Powell* (Oxford: Oxford University Press, 2001), 141. Artemus Ward speaking to Leavenworth Typographical Union Wilder, *Annals of Kansas*, 420; *Mercantile Guide and Directory for Virginia City, Gold Hill, Silver City and American City*, comp. Charles Collins (San Francisco: Agnew and Deffenach, 1864–65), 33; Mills, "Reminiscences of an Editor," 273, 274, 275, 274–278nn, 279–80; "Hugh McQuaid Told World of the Custer Massacre: Pioneer Newspaper Man Scoops War Department on Terrible Battle," *Contributions to the Historical Society of Montana* 4: 287; "Sacramento, Cal.," "Breaking into the U.S. Marines," *Typographical Journal* 53 (July–August 1918): 48, 149.

25. "Many men will pass through life without ever making any use of their reason, beyond the best method of getting money and how to enjoy it, leaving all the rest unknown or unheeded." Others "think it is enough to do as they are ordered." Seaver, *Occasional Thoughts*, 36.

Index

MARK A. LAUSE is a professor of American history at the University of Cincinnati. He is the author of *A Secret Society History of the Civil War* and *Race and Radicalism in the Union Army*.

THE WORKING CLASS IN AMERICAN HISTORY

Worker City, Company Town: Iron and Cotton-Worker Protest in Troy and Cohoes, New York, 1855–84 *Daniel J. Walkowitz*

Life, Work, and Rebellion in the Coal Fields: The Southern West Virginia Miners, 1880–1922 *David Alan Corbin*

Women and American Socialism, 1870–1920 *Mari Jo Buhle*

Lives of Their Own: Blacks, Italians, and Poles in Pittsburgh, 1900–1960 *John Bodnar, Roger Simon, and Michael P. Weber*

Working-Class America: Essays on Labor, Community, and American Society *Edited by Michael H. Frisch and Daniel J. Walkowitz*

Eugene V. Debs: Citizen and Socialist *Nick Salvatore*

American Labor and Immigration History, 1877–1920s: Recent European Research *Edited by Dirk Hoerder*

Workingmen's Democracy: The Knights of Labor and American Politics *Leon Fink*

The Electrical Workers: A History of Labor at General Electric and Westinghouse, 1923–60 *Ronald W. Schatz*

The Mechanics of Baltimore: Workers and Politics in the Age of Revolution, 1763–1812 *Charles G. Steffen*

The Practice of Solidarity: American Hat Finishers in the Nineteenth Century *David Bensman*

The Labor History Reader *Edited by Daniel J. Leab*

Solidarity and Fragmentation: Working People and Class Consciousness in Detroit, 1875–1900 *Richard Oestreicher*

Counter Cultures: Saleswomen, Managers, and Customers in American Department Stores, 1890–1940 *Susan Porter Benson*

The New England Working Class and the New Labor History *Edited by Herbert G. Gutman and Donald H. Bell*

Labor Leaders in America *Edited by Melvyn Dubofsky and Warren Van Tine*

Barons of Labor: The San Francisco Building Trades and Union Power in the Progressive Era *Michael Kazin*

Gender at Work: The Dynamics of Job Segregation by Sex during World War II *Ruth Milkman*

Once a Cigar Maker: Men, Women, and Work Culture in American Cigar Factories, 1900–1919 *Patricia A. Cooper*

A Generation of Boomers: The Pattern of Railroad Labor Conflict in Nineteenth-Century America *Shelton Stromquist*

Work and Community in the Jungle: Chicago's Packinghouse Workers, 1894–1922 *James R. Barrett*

Workers, Managers, and Welfare Capitalism: The Shoeworkers and Tanners of Endicott Johnson, 1890–1950 *Gerald Zahavi*

Men, Women, and Work: Class, Gender, and Protest in the New England Shoe Industry, 1780–1910 *Mary Blewett*

Workers on the Waterfront: Seamen, Longshoremen, and Unionism in the 1930s *Bruce Nelson*

German Workers in Chicago: A Documentary History of Working-Class Culture from 1850 to World War I *Edited by Hartmut Keil and John B. Jentz*

On the Line: Essays in the History of Auto Work *Edited by Nelson Lichtenstein and Stephen Meyer III*

Labor's Flaming Youth: Telephone Operators and Worker Militancy, 1878–1923 *Stephen H. Norwood*

Another Civil War: Labor, Capital, and the State in the Anthracite Regions of Pennsylvania, 1840–68 *Grace Palladino*

Coal, Class, and Color: Blacks in Southern West Virginia, 1915–32 *Joe William Trotter Jr.*

For Democracy, Workers, and God: Labor Song-Poems and Labor Protest, 1865–95 *Clark D. Halker*

Dishing It Out: Waitresses and Their Unions in the Twentieth Century *Dorothy Sue Cobble*

The Spirit of 1848: German Immigrants, Labor Conflict, and the Coming of the Civil War *Bruce Levine*

Working Women of Collar City: Gender, Class, and Community in Troy, New York, 1864–86 *Carole Turbin*

Southern Labor and Black Civil Rights: Organizing Memphis Workers *Michael K. Honey*

Radicals of the Worst Sort: Laboring Women in Lawrence, Massachusetts, 1860–1912 *Ardis Cameron*

Producers, Proletarians, and Politicians: Workers and Party Politics in Evansville and New Albany, Indiana, 1850–87 *Lawrence M. Lipin*

The New Left and Labor in the 1960s *Peter B. Levy*

The Making of Western Labor Radicalism: Denver's Organized Workers, 1878–1905 *David Brundage*

In Search of the Working Class: Essays in American Labor History and Political Culture *Leon Fink*

Lawyers against Labor: From Individual Rights to Corporate Liberalism *Daniel R. Ernst*

"We Are All Leaders": The Alternative Unionism of the Early 1930s *Edited by Staughton Lynd*

The Female Economy: The Millinery and Dressmaking Trades, 1860–1930 *Wendy Gamber*

"Negro and White, Unite and Fight!": A Social History of Industrial Unionism in Meatpacking, 1930–90 *Roger Horowitz*

Power at Odds: The 1922 National Railroad Shopmen's Strike *Colin J. Davis*

The Common Ground of Womanhood: Class, Gender, and Working Girls' Clubs, 1884–1928 *Priscilla Murolo*

Marching Together: Women of the Brotherhood of Sleeping Car Porters *Melinda Chateauvert*

Down on the Killing Floor: Black and White Workers in Chicago's Packinghouses, 1904–54 *Rick Halpern*

Labor and Urban Politics: Class Conflict and the Origins of Modern Liberalism in Chicago, 1864–97 *Richard Schneirov*

All That Glitters: Class, Conflict, and Community in Cripple Creek *Elizabeth Jameson*

Waterfront Workers: New Perspectives on Race and Class *Edited by Calvin Winslow*

Labor Histories: Class, Politics, and the Working-Class Experience *Edited by Eric Arnesen, Julie Greene, and Bruce Laurie*

The Pullman Strike and the Crisis of the 1890s: Essays on Labor and Politics
Edited by Richard Schneirov, Shelton Stromquist, and Nick Salvatore
AlabamaNorth: African-American Migrants, Community, and Working-Class Activism in Cleveland, 1914–45 *Kimberley L. Phillips*
Imagining Internationalism in American and British Labor, 1939–49 *Victor Silverman*
William Z. Foster and the Tragedy of American Radicalism *James R. Barrett*
Colliers across the Sea: A Comparative Study of Class Formation in Scotland and the American Midwest, 1830–1924 *John H. M. Laslett*
"Rights, Not Roses": Unions and the Rise of Working-Class Feminism, 1945–80 *Dennis A. Deslippe*
Testing the New Deal: The General Textile Strike of 1934 in the American South *Janet Irons*
Hard Work: The Making of Labor History *Melvyn Dubofsky*
Southern Workers and the Search for Community: Spartanburg County, South Carolina *G. C. Waldrep III*
We Shall Be All: A History of the Industrial Workers of the World (abridged edition) *Melvyn Dubofsky, ed. Joseph A. McCartin*
Race, Class, and Power in the Alabama Coalfields, 1908–21 *Brian Kelly*
Duquesne and the Rise of Steel Unionism *James D. Rose*
Anaconda: Labor, Community, and Culture in Montana's Smelter City *Laurie Mercier*
Bridgeport's Socialist New Deal, 1915–36 *Cecelia Bucki*
Indispensable Outcasts: Hobo Workers and Community in the American Midwest, 1880–1930 *Frank Tobias Higbie*
After the Strike: A Century of Labor Struggle at Pullman *Susan Eleanor Hirsch*
Corruption and Reform in the Teamsters Union *David Witwer*
Waterfront Revolts: New York and London Dockworkers, 1946–61 *Colin J. Davis*
Black Workers' Struggle for Equality in Birmingham *Horace Huntley and David Montgomery*
The Tribe of Black Ulysses: African American Men in the Industrial South *William P. Jones*
City of Clerks: Office and Sales Workers in Philadelphia, 1870–1920 *Jerome P. Bjelopera*
Reinventing "The People": The Progressive Movement, the Class Problem, and the Origins of Modern Liberalism *Shelton Stromquist*
Radical Unionism in the Midwest, 1900–1950 *Rosemary Feurer*
Gendering Labor History *Alice Kessler-Harris*
James P. Cannon and the Origins of the American Revolutionary Left, 1890–1928 *Bryan D. Palmer*
Glass Towns: Industry, Labor, and Political Economy in Appalachia, 1890–1930s *Ken Fones-Wolf*
Workers and the Wild: Conservation, Consumerism, and Labor in Oregon, 1910–30 *Lawrence M. Lipin*
Wobblies on the Waterfront: Interracial Unionism in Progressive-Era Philadelphia *Peter Cole*
Red Chicago: American Communism at Its Grassroots, 1928–35 *Randi Storch*
Labor's Cold War: Local Politics in a Global Context *Edited by Shelton Stromquist*

Bessie Abramowitz Hillman and the Making of the Amalgamated Clothing Workers of America *Karen Pastorello*
The Great Strikes of 1877 *Edited by David O. Stowell*
Union-Free America: Workers and Antiunion Culture *Lawrence Richards*
Race against Liberalism: Black Workers and the UAW in Detroit *David M. Lewis-Colman*
Teachers and Reform: Chicago Public Education, 1929–70 *John F. Lyons*
Upheaval in the Quiet Zone: 1199/SEIU and the Politics of Healthcare Unionism *Leon Fink and Brian Greenberg*
Shadow of the Racketeer: Scandal in Organized Labor *David Witwer*
Sweet Tyranny: Migrant Labor, Industrial Agriculture, and Imperial Politics *Kathleen Mapes*
Staley: The Fight for a New American Labor Movement *Steven K. Ashby and C. J. Hawking*
On the Ground: Labor Struggles in the American Airline Industry *Liesl Miller Orenic*
NAFTA and Labor in North America *Norman Caulfield*
Making Capitalism Safe: Work Safety and Health Regulation in America, 1880–1940 *Donald W. Rogers*
Good, Reliable, White Men: Railroad Brotherhoods, 1877–1917 *Paul Michel Taillon*
Spirit of Rebellion: Labor and Religion in the New Cotton South *Jarod Roll*
The Labor Question in America: Economic Democracy in the Gilded Age *Rosanne Currarino*
Banded Together: Economic Democratization in the Brass Valley *Jeremy Brecher*
The Gospel of the Working Class: Labor's Southern Prophets in New Deal America *Erik Gellman and Jarod Roll*
Guest Workers and Resistance to U.S. Corporate Despotism *Immanuel Ness*
Gleanings of Freedom: Free and Slave Labor along the Mason-Dixon Line, 1790–1860 *Max Grivno*
Chicago in the Age of Capital: Class, Politics, and Democracy during the Civil War and Reconstruction *John B. Jentz and Richard Schneirov*
Child Care in Black and White: Working Parents and the History of Orphanages *Jessie B. Ramey*
The Haymarket Conspiracy: Transatlantic Anarchist Networks *Timothy Messer-Kruse*
Detroit's Cold War: The Origins of Postwar Conservatism *Colleen Doody*
A Renegade Union: Interracial Organizing and Labor Radicalism *Lisa Phillips*
Palomino: Clinton Jencks and Mexican-American Unionism in the American Southwest *James J. Lorence*
Latin American Migrations to the U.S. Heartland: Changing Cultural Landscapes in Middle America *Edited by Linda Allegro and Andrew Grant Wood*
Man of Fire: Selected Writings *Ernesto Galarza, ed. Armando Ibarra and Rodolfo D. Torres*
A Contest of Ideas: Capital, Politics, and Labor *Nelson Lichtenstein*
Making the World Safe for Workers: Labor, the Left, and Wilsonian Internationalism *Elizabeth McKillen*
The Rise of the Chicago Police Department: Class and Conflict, 1850–1894 *Sam Mitrani*
Workers in Hard Times: A Long View of Economic Crises *Edited by Leon Fink, Joseph A. McCartin, and Joan Sangster*

Redeeming Time: Protestantism and Chicago's Eight-Hour Movement, 1866–1912
William A. Mirola
Struggle for the Soul of the Postwar South: White Evangelical Protestants and Operation Dixie *Elizabeth Fones-Wolf and Ken Fones-Wolf*
Free Labor: The Civil War and the Making of an American Working Class *Mark A. Lause*

The University of Illinois Press
is a founding member of the
Association of American University Presses.

Composed in 10.75/13 Bulmer
with Inflex display
by Jim Proefrock
at the University of Illinois Press
Manufactured by Cushing-Malloy, Inc.

University of Illinois Press
1325 South Oak Street
Champaign, IL 61820-6903
www.press.uillinois.edu